MORONI AND THE SWASTIKA

MORONI AND THE SWASTIKA

Mormons in Nazi Germany

DAVID CONLEY NELSON

University of Oklahoma Press : Norman

Library of Congress Cataloging-in-Publication Data

Nelson, David Conley, 1953–
    Moroni and the swastika : Mormons in Nazi Germany / David Conley Nelson. — First [edition].
        pages cm
    Includes bibliographical references and index.
    ISBN 978-0-8061-4668-3 (cloth)
    ISBN 978-0-8061-6575-2 (paper)
    1. Church of Jesus Christ of Latter-day Saints—Germany—History—1933–1945. 2. Church and state—Germany—History—1933–1945. 3. Church of Jesus Christ of Latter-day Saints—Foreign relations—Germany. I. Title.
    BX8617.G4N45 2014
    289.3'4309043—dc23
                            2014024515

The paper in this book meets the guidelines for permanence and durability of the Committee on Production Guidelines for Book Longevity of the Council on Library Resources, Inc. ∞

Copyright © 2015 by the University of Oklahoma Press, Norman, Publishing Division of the University. Paperback published 2020. Manufactured in the U.S.A.

All rights reserved. No part of this publication may be reproduced, stored in a retrieval system, or transmitted, in any form or by any means, electronic, mechanical, photocopying, recording, or otherwise—except as permitted under Section 107 or 108 of the United States Copyright Act—without the prior written permission of the University of Oklahoma Press. To request permission to reproduce selections from this book, write to Permissions, University of Oklahoma Press, 2800 Venture Drive, Norman, OK 73069, or email rights.oupress@ou.edu.

For two people in my life who gave me second chances:
To Professor Arnold P. Krammer, whose kind patience granted
many deadline extensions that ultimately allowed me to
finish my doctoral dissertation in history.
But, much more importantly, to my beloved wife, Ruth,
whose devotion gave me a second opportunity
for marriage and fatherhood.

And to be perfectly frank, there have been times when members or leaders in the Church have simply made mistakes. There may have been things said or done that were not in harmony with our values, principles, or doctrine.
 —Dieter F. Uchtdorf, Second Counselor in the First Presidency,
 The Church of Jesus Christ of Latter-day Saints,
 October 5, 2013
 Elder Uchtdorf is a former German citizen.

Contents

List of Illustrations xi

Preface xiii

Introduction: Deliverance on the Night of Broken Glass 3

Part I. The Mormon *Sonderweg:* The Road to Nazi Germany

1. Mormonism's Long Nineteenth Century in Germany: From Pariahs to Skilled Survivors 19
2. German Mormons in the Great War: Lessons Learned in the Crucible of Combat 49
3. Mormons in the Weimar Republic: Honing Survival Skills in a Fledgling Democracy 59

Part II. The Prewar Nazi Years, 1933–1939: A Forgotten History

4. The Mormon Battle Plan in the Third Reich 93
5. Genealogy: Promoting a Common Worldview on Earth and in the Afterlife 105
6. Mormon Basketball Diplomacy in Hitler's Reich 116
7. Boy Scouting: The Mormons' Only Unconditional Surrender to the Nazis 123
8. The *Führer's* Chosen People? The Mormons' Hitler Myth 135
9. A Countervailing Myth: Nazi Persecution of the Mormons 167
10. God's *Oberführer:* The Mormon Mission President 185

Contents

11. J. Reuben Clark: Mormon Ambassador Plenipotentiary and His Entourage   209

Part III. Beacons of Mormon Memory in Nazi Germany

12. The Second World War and Its Aftermath   223
13. Forgotten Heroes and Rediscovered Villains   253
14. Mormons and Jews: An Inconvenient Association   272
15. Helmuth Hübener: A Memory Beacon with a Dimmer Switch   288
16. A Premature Curtain Call   318

    Conclusion: To Save the Church?   339

    Abbreviations   345
    Notes   347
    Bibliography   385
    Index   403

Illustrations

Figures

Max Reschke with his father, Theodor   145
Basketball players giving Hitler salute   146
Willie Ludwig and Clemens Hegewald   147
Relief Society meeting, Stettin   148
Stettin Branch boat trip on the Oder River   149
Alfred C. Rees and Joseph Fielding Smith   150
Thomas E. McKay   151
Mormon prophet, seer, and revelator Heber J. Grant   152
American Mormon missionaries in Durlach   153
J. Reuben Clark, Jr.   154
Senator Elbert D. Thomas of Utah   155
Commemoration in 1939 at Ft. Douglas, Utah   156
"Jews are not allowed"   157
Frankfurt city hall during a Mormon conference   158
Karl Herbert Klopfer   159
Wedding party in the Spandau city hall   160
Rudi Wobbe, Helmuth Hübener, and Karl-Heinz Schnibbe   161
St. Georg Branch of Hamburg   162
Helmuth Hübener   163
Helmuth Hübener-Haus in present-day Hamburg   164
Helmuth-Hübener-Weg in present-day suburban Hamburg   165
Thomas S. Monson and Erich Honecker   166

Illustrations

Tables

10.1. Mission presidents during the prewar National Socialist period, 1933–1939   188

15.1. German-speaking Mormon immigration to the United States during the post–World War II era   315

Maps

Imperial Germany, 1871 to 1918   40–41
The Weimar Republic, 1918 to 1933   74–75
Nazi Germany, September 1, 1939   168–69

Preface

This book began with a question posed more than two decades ago by my adopted stepson Jeff, then a thirteen-year-old junior high school student taking his first world history class. He learned that prisoners in Hitler's concentration camps wore triangular symbols on their armbands. The color corresponded to their reason for confinement. Common criminals wore green triangles, political prisoners red, the "work shy" black, homosexuals pink, Jehovah's Witnesses purple, and the Jews a yellow Star of David—which could be seen as one yellow triangle atop another. Jeff's adolescent logic sought to forge a link between this new knowledge and what he had been taught in Sunday school. A descendant of the Mormon pioneers, he had learned the orthodox interpretation of his denomination's history: His nineteenth century co-religionists trekked west to escape American persecution, and their missionaries had often been mistreated in foreign lands. Certainly, he thought, Mormons must have suffered the same fate in Nazi Germany.

One evening, as our typically large Latter-day Saint family gathered around the kitchen table, Jeff asked: "Dad, what color triangles did the Mormons wear in the concentration camps?" That question became my impetus for a research paper several years later, subsequently an award-winning presentation at the Mormon History Association's annual conference, then my shift of emphasis from French to German history, and ultimately my doctoral dissertation—upon which this book is based.

My dissertation advisor took up where Jeff's inspiration left off. Arnold P. Krammer understands concentration camp insignia in a way unmatched by many academics. Most members of his large, extended

Hungarian Jewish family perished after they boarded boxcars for Auschwitz in 1944. When he cracks a shoebox lid and places carefully handstitched Stars of David into the palms of his students, the seminar room becomes eerily quiet. Meant as badges of shame by the Nazis, those fragile, seventy-year-old yellow patches today constitute memorials of pride, crafted by a physically doomed yet spiritually resilient people who refused to allow fear of their impending fate to degrade their detailed workmanship. My mentor asks that his students draw insight and fuel their work ethic from the example of those who meticulously stitched and unashamedly wore such emblems.

My deepest gratitude extends to Jeff, who got this project rolling with youthful curiosity, and to Professor Krammer, whose mature guidance helped my graduate education bridge twin chasms imposed by my airline career and my midlife divorce and remarriage. Without many others named subsequently, this work would have emerged in a different form. Without these two, it would not exist.

Other members of Texas A&M University's faculty taught me the entry-level skills of the historical profession. Masters and doctoral committee members Chester Dunning, Walter Kamphoefner, Peter Hugill, H. W. Brands, Lora Wildenthal, Harold Livesay, James Rosenheim, and Richard Golsan figure prominently among those. Two previous chairs, Cynthia Bouton of my MA committee and Sarah Fishman, who guided my undergraduate thesis at the University of Houston, deserve special gratitude. Professor Fishman's Houston colleague, Robert Zaretsky, inspired me to become a historian.

D. Michael Quinn, who journeyed from California to Texas for my examinations and stood ready to help by phone and email during the interim, served as my Mormon history specialist, a billet that could not be filled in College Station. One of the best living scholars of Mormonism, Professor Quinn could be described as the Job of the historical profession. He has suffered prodigiously for the sin of writing Mormon history according to his primary sources, rather than in conformance with the faith-promoting paradigm necessary for survival among co-religionists in that field. The previously named scholars are my role models. Mike is my hero.

German teachers at Texas A&M and the Goethe Institute in Munich struggled to help an older student undergoing a midlife language crisis—who had entered graduate school with a freshly minted BA in French,

Preface

thinking that would be his primary research language. Norbert Feltes, a native German speaker from Luxembourg who married into my wife's family, helped fill the gap. He shared budget accommodations with me while we mined the German language documents in the LDS Church archives. I also express gratitude to my lifelong friend from high school, Mark Earnest, who read chapters of this work and offered criticism.

The European Union Center of Excellence (EUCE) awarded a research fellowship that paid hostel and campground bills in Salt Lake City, as well as many hamburger meals. The Department of History at Texas A&M bestowed a generous research grant. I thank Johan Lembke of the European Union Center of Excellence and Walter Buenger of the history department for this valuable funding. I'm equally grateful to the late Robert Calvert, a Freedom Rider during the Civil Rights era and an inspiration to legions of graduate students since then, for admitting a man in his late forties to a graduate history program normally reserved for younger scholars.

I am grateful to the editors and staff at the University of Oklahoma Press, who embraced a first-time author with the kindness and consideration that might only be expected by one who had published many books. Jay Dew was an enthusiastic acquisitions editor who walked me through the process of peer review and committee approval. Then Chuck Rankin, Editor-in-Chief of the OU Press, provided the expert mentoring and occasional reassurance that a rookie author needed as this book became a reality. Emmy Ezzell and Stephanie Attia shepherded my work through the production process, and copyeditor Rosanne Hallowell's sharp eye helped me find mistakes and clarify ambiguities that I just could not discern in my own writing. My cartographer, John Gilkes, drew up simple but handsome maps that pictorially illustrate the otherwise esoteric subject of Mormon history in Germany.

I chose the OU Press because of its reputation for publishing the works of talented historians who have enriched the field of Mormon Studies—those who have written from the viewpoint of believers, as well as those who wrote nonconforming histories. I am honored to have my book bear the same publishing trademark that embosses the works of Richard E. Bennett, Thomas Alexander, Polly Aird, Gary Topping, Juanita Brooks, Newell Bringhurst, Will Bagley, David Bigler, Dale Morgan, and others.

I am also thankful to the historians, archivists, library staff, and fellow patrons at the Church History Department of the LDS Church, to active

xv

Preface

and retired faculty members at the Mormon Church's flagship university, Brigham Young University, and to members of the German-American Mormon immigrant community in Salt Lake City. I have chosen not to name them, for fear that some may encounter the professional and personal recrimination that occasionally befalls faithful Latter-day Saints who assist in scholarly endeavors that are not faith-promoting. Nevertheless, I value their help considerably, as without it I would not have been able to write this book.

I could not have persevered in this project without the loving support of the twin lights of my life—my wife Ruth and daughter Megan—plus the world's two greatest stepchildren, Brittany and Kyle Ray. My second family adopted my dreams as theirs and unselfishly endured my weeklong sojourns that cut into planned home time between airline trips. "Daddy is doing research," entered precious little Megan's vernacular at too young an age, especially when her father would finish piloting a flight from Paris and then board an airplane to Salt Lake City—with intervening time for not much more than a kiss.

My parents blessed me with a modicum of intelligence and copious doses of instruction in the art of discernment. My mother reared me to avoid prejudice despite my racist Louisiana roots in the 1950s. She also emphasized the difference between believing in God and adhering to the dictates of religion. My late father, who searched for accommodation between spirituality and intellect throughout his long life, simply admonished me—on the eve of my decade-long sojourn into Mormonism—not to allow "the church," any church, to do my thinking for me.

To answer Jeff's query after all of these years, most Mormons in Nazi Germany had little to do with the concentration camps, but the few who did were as likely to have been guards as prisoners. German Mormons and their prewar American missionaries avoided persecution by skillfully collaborating to a degree that ensured their survival but did not subject them to postwar retribution. As this narrative describes, sometimes their enthusiastic embrace of Hitler's regime exceeded the necessities of survival. In doing so, they emerged as the most successful foreign-based "new religion" during the Third Reich and inspired faithful historians who emphasized their wartime heroism and suffering, while masking the less admirable aspects of their behavior. Thank you, Jeff, for helping me discover a collective memory that needs to be challenged, and for inspiring me to write this story in a different way.

MORONI AND THE SWASTIKA

Introduction
Deliverance on the Night of Broken Glass

On the evening of November 10, 1938, while Germans were sweeping the broken glass and dousing the smoldering embers of *Kristallnacht*,[1] a nondescript sedan crossed the Swiss border. A young Jewish couple from Hanover crouched in the back seat, thankful for deliverance from the nationwide pogrom that destroyed their small business and sent thousands of fellow Jews to concentration camps. The leader of a local Mormon congregation had driven more than four hundred kilometers that night, risking his life to save his friends from brown-shirted Nazi storm troopers.

During Hitler's twelve-year Reich, Max Reschke not only rescued the Hanover couple but also sheltered a prominent local Jewish banker and sent his children to care for the banker's wife in the Hanover ghetto. He later shielded a Russian prisoner of war and protected a Polish slave laborer who had been assigned to work in his industrial plant. For harboring the Jewish banker, he suffered arrest and temporary concentration camp imprisonment. As a factory foreman he resisted the Nazi Labor Front's attempts to organize his workers, and as a Boy Scout leader he opposed the Hitler Youth's attempts to take over his Mormon Church scouting troop. Both efforts also resulted in trouble with the Nazi authorities.

Despite courageous resistance that sometimes bordered on foolhardiness, Reschke's acts remain unheralded today, acknowledged within his family circle but mostly unknown to fellow Mormons or to Jews, Poles, or Russians whose countrymen or coreligionists he heroically protected. His name does not appear in Righteous Among the Nations, Israel's *Yad*

Vashem list of those non-Jews who rescued Jews from the Nazis. He receives scant mention in the apologetic history, written by both faithful Mormon scholars and amateur historians, who instead tread lightly regarding the relationship of their coreligionists with the government of Nazi Germany.

Reschke diverged from his church's methodology for dealing with Adolf Hitler's government. In doing so he not only violated a coordinated survival strategy mapped by his ecclesiastical leaders, but also transgressed against an important religious tenet. The Twelfth Article of Faith and parts of the 134th Section of the Doctrine and Covenants function as Mormonism's equivalent of the biblical admonition to "render unto Caesar," a charge to cooperate with civil government however onerous it may be. Isolated cases of Mormon rebellion against the Third Reich met with fear, disapproval, or outright hostility from congregants who saw such nonconformity not only as endangering a vulnerable sect that the Nazis could have easily squashed, but also as a violation of God's will.

Max Reschke's heroics lead this narrative not because he typified Mormons in Nazi Germany but instead because he differed so much from them.[2] Unlike this rebellious Hanover branch president,[3] many Mormon officials strove to fit into the Third Reich by emphasizing points of congruence between their church and Hitler's regime. These were not spontaneous or localized efforts, but instead reflected a centralized strategy mandated by senior ecclesiastical leaders—the American Mormon mission presidents who acted under guidance from church headquarters in Salt Lake City. Their attempts proved successful. The Nazis banned no Mormon congregations from worship and persecuted few individual members. When a German Mormon or an American missionary ran afoul of the government, it was because of an individual transgression that would have imperiled any ordinary German during the Nazi regime. German Latter-day Saints and their American ecclesiastical leaders learned how to live under periodic state surveillance but succeeded in surviving this scrutiny.

However, in the process of proving that Mormonism posed no threat to the German state, especially in the prewar period from 1933 to 1939, LDS Church leaders exceeded the effort necessary for survival. The historical record reveals numerous efforts to court favor with the Nazi state, from stressing common interest in genealogical research to professing admiration for Hitler's carefully cultivated image as a nonsmoking, nondrinking devotee of healthy living. One American mission president, Roy Welker, in his writings and pulpit pronouncements, openly professed his belief that Hitler showed favoritism to his sect. When his wife Elizabeth wrote the Nazi women's leader to express her concerns over alleged sexual lasciviousness in Party youth camps, Gertrude Scholtz-Klink responded by inviting her to ride with Hitler in the Führer's limousine on the way to Nazi youth rallies. Another more sophisticated American mission leader, Alfred C. Rees, cultivated contacts in the Nazi's propaganda ministry that allow him to publish an article in the official Nazi daily newspaper, the *Völkischer Beobachter*. The article stressed points of congruence between Utah Mormon and German Nazi society.

Assured by their church leaders that there was no conflict in being a good Mormon and a good citizen of the Nazi State, German Mormons dutifully served in the Nazi Labor Corps and the German military. Other Latter-day Saints enthusiastically donned the brown shirts of Hitler's *Sturmabteilung* (SA), an organization that bashed heads in the streets and vandalized Jewish businesses. Some joined for more benign reasons, such as the Hamburg congregants who enjoyed playing in the local SA band. Other Mormons obtained membership in Hitler's elite group of personal guards, the black-shirted *Schutzstaffel* (SS), an organization that expanded to play a leading role in the Holocaust. One Hamburg member, infamous among his fellow congregants for having killed one of Hitler's political opponents in a street fight, enlisted in the *Totenkopfverbände*, the Death's Head SS brigades that ran the extermination camps. Another Mormon appeared in an early scholarly article as an "expert mechanic" who "install[ed] specialized machinery" at Auschwitz.[4] In the parlance of Nazi Germany, that is a euphemism for someone who set up gas chambers and crematoria.

Some young American LDS missionaries rendered the stiff-armed Hitler salute with the encouragement of their leaders, not necessarily out of genuine sympathy with the regime, but instead to avoid conflict.[5] Other missionaries refused to perform that sign of loyalty to the government, which occasionally caused them difficulty with the Nazis they encountered. That divided opinion within the missionary corps reveals an awareness of the political ramifications of such a display. It argues against the position that spiritually minded American Mormons lacked knowledge of political reality in the Third Reich. One young American missionary, Alvin Schoenhals, suffered imprisonment in a local jail for three weeks after postal censors read his politically astute but intemperate anti-Nazi remarks in a letter he sent home to Utah. Communication from mission presidents to the church hierarchy in the United States reveals a sophisticated understanding of what was transpiring in Nazi Germany. The Mormons strove to continue their congregational worship and missionary efforts in one of the world's most oppressive regimes with renewed vigor each time the Nazi government posed a challenge. The LDS leadership's politically shrewd responses were overwhelmingly successful.

Mormons in Germany also changed liturgical practices and missionary efforts to accommodate the Nazi state's anti-Semitic bias. Ecclesiastical leaders purged German-language hymnals of references to Zion and Israel that had existed since Mormon Church music had been translated into German during the nineteenth century. They sanitized church publications of words and phrases that the Nazis found repugnant. When a lesson manual appeared that contained a Jewish reference, one of the mission presidents directed that the offending page be cut out and the adjoining pages pasted together. Aware that the Nazis recognized no rite of religious conversion for Jews, some German Mormon leaders refused to baptize prospective Jewish members. In one case, a congregation reluctantly said goodbye to a convert from Judaism who, in the years before Hitler came to power, had considered himself fully assimilated and acculturated into his new faith. Regret did not extend to another local Mormon leader, also a supporter of the Nazi Party, who erected a sign outside of the meetinghouse: "Jews Are Not Allowed!" The same branch president once tried to mount a picture of Adolf Hitler in a congregational chapel, in the spot that had previously displayed pictures of Jesus Christ and Mormon founder Joseph Smith. He interrupted services whenever Hitler gave a speech on the radio, compelled his congregants to listen, and locked the church doors to prevent them from leaving. During choir rehearsals, he sent children around the room to spy on the adults, to report whether they were singing the Horst Wessel Song (the Nazi Party anthem) with the same enthusiasm as they did the church music.

On the eve of the Second World War, the second in command of the LDS Church, a former diplomat and undersecretary of state, J. Reuben Clark, ignored the pleas of at least two German-speaking Mormons

Introduction

—converts from Judaism—for documentation that would help them leave prewar Nazi Germany. Rarely accessible correspondence files of the Mormon first presidency, available to Clark's authorized biographer, reveal these heart-rending appeals and boilerplate refusals by Clark—at a time when tens of thousands of Jews left prewar Nazi Germany with nominal foreign assistance. Clark, whose records bequeathed a long paper trail of anti-Semitic sentiments, asked on behalf of his church to be "excused" from taking action on such requests. Concurrently, Clark urged the U.S. State Department to facilitate the emigration of non-Jewish German-speaking Mormons, whom he referred to by the term "Aryans."

When the Mormons' American leadership and its missionaries evacuated Europe one week before Hitler's tanks rolled into Poland, the emphasis shifted to surviving the war. German Mormons hunkered down but still cooperated with the state to the same extent as their fellow citizens. They sent their husbands and sons into military service, prayed in church for a German victory, served in neighborhood civil defense positions, and rendered whatever mutual assistance they could to survive Allied bombing raids. When meetinghouses crumbled and burned under aerial bombardment, small congregations consolidated in the surviving buildings. Mormon women, ineligible for the top leadership positions, provided the cohesion that sustained organized worship. Mothers assigned their teenaged sons to duties normally reserved for older male priesthood authorities and then ensured that those tasks were accomplished with the customary efficiency.

When the Allies proved victorious, German Mormons welcomed their American spiritual cousins back with open arms. Survival remained paramount, but in the midst of a challenging postwar recovery, efforts to expand the church resumed. Members embraced former missionaries who appeared at Sunday services wearing the uniform of the conquering power, as if no conflict had ever occurred. The Salt Lake City church leadership mobilized American and Canadian Mormons to provide a massive relief campaign that sent food and clothing to Germany in quantities that dwarfed LDS-sponsored relief efforts elsewhere on the continent. Ezra Taft Benson, a member of the Mormons' ruling "Quorum of the Twelve Apostles," who would later become Dwight Eisenhower's secretary of agriculture and subsequently the Mormon church president, visited Germany in 1946 and rallied the vanquished and bombed-out

Latter-day Saints. The American ecclesiastical leadership quickly reestablished centralized control of German church units, an important first step toward resuming the missionary effort, rebuilding church structure, and reestablishing American authority.

The Mormon *Sonderweg*: The Road to Nazi Germany

Historians have often referred to a *Sonderweg*, a special path that differentiates the development of German democracy from other European systems. Mormon history in Germany followed its own unique route, one in which Mormon–state relations in Imperial Germany were inexorably linked to difficulties that Latter-day Saints experienced on the American frontier. That road began with a pronouncement from Mormonism's founder, Joseph Smith, an intelligent albeit informally educated young man with a vivid imagination and a magnetic personality. Having declared himself a prophet of God, he uttered several "revelations" regarding the German language and the people who spoke it—including his speculation that the Germans were particularly qualified to attain the Mormon status of post-mortal godhood. Brigham Young, Smith's successor, saw nothing divine in the Germans, only hard workers who, as migrants, helped build the American Zion in the Mormon Culture Region.[6]

The nascent German branches of the LDS Church and their American missionaries encountered considerable opposition from the German state governments and mainline Christian priests and ministers. Polygamy was the most significant provocation. Mormons never practiced "plural marriage" in Germany. However, officials of the various German states argued that if Latter-day Saints could not obey the law in their own country, they were not likely to be law-abiding abroad. The emigration of young, military draft–age men also concerned civil authorities who thought German Mormon men were converting and emigrating to avoid army service. Ministers and priests naturally took offense at any attempt to convert their congregants. But for religious authorities, their most impassioned denunciations cited sensationally embellished stories of Mormon polygamous harems in the Utah desert, and fanciful rumors of German women held against their will by lascivious Mormon elders.

Introduction

The recurring conflict between the Mormon missionaries and their German hosts during the nineteenth century illuminates an important point when one examines how the Mormons later conducted themselves during the Third Reich. Before the First World War, Latter-day Saints ignored the Twelfth Article of Faith in their dealings with German governmental authorities. When a Mormon missionary found himself banished from a German city, he transferred to another. When a local censor refused to approve printing of a pamphlet, missionaries had it printed elsewhere and then circulated it under the nose of the original censor. The Mormon Church had so much difficulty with German officials that it established its first permanent mission headquarters across the border in German-speaking Switzerland, in the border town of Basel. In that era, the Mormons justified defying civil government in deference to "higher authority." God's law trumped civil law.

The Mormons learned other important lessons from their nineteenth century experience that they successfully applied during the Third Reich. The first missionaries to Germany struggled to learn the language, while their mission presidents suffered from scant cultural knowledge. There was no formal missionary training program, nor did young men undergo medical screening in anticipation of long days trekking on foot. A formal system of financial support had not yet been worked out; missionaries often depended on the good graces of German congregants to provide food and shelter. As the years passed, the Mormons began sending mission presidents to Germany who understood the language and culture. These leaders were German émigrés who received spiritual seasoning in the Mormon Culture Region, and who then agreed to return to their native lands to direct the proselytizing efforts. Formal training and financial support regimens did not occur until the first decades of the twentieth century.

The First World War and the Weimar Republic served as a bridge to legitimacy for Mormons in Germany, as they assumed responsibilities of citizenship in both war and the nascent democracy that followed. Some fifty-five German Mormons died on the battlefield for the Fatherland during the war, allowing the Latter-day Saints an authentic claim of patriotism during both the fledgling republic and the Nazi dictatorship that followed. During the Weimar Republic, Mormons enjoyed the benefits of the German constitutional democracy that allowed them to challenge expulsion decrees and seek civil redress for harassment by hostile clerics. The increase in German immigration to the American Zion also provided an impetus to develop the core of native Germans who eventually steered the LDS Church through the Second World War. By the time Hitler rose to power early in 1933, German citizens once again led most German ecclesiastical units at the branch (parish) and district (diocesan) level—as they had done in the First World War after the Americans left.

During the Weimar Republic, Mormon leaders demonstrated their growing willingness to comply with secular authority by disciplining members and missionaries who transgressed, and by improving supervision of subordinates. They also instituted training programs for newly arrived missionaries in Germany, formalized the system of financial support for these young emissaries of the gospel, and perfected a routine by which the American mission presidents would tour their jurisdictions periodically in order to supervise ecclesiastical activities. Mission presidents developed a working relationship with American consular officials in Germany, upon whom they could rely to intercede with both the Weimar and Nazi governments when missionaries experienced difficulty.

It would be a mistake to conclude, however, that missionaries and congregants obeyed solely because of improved supervision or fear of adverse consequences. The growth of the German LDS Church convinced young American elders and German converts that the Spartan missionary lifestyle and increasingly rigorous membership standards met with divine approval. Reports of miraculous healings, godly interventions in the face of danger, and mystical promptings provided the confirmation that these true believers needed to sustain their faith and endure conflict with German civil and religious authorities. A foundation was being laid, albeit unknowingly, for Mormonism's survival and arguable prosperity under the Nazi regime.

The Prewar Nazi Years, 1933–1939: A Forgotten History

The Mormons had not intended to partner with the National Socialist government. Reports dispatched by mission presidents in the late Weimar period expressed fear that a Nazi political takeover would impede

Introduction

the American missionary effort and disrupt Salt Lake City's control over German congregants. Initial efforts to maintain mastery of their own affairs morphed into an endeavor to exploit commonalities between the small American sect and the Nazi behemoth. As Christine Elizabeth King observed in one of the first scholarly articles on this subject, the Nazis and the Mormons shared a common *Weltanschauung*, a conjunction of worldviews.[7] National Socialist policies presented opportunities that were too attractive for the Mormons to let pass.

The Mormons in prewar Nazi Germany established a pattern for dealing with problems posed by the government. At first a challenge would arise that threatened the Mormons' ability to continue liturgical worship, church auxiliary activity, or missionary work. In the course of solving the problem at the lowest level of government officialdom, new opportunities would occur to exploit mutual areas of interest between the church and the regime, such as genealogical research and basketball, as described in chapters 11 and 12. In doing so, the Mormons often seemed oblivious to the implication of collaborating with the Nazi state. Often, articles would appear in a church publication, including the Church Section of the *Deseret News*, the Mormon Church-owned daily newspaper in Salt Lake City, which celebrated the success that the Latter-day Saints were enjoying in their relationship with the National Socialist government. At the same time, the news columns of the *Deseret News* were running wire-service stories that detailed the persecution that Germany's Jews were experiencing. The steady rhythm of disturbing news from Germany never discouraged the newspaper's religion section from publishing articles and pictures that celebrated the burgeoning relationship between the Mormon Church and the Nazi State. In 1937, a picture of the prophet, seer, and revelator Heber J. Grant, seated in front of a large Swastika banner during a banquet in Frankfurt, appeared in the Salt Lake City daily newspaper. That was one year after a similar picture of the European Mission President, Joseph Merrill, speaking at a Berlin podium adorned with a large swastika, ran in the same publication.

Such a symbiotic relationship would have helped the Mormons only to a limited degree without the guidance of skilled American leaders—well-educated mission presidents and other powerful Americans with strong political connections. Of the seven American mission leaders who served in prewar Nazi Germany, six were college graduates and two had earned additional professional degrees. All had served prior missions in Germany, and each was fluent in the language. During the peacetime National Socialist years before the Second World War, the Mormons also dispatched to Germany a parade of influential prelates, politicians, and professors. The message to the Third Reich was twofold: We will obey your laws and support your government, but we also have powerful friends in America who will notice if you mistreat us.

Two U.S. senators from Utah made their connection with Mormonism known. Reed Smoot, who served for three decades, wrote an article in the German-language Mormon weekly that extolled the virtues of genealogical research and made an anti-Semitic reference.[8] Elbert Thomas, who defeated Smoot in the 1932 elections, toured Germany for several weeks, consulting with government officials, academics, and the American ambassador. The most influential Mormon ambassador to Germany may have been J. Reuben Clark, who made two trips to Germany to negotiate with *Reichsbank* president Hjalmar Schacht, Hitler's finance minister. Unofficially on leave from the Mormon first presidency to represent the interests of America's small bondholders whose investments were imperiled in the Great Depression, Clark spent off-duty time addressing German members and American missionaries. The Gestapo, the secret police of Nazi Germany, could not have failed to notice the prominent American's access to powerful government officials and concomitant interest in Germany's Mormons.

Influential Americans such as Clark, who corresponded regularly with the Nazi finance ministry on bondholder business, helped differentiate the Mormons from other small American sects who had few friends in powerful positions abroad. Two of those, the Christian Scientists and the Seventh-day Adventists, suffered suspension of worship or curtailment of their privileges in Germany. Another sect, the Jehovah's Witnesses, fell victim to overt persecution that lead to the death of up to one-quarter of their German members. The compliant Mormons, unlike the Witnesses who refused to salute the swastika flag or serve in the army, knew when they could stand their ground and, conversely, when it was prudent to surrender to the Nazis' indomitable will. As an example of the latter, the Mormons disbanded their cherished Boy Scout troops, which they regarded as a vehicle of religious instruction. The Hitler Youth had demanded control over all youth organizations for boys, but through skilled negotiating the Mormons were able to retain their activities programs for adolescent girls.

From the top to the bottom of the ecclesiastical chain, Mormons in prewar Nazi Germany cooperated to survive and prosper. Many happily believed that they were favored citizens in a police state. Some ordinary congregants convinced themselves that Hitler had read the Book of Mormon and was a secret church member. Mission President Roy Welker, whose wife rode with Hitler in the Führer's limousine, told a civic meeting in Salt Lake City in 1937 that "Jews are safer today in Germany than they are in many parts of the world."[9] Such absurdities do not seem as preposterous when viewed through the eyes of those dedicated to serving causes bigger than them—Mormonism and Nazism.

Beacons of Mormon Memory in Nazi Germany

When Mormon missionaries began evacuating Europe during the week prior to the beginning of the Second World War, the detailed accounting of their activities—fastidiously recorded in personal journals and mission historical records—ceased. Extensive firebombing of German cities destroyed many records kept by the church members who remained. What survived was memory, which can be tricky. It is more difficult to manipulate information recorded on paper, protected and shared by archivists, and interpreted by historians. Recollection, what is remembered and what is repressed, can change as time passes. In the new collective memory of Mormons in Nazi Germany, fourteen thousand German Mormons were victims of the Second World War.[10] This storyline has its logical appeal. The war impacted Latter-day Saint life on the same scale that it affected most citizens of the Third Reich. Mormon husbands and sons fell on the battlefield. Church members died or lost their homes in bombing raids, made perilous escapes from burning cities, sent their children to live with relatives in the countryside, and feared advancing Red Army soldiers.[11]

The war also interrupted the religious life of small LDS congregations. It cut the ecclesiastical chain of authority through the removal of American missionaries. Military conscription of priesthood leaders disrupted the replacement German leadership structure. The loss of lives and meetinghouses to aerial bombing also destroyed the process of accountability. Author Gilbert Scharffs estimated that almost five hundred German Mormon soldiers and more than one hundred civilians died as the result of the hostilities.[12] Earlier records revealed a lower total of German Mormon casualties: 184 killed in combat and 120 who died on the home front.[13] Because of the catastrophe of war, no one knows exactly how many Mormons were killed or injured in the hostilities.[14]

Instead of a detailed chronicle punctuated with statistics, the favored stories of the Mormons in Germany during the Second World War unfold through a series of memory beacons:[15] courageous *Wehrmacht* soldiers who endured battlefield hardship without firing a shot at the enemy; resilient civilians who sheltered bombed-out co-religionists and took in evacuating Saints from the east; German priesthood holders who stepped into the role of the departed prewar American leadership; missionaries who returned as gracious occupation soldiers; and a massive church-sponsored relief campaign that transpired as the American ecclesiastical leadership returned to impose Zion's spiritual authority over its vanquished German congregants. Memory beacons that would not be so faith-promoting are conveniently omitted from the new collective memory. The suffering that German Mormons experienced during the war provides stories to tell that obscure other accounts that might not be spiritually stimulating.

These memory beacons come equipped with a dimmer switch, a rheostat by which memorialization can be dialed up or adjusted downward in the postwar period to meet the comfort level of surviving Mormons —be they ordinary family members, groups of German immigrants to the American Zion, or senior church leaders. The family of Max Reschke, the branch president who saved lives with his heroics but could not save his marriages or church membership because of his serial philandering, set their family patriarch's dimmer switch at a low level. His son authored a privately published book made available only to relatives and trusted friends, lectured at least once to a university class, and wrote a few articles for obscure genealogical magazines. He eschewed opportunities to seek a more public degree of memorialization for his father.

Chapter 13 profiles a Mormon memory beacon whose illumination had been totally darkened until a distant relative uncovered the story of an LDS commandant of a "wild" concentration camp in Berlin. Erich

Introduction

Krause had joined the Mormon Church in 1923 and then enrolled in the Hitler's brown-shirted SA five years later. Mormonism and Nazism became his twin passions. Krause was the commandant of Berlin's Pape Street prison in the mid-1930s, where he murdered and tortured Hitler's political opponents. Communists and Social Democrats were the main targets of his sadism while Hitler consolidated his power. Then, during the war years, Krause sent postcards home to his family from Poland, where he served as a military policeman in a city where the *Einsatzgruppen* liquidated the ghetto and loaded Jews on boxcars destined for the extermination camps. The cards reminded his children to attend their Mormon Sunday school lessons and say their prayers.

After the war, when Krause faced charges for crimes against humanity, an American Mormon mission president funded his pretrial bail from church funds and wrote letters to the court attesting to Krause's good character. He escaped punishment on a legal technicality and started a new life. He became a trusted genealogical researcher in his German Mormon congregation before he died in the early 1980s. Krause's memory beacon illuminated when his distant relative's unwelcomed book blindsided Krause's adult children, four of whom he had sired with his third wife after the war. They had immigrated to the United States without a clear knowledge of their father's hidden history.

The most prominent memory beacon in this narrative is an intelligent, idealistic, faithful young Mormon named Helmuth Hübener, sixteen years old when he began listening to the forbidden wartime broadcasts of the British Broadcasting Corporation. Convinced that the Nazi propaganda machine did not truthfully account for German wartime losses, he used his congregation's typewriter to produce anti-Hitler tracts that he and three friends—two of whom were Latter-day Saints—scattered around Hamburg. Convinced, as early as 1942, that Germany was losing the war, Hübener wanted to incite a popular rebellion against the Nazis. Betrayed by a colleague at work, Helmuth Hübener was tried by a Nazi tribunal and guillotined. Before his execution at age seventeen, his LDS congregational leader excommunicated the boy from the Mormon Church.

Chapter 16 recounts the heavy hand of Mormon officialdom on the dimmer switch of Hübener's memory beacon, alternately darkening and brightening Hübener's memorialization to meet the church's later twentieth century requirements—diplomatic relations with the communist East German Government, and domestic relations back home where German immigrants did not wish to be judged for their support of the Nazi state. In the twenty-first century, Hübener's memory beacon shines brightly, but behind a powerful filter. These days, books and videos tell the faithful of his courageous resistance against Hitler, while soft-peddling the fact that he rebelled as strongly against Nazi sympathizers in his Hamburg congregation as he did against the government. In the juxtaposition of faith and history in Mormondom, faith usually prevails.

PART I

The Mormon *Sonderweg*
The Road to Nazi Germany

1

Mormonism's Long Nineteenth Century in Germany

From Pariahs to Skilled Survivors

Joseph Smith had fewer than ten weeks to live when he preached his most significant sermon as the organizer of what would become the largest and most influential religious organization founded on American soil. Speaking on April 7, 1844, at the funeral of a friend, Smith outlined the doctrinal issues that separated Mormonism from mainstream Christianity. Elements of the "King Follett Discourse" had been introduced into LDS theology during the fourteen years that followed the church's founding, but never before had Smith expressed them all in one sermon. The importance of Smith's address extends beyond a public summation of the LDS Church's more controversial tenets: the nature of God, how the world was created, and humankind's relationship to God in the afterlife. Less prominent passages of that sermon suggest why Smith considered German-speaking converts so important to the future of his fledgling religion.

Smith delivered the funerary oration on a Sunday afternoon in a tree-lined amphitheater on a bluff overlooking the Mississippi River town of Nauvoo, Illinois. Mormonism's founder described his faith's idea of the deity, which differed from traditional Christianity's Trinitarian concept. God the Father, whom Smith referred to using the Old Testament name of Elohim, was not a spirit but instead a corporal entity—blessed with a perfect, everlasting body of flesh and bones. His son, Jesus Christ, according to Smith, also possessed a physical body. The Holy Spirit was the only member of the Mormon godhead that did not manifest a physical presence.

The creation story told in the Book of Genesis revealed only part of the truth, Smith maintained, for God had not formed the entire universe from nothing, nor did he do it alone. Rather, when Elohim created the earth, he did so as a member of a group of gods, each of whom had ascended to divinity after a probationary period as men who lived in worlds similar to earth. As Elohim had once been a man who became a god, all humans who inhabit the earth have the potential to achieve godhood in their own right and to preside as Supreme Being over worlds of their own. In contemporary times, Smith preached, that path wound through the church he had established.[1]

Then, in a section of the King Follett Discourse that most scholars ignore, Smith maintained that the German version of the Bible, as adopted by members of the Evangelical Church, is "the most nearly correct translation, and corresponds to the revelations which God has given me for the past fourteen years." In remarks made to a smaller group a few days later, Smith expounded on his belief that the German Bible provided scriptural justification for his sect's deviations from orthodox Christianity: "The old German translators are the most nearly correct, and the most honest of any of the translators."[2]

Smith's fascination with biblical German may have stemmed from association with Peter Whitmer. Smith and his wife Emma lived in Seneca County, New York, with the Whitmer family in 1829 while Smith ostensibly translated the Book of Mormon from golden plates he had obtained during an apparition of the Angel Moroni. Peter, along with five of his sons and one son-in-law, comprised seven of the original eleven "witnesses" who claimed they had seen the golden plates. Whitmer, who had grown up in Pennsylvania while speaking German as his first language, belonged to a German Reformed congregation before he became a believer in Mormonism. All members of the Whitmer household spoke English with a German accent. A few years later, Smith studied German under the tutelage of Mormonism's first Jewish convert, Alexander Neibaur, who converted in England and emigrated to America in 1838. Neibaur, a dentist, had capped Smith's tooth, broken several years earlier when Smith had been beaten, tarred, and feathered by a mob in Ohio.

A former rabbinical student, Neibaur may have prompted Smith's belief in polytheism: Elohim, in Old Testament Hebrew, is plural.³

While speaking to that small group of believers in Nauvoo several days after he delivered the King Follett Discourse, the Mormon prophet enlarged the scope of his remarks from German-language scripture to the German people themselves, pronouncing what may have been his rationale for ordering an intensive nineteenth-century conversion effort in the territory of the German states prior to unification: "The Germans are an exalted people!"⁴

Exaltation, in Mormon theology, refers to achieving the highest degree of God's favor in a stratified heavenly afterlife. An adherent whose earthly faith and good works earns postmortal residence in the Celestial Kingdom would also qualify to progress to godhood as Elohim had done.⁵ Joseph Smith proclaimed the German potential for exaltation, but no record has been discovered that documents Smith's evaluation of the prospects for godhood among the other particular nationalities and linguistic groups that his church targeted for conversion.

The importance that Mormons placed on converting Germans, either because of Smith's belief in their potential for divinity or because they subsequently became hardworking settlers on the American frontier, drove the missionary effort in Germany. The more missionaries they sent to the German states, the more converts those efforts produced, and thus, the German influence on Mormonism intensified. From the beginning of missionary work in the mid-nineteenth century until 1950, more German speakers joined the Latter-day Saints than any linguistic group other than English speakers. Residents of German-speaking lands made up the third most populous group of immigrants to the American Zion, after residents of the British Isles and Scandinavia.⁶

Successor Mormon prophets have reemphasized the importance of catering to the spiritual needs of the large German ethnic minority that populated the Mormon Culture Region, as well as to German Mormons living abroad. Joseph F. Smith, a member of the church's three-member ruling council who would later ascend to the office of prophet, seer, and revelator, visited the Swiss and German Mission in 1875. He did this in the midst of German harassment of Mormon missionaries in states that ranged from Schleswig-Holstein in the north to Bavaria in the south, and from the Rhineland in the west to East Prussia. As part of a visit to Great Britain and continental Europe in 1937, Heber J. Grant, the last polygamous church president, visited both German-speaking Switzerland and Nazi Germany during a period in which Hitler's government threatened the existence of other small, American-based new religious groups in Germany.[7] In 1951, David O. McKay, by this time the prophet, seer, revelator, visited Germany and dedicated new church construction projects. In 1973, Harold B. Lee, the eleventh church president, spoke to an assemblage of East German Mormons who had been granted special dispensation to attend a conference in Munich during the height of the Cold War. He urged them to remain loyal to both their civil government and their religious tenets, and to return to their homes behind the Iron Curtain.[8]

Shortly after the Second World War, Thomas S. Monson, who later became the Mormon Prophet in February 2008, began his adult church service as the bishop (lay minister) of a metropolitan Salt Lake City ward (congregation) made up of many descendants of German immigrants. During the 1960s and 70s, he served as Mormonism's visiting emissary to East Germany, where he catered to the needs of German Latter-day Saints who struggled with the challenges of practicing an American religion in a communist state. He eventually negotiated an agreement to build a Mormon temple in Freiberg, Saxony, the first such structure erected behind the Iron Curtain, as well as an agreement for a reciprocal exchange of Mormon missionaries between East and West Germany—some four years before the fall of the Berlin Wall.[9] When Monson became church president, he chose a former German citizen and Lufthansa Airlines pilot, Dieter Uchtdorf, as the Second Counselor in the First Presidency—the number three leadership position in Mormon hierarchy.

In order to understand why the Mormons cooperated eagerly with the government of the Third Reich, one must start at the beginning, at the religion's founding on the American frontier. Although the effort to win converts far away on German soil proved to be difficult, missionaries continued to follow Smith's admonition to cultivate an "exalted" strain of Germanic adherents. After Smith's death the Mormons, with their pragmatic worldview, continued to embrace Germans as productive converts and immigrants whose temperaments fit well with the church's authoritarian leadership style. But as Smith made clear in one of his last public pronouncements before being killed by a jailhouse mob two months later, God's prophet on earth viewed Germans as a breeding stock for deity.

American Frontier Mysticism and the Roots of Early Mormonism

On the American frontier in the early nineteenth century, during a period religious historians call the Second Great Awakening, pioneers found restorationist Christianity to be an appealing concept. The Millerites, Seventh-day Adventists, and Shakers, in addition to the Mormons, claimed to correct erroneous beliefs and practices promulgated by the mainline Protestant churches of the day. As a fourteen-year-old boy in 1820, Joseph Smith proclaimed that God the Father and Jesus Christ had visited him one day in a grove in western New York, to answer his prayerful pleading for guidance as to which church he should join. They told him to affiliate with no established religion, as all were wrong. Later, Smith claimed to have conversed with John the Baptist and the apostles Peter, James, and John, who ordained him to various levels of the priesthood.

Smith had the background to establish what has become the most successful religious denomination conceived entirely on American soil. He grew up in western New York's "burned over district," so designated because during his boyhood itinerant evangelists and circuit-riding preachers peddled their spiritual wares as fervently and frequently as traveling tradesmen sold goods. Thus, Smith had the advantage of knowing the burning theological questions of the day. One of the hottest topics was the origin of the American Indians. As Smith's most widely read biographer, Fawn McKay Brodie, maintained, some of the most prominent clerics of early America—William Penn, Cotton Mather, Roger Williams, and Jonathan Edwards—preached that the natives they encountered were the descendants of the ten lost tribes of Israel. As a boy, Smith had access to private lending networks that allowed books to circulate for hundreds of miles. One of those, *View of the Hebrews*, published in two editions in 1823 and 1825, became popular during his late adolescence. Author Ethan Smith, unrelated to Joseph, argued that the American Indians were Jews, and that the gospel of Christ had been preached in ancient America. He further contended that the Western Hemisphere had been populated by early inhabitants who undertook long sea voyages for religious reasons, and that these Semitic migrants had divided themselves into warring tribes, some that were highly civilized and others less so. All of these claims are central themes of the Book of Mormon.[10]

A Distinctly American Church Relies Extensively on Foreign Converts

Joseph Smith founded the Church of Jesus Christ of Latter-day Saints on April 6, 1830, in Peter Whitmer's house in western New York. Six charter members enrolled. Smith bestowed upon himself the spiritual title of prophet, seer, and revelator, as well as the temporal position of church president. Later, when he sent his brother Samuel from town to town selling copies of the Book of Mormon, the younger sibling preached the doctrine of a new faith: The "American Prophet" would restore the doctrinal beliefs and priesthood authority that the early Christian church enjoyed before it became corrupted under the influence of the Roman emperor Constantine.

By the autumn of that year, four full-time missionaries proselytized among the American Indians, and the first Mormon missionaries to preach outside of the United States began recruiting converts in Canada. According to Columbian University historian Richard L. Bushman, these missionaries "went without training or indoctrination. . . . No education was required." Their fresh converts quickly became the newest missionaries. An early Mormon elder, Eber D. Howe, described the quality of these first emissaries of the faith: "Nearly all of their male converts, however ignorant and worthless, were forthwith transformed into 'elders,' and sent forth to proclaim, with all their wild enthusiasm, the wonders and mysteries of Mormonism."[11]

Through determined efforts by these crudely polished converts, several hundred new members joined by the end of the church's first year. Domestic missionary efforts continued unabated, and by the end of the church's fifth year in 1835, membership had grown, astonishingly, to 8,835.[12] During this period, preliminary preparations for overseas missionary work commenced with the conversion of immigrants from Europe, whom Smith and his lieutenants hoped would provide a foundation of expertise to send missionaries worldwide. In 1837, Joseph Smith dispatched Heber C. Kimball to open a mission to the British Isles. By the end of 1841, nine of the serving members of the Quorum of the Twelve, whom the Mormons considered to be the modern-day equivalent of the twelve apostles, had relocated to Great Britain for the purpose of recruiting new members who would move to the United States.[13] As the year 1842 concluded, some 5,500 British subjects had become Mormons, and by 1857 more than fifteen thousand Britons had converted.[14] Most subsequently sailed for the new American Zion.[15] By the end of the 1850s, Smith and his successor, Brigham Young, had sent missionaries to Austria, Canada, Chile, China, France, Germany, Gibraltar, Great Britain, Hawaii, India, Italy, Jamaica, Malta, Palestine, Scandinavia, South Africa, the islands of the South Pacific, and Switzerland.[16] Each dispatched the majority of its converts to Zion, which by 1847—because of constant Mormon conflict with neighbors in New York, Ohio, Missouri, and Illinois—had relocated to the barren northernmost outpost of Mexican territory in the North American Intermountain West.

The First German Missionary Efforts: A Template for Later Success

James Howard, a recent English convert to Mormonism, took a job in a Hamburg foundry in September 1840. He tried missionary work but soon became discouraged. "I am too weak a creature to do anything with them," Howard wrote to Joseph Smith before he returned home, admitting defeat as the first Mormon who tried preaching in the territory that later became unified Germany.[17] Nine months later, Mormon Apostle Orson Hyde stopped in Frankfurt on his way to Jerusalem, where he planned to "dedicate Palestine for the return of the Jews." Mormons believe an interpretation of the New Testament Book of Revelation that requires the return of the Jews to their historical homeland, a prerequisite to the thousand-year reign of Christ on earth prophesized to occur prior to the Apocalypse.[18] While Hyde waited for his visa to visit the Holy Land, he claimed to have attained a remarkable mastery of German in the astonishingly short period of five days, which he used upon his return from Jerusalem to author the first German-language LDS religious tract. When he presented *Ein Ruf aus der Wüste*, A Cry out of the Wilderness, to a printer in Regensburg, the city's censor rejected it as "likely to cause excitement and unrest among the people."[19]

These first two ambassadors of Mormonism in the German-speaking world, Howard and Hyde, illustrate several key aspects of Mormon experience that recurred with regularity in the nineteenth and early twentieth centuries. Early LDS histories in German-speaking lands abound with miraculous tales: healings of the sick, fervent prayers that provoke divine intervention with recalcitrant authorities, and the "gift of tongues"—in Mormon theology the God-given ability to master foreign languages rapidly for missionary purposes. Apostle Hyde's claim of miraculous short-term German language mastery seems to have provoked skepticism, even by author Gilbert Scharffs, who is otherwise known for his faith-promoting historical accounts and apologetic argumentation.[20] "Elder Hyde must have made amazing progress in learning German," Scharffs declares, "because those with whom he stayed found it hard to believe he had neither spoken nor studied the language prior to his arrival in Frankfurt."[21]

Hyde's experience with the censors also marked the first of many recorded clashes between Mormon missionaries and German authorities. Mormons employed many techniques to surmount opposition, such as the reassignment of barred missionaries to different locations, where expulsions from other German kingdoms were not recognized. Also, missionaries appealed to parallel or higher authority to overcome official proscription. In the case of the banned pamphlet, Hyde simply took his rejected text to Frankfurt and found both a printer and a censor who approved.

Throughout Mormon history, an initial lack of success in missionary work usually provoked intensified corrective efforts directed by higher authority and entrusted to emissaries with a greater degree of ecclesiastical authority and interpersonal skill. Joseph Smith dispatched Apostle Hyde to Palestine shortly after receiving an apologetic letter from Howard, the British foundry worker in Hamburg whose mission had failed. Smith understood that Hyde would also proselyte in the Mediterranean region and Eastern Europe. Hyde was one of the few members of the Quorum of the Twelve who had remained in the United States when most of his fellow Apostles participated in the intensive effort during the 1840s to convert and attract English-speaking converts from the British Isles. Smith's willingness to dispatch abroad one of his remaining assistants demonstrates the importance the early Mormons placed on recruiting members from Germany.

As Mormonism became increasingly controversial in the United States, its reputation followed missionaries dispatched overseas, resulting in increased difficulties with civil and religious authorities. The practice of polygamy and the deteriorating relationship between the church and the U.S. government, especially during the 1857–58 Utah War, became a reason for German officials to oppose Mormon missionary work. Although the existence of Mormon polygamy had been rumored since Joseph Smith took his first "plural wife" in 1833, it became public knowledge in 1842 with the publication of a scandalous expose written by John Bennett, a disaffected Mormon militia leader, who was promptly excommunicated. Another ten years transpired before the LDS Church issued its first public statement on the practice, Orson Pratt's August 29, 1852, address in Salt Lake City that defended both the spiritual attributes and legality of plural marriage.[22] Officials of the German states also knew of the Mormons' historical difficulty with civil authorities, and with ordinary neighbors, wherever they had lived—in western New York, Ohio, Missouri, and Illinois.

As its missionaries and new converts suffered civil harassment in Germany and elsewhere in Europe, the church hierarchy dispatched more missionary and supervisory personnel to overcome the opposition. This, in turn, created more opportunities for conflict with local clergy and government officials. As Mormon missionaries converted more Germans, and as the new converts emigrated, German Protestant ministers and Catholic priests increased their pressure on officials of local government to clamp down on the activities of these conspicuous representatives of a strange foreign religion. This cycle repeated itself for the duration of the Mormons' "long nineteenth century" in Germany, and was interrupted only when the First World War forced the withdrawal of American missionaries from German soil.

The First Mormon Mission in Germany

On April 3, 1852, the first designated Mormon mission president for the German states arrived in Hamburg. Daniel Carn, a German immigrant who converted to Mormonism in the United States, had been the first leader of the initial German-speaking ecclesiastical unit in Nauvoo, Illinois. He quickly established a congregation of twelve Hamburg converts and just as rapidly got into trouble with the law. On eight separate occasions, he appeared before the police and officials of the Hamburg Senate. Eventually, after refusing to leave Hamburg, Carn went to jail. His temporary imprisonment prompted another defensive measure the Mormons employed repeatedly to meet official opposition from the mid-nineteenth century through the Nazi years: he sought and received the intervention of American diplomatic officials. After U.S. Consul Samuel Bromberg obtained Carn's release on the condition that the Mormon mission president leave Hamburg, Carn fled to the city's suburb of Altoona, which at the time was under Danish governance. Based there, he continued to preach and win converts, and occasionally visited stealthily the congregants and the missionaries sent to replace him in Hamburg.[23]

The first thirty years of Mormon history in the German states unfolded as the story of relentless proselyting by missionaries who endured against clerical and governmental opposition, the emigration of their converts from Germany to the American Zion, and the reaction of authorities who subsequently harassed, jailed, and expelled the missionaries. Young Mormon missionaries who arrived to take their place convinced common, uneducated townspeople and countryside peasants to change their religious beliefs, leave extended family behind, and seek a life of hardship in a new land half a world away, where they would have to adopt a strange language. One of these missionaries was John Beck, who had emigrated from Germany, converted to Mormonism while in the United States, and then returned to Germany as a missionary—only to be jailed three times in his hometown of Stuttgart. Another missionary, Ernst Mueller, went to jail eleven times in three months. In Hamburg, a successor mission president, George Reiser, received a two-week prison sentence for "being dangerous to our government," but called upon a familiar ally, American consul Bromberg, who negotiated his release in exchange for Reiser's expeditious departure from the country.

Survival, physical and financial, also plays a key role in this story. Reiser once avoided an angry contingent of hostile former converts who sought to confront him at a railroad station. He evaded the mob by taking an alternate exit from the train platform.[24] In later decades, missionaries would receive regular disbursements of money from relatives in America, but in the early days, they relied on the goodwill of their German converts for support. In Karlsruhe, an entire congregation of Germans abandoned their Mormon faith seemingly overnight, and suddenly refused to feed or house the missionaries.[25] Despite tales of harrowing escapes from the police and mobs of apostate members turned foes, no Mormon missionary in Germany during its first fifty years of proselyting lost his life in the line of duty—a circumstance that only gave rise to more faith-promoting stories of miraculous preservation from the Lord's enemies.

German Mormonism during the Era of Unification: A Semblance of Permanence

The reality of German opposition to Mormon proselyting dictated the necessity of establishing a headquarters operation in another country. In 1853 a (failed) Mormon attempt to obtain an audience with King Friedrich Wilhelm IV disturbed the Prussian state authorities to the extent that they issued a formal decree, a *Runderlass*, that denied legal status to the LDS Church.[26] It became the basis for the periodic ejection of Mormon missionaries from Prussia for the next half-century. The events leading to that expulsion order represented an important lesson that the Mormons learned well, and which they used to their advantage in dealing with German governments in subsequent periods, including the Third Reich. In essence, the LDS Mission leadership learned to avoid "overplaying its hand," and to seek resolution of problems on the lowest possible local governmental level, eschewing undue attention from powerful state authorities.

In the church-wide General Conference of January 1853, Brigham Young announced the dispatch of two emissaries—Orson Spencer and Jacob Houtz—to Berlin with instructions to seek an audience with the Prussian monarch. Young had been told that Friedrich Wilhelm IV had expressed, through a diplomatic legate, some interest in Mormonism. Young hoped to facilitate the emigration of Germans and establish a cordial relationship with their government. The mission of the two Mormons caused a stir in the German press, which in turn apparently agitated officials of Germany's Evangelical Church. Evidently, the Prussian government had learned of their plans early, as news of the emissaries' trip—such as their arrival in St. Louis from Salt Lake City—appeared in German newspapers. Prussian secret police exercised an effective spy network, which presumably included German expatriates in the United States. Six days after their arrival in Berlin, having been unsuccessful in gaining an audience with Friedrich Wilhelm IV, Orson and Houtz were hauled before a police court, questioned, and expelled from the kingdom.[27]

Three months later, on April 26, 1853, the Prussian interior ministry issued the *Runderlass* (a circular stating official government policy) that denied the Mormons legal status in Prussia and that, in effect, became a standing expulsion order that authorities used to harass, detain, and deport the church's missionaries. This occurred less than one year after Mormon Apostle Orson Pratt had publically admitted, at a church general conference, the existence of the doctrine of plural marriage. The decree found the Mormons objectionable on the grounds that they encouraged immigration to the United States, not specifically because of young women who would enter into polygamous marriages, but instead because of what the authors perceived as politically motivated Mormon recruitment of German citizens. As Michael Mitchell, in a master's thesis written at Brigham Young University, said: "The language of the decree focused not on doctrines and practices, but on a perception of the Prussian government that church leaders in Utah desired political independence from the federal government. If missionaries could attract a large enough immigrant population to qualify as a state, Utah would be subject to its own local laws rather than federal decrees hostile to the Mormon way of life."[28]

The decree was based on Paragraph 114 of the Prussian Criminal Code, which punished military deserters and discouraged emigration of workers with critical skills. Throughout the nineteenth century, Mormons clashed with German authorities over emigration, not only because of the emotional issue of German women becoming polygamous concubines, but also because of Mormon emigration's effect on draft-eligible men. American diplomats in Germany often had to intercede on behalf of native Germans, Mormons and non-Mormons, who had become naturalized American citizens. When these German expatriates returned to their native land to visit relatives, some become embroiled in the issue of whether they had fulfilled their German military obligations.[29]

In 1861, the Mormons established the Swiss-Italian-German Mission, which in reality was a mission to the Swiss with limited outreach to Germans and Italians. Brigham Young University church history and doctrine professor Bruce A. Van Orden explained: "In the German states, persecution had become so intense that most members had gathered to Zion and missionary work there was close to nonexistent. . . . A rotation system kept missionary efforts there alive. When one missionary was persecuted or banished, he left for Switzerland and another arrived to replace him."[30]

When Mission President Joseph S. Horne arrived in Basel in the mid-1860s, he toured Mormon congregations in the Swiss cantons, but according to mission records, "did not risk going into Germany."[31] Only five American missionaries were at work in the German states at the time, and the most recent attempt to send a missionary to Germany had failed when the young man ran out of funds. In 1867, only 464 members resided in the entire mission that included Switzerland, and the largest German branch, at Karlsruhe, had only nineteen members.[32]

The use of Switzerland as a base for dispatching missionaries into hostile German territory represented an important and long-lasting step that Mormons undertook in order to continue their missionary work on German soil. Mormons also clashed with Swiss authorities during the 1840s and 50s, but in 1864, a decree of the Federal Council of Switzerland granted Mormons rights equal to those enjoyed by other churches with regard to holding church services and the baptism of converts.[33] From 1861 until 1898, and again from 1904 to 1925, LDS missionaries in Germany reported to a mission president who took shelter in the relatively safe cities of Geneva and Basel.[34] From 1925 until 1937, when missionaries in the eastern part of Germany reported to a mission president in Dresden and then Berlin, Basel also served as Mormon missionary headquarters for western Germany as well as the German-speaking cantons of Switzerland. During the First World War, when the church pulled its foreign missionaries out of Germany, the Swiss mission office kept in touch with German members as best it could by mail and through interviews with occasional travelers. During the last years of the Weimar Republic and the first years of the Third Reich, the office of the German-Austrian Mission operated under the watchful eye of the German government, but missionaries who proselytized in the western half of Germany always knew a safe haven existed across the border in Switzerland. At the outbreak of the Second World War, when Mormon missionaries again evacuated—this time not only from Germany but the rest of continental Europe—European Mission President Thomas E. McKay oversaw the shutdown of missionary affairs from his Swiss base for months before leaving for the United States in the summer of 1940.

Skilled Leaders Bring Stability to Missionary Efforts

As the nineteenth century progressed, LDS leaders became aware of the need to send culturally and linguistically skilled emissaries to the foreign mission field throughout the world. Although front-line proselytizing missionaries would still arrive in foreign lands with inadequate knowledge of the local language and customs, a small group of proficient leaders began to emerge.[35] Early mission presidents had come to Germany with no knowledge of the language or, if they were native-born Americans whose childhood tongue was German, they had no experience living in the land of their ancestors. As Mormonism aged sufficiently to allow European converts to mature in their newfound faith by joining the main body of Latter-day Saints in America, a corps of native German speakers with the desired European cultural knowledge became available to return as leaders in the mission field. Karl Maeser, the most revered German mission president of the nineteenth century, and his brother-in-law, Edward Schoenfeldt, typified these new leaders.

Because of his education, Maeser was an unusual early convert. Most nineteenth century Germans were literate but enjoyed limited formal schooling.[36] Maeser, by contrast, was a well-educated intellectual who eventually rose to the position of president of Brigham Young Academy, the forerunner to Brigham Young University (BYU). Born in 1828 in Saxony, he became an accomplished linguist and musician. His parents provided years of private tutoring, plus an impressive formal education for the time—two years at the Krenz Schule in Dresden before he graduated with distinction from the Friederich Stadt normal school. He became proficient in Latin, French, and Italian, played the piano and organ, and conducted choral groups and orchestras. As a young man, he taught school and offered private tutoring.[37]

An early missionary tract stimulated Maeser's interest in Mormonism. It contained grammatical errors and a writing style that betrayed the author as someone whose native language was not German. Maeser's intellectual curiosity led to correspondence with Mormon missionaries in Copenhagen and Geneva, and the eventual dispatch of a missionary to meet Maeser. Because Mormons were banned from Saxony at the time, missionary William Budge traveled surreptitiously, posing as an English instructor, and confirmed Maeser's identity by matching his half of an irregularly cut card with the other half that had been mailed to Maeser. Budge did his best to teach Maeser the principles of Mormonism, as well as could any Englishman who spoke no German. Despite difficulties in communicating with his tutor, Maeser embraced the new faith. In order to avoid attention, he consented to be baptized in the Elbe River at midnight on October 11, 1854.

Maeser quickly assumed an unusual position for a newly converted member, that of Dresden branch president, but because of disfavor encountered by Mormons in his native state, he eventually agreed to emigrate with his family in 1856. Learning English quickly, he served as a missionary in Great Britain before sailing for Philadelphia in 1857. Because he had no money for overland passage to Utah, he accepted a calling to proselytize in the American Southern States Mission and earned his living by giving music lessons. While demonstrating a piano in a Virginia music store, he was approached by John Tyler, a former president of the United States, who hired Maeser to teach piano lessons to his daughters. Eventually, Maeser moved to Salt Lake City, where he became a private tutor to Brigham Young's children.[38]

Ten years after he immigrated to the United States, and after attaining sufficient expertise with his adopted religion, Maeser answered Young's call to become president of the Swiss-Italian-German Mission. When Maeser and Octave Ursenbach, who had also been converted in Germany before emigrating, arrived in Geneva in September of 1867, they found the mission's affairs in a deplorable state. Membership in all of Switzerland and Germany had fallen from 700 at the onset of the mission at the beginning of the decade to only 464 upon the new mission president's arrival. An average of 35 baptisms occurred each year, with an equal number of emigrations and excommunications. Only five American missionaries were at work, and they mostly preached on the Swiss side of the border.

Maeser's understanding of German culture led him to pursue available avenues of success and eschew strategies that led to confrontations with government officials and rival clerics. He arranged speaking engagements in Switzerland and Germany, not proselytizing *per se*, but instead educational lectures. These attracted the curious without threatening the religious status quo.[39] Twentieth century Mormon missionaries would follow his lead by giving presentations on the geological wonders of the State of Utah, and the health benefits of the Mormon Word of Wisdom, which prescribes abstinence from alcohol, tobacco, coffee, tea, and dangerous drugs. Of course, missionaries in Maeser's day and thereafter always stood by to provide follow-up religious instruction if attendees asked. In January 1869, he started the monthly Mormon religious publication, *Der Stern* (The Star), printed without the censor's constraints in Switzerland. The mission office in Basel distributed *Der Stern* by mail where the postal inspectors would allow, and by hand when necessary. The name closely paralleled its English-language cousin, *The Millennial Star*, which began publication in London in 1840, and from which *Der Stern* editors translated many articles into German. *Der Stern* published continuously from 1869 until it suspended publication for the duration of the Second World War.[40]

Maeser dropped the reference to Italy from the mission's title and renamed it the Swiss and German Mission. That name remained from 1868 until 1897, the longest continuity of a German-speaking Mormon mission since the first missionary arrived in 1840. Maeser reported the founding of congregations in Bavaria and Württemberg at a time that Mormonism was shrinking or nonexistent in the rest of Germany. Records show some six hundred conversions, mostly German-speaking Swiss, during the two and one-half years of Maeser's mission. When he returned to the United States in 1870, he did so as the leader of a party of some eighty-five emigrants. When he arrived in Salt Lake City, Utah, he became the branch president of a German-speaking congregation that enrolled many of his converts. Maeser left the mission in the hands of his brother-in-law Edward Schoenfeldt who, like Maeser, had converted in Germany, migrated to the American Zion, and returned to preside over mission efforts with the cultural understanding that only a native German could provide.[41]

By the 1870s, forty years after the church's founding, the pool of linguistically and culturally aware mission presidents with spiritual seasoning in the American Zion had increased to a level adequate to staff its overseas missions. Conflict with civil and religious authorities in Germany and elsewhere abroad would continue through the first decades of the next century, but this new brand of missionary leader had the knowledge and experience to choose his battles with discretion.

Mormon Polygamy: The Elephant in the German Parlor

Legend recounts that when Karl Maeser left on his mission to Germany in 1867, he gave his wife Anna his last fifty-cent piece and that when she met him upon his return to Utah in 1870, she gave it back to him.[42] Five years later in 1875, Maeser "rewarded" his wife's loyalty and frugality by giving her a "sister wife." Like so many Mormon elders of the time, he became a polygamist. His bride was Emilie Damke, a fellow German immigrant twenty-three years younger than Anna. No publically available record reveals his first wife's reaction, but this marriage marked an important dichotomy. A culturally aware, well-educated German used his native skills to help the Mormons succeed in the mission field, but then surrendered one facet of his German identity: he adopted the Mormon practice of taking more than one wife.

For Mormons attempting to gain traction as a legitimate religious organization in Germany, no facet of their faith inspired more fear, loathing, and determined opposition than the doctrine of polygamy. Leaders of Germany's two largest Christian denominations, Catholicism and Lutheranism, civil authorities from parliamentarians to policemen on the street, and opinion leaders such as journalists and professors had no need to investigate or to invent reasons to fear the Mormons. If the fact that one man could marry more than one woman were not sufficiently inflammatory, Mormonism's many detractors could choose among a plethora of rumor, innuendo, and sensationalistic fiction being promulgated in the popular press, over conversations at the beer hall, or in Sunday sermons.[43]

When President James Buchanan sent Colonel Albert Sidney Johnson and a contingent of army troops to the Salt Lake Valley in 1858 to facilitate the installation of territorial governor Alfred Cumming, the purpose was to insure a smooth transition from the theocratic outgoing governor, the Mormon prophet Brigham Young. Articles in the German press of the time, however, said the troops were being sent to rescue German immigrants who were being held hostage. When German newspapers reported the driving of the "golden spike" at Promontory Summit, Utah, in 1869, marking completion of the Transcontinental Railroad, some editors speculated that Americans were building a railroad in order to dispatch troops to combat the Mormons.[44] Agitation over polygamy, especially rumors of its practice being forced upon unwilling young women, played a role in popular fiction of that era that eventually found its way into German translation. As historian James B. Allen said: "Throughout the nineteenth century the Church and its members were presented to the public in popular magazines and novels that stressed the sensational. Many readers gained their only conception of Mormonism from articles condemning polygamy or criticizing the leaders as autocrats and denouncing the church as un-American."[45]

The second half of Conan Doyle's first Sherlock Holmes detective novel, *A Study in Scarlet*, takes place in the Utah territory and spins the fictional account of a young woman unwillingly taken into a polygamous marriage and her efforts to escape her husband and the Mormon secret police, the Danites. She eventually commits suicide.

In 1862, Congress passed the Morrill Anti-Bigamy Act, but its enforcement proved impossible in Utah courts composed of faithful Mormons.[46] The executive branch showed no enthusiasm for instigating another internal American conflict during the Civil War. As historian James B. Allen points out, Abraham Lincoln told a visiting Mormon: "You go back and tell Brigham Young that if he will leave me alone, I'll leave him alone."[47] Lincoln's unwillingness to enforce the new anti-polygamy law did not diminish the intensity with which German authorities harassed Mormon missionaries. While the congressional bill was being debated, two missionaries near Durlach in Baden-Württemberg spent five days in jail for distributing unauthorized religious material. Authorities in Karlsruhe prohibited members from holding church meetings in their own homes and forbade their contact with missionaries. Another missionary in southern Germany went to jail three times during 1862. In Adorf, a village in southwest Saxony, Elder Ernst F. Mueller scheduled a lecture, only to learn that some of his audience had arrived with the intention of killing him. One German mother became so upset by the conversion of her son to Mormonism that she submitted a bottle of consecrated oil, used in religious healing ceremonies, to a chemist to determine if her boy had been drugged.[48]

In 1872, Mormon polygamy again made headlines in the United States and abroad when federal prosecutors, under the auspices of the Morrill Act, obtained an indictment against Brigham Young for adultery, but the Supreme Court quashed Young's and others' indictments on a technical point of law. Two years later, the federal Poland Act weakened the Mormons' ability to defend themselves against polygamy charges by removing jurisdiction from the local probate courts and awarding it to the federal judiciary.[49] In 1882, Congress passed the Edmunds Act, which added unlawful cohabitation to the proscription against polygamous marriage, and prescribed a $500 fine and five-year jail term for either marrying a new polygamous wife or living with an existing one. New voting regulations disenfranchised some twelve thousand Utahns. In Germany, where accounts of these measures appeared in the newspapers, the Mormons experienced increased legal scrutiny and some mob violence. In Bavaria, a Mormon missionary was conducting a church service in a private residence when a group of some thirty men surrounded the house, broke open the door, dragged him out, and beat him. Bavarian authorities expelled two other missionaries at approximately the same time. Another missionary in Kiel languished in solitary confinement for three weeks on a nebulous charge of "baptizing" before his acquittal at trial.[50]

The 1880s proved to be a watershed decade for Mormon polygamy. This was the "underground period" in the American Zion, when otherwise lawful Mormon men either suffered imprisonment for polygamous cohabitation or moved away with their families to escape the wrath of federal judges appointed to enforce the recently enacted laws. Even the prophet, seer, and revelator John Taylor—who ascended to the church presidency after Brigham Young's death in 1877—moved from place to place to avoid capture. He ruled the LDS theocracy by postal dispatch.

The Edmunds-Tucker Act of 1887 dissolved the Church of Jesus Christ of Latter-day Saints as a corporate entity and seized most church property. It legalized a wife's testimony against her husband, abolished women's suffrage in the Utah territory, and dissolved both voting districts and local control of schools.[51] It also seized the Church's assets and shut down the Perpetual Emigration Fund that loaned money to those desiring transoceanic passage and provided start-up funds once the immigrant arrived in Zion.[52] At one point during this decade, more than thirteen thousand Mormons were imprisoned in the Utah territory for plural marriage or "cohabitation."

German officials took notice and used the Mormons' difficulties with their own government as an excuse to consider the church an undesirable organization. When a missionary named Francis D. Lyman went on trial for advocating polygamous marriage, the German prosecutor said: "The United States government is legislating against you; why shouldn't we?" A missionary in Nuremberg reported that police detectives kept him under surveillance, and when he later appeared before the police commissioner for Bavaria, he learned that the police intelligence branch had documented his day-to-day activities since his arrival in the country. According to reports submitted by the mission office to headquarters in Salt Lake City, German newspapers during this period reported many incidents of exploitation of émigrés who had settled in Utah, which church officials countered by submitting hundreds of affidavits from expatriates attesting to their proper treatment in America.[53]

Throughout their history in Germany, Mormon missionaries seemed to be of two minds with regard to their relationship with the Twelfth Article of Faith, a tenet of their religion that mandated loyalty to civil government and obedience to the law of the land. Whenever a mission leader found himself confronted by local civil authorities, he proclaimed his willingness to obey civil authority as a scriptural mandate. That occurred in the days of the first mission president, Daniel Carn, in the early 1850s, through the turn of the twentieth century, when Mission President Hugh J. Cannon told Berlin police of "the church's belief in subjugation to local police and noted that the well-being of the Imperial Government was the object of their daily prayers."[54]

Nevertheless, whenever a chance occurred to achieve success in a "higher calling," adherence to statute law and the dictates of civil authorities became secondary. In 1875, European Mission president Joseph F. Smith, a member of Quorum of the Twelve who would later ascend to the office of prophet, seer, and revelator, visited the Swiss and German mission's headquarters in Basel. Informed that missionary work in the Prussian state of unified Germany still suffered from the *Runderlass* decree of 1853 and the resulting banishments of missionaries, he chose to reference instead an 1850 decree of the Prussian parliament that declared religious liberty in that state. He proclaimed: "Hereafter, the Elders will not stop to ask permission of the Authorities of Germany to preach the Gospel there but they will *go and do it* the Lord helping them and opening the way. The law gives them the *legal right*, and if denied by the bigotry of priests or rulers, contrary to the law, they will claim it at the hand of God, for it is HIS WORK" (emphasis in original).[55]

The missionaries, although harassed officially in Prussia and on an ad hoc basis in the other German states, took Smith's words to heart. They made fourteen new German converts in 1875, while none in Prussia had been recorded for the previous five years. However, official sanctions followed as a consequence of their success. In Berlin, police broke up Sunday services, detained the missionaries, and eventually ordered them out of the city under threat of a four-week jail sentence. In the Schleswig-Holstein city of Kiel, elder Ludwig Suhrke served thirty-eight days in prison after being arrested for a third time, and after having previously been banished twice. The authorities apparently thought the contagion of Mormonism posed a threat sufficient to warrant dispatching several dozen policemen to surround the house where he was staying.[56]

Over the next twenty years, despite a spate of official opposition, Germany overtook Switzerland as the home of the majority of German-speaking Mormons. During one three-month period in 1876, while a steady stream of bad publicity from America appeared in German periodicals, missionaries in the Mannheim-Ludwigshafen region reported thirty-one baptisms. The press took notice. "The Mormons are thriving and preaching polygamy," stated an article in the *Ludwigshafen Tageblatt*.[57] The next year, 1877, saw Mormons baptize forty-seven out of its 243 German-speaking converts within the borders of a unified Germany, and in the following year, that number grew to fifty-five. Authorities in

The German Empire after Unification until the end of the First World War, 1871 to 1918. Map by John Gilkes.

Bavaria shut down all Mormon meetings in 1879, but across the country in the Rhineland, the congregation in Ludwigshafen grew to ninety-seven members. By the end of 1880, German members composed one-third of the membership of the Swiss and German mission.

In 1882, the same year that the American Congress passed legislation that criminalized, after the fact, existing polygamous marriages, the Nuremberg branch reached a membership total of 218, which surpassed Switzerland's Bern as the largest German-speaking congregation in Europe. Some 466 of the 1,091 members registered with the Swiss and German mission lived in Germany that year. At the same time, local police in Hamburg and Bremen refused to allow traveling Mormon elders to spend the night in either city.[58]

Despite official harassment and mob vigilantism that resulted from reports of Mormon polygamy abroad and successful conversion efforts in Germany, progress continued incrementally each year. By 1893, more than fifty percent of the membership that fell under the jurisdiction of the Swiss and German mission president resided in Germany. Five of the seven German speaking ecclesiastical units, called "conferences" during that period, were based on the German side of the border.[59] This occurred despite periodic government shutdowns of church meetings, which happened in Berlin in the 1890s, and banishments of missionaries from Bavaria in 1894. The latter happened after a local newspaper complained that "Mormon baptisms were polluting the water of a canal" that ran through the King of Bavaria's property.[60]

Despite a persistent rhythm of success followed by disappointment, of conversions followed by excommunications and apostasies, of the organization of church units followed by their banishment, German-speaking Latter-day Saints were on the verge of a growth spurt that would see them become, through emigration, the third-largest linguistic group to populate the Mormon Culture Region.[61]

Polygamy Dies but Its Legacy Lives On

Early in the year 1890, a United States congressman from Illinois and another from Iowa proposed legislation that, although not enacted, served to break the back of polygamy and change the face of Mormonism worldwide. The Cullom-Struble Bill, if it were not for the intervention of Secretary of State James G. Blaine, would have revoked the right to vote for every Mormon—single, monogamist, or polygamist—in the Utah territory. Up to this point, the Mormon hierarchy had stubbornly refused to modify the religious doctrine of polygamy—despite the fact that thousands of its elders were incarcerated in territorial penitentiaries, thousands more had scattered with their families to Mormon colonies from Canada to Mexico, Utah courts and school systems had been federalized, and the church's property was in receivership. The prospect of Mormons effectively losing their rights as American citizens motivated the fourth prophet, seer, and revelator, Wilford Woodruff, to call a meeting of the Quorum of the Twelve on September 24, 1890.[62] That afternoon a telegraph operator in Salt Lake City sent a dispatch to the Associated Press in Chicago: The Church of Jesus Christ of Latter-day Saints announced its intention to comply with the law of the land. There would be no more polygamous marriages.[63]

Observers in the United States and abroad regarded the announcement with skepticism. Gradually, however, sensational stories about Mormons disappeared from newspapers and public consciousness, giving the missionary effort new life. But clergy and constables were slow to forget. As missionaries began to walk the streets of Germany freely, they made more converts, but their proselyting success garnered increased attention. That fueled a backlash from pulpits and police stations. As life at home became harder for new German converts, they were more prone to emigrate, which attracted even more scrutiny. An increasing number of missionaries arriving in the country drew even more attention. In the last decade of the nineteenth century, some six thousand missionaries left the safety of the Mormon Culture Region to preach the gospel all over the world. By 1901, eighty were recruiting converts in Germany. They were a conspicuous lot. As Thomas G. Alexander notes, "Church rules did not allow missionaries to wear suits and ties; they were expected to don a Prince Albert coat and top hat . . . which singled out the missionaries for disfavor and constituted a sizable financial burden."[64]

Nevertheless, the outlook for missionary work in German-speaking countries of Europe appeared so favorable at the turn of the century that Mormon officials decided to split the Swiss and German Mission into separate contingents for each country. For six and one-half years, the newly designated German Mission produced a record number of baptisms: 2,246. By 1904, German membership reached an all-time high, 2,863, and this number did not include those members who had emigrated. For the short-lived German Mission, an average of ninety-five missionaries proselytized each year, with maximum number of 137 in 1902.[65] However, as a consequence of the mission's success, opposition from clerics and police increased. Six elders had recently been expelled from the mission headquarters city of Hamburg in 1901, when missionaries William Owen and Charles Morris were jailed and subsequently chained together as they were driven out of town. Seeking a friendlier venue, Mission President Hugh J. Cannon transferred the mission headquarters to Berlin in 1902, but that did not prove to be a fortuitous move. Within months, Prussian authorities expelled some twenty elders. Officials told the missionaries: "You are Mormons; the pastors have demanded your banishment."[66]

Success did not always help the missionary effort; more often than not, it drew unwelcomed attention. Such was the case when, encouraged by increasing numbers of baptisms, Mormon mission presidents and their missionaries tested German tolerance by holding a European conference in Berlin on January 5, 1902. The convergence of so many American Mormons on the Prussian state capital, although vastly successful from a spiritual standpoint, alarmed officials of the Interior Ministry and the Ministry of Religion. Local pastors also met in conference and planned to respond by appealing to civil authorities to restrict Mormon proselyting.[67]

Two months later, when a Prussian judge banished two Mormon missionaries from his jurisdiction, the Mormons pursued legal and diplomatic channels, involving not only the local American consul general, but also the highest echelons of the American State Department. Apostle Reed Smoot, who would soon play a controversial role in the next Mormon scandal to draw worldwide attention, approached Secretary of State John Hay. He asked Hay to instruct U.S. Ambassador Charlemagne Tower, Jr., to intercede on behalf of the mission. Another influential Mormon, Apostle John Henry Smith, obtained an audience with President Theodore Roosevelt, who promised that law-abiding missionaries would receive all of the diplomatic protection the American government could muster.[68] The American embassy, working through the German

Foreign Ministry, intervened. It requested that the Prussian state government adopt a uniform policy regarding the treatment of Mormon missionaries.

The strategy backfired. As in 1853 when Brigham Young sent emissaries to see the Prussian King, the Mormon leadership had overplayed its hand. Late in 1902, the Prussian Minister of the Interior released a memorandum entitled *Ausweisung der Mormonen*, Banishment of Mormons. Old reasons, such as encouragement of emigration, played a part in his decision. He also cited the input of the Minister of Religion, who argued that despite the 1890 Manifesto, "polygamy had not been eradicated in Mormon theology, and therefore the missionaries had no business in Prussia."[69] It probably did not help that Cannon, the mission president, had taken a bride in a polygamous union after the Mormon Prophet had issued the Manifesto but before he arrived in Germany.[70] Prussian police intelligence was skilled enough to trace and record numerous comings and goings of American missionaries, often from the time they left their homes in Utah. Undoubtedly they knew about Cannon's subsequent marriage. The Interior Minister declared that the 1853 expulsion order, the *Runderlass*, was still in effect.[71]

LDS officials appointed a German priesthood leader to take charge of the Berlin church affairs while Cannon, the American mission president, retreated to the safety of Switzerland. Missionaries were allowed to return to Berlin in 1905, but by 1907 the expulsions had resumed. In 1909 Smoot, by this time an influential United States Senator, again intervened with Secretary of State Philander Knox. The American consul in Hanover conferred with the German government to determine the reasons for continued harassment. Officials told him missionaries were guilty of "encouraging emigration" and "disorderly conduct."

Another explanation for renewed maltreatment undoubtedly resulted from reemergence of the missionaries' old nemesis: hysteria emanating from polygamy's return as an issue in the popular press, and the fear that converted German women were being forced into plural marriages by lecherous Mormon elders hiding their harems behind the parapet of the American Intermountain West. The tumultuous controversy arose again in 1903 when Utah's legislature appointed Reed Smoot to fill one of the state's two seats in the United States Senate.[72] Smoot was a member of the LDS Church's Quorum of the Twelve, an apostle in

Mormon parlance. Although he was a monogamist, the appointment of a Mormon who held such a high ecclesiastical rank provoked a firestorm among Protestant Easterners who, as part of America's emerging Progressive movement, campaigned assiduously against what they considered the twentieth century's twin pillars of barbarism: alcoholic drink and residual Mormon polygamy. The Woodruff Manifesto of 1890 merely forbade subsequent polygamous marriage ceremonies. Most Mormon elders continued to live with their multiple wives and father children by them. In fact, the first prophet, seer, and revelator who had never taken a plural wife was George Albert Smith, who became church president in 1945.

The sensational subject of Mormon polygamy once again returned to the front pages of the world's newspapers when the United States Senate challenged Smoot's credentials. Senators argued that the appointment of such a high-ranking LDS Church official indicated that Utahns had not sufficiently eschewed theocracy or embraced secular democracy. Fueling their opposition were persistent rumors that church officials continued to perform secret plural marriage ceremonies.[73] For three years, from 1904 to 1907, the Senate held a series of hearings on Smoot's fitness to represent Utah. Senators dredged up and regurgitated old history that became fodder for journalistic sensationalism in the United States and abroad: Brigham Young's multiple wives, the Mountain Meadows Massacre, the Danites, and the Mormon temple's endowment oath to avenge the death of the Prophet Joseph Smith.

In 1904, in response to the Smoot controversy, the reigning prophet, Joseph F. Smith, issued a Second Manifesto that threatened excommunication for any Mormon who subsequently took a polygamous partner and for any church elder who officiated. This became the basis for aggressive anti-polygamy enforcement in Utah and elsewhere in the Mormon Culture Region, to include both civil sanctions and spiritual excommunication, which the church hierarchy pursued for the remainder of the twentieth century. Nevertheless, any hopes that Mormons in the mission field may have had to quell the furor over polygamy after 1890 died when the Smoot hearings aired the controversy's scurrilous legacy once again. The hearings in Washington lasted until 1907, when Smoot was finally seated, but the reverberations abroad affected Mormon missionary work for many years afterward.

Until missionary activity was suspended at the beginning of the First World War, the Mormons and German civil authorities continued to engage in the same cyclical struggle. Missionaries preached the gospel, made converts, and dispatched emigrants to America. In doing so, they attracted the attention and the wrath of religious and civil authorities. The police and courts then arrested and imprisoned the offending missionaries, who shortly thereafter obtained their release, often with consular help contingent on a promise to leave the city or the district. The expelled missionaries soon found themselves reassigned to other parts of Germany, their vacancies filled by fresh faces—newly arrived from America or recently expelled from other parts of the nation. Then, after a period of relative quiet ensued in which the antagonistic German preachers and their allies in the justice system seemed to lose interest, the replacement missionaries would begin making converts and dispatching them overseas.

This process seemed to repeat itself endlessly, but with each cycle, the Mormons gained strength incrementally. While some converts left for the American Zion, others stayed and built a permanent church membership in their own land. During the short life of the independent German Mission, total church membership among German citizens rose from 1,018 in its first year in 1898 to 2,863 in its final year of 1904.[74] The Mormons gained strength because they fought a single-minded, full-time, unitary struggle to spread what they considered to be the restored gospel of Jesus Christ. Opponents in the pulpits and the police stations had other, far more wide-ranging concerns. Furthermore, Germany's federal structure provided for powerful state governments with expansive police powers within their own boundaries, but without a nationwide law enforcement structure.

In 1910, just four years before the war began, a few incidents illustrated the progress Mormons had made during the history of their missionary work in Germany—offset by the frustration they experienced at continued official harassment. In April of that year, the new Swiss and German Mission president, Thomas E. McKay, embarked upon a two-month tour of Mormon congregations. Conditions had improved enough that the American ambassador in Berlin, David Jayne Hill, felt comfortable in furnishing the newly arrived mission president with an embassy car for the trip. In the interest of improving relations with civil authorities,

McKay visited police stations in Berlin, Dresden, and Leipzig.[75] Later that month, the president of the Danish-Norwegian Mormon mission, traveling as a tourist, enjoyed unrestricted passage and a visit without incident when he attended the Oberammergau Passion Play in Bavaria.[76]

By the end of the first decade of the twentieth century, a Mormon official traveling in Germany who advocated neither polygamy nor emigration could be assured of safe passage without harassment. That signified progress, but hardly the respect that Joseph Smith had hoped for when he proclaimed German Mormons worthy of exaltation into godhood. The next steps would be prompted not by the Latter-day Saints but instead by the German nation, as the First World War and the Weimar Republic afforded the LDS Church the opportunity to develop the tools it would need to survive National Socialism.

2

German Mormons in the Great War
Lessons Learned in the Crucible of Combat

The events that triggered the First World War caught Germany's Mormons and their American missionaries by surprise. When compared to building God's earthly kingdom or saving souls for the afterlife, the obscure, far-away assassination in Sarajevo of the heir to the throne of the Austro-Hungarian Empire seemed of little consequence. As the tension of the July Crisis of 1914 unfolded, at first quietly among diplomats and generals' staffs, and only later in the consciousness of the European population, the Swiss and German Mission's leadership paid little heed—even as the world spiraled precipitously down into war. Only in the final week of the crisis did the Mormon leadership in Basel, Switzerland, become aware. On July 25, as the German government urged Austria to take immediate military action against Serbia, Rose Ellen Valentine, the wife of Swiss and German Mission President Hyrum Valentine, wrote in her journal as she sat safely across the Swiss border: "There are rumors of war in Germany." One day later, as Russian Tsar Nicholas II ordered partial mobilization in four large cities, she added: "War seems inevitable."[1]

Her husband, Mission President Hyrum Valentine, encountered more than rumors of war; he observed firsthand the reaction of Germany's populace to the outbreak of Europe's first continent-wide armed conflict since the days of Napoleon Bonaparte. On August 1, when Germany formally declared war on Russia, Hyrum Valentine was touring the German congregations in the company of Hyrum Mack Smith, the Mormons' European mission president, who had come to Germany from his headquarters in Liverpool, England. On August 3, the day Germany declared war on France, Smith's European mission office in Liverpool received an overnight cable dispatched from Salt Lake City the previous day. It instructed mission presidents to remove missionaries from all regions where they could face danger.[2] Smith was not there to read it; he would not view that directive from his superiors in the LDS hierarchy until he returned to England on August 22.[3] The declaration of war caused communications between the United States and Germany to be severed. Events had overtaken the church leadership's ability to respond.

The war declarations quickly stoked patriotic fever and nationalist hysteria throughout the combatant nations. By the time Great Britain declared war on Germany on August 4, anyone caught speaking English on the streets of Germany risked attracting suspicion at best and mob reprisal at worst.[4] Indeed, German police arrested the two mission presidents, Valentine and Smith, together with a young companion missionary, and charged them with being spies. Valentine and the young missionary were able to produce their American passports, but when Smith could not do so immediately, it required the intervention of the American vice consul to convince the German authorities that the European Mormon mission president was not engaged in espionage for the British.[5]

In the absence of guidance from Salt Lake City, the two mission presidents suspended all meetings between the American missionaries and their German congregants. American diplomats advised the missionaries to seek protection in neutral countries, but overland passage proved impossible. Germany's soldiers jammed all available trains, enacting a mobilization plan for fighting a two-front war against the French and the Russians. Valentine could not book passage back to Switzerland until twelve days after the war started.

Meanwhile, some missionaries in northern Germany, aided by funds dispatched by Mission President LeGrand Richards in The Netherlands, were able to arrange travel through that country on their way to Liverpool.[6] Nevertheless, for more than a month after the outbreak of hostilities, Mormon missionaries remained haphazardly scattered about wartime Germany, forbidden to carry out their duties for fear of provoking reprisals against foreigners and cut off from their source of financial support by the suspension of postal and telegraphic service.

It was only upon Valentine's arrival back at mission headquarters in Basel, following receipt of cables from church headquarters in Salt Lake, that the Swiss and German Mission president received what he considered to be the proper ecclesiastical authorization to evacuate the young Americans. That required a potentially hazardous ten-day trip back into Germany. Valentine withdrew twenty thousand Imperial Marks from the mission's bank account and began tracking down the remaining dispersed missionaries, arranging for their safe passage home, and appointing native German convert members to assume leadership posts in the congregations and in the missionary work. Valentine found most of the American missionaries secure, unaffected by the war, and protected by German members.[7] By October 15, 1914, the German-language Mormon periodical published in Basel, *Der Stern* (The Star), had compiled a list of 152 evacuated missionaries.[8]

After the removal of all American missionaries from Germany, the next challenge became maintaining contact with the membership. Foreign mission work had relied on regular visits by the mission president and his assistants, who toured the various branches and districts on a regular basis in order to ensure compliance with proper liturgical practices and church directives issued in Salt Lake City. Although some progress had been made in the first decade of the twentieth century regarding the installation of converted German members into positions of authority on the local level, often young American missionaries had assumed the position of branch or district president in the absence of competent local priesthood authority. This became impossible upon the evacuation of missionary personnel, and necessitated trust in native German leaders who would henceforth receive only sporadic counsel from higher authority.

From time to time, despite great odds and potential penalties, a German soldier of the Mormon faith would succeed in crossing the border for a visit to the mission president. An entry in Rose Valentine's diary in the summer of 1915 tells of one such encounter with a recently discharged army veteran: "In the evening Brother Edward Hoffmann came in. (Bro. Hoffmann had been an earnest local missionary before being called into the war.) I felt like taking him into my arms . . . with a feeling of laughing and weeping, joy and sadness—a soldier who had lost his right leg (amputated under the knee), a soldier for truth and a missionary. 'Not one shot have I fired on the enemy,' he said, and this sentence brought a glorious light into his face. We talked and talked; he ate a bite and retired."[9]

The Mormon Sonderweg

Mail service between combatant Germany and neutral Switzerland eventually resumed, allowing Valentine to coordinate with appointed German ecclesiastical leaders by postal dispatch. Communication was intermittent at first but then flowed more regularly. The first full reports of branch conferences, held in 1915, indicated a resumption of normal church functioning. Those reports appear in a January 2, 1916, entry in the Swiss and German Mission Manuscript Histories as a consolidation of the previous year's events.[10] By Easter of 1916, from the safety of his office in Basel, the mission president directed Sunday school conventions in Berlin, Zwickau, Freiberg, Frankfurt, Hanover, Königsberg, Hamburg, Munich, Cologne, Breslau, Stuttgart, and Spandau.[11]

The mail also brought unwelcome news of Mormon deaths on the battlefield, which the Latter-day Saints would subsequently exploit to demonstrate their loyalty to the government. Shortly after hostilities commenced, the mission office in Basel began compiling a list of faithful Mormon priesthood holders who had fallen for the Fatherland. Most surviving records reveal only the name of the soldier, his local congregation, and his date of death. Some contained a few sparse details. For example, Friedrich Wehnes of Frankfurt "stepped on a mine" and perished on October 2, 1915. Helmuth Friedrich Michael Walter Kererbeck of Hamburg "succumbed to typhoid fever while in the military" on June 28, 1915. The entry for Friedrich Dahl of Karlsruhe reveals that he was "shot through the stomach and died on the battlefield."[12] In subsequent years, and especially in reaction to the rise of National Socialism, Mormons stressed the loyalty their German members displayed to the Kaiser by their service and sacrifice on the battlefield during the Great War. The ability to remain loyal to the state and to the church simultaneously, along with the skill of the leaders who brought this message to the government, became the hallmark defense of this American-based religion that aroused so much suspicion in Germany.

The experience of Wilhelm Kessler, a native German who immigrated to the United States and then returned to service in his native country —first as a Mormon missionary and then as a soldier for the Kaiser— demonstrates that maintaining such dual fidelity was not always easy. Some decisions were gut-wrenchingly painful. At the outbreak of the First World War, Kessler faced a stark choice: evacuate Germany, remain in missionary service with his American church in Switzerland,

and eventually return to his adopted American home, or answer a call to military service from his native land. He chose the latter, expressing profound feelings of guilt for abandoning his church and newfound country, and subsequently paying for the decision by sacrificing his life on the battlefield.

Kessler, born in Neunkirchen, converted to Mormonism at age twenty in 1907. He moved to Salt Lake City in 1910 and worked as a bookkeeper for a candy company. Two years later, the church called him on a mission. He proselytized in Germany during 1912 and subsequently moved to Basel, where his bilingual skills helped him edit the weekly German-language church periodical, *Der Stern*.

When war broke out, Kessler, at work in Basel, attempted to telegraph Valentine, who was touring Germany, to seek counsel about enlisting in the German army. But communications links had been severed at the outbreak of hostilities, leaving the young German-American missionary solely with the guidance he could receive through prayer.[13] When Valentine returned to Basel, he found a letter Kessler penned before departing for the front lines that explained the young man's anguished deliberation and tortured decision: "I could not look my countrymen in the face and stand here when they call me to render assistance. It is true that I have been sent here to do missionary work . . . there is nothing here but turmoil. I don't know but that tomorrow the French will rush over the boundary into Basel; they will discover I am a German citizen, and I will be taken a prisoner of war and interned. I don't know but tomorrow the Germans themselves will cross over the boundary . . . and could come here and take me as a traitor to my country. I may be cast into prison, I may be executed. It matters not. I must go!"[14]

Kessler was wounded in battle on September 19, 1914, for which he received the Iron Cross, Second Class. After recovery in hospitals at Karlsruhe and Labry, the former missionary again served on the front lines. Kessler then attended officer candidate school, from which he graduated and subsequently received a promotion to first lieutenant on June 16, 1916.

One month later, Valentine reluctantly penned the following dispatch to Salt Lake City: "Wilhelm Kessler, a local elder of the Church, was killed in battle on the west front, near Mametz and Montauban, in France."[15] That happened on July 1, the first day of the Battle of the Somme, in which the Germans eventually lost half a million soldiers, the

British four hundred thousand, and the French two hundred thousand. Kessler's death made such an impression on Valentine that he made it a subject of his address to the LDS Church's General Conference in Salt Lake City on April 8, 1917, after the mission president returned from his duties.[16] Valentine's speech took place the day after the United States declared war on Germany, but that did not prevent the former mission president from extolling the loyalty of German-Americans to their native country. Such declarations from the pulpit at the Salt Lake Tabernacle would occur regularly in the years that followed, especially during the prewar Nazi years (1933–39), when church leaders emphasized the loyalty of German Mormons to their country.

The Mormons were well aware that much of their nineteenth century history in Germany reflected confrontations with local authorities and defiance of government directives; in the twentieth century, the emphasis shifted to compliance and coexistence. Records of the Swiss and German Mission indicate that Wilhelm Kessler was one of seven ordained German missionaries who quit church service in favor of military enlistment at the beginning of the war; others undoubtedly followed in subsequent years. The same records indicate that eleven Mormon priesthood holders died on the battlefield for the Fatherland in 1914, twenty in 1915, fourteen in 1916, thirteen in 1917, and seventeen in 1918. These casualties do not include the number of wounded LDS soldiers who survived.[17] The willingness of faithful Mormons to serve in the German military and to spill their blood on the field of battle became a strong arguing point for the survival of LDS congregations in the subsequent Weimar and National Socialist eras.

The Mormons' postwar relief effort served as a trial run for a larger relief effort undertaken for German members after World War II. Although most of the Great War's battles occurred away from German soil, continuing Allied naval blockades, enacted to pressure the German government to accept the terms of the Treaty of Versailles, caused widespread hunger and deprivation for more than a year after the armistice. Although the first postwar American missionaries would not arrive to proselytize in Germany until 1921, the new mission president, Angus J. Cannon, busied himself not only with the reestablishment of ecclesiastical supervision over the German branches and districts, but also with the provision of relief supplies obtained from Switzerland and the Americas.

On September 2, 1919, Cannon cabled the church hierarchy in Salt Lake City: "Eight thousand Saints of this mission are in immediate need of flour, corn-meal, condensed milk, fats, dried fruit, beans, peas. Can the Saints at home send such supplies immediately?" Cannon followed it with a postal dispatch: "I am certain that [yesterday's] telegram might cause some surprise because the home papers spread the idea that the people in Germany are well fed and cared for. According to reports we have received from the Saints, we fear their fate is doubtful. They almost beg that their brethren in Zion may help them. One sister, the president of the Relief Society in Chemnitz, writes: 'A few cans of condensed milk would make us dance like children and our gratitude would reach to the high heavens.'" Cannon's dispatch emphasized the self-reliance attempted by local Mormons, and how French-speaking Mormons from western Switzerland had been the first to respond by sending local relief items to their fellow German congregants.[18]

Church leaders responded by utilizing a resource not available during the rebellious period of the nineteenth century, when their defiance of American anti-polygamy laws won them few friends among American politicians. The Mormons turned to political leaders who had emerged with the advent of Utah statehood in 1896. Reed Smoot, seated as a United States Senator upon the intervention of President Theodore Roosevelt after a three-year Senate investigation in 1907, concluded in concert with church officials that the most efficient way to obtain relief supplies would not be to seek donations in America, where they would have to deal with the futility of purchasing passage on already burdened postwar ships. Instead, Smoot used his political connections to help the church purchase provisions from the American Expeditionary Forces that had joined the war in late 1917.

Said Smoot in a cable to the First Presidency in Salt Lake: "War Department wired Judge Parker, United States Liquidation Commissioner, Paris. . . . I have guaranteed payment. Wired Cannon to get in touch with Parker. Have given him the address of the Commissioner."[19]

The relief effort provided one vehicle by which the American mission president reestablished ecclesiastical control over German Latter-day Saints who had acted independently of centralized authority for nearly five years. Cannon appointed Elder Johannes Borkhardt to take charge of distributing relief supplies. No figures document the value of relief supplies provided from Swiss members and American Army sources, but one invoice from the American military garrison in Koblenz provides an approximation of the magnitude of a typical local effort: Church funds purchased fifty thousand pounds of flour, fifteen thousand pounds of rice, five thousand pounds of oleo margarine, twenty thousand pounds of prunes, and twenty thousand cans of condensed milk.[20]

German Latter-day Saints during the war not only served their country well, but also attended conscientiously to church business. Baptisms remained relatively stable and tithing collections increased, despite the fact that the American missionaries had departed for home and young German priesthood holders had left for the battlefield. Local missionaries conducted proselytizing activity, and many Mormon soldiers preached the gospel to fellow military personnel. During a seven-year period from the outbreak of the war until the first arrival of foreign missionaries in 1921, German Mormons averaged 430 baptisms per year, quite a remarkable accomplishment for a nation in the throes of war and postwar recovery. By contrast, during the prosperous prewar years of 1912 and 1913, with the aid of foreign missionaries, baptisms averaged 564. In 1915, Germany's first full calendar year of war, tithing collections increased over the immediate prewar period.[21] In 1920, in the midst of the American church's relief effort but absent supervision from American ecclesiastical leaders, baptisms almost doubled to 1165.[22]

Thus, to the observer not acquainted with the culture of Mormonism, it may be surprising that the American mission president, upon the reestablishment of centralized church authority over the formerly isolated wartime congregations, would reorder the local ecclesiastical leadership. Mission President Cannon's successor, Serge Ballif, embarked in 1921 upon a program of wholesale leadership changes at the branch and district level, replacing Germans with Americans. Jeffery L. Anderson speculated that the desire to replace these native German leaders might have stemmed from congregational discord observed by the returning missionaries, driven by the American cultural belief that Germans tend to be dogmatic and inflexible.[23]

Another factor may have been the spike in patriotic German meetinghouse pronouncements that made the American leadership uncomfortable after the United States joined the war in 1917. An article in the German-language church periodical, *Der Stern*, which published continually from Switzerland throughout the war, mentions a commendation from the Kaiser bestowed upon a German Mormon for authoring poetry with a patriotic tone.[24] Another article cited the tendency of congregants to pray for a German victory.[25] Although the Mormon leadership always stressed the loyalty of converts to their secular government, such pronouncements occurred as part of a strategy coordinated by the hierarchy. When Germans expressed patriotic fervor for their native land during a war with the United States, those declarations could have disturbed the American leadership—even if they were read, after the fact, in written records of wartime church services.

The most alarming reason for the reversion to American congregational leadership, however, may have been the tendency of the German wartime priesthood—often converts who had limited Mormon Church experience prior to the departure of the American missionaries—to modify ironclad liturgical practice in accordance with their previous Christian experiences in the Catholic or Protestant churches. In Hamburg, for example, the local branch president began withholding the sacrament of bread and water from members of the congregation who did not pay a ten percent tithing.[26] The same leader began pronouncing "prophesies" regarding the fate of Germany's enemies in the postwar period.[27] Mormons believe in the authenticity of personal prophecy for oneself and one's own immediate family, but such wide-ranging, global predictions of the future are usually reserved for the prophet, seer, and revelator—the church president. In Bremen, the simple sacrament ceremony found itself upgraded to a Catholic- or Evangelical Church-style presentation, with candles on a sacrament table adorned with a gilded tablecloth, water consumed from a crystal chalice, and a musical accompaniment.[28] Today, the Mormon sacrament is served in silence.

The First World War served as a dress rehearsal for Mormon survival after the Nazi seizure of power and the Second World War that followed. In 1914, and again in 1939, missionaries were suddenly and expeditiously withdrawn upon the outbreak of hostilities, leaving local congregants accustomed to close supervision to wield church governance on their own, which they did quite successfully on both occasions. With American missionaries gone, persecution by religious prelates and the police waned. German Mormons enlisted in the armed services and supported their country's war efforts during both conflicts, demonstrating genuine patriotism and dedication to mutual support by the members. Customary German immigration to the United States halted during both conflicts, only to begin again after peace was restored. After both wars, the church moved aggressively to reestablish ecclesiastical supervision of members and institute effective material aid to its German members in a war-ravished country. Following both world wars, improvements in constitutional democracy gave the Mormons more freedom of action to promote their church programs and missionary conversion efforts in both postwar periods.

The First World War proved to be a crucible in which German Latter-day Saints demonstrated they could survive as a foreign-based religious sect without direct guidance of their traditional mentors. However, it took the return of that American leadership, and the political savvy it had developed after the demise of polygamy, to provide the German church with the mettle it would need to survive National Socialism in both peacetime and war. The test bed was the Weimar Republic, that experiment in democracy that Germany ultimately failed but that the Mormons used so effectively.

3

Mormons in the Weimar Republic
Honing Survival Skills in a Fledgling Democracy

Critics of the Weimar Republic—that fourteen-year experiment in German democracy born of devastating defeat in the First World War, and ultimately crushed in the catastrophe of National Socialism—often refer to it as a "republic without republicans."[1] The degree to which German society was ready for constitutional democracy lies beyond the scope of this narrative, but the freedom afforded by the new republic appeared fortuitously timed to benefit a struggling American religious sect hampered by its inconvenient past and a history of persecution. Mormon society, a theocracy governed by rigid, centralized authority, did not require all of the constitutional freedoms ostensibly guaranteed by the new German republic; it needed only some breathing room. This is what the German LDS Church received when Friedrich Ebert, the state president, affixed his signature to the Weimar Constitution on August 11, 1919. Henceforth, although Mormons would still encounter resistance from offended Protestant and Catholic ministers and priests, and the occasional policeman would still take an elder into custody, there would be no question of a law-abiding American's right to preach his version of the gospel on German soil.

Mormons had been their own worst enemy during the nineteenth century; their doctrine of polygamy was a self-inflicted wound. Latter-day Saints, branded as outlaws in their own country, could hardly have expected to receive recognition of legitimacy in Imperial Germany. Although the First Manifesto prohibited new plural marriages in 1890, and the Second Manifesto in 1904 cleaned up hierarchical resistance to the new doctrine of monogamy, skepticism in Germany remained. The conduct of Mormon missionaries did little to convince officials otherwise. For example, during the first decade of the twentieth century, young Americans from Utah were registering themselves as "English teachers" rather than missionaries in order to circumvent a banning order in Prussia.[2]

Hugo Preuss, a respected left-wing politician, Secretary of State of the Weimar Republic, and a Jew, drafted a constitution that challenged the Mormons and their German antagonists to adhere to a higher standard of conduct. The freedom to proselyte in Germany carried with it a responsibility to respect the sensitivities of Germans toward emigration of young, single, female citizens to distant lands. The policeman who investigated an incensed Lutheran minister's hysterical and unsubstantiated complaint against a young Mormon missionary could also become a resource that helped the same emissaries of the gospel locate and rent a schoolhouse for Sunday meetings.[3] When a town mayor did not respect the lawful right of a young missionary to conduct his religious teachings, the Mormon leadership bore the responsibility to hire an attorney or seek help from the American consulate, rather than sneak the young man out of town and clandestinely replace him with a surrogate. The responsibility fell upon the church leadership to effect a strict code of conduct for missionary work and employ skilled and sensitive mission presidents who would enforce it. For the most part, the Mormon hierarchy met this challenge successfully by instituting more stringent selection, training, and supervision of missionaries.

Members of the church leadership in Salt Lake City had discussed problems pertaining to the quality of missionaries since the turn of the twentieth century. Only after the First World War did concrete reforms find their way into the process. The reliance on volunteers without sufficient spiritual, moral, or health screening resulted in embarrassing incidents that occurred in the foreign mission field prior to World War I. Some missionaries in Switzerland and Germany, just before the outbreak of hostilities in 1914, surreptitiously violated the church's health code, the Word of Wisdom, by drinking tea and coffee, smoking cigarettes, and enjoying an occasional beer. Earlier that same year, the mission president in Japan reported that five of his missionaries "had visited houses of prostitution and that one had contracted a venereal disease."[4] Other well-meaning missionaries had reported for duty in questionable health, and found themselves unable to keep up with fourteen-hour days of going door-to-door, preaching on street-corners, and walking across town to attend meetings. Only after 1922 did the church require that prospective missionaries submit a statement of fitness from a medical doctor, and by 1926 authorities added the requirement for vaccination against smallpox and typhoid fever.[5]

Prior to World War I, new missionaries arrived in the field with only the preparation they had received in church, Sunday school, or at family devotionals. A turn-of-the-century effort to offer missionary training at church-operated colleges and normal schools collapsed because of the students' financial burden, failure to complete the course, or decision not to pursue a call to missionary service after graduation. The only recourse was the anonymously written *Elder's Reference* or *Notes for Missionaries* by Apostle Francis M. Lyman. In 1925, missionaries and mission presidents called from the Mormon Culture Region began attending a one-week course of instruction at Mission Home in Salt Lake City.[6] By January 1927, newly arrived missionaries in the recently established Swiss-German Mission, responsible for the western half of Germany but headquartered in Basel, Switzerland, began attending a four- to six-week instructional program in Cologne. The curriculum stressed missionary responsibilities, teaching strategies, and rudiments of the German language.[7]

Disciplined, Knowledgeable Mission Presidents Lead the Way

When Oliver Budge hurriedly closed his oral surgery practice in Utah's Cache Valley late in the summer of 1930, having agreed on only two months' notice to become an emergency replacement for the Mormons' Dresden-based mission president, he hardly expected that his first duty would involve quelling a congregational revolt.[8] Having spoken little German since returning from a youthful mission just prior to the turn of the twentieth century, Budge found his linguistic, diplomatic, and managerial skills abruptly challenged when a thirty-three-member faction in the Breslau Central Branch demanded that it be allowed to split off from the main body of local worshipers and elect its own local leadership.[9]

That constituted a surprising degree of rebellion almost unheard of in a Mormon congregation, especially one located in the foreign mission field, where the local faithful obediently submitted to close supervision from the American mission president.[10]

The fifty-eight-year-old bespectacled dentist—the first in Logan, Utah, to own his own X-ray machine, and one of the first in the state to administer local anesthetic to patients before a tooth extraction—handled the schismatic congregants with a degree of interpersonal skill befitting an experienced practitioner of the healing arts.[11] Yet, as a ten-year veteran stake president, the equivalent of a Catholic bishop who oversees a diocese, he also displayed the authoritarian manner characteristic of a Mormon ecclesiastical leader.[12] His first order of business was to reestablish respect for the church's chain of command; only then did he address the underlying cause of the discontent.

Three days after disembarking from the ocean liner SS *America* in Hamburg, Budge repacked his suitcase for the trip to Breslau in Lower Silesia. There, on the train platform, Budge met with one of his stalwart missionaries, Donald C. Corbett, the mission secretary who assumed command after illness struck the wife of Budge's predecessor, forcing the previous mission president to leave for America ten weeks earlier. The youthful Corbett had been trying unsuccessfully to quell the schism. He identified the two instigators of the hostilities as local members, both long-time residents of the German city that later became Wroclaw, Poland.[13]

The members' complaints seemed understandable. Older, married German priesthood holders and their wives objected to their branch being led by younger, single American missionaries.[14] Undertones of matrimonial jealousy permeated the obvious friction between German members, many of whom had recently converted to the LDS faith, and the younger American missionaries who had been born into the church regimen of the Mormon Culture Region. The petitioners wished to elect their own local leadership, which would subject itself to the counsel of the American mission president and use tithing money to rent a separate meetinghouse. An unauthorized search had already resulted in the selection of one property.[15]

On the first day of his journey to quash the rebellion, Dr. Budge prescribed vinegar for the miscreants, and on the second, honey for the congregants. He instructed Corbett to assemble the petition leaders, Paul Köhler and Karl Hübner, and then called in each individually. Budge's memoirs describe the confrontation, recounting how he patiently listened to each member and then forcefully but tactfully warned of the absolute necessity to obey church authority—and the implied threat of the consequences to their church status for failing to conform. Budge recalled his approach to the first man: "After he had finished his story, I commenced to talk, 'Brother,' I said, 'your attitude in this matter is not what it should be. If you value your Priesthood and the Gospel, you should be willing to take the advice of your Mission President.' After talking to him for some time, he softened."

Budge's admonition is familiar to anyone reasonably fluent in Mormon parlance. By questioning how the errant member cherished his religious values, Budge warned him that rebellion not only endangered his church membership but also his eternal salvation. Faced with that ultimatum, the believing member relented. Budge took a similar tack with the second instigator: "I used the same procedure that was so successful with the first man. He became so excited at times that he jumped off his chair and danced around like a centipede on a hot stove. Several times I had to ask him to sit down. . . . After I had explained to him what it meant to be a Latter-day Saint, to hold the Priesthood, and to enjoy the blessings which follow a consistent Priesthood holder, he became calm and apparently repentant."

The next evening, after giving the malefactors an opportunity to think about the consequences of rebellion and allowing the news of his corrective action to circulate among the congregants, Budge summoned the entire branch membership. Undoubtedly, Corbett had told Budge that many had not supported the disgruntled members. Exploiting the congregational division, the American leader downplayed admonition and instead urged the flock to avoid factionalism. He assured everyone that recent disagreements had been settled to everyone's mutual satisfaction. Then he asked for and received the congregation's sustaining vote.[16] According to official reports of the German-Austrian Mission, "A few left the meeting in a bad spirit, but . . . no more trouble was experienced." The congregants of the Breslau Central Branch eventually received their desired all-German ecclesiastical leadership, but that did not occur until four years later in 1934, after the American leadership had emphasized the training and development of German members for leadership positions in their own congregations.[17]

Budge had arrived in Germany in 1930, in the midst of the Mormons' gradual but steady rebuilding of its church network after the American leaders and their missionaries had fled the country at the outbreak of the First World War. Like those who preceded and followed him as mission presidents, he governed both his missionaries and German church members lovingly but firmly. He traveled the expanse of the mission's territory, visiting congregations and extolling the virtues of faithfulness and obedience. He disciplined errant missionaries. He presided over church courts that excommunicated or dishonorably released missionaries from their callings. He never hesitated to send a young man home on the next transatlantic steamship if his behavior violated mission standards or threatened to embarrass the church. He managed the German church's meager resources during the country's decline into the Great Depression, which struck industrialized Germany with rapidity unmatched in more agrarian European countries. Despite their financial hardship, Budge never relented in his appeal to the German Latter-day Saints to continue their tithing and other church offerings. He continued an ongoing process of integrating newly converted German Mormons into the governing structure of their local congregations, a process impeded by the steady stream of emigration by many faithful Germans. He interacted with government officials when his missionaries faced legal challenges to their right to proselytize. He cultivated contacts among American consular officials, employed German lawyers, and used the local court system to defend the church's interests when necessary.

Budge's skill in dealing with the government proved valuable upon Adolf Hitler's appointment as Chancellor on January 30, 1933. This sudden change of regime focused new suspicion on foreign religious groups operating in Germany. Budge's tact in dealing with Nazi officials, which will be discussed in the following chapter, bespoke the kind of leader the Mormons dispatched to the foreign mission in the twentieth century. That Budge possessed this critical ability, as did his immediate predecessor and successor mission presidents, explains to a large degree why the Mormons were able to succeed in their dealings with the National Socialist state. Their experience contrasts with that of other foreign-based small religions, which suffered persecution or suspension of their rights to worship.

Missionary and Member Discipline

When twenty-four-year-old American missionary Reed Galli of Midway, Utah, appeared for his church court—an ecclesiastical disciplinary tribunal in Dresden on February 19, 1927—fanciful tales still circulated widely in Germany about lecherous Mormon elders preying on meek and defenseless young German women and shipping them off to the wilds of Utah for sexual service in polygamous harems.[18] Priests and ministers still condemned the better-documented lasciviousness and misjudgment of church founder Joseph Smith, whom various modern scholars have credited with marrying from thirty-four to eighty-four times, and Brigham Young, said to have married between twenty-five and fifty-five times.[19]

Hyrum Valentine, on his second tour as a Mormon mission president in Germany, officiated that winter morning in Saxony over a jury of ten young Mormon elders, who would hear testimony and render judgment on Galli, a peer who stood "charged before this tribunal with serious violations of missionary rules and regulations, to wit: sexual sin, committed three times in the city of Dresden, according to his own admission of guilt. All done at the time that he has been commissioned as an emissary of the Meek and Lowly Master, contrary to each and every suggestion given the missionaries, and in violation of our mutual sacred covenants and obligations."

Faced with Galli's guilty plea to all three specifications and unambiguous instructions by the First Presidency concerning convictions for adultery and fornication, the disciplinary tribunal pronounced its only allowable sentence: excommunication.[20] Excommunication from the Church of Jesus Christ of Latter-day Saints in that epoch not only severed one's church connections in the temporal existence and chances for spiritual exaltation in the afterlife, but it also pinned a badge of shame on a young missionary who returned to his community. Elder Galli or his parents faced the immediate burden of paying for the errant young man's transatlantic passage back to the United States, as the church immediately disavowed any connection with or responsibility for him.

Once he returned to his small community in Utah's Heber Valley, he would have been welcome to attend services at this church ward, but everyone would know about his shameful excommunication, and eventually the reason would become common knowledge. Many would avoid eye contact, and verbal greetings would be embarrassingly perfunctory. More than likely, concerned elders would have advised the disgraced young man to seek a new life away from the community.

Apparently, the resiliency of youth allowed Galli to overcome some of the worst consequences of excommunication, but a short, bittersweet life followed. By June 1928, some sixteen months after being dismissed from his mission, the young man apparently had regained his church membership—a remarkably short period of spiritual renewal in twentieth-century Mormonism, when rehabilitation from excommunication usually required a much longer period of repentance. Galli used that privilege to marry a young Salt Lake City native of Danish descent in the Salt Lake Temple, a religious venue where Mormon marriages could be solemnized for eternal duration.[21] Nevertheless, the young couple had no children, and the best employment the young man could attain, given the dual consequences of the Great Depression and a dishonorable mission release, was the position of custodian at a newspaper office. Records of the Salt Lake City municipal cemetery authority reveal that Reed Galli died prematurely at the age of thirty-two in the year 1935.[22] His death certificate indicates he suffered from chronic leukemia and Vincent's infection (trench mouth).[23] Victims of trench mouth usually manifest several accompanying symptoms: emotional stress, poor oral hygiene, and poor nutrition. Probably, Galli never recovered from the emotional consequences of his indiscretion and resulting banishment from missionary work.[24]

Mission presidents were no more tolerant of other young missionaries who stepped out of line during a period when the church was trying to stress its conformity with the law and social customs. One month after Galli's excommunication, the same German-Austrian mission records describe the release of another missionary who fared slightly better at the disciplinary tribunal. Twenty-one-year-old Elder Rulon W. Jenkins faced charges of "despoiling a wife, dishonoring a mother, and destroying a home. You have made a mockery of things divine, by baptizing a woman as a penitent sinner, which placed you in the position of her spiritual adviser, and thus you have despoiled her. You have greatly aggravated the situation already strained by again meeting with her clandestinely after having somewhat of an understanding with her offended husband."

The record of the church court then got specific and graphic regarding Elder Jenkins' transgression: "According to a statement by Willie Zacheile, Ludwigstrasse 26, Chemnitz, which he read to the tribunal, Rulon Jenkins was charged with several clandestine meetings with Sister Zacheile, and of handling her sexual organs, and hugging and kissing her, taking her out several times late at night at which times she returned home in a drunken condition, and even after having been taken to task by the husband of this woman, of meeting her later and indulging in these liberties with her."

This tribunal handed down a different sentence than the court that had convicted Elder Galli one month previously. It dishonorably released Jenkins from his mission, asked him to surrender his missionary credentials, and required his return home at his own expense. But he was not excommunicated, and thus remained a full-fledged member of the church who would eventually be able to marry in the temple and regain the full fellowship of his congregants, on earth and in the life to come.

Why was this church court more lenient? The record indicates that Jenkins "acknowledged all of the pertinent points of these charges, taking exception to one or two . . . but admitted them generally. The accused was then questioned as to whether he had committed adultery, to which he solemnly replied he had not. He was then questioned, 'Has your sexual organ been placed next to hers?' to which he replied, 'No.'"

Although Elder Galli had admitted to three sexual liaisons, nothing in the record of his disciplinary tribunal indicates he had done so with married women. There is no record of a pregnancy. Galli was an ordinary missionary. By contrast, Jenkins was a branch president, had baptized the woman with whom he had a relationship, and had become her spiritual adviser. The woman's aggrieved husband testified at Jenkins' hearing. Nevertheless, because of the distinction drawn between tactile and coital sex, Jenkins' membership remained intact.

The social consequences once Jenkins returned home were also different. He would not be allowed to speak triumphantly from the podium in his home ward, as befitting honorably released missionaries upon their successful return. He would have to answer to his parents and local ecclesiastical leaders for his dishonorable release. Astute congregants would have noticed that he returned home earlier than scheduled. But his ability to partake of the sacrament, speak and pray aloud in church, and eventually obtain his bishop's endorsement to attend the temple would have facilitated his acceptance back into his local social and religious circles. Unlike Reed Galli, who died five years after his excommunication, Rulon Jenkins lived to the age of eighty-six.[25]

One did not have to partake in illicit sexual relations in order to run afoul of the new orthodoxy being enforced by Mormon mission presidents in the Weimar period. Merely becoming engaged to a local German girl and marrying her at the conclusion of one's missionary service was sufficient to deny a missionary an honorable release and a church-funded steamship ticket home.

The case of Elder Edgar C. Schwab illustrates how far the mission leadership was willing to pursue this policy. Schwab, a native of Smoot, Wyoming, arrived in Dresden in February 1926 and immediately fell into disfavor because he smoked cigarettes. The mission president assigned him to be supervised by "one of the best men in the mission" as a companion, but he was soon discovered smoking in a railway station restaurant while seated with an empty glass of beer in front of him. The mission president then transferred Schwab to Berlin, where he would work under another missionary with an excellent reputation. At this point he repented somewhat and continued his missionary work for the better part of two years before falling sick early in 1928 and being granted an honorable release based on ill health.

When Mission President Valentine learned, two days after Schwab had sailed from the port of Bremen, that the former missionary had been married between his last contact with mission authorities in Dresden and his departure for America, he took the extraordinary step of writing the First Presidency in Salt Lake City. Ostensibly, that correspondence would be forwarded to Schwab's ecclesiastical leadership in Wyoming. Valentine sought the return of the young man's certificate of honorable release and forwarded a demand for reimbursement of funds expended by the church to send him home. Valentine was particularly incensed that Schwab had left his new wife in the care of relatives while she resolved difficulties with her visa. Instead, Schwab traveled home in the company of his wife's sixteen-year-old sister, who faced no difficulties with immigration procedures. Schwab's father, who had relatives in Germany, had joined his son and new wife in Bremen for the wedding and transatlantic passage home. Elder Schwab's last contact with mission authorities had occurred on February 11, 1928, when he received his certificate of honorable release. He married on March 8 with full knowledge of both sets of parents. Said Valentine in that correspondence: "The taking of this 16-year-old girl, a sister of his wife, as far as New York is an unpardonable indiscretion and wholly uncalled for, even though it was done with the consent of her parents, who are faithful members of the church in long standing."[26]

Valentine's rant was motivated by two factors. First, he knew that the Mormon Church in Germany had been criticized severely for its recruitment of young, single women who then emigrated. Elders taking German brides home, even if their courtship had adhered to all standards of Christian premarital chastity, did not seem consistent with the church's stated twentieth-century goal of merely spreading the restored gospel of Jesus Christ. Valentine's second desire was to maintain control. As he stated in the letter he sent after Schwab's departure: "Missionaries generally should be made to feel that their mission begins, and terminates if at all, in the ward from which they are accredited. The technicality of 'release' does not permit them to do that the next second, which they are not permitted to do as missionaries."[27]

Apparently, Mormon mission presidents applied the same rules to native German missionaries serving on their home soil. In January 1928, Albert Zenger received a dishonorable release for "marrying a local member."[28] Another German missionary, Bruno Böhm, released dishonorably for unspecified reasons one month later, reacted with unusual defiance. He sued the mission president for having made "insulting remarks." In April, the local judge dismissed the litigation.[29]

From time to time, groups of proselytizing elders misbehaved, which required the mission president to travel to the scene to investigate and reorganize the ecclesiastical units that he purged of the malefactors. In November 1930, German-Austrian Mission President Oliver Budge summoned by telegram the missionaries serving in the West Pomeranian hamlets of Prenslau and Stargard to meet him in Stettin, where he held an inquiry pertaining to facts not disclosed by the mission records. He sent the district president home on the next transatlantic sailing without a certificate of honorable release and then demoted and reassigned the rest of the offending missionaries.[30]

Discipline of errant German members occurred even more frequently, and often without the same degree of due process from the mission president and his top-level assistants. Although the mission president would eventually have to approve an excommunication, the disciplinary courts would almost always be held at the district level, where young, single American missionaries in their twenties would sit in judgment of older, married German members. The three most frequently cited reasons for depriving congregants of their membership—their ticket to paradise in the afterlife—were adultery or fornication, disrespect or disobedience to proper ecclesiastical authority, and acquiescence to a member's request that his name, or the names of his entire family, be removed from the membership rolls.

Much of the verbiage that appears in the official mission historical records is curt and lacking in detail, and gives the impression that separating these members was a routine act of culling the flock: "Marie Elizabeth Rattei was excommunicated from the church for immorality," said one entry.[31] Both parties in a German couple, who had apparently separated and sought companionship with others without taking the trouble to file for divorce, were "excommunicated for committing adultery," according to another record.[32] Eight members of one family in the Swiss-German Mission were excommunicated together on one day in May 1929, apparently at the behest of the parents.[33] Two days later, a single entry in the German-Austrian Mission's records names nine unrelated German members who were "excommunicated at their own request."[34]

Recording the details of a German member's excommunication became more important, however, when that individual became a public apostate or heretic, or when he stole money from the church. Paul Seifert of Dresden serves as an example of the first category, when in August 1930 a priesthood tribunal found him guilty of "vigorously fighting against the church and excommunicated him." Having fallen out of favor in his local congregation, but not having bothered to request the termination of his own membership, he voiced his opposition publicly by authoring "many vile articles that appeared against the Church in newspapers around the country."[35]

Theft and embezzlement rated an even more extensive accounting of the miscreant's disciplinary hearing. Immediately after the end of the First World War, the Latter-day Saints had tried unsuccessfully to become certified as a church by the German government, but resistance from bureaucrats and religious leaders forced the Mormons to apply instead for recognition as a *Verein*, or an association or club. The government's rejection stated that for a foreign religious organization to receive German accreditation, it must first be recognized as a church in its home country. Since the United States did not certify churches, the Mormons could not receive such recognition in the Republic.[36]

The LDS Church obtained its status as a legal association in 1923, which allowed the purchase of the Dresden mission headquarters and an attached meeting hall. However, the laws that governed the recognition and operation of a *Verein* required that its officers and directors be German citizens. Earlier mission presidents had appointed ostensibly loyal German church members to the "Board of Control," with the understanding that they would control nothing. Instead, they were expected to defer to the American mission president regarding important decisions.

In January 1928, a Dresden resident and prominent church member, Bruno Ernst Richter, received a seat on the board.[37] In September 1931, in the midst of the Great Depression, German-Austrian Mission President Oliver Budge decided that expenses required for the upkeep of the mission headquarters building on *Königsbrückerstrasse* in Dresden were placing an undue burden on the church's finances. More desirable property had been identified in Berlin, and Budge decided to move the mission office to the nation's capital. However, when the sale of the Dresden property closed on December 19, 1931, church officials learned that Richter had used his authority as a legal owner of the property to mortgage it and abscond with the proceeds.[38]

Richter's church court, which tried him in absentia, convened on January 19, 1932, with a prayer, followed by the well-known LDS hymn, *Do What Is Right*. Marvin A. Ashton, the designated prosecutor, accused Richter of misappropriating several thousand *Rentenmarks* by mortgaging the mission headquarters and "spending the money on riotous living." His estranged wife, with whom Richter apparently did not share the proceeds, testified that her husband "had led an indecent life and had previously been punished by city and other governing officials for dishonesty." Then, in an effort to increase the severity of Richter's sentence, Ashton accused him of "being an apostate at heart" and of drinking and smoking. The tribunal returned a guilty verdict and unanimously prescribed excommunication.[39]

The twin pillars of ecclesiastical discipline and unbridled faith, combined with less harassment from civil authorities, functioned to help the Mormons maintain a steady growth of membership numbers during the fourteen-year duration of the Weimar Republic. In 1920, with 9,100 members, Germany ranked third among the world's nations in total number of Mormons residing within its borders. By 1930, with 11,596 members, Germany had surpassed Canada and ranked second only to the United States in the number of registered LDS Church members.[40]

That number is deceiving, however. It does not account for a steady stream of emigration, which paradoxically represents a triumph of faith over obedience to the church hierarchy. At a time when Salt Lake City was proclaiming the end of "the gathering," and instead encouraging Mormons to build the church organization at home, German Mormons immigrated to the United States in record numbers. A total of 2,827 Latter-day Saints made the passage during the Weimar years. When one discounts two periods of economic hardship, the first associated with the end of the First World War through the end of hyperinflation (1918–23), and the second beginning with the Great Depression and ending with the advent of the National Socialist regime (1929–33), an average of 343 Latter-day Saints per year left the German-speaking missions.

The emigration of German Mormons during the Weimar Republic illustrates an important limit of obedience by Latter-day Saints. Mormons struggled to tolerate a mandate that conflicted with longstanding Church tradition on emigration, in much the same way that many found the abolition of polygamy impossible to accept decades earlier. Failure to discontinue the blessing of new polygamous marriages resulted in many individual excommunications and several schismatic movements, but no record exists of any attempt to discipline a Mormon for emigrating once church leaders changed their stance. Church leaders learned when it was important to enforce conformity in order to save the church organization from government reprisal, and conversely, when enforcement of lockstep obedience might temper spiritual enthusiasm.

Miracles, Miraculous Faith, and the Limits of Obedience

On a warm East Prussian day in July 1926, Elder William Porter and a companion missionary were going door to door in the city of Tilsit, preaching the gospel to anyone who would listen.[41] When they entered a yard, a large, agitated dog—frothing at the mouth—attempted to pounce on them but found its range limited by the chain attached to its collar. Assuming that the beast was adequately restrained, the two Mormon missionaries approached the house when, suddenly, the raging canine broke free of its chain and pounced on Elder Porter's companion. As it tried to tear into the young man's flesh, the dog discovered that its mouth would not open. Frustrated, the enraged animal then turned on Elder Porter, but again it could not open its mouth to bite. Having survived the attack unharmed, the two emissaries of Joseph Smith's restored gospel delivered their message to the house's human inhabitants and then departed, giving thanks for the divine intervention that held closed the jaws of the savage canine.[42]

Stories like this appear regularly in the chronicles of young Americans who ministered in the Mormon missions of the Weimar Republic. They served to buttress the faith of postadolescent foreigners, far from home with few possessions and often short of money, promoting conversion to a strange New World religion in a tradition-bound Germany hostile to the concept, and in a German tongue that most were still learning. For their German congregants, whose choice to abandon their childhood Catholicism or Protestantism often estranged them from neighbors and sometimes from their relatives, such miracles discussed during weekly meetings provided the hope that they would, one day, be able to immigrate to the American Zion, where they expected miraculous happenings to become commonplace, and where their adopted Mormonism would place them into the majority.

In most cases, recorded "miracles" occurred after a German church member sought a blessing of comfort and healing. The liturgical procedure required one missionary to apply a few drops of consecrated oil, usually high-grade olive oil that had been blessed previously during prayer, to the forehead of an afflicted believer. The other missionary would then place his hands upon the head of the troubled congregant, say a prayer,

The Weimar Republic, 1918 to 1933. Map by John Gilkes.

and thus "seal the anointing." Such a Mormon priesthood ordinance could be counted upon to heal both sickness and injury, and to be effective on all age groups, from children suffering the onset of infantile paralysis to those afflicted with the maladies of old age.[43] Sometimes, the records indicate only that the missionaries prayed with their congregants, but that healings were nevertheless achieved.

In July 1927, Sister Schüler of the Hohenstein Branch felt so near death that she called all her close relatives in order to say goodbye. She had vomited blood continuously for three days and was unable to sleep. When the missionaries arrived and blessed her, she fell asleep immediately. Within fifteen minutes, she awoke refreshed, "was without pain and was not troubled with further vomiting." She made a complete recovery.[44]

On several occasions, missionaries helped cure faithful members who had been sick for much longer periods. On April 30, 1926, the mission president, Frederick Tadje, blessed a female member of the Leipzig Branch who had undergone several surgical procedures and had been bedridden for one year. Within two weeks of his visit, she had regained her health.[45] In the Chemnitz Central Branch in July 1927, a lady who had been confined to bed for six months summoned Elder Ray H. Adams and his companion. Within one day of their blessing, "she was up and doing her washing," and the healing was "a topic of conversation in her neighborhood for some time."[46]

Sometimes, records indicate that the healing actions of Mormon missionaries confounded and amazed German medical practitioners. When Frau Ackermann, who was considering joining a church congregation in Chemnitz, called upon the elders to help her with a troubled pregnancy, the result caused her obstetrician to cancel plans for surgical delivery of her baby. "The doctor examined her and to his great surprise," the mission records state, "found the unborn child in proper position and the mother in perfect condition." Reportedly, when she told her physician of the blessing, he took the names of the ministering elders and set out to investigate this "supernatural method of healing."[47] When Sister Kant of Stettin suffered from the infirmities of aging, her doctors prescribed steady doses of morphine as the only remedy for her constant, excruciating pain. When the missionaries blessed her, however, "the pain left her body" and she was able to attend church services the next day. Additional commentary in the mission records noted: "The power of the Lord can go a lot further than the best of doctors."[48] In Bern in July 1931, doctors had given up hope for the recovery of an ill child who had not eaten in ten days. According to mission historical records, the next day the missionaries administered a blessing to the famished youth, which subsequently caused the same doctors to concede that a miracle had happened and predict that the child would fully recuperate.[49]

Occasionally, members did not need to call the missionaries. Instead, these young ministers of the gospel received spiritual "promptings" or premonitions that their priesthood powers were needed. In the Schleswig-Holstein city of Husum in October 1927, Elders Edwin H. Calder and Norman W. Forsberg borrowed bicycles in order to visit the rural home of a church member. On the way, one claimed to have received a prompting that they should visit a different member. His companion protested that they would be late for their original appointment, but the young man who felt divine direction prevailed. When they arrived at the home of Sister Albertsen, they found her seven-year-old child "laid out on the table, having just fallen from an upstairs window to the stone below." The elders applied consecrated oil and gave the child a blessing. When they returned the next day, they found the youngster playing normally. A story about the miraculous healing subsequently appeared in a local newspaper.[50]

Missionaries in Silesian city of Schweidnitz needed neither oil nor water to successfully intercede after an enraged Brother H. Popel attempted to cut his girlfriend's throat one Sunday afternoon after church. When they arrived on the scene, Walter Rathke and Ossman Elgren deduced that this was not a case of domestic abuse but rather possession by the Devil. "Brother Rathke recognized the condition and immediately demanded 'in the name of Jesus Christ' that the spirit leave Herr Popel's body. Immediately, Brother Popel fell limp on the sofa and later came to consciousness."[51] Likewise, when a "poison fly" flew into the chapel during services of the Chemnitz Central Branch and stung a female congregant, recovery from her allergic reaction required neither medicine nor consecrated oil. Instead, elders John Roderick and Theron Covey simply "commanded" her to begin using her paralyzed arm and hand. She did so almost immediately.[52]

Stories like these, however fanciful, fell into the Mormon pattern of "expect a miracle." Mormon history is replete with tales of divine delivery from the dual threats posed by nature on the trek to the American West, and by the persecution of neighbors who felt threatened by the Mormons' economic collectivism and practice of polygamy. Faithful members who strove to live in obedience to the gospel and to the church leadership expected God to take care of them.

Church–State and Ecclesiastical Relations during the Weimar Republic

When Karoline Uder, a member of the Stadthagen congregation near Hanover, died during the summer of 1925, her family wanted to bury her in the local municipal graveyard. They also asked the local Mormon missionaries, who held leadership positions in the Stadthagen Branch, to officiate at the funeral. However, because of the blurred lines of authority that marked church–state relations in Germany, a local pastor felt free to deny Uder not only a final resting place in the city's cemetery, but also use of the only hearse in town. In the minister's view, she had apostatized in favor of a scandalous foreign-based religion, for which he felt justified in denying her burial in a Christian graveyard and transportation in the hearse that had carried so many faithful believers to their graves. Under no circumstances would he allow heretical young missionaries from a controversial overseas sect to conduct a religious service in her honor.

This is where the story would have ended in Imperial Germany. There would have been no avenue of appeal. Given their newfound Weimar Republic constitutional liberties, however, Uder's family and its Mormon spiritual advisers petitioned to overturn the autocratic pastor's decree. A spirited debate occurred in the town council and a compromise ensued. Frau Uder would be allowed burial in the town cemetery and a ride to her grave in the municipally owned hearse. The Mormon missionaries would be permitted to pray silently at the gravesite if they agreed not to perform any kind of liturgical funeral service. To ensure the tranquil dignity of the burial, the council dispatched local police to the cemetery on the day of Uder's funeral.[53]

As a previous chapter relates, from the establishment of Mormonism in Germany until the First World War, pastors, policemen, and politicians colluded to harass, suppress, and expel representatives of a foreign sect that encouraged Germans to abandon the faith of their birth and migrate to a strange land. After the establishment of the Weimar Republic, Mormons still faced opposition from all three of these traditional nemeses, but their newfound constitutional liberties allowed them to exploit statutory divisions of authority between religious and governmental officials, often with the assistance of American consular officials or embassy diplomats. This freedom allowed the Mormons to pick their battles, and sometimes isolate and wear down their antagonists. The Mormons did not win every confrontation; sometimes they chose to withdraw missionaries from a particular town, as they had done in the nineteenth century. But on many occasions during the Weimar period, surrender was not the only option.

In Imperial Germany, established German Mormon congregations could offer limited help to missionaries that many officials saw as being in the country illegally. After the constitutional changes that followed the First World War, the presence of German citizens as missionary companions to young American elders provided a legal basis for local officials and police to assert the right of the LDS Church to proselytize and organize congregations in German municipalities. For example, in December 1926, police in Kassel responded to the complaint of a local pastor that the missionaries were in town "to entice young girls to go to America." They arrested Elder Otto Seifart, an American citizen of German extraction, but released him when they found his passport and visa to be in order. They could find no evidence of illegal activity regarding his companion, Albert Schmuhl, who asserted his rights as a German citizen. When the American consul in Hanover intervened on behalf of Seifart, the authorities dropped all charges, much to the annoyance of the local pastor, who continued to warn his congregation that the Mormons were engaged in the white slave trade.[54]

Often during Sunday services, a lone heckler would suddenly interrupt the speaker, such as when a man claiming to be a Jesuit priest lodged a loud protest one Sunday morning in Hindenburg. He claimed to be an American citizen who had "studied Mormonism."[55] Usually, local congregants were able to escort such malefactors out of the building. On one occasion, several local Lutheran ministers in the Berlin suburb of Bernau attended Mormon Sunday services accompanied by members of their congregations. Upon a prearranged signal, the Lutheran parishioners all stood up and walked out of the meeting while their ministers filibustered loudly.[56] Once, in the Bavarian city of Bamburg, opponents apparently employed a gang of hooligans and ne'er-do-wells to disrupt Sunday worship by carrying on in an irreverent manner, "smoking, stalking, and laughing as if they were on the street, and mixing politics with religion." When the Mormon missionaries visited the local police department the next day, they received assurances of protection from subsequent boorish behavior.[57]

Sometimes, Mormons stood their ground when opposing pastors disrupted worship services or organized municipal opposition. In the East Prussian town of Heiligenbeil, visiting elders from Königsberg spent days preaching and distributing literature on the street. Some five hundred local residents attended subsequent Sunday meeting, as did several local ministers who tried to disrupt the service. However, the Mormons successfully engaged their interlocutors in debate.[58] In the Thuringian town of Greiz, local ministers attending a Mormon Sunday service disrupted the proceeding by demanding a "sign," to which the missionaries replied by quoting the New Testament admonition against "a wicked and adulterous generation [that] looks for a miraculous sign."[59]

One of the more effective instances of ecclesiastical opposition came from a fellow American sect, a breakaway Mormon denomination known as the Reorganized Church of Jesus Christ of Latter Day Saints. Founded in 1860 by followers of Joseph Smith who refused to accept the leadership of Brigham Young, and who remained in the American Midwest while the larger body of Mormons trekked to Utah, this group began establishing small congregations in Germany shortly after the turn of the twentieth century. German RLDS membership numbered less than one thousand in the early 1930s, whereas LDS membership was more than ten times as numerous. However, before the ascension of Hitler to the chancellorship in 1933, Reorganized Church missions or congregations existed in Berlin, Brandenburg, Breslau, Augsburg, Hanover, Offenbach, Einbeck, Plauen, Braunschweig, Elmshorn, Tilsit, Groß Wartenberg, and Großräschen.[60]

From time to time, LDS missionaries encountered difficulties with the professional ministers and missionaries sent to Germany by RLDS officials intent on convincing already-baptized Mormons that their breakaway church had inherited the true mantle of restored gospel preached by Joseph Smith. In the early 1930s, this resulted in a running battle for the loyalty of converted Mormons in a few strategically selected places, one of which was the southwestern Bavarian city of Augsburg. Records of the local LDS congregation reveal a concentrated effort in January of 1931, during which RLDS missionaries convinced several Latter-day Saints to switch allegiance, allegedly based on an inducement involving plots of land in the United States.[61] By July of that year, RLDS activity had driven a wedge into the existing LDS branch in Augsburg, which reported several more "apostasies" of German Mormons who changed their membership to the Reorganized Church.[62]

Despite the fact that records of both LDS missions in Germany reveal numerous instances of conflict with civil and religious authorities in Weimer Germany, not all such incidents had unfavorable endings. The same police who arrested Mormon missionaries on trumped-up charges occasionally became their friends and allies, or at least neutral arbiters of disputes. Police in the northern Rhineland city of Bielefeld, acting on a tip from law enforcement officers in another jurisdiction, investigated the missionaries in late 1926. They found no evidence of illegal activity, and in fact became so impressed with the young Americans that the officers helped the missionaries locate a suitable place for the fledgling congregation to hold its Sunday meetings.[63] In July 1931, police in Ludwigsburg arrested two missionaries on charges of engaging in illegal commerce, more than likely the sale of Books of Mormon or other religious materials. When local citizens intervened on the young Americans' behalf, the police officers "apologized and withdrew."[64] Even when two American missionaries committed the *faux pas* of trying to present a religious tract at the home of the police commissioner of the city of Mühlhausen in Thuringia, police soon dropped the ensuing vagrancy charges and helped negotiate a settlement with local citizenry in a town where the Mormons' relationship with the local populace had been strained.[65] No such compromise was necessary in the Brandenburg city of Forst, where the town council gave the Mormons free use of school buildings for religious meetings, and invited the church's youth organizations to participate in municipal leagues—membership in which allowed the use of civic libraries, gymnasiums, and other facilities.[66]

The Mormon Sonderweg

Consular Officials Befriend the Mormons

The Mormons did not have to go it alone when they faced opposition from German government officials. As early as the mid-nineteenth century, mission presidents sought the help of American diplomats and consular officials in major German cities when their missionaries ran afoul of local authorities. Such diplomatic interaction generally proved ineffective, as German officials justifiably reasoned that a small foreign religious sect that was at odds with its own government had little justification to argue it would obey the laws of the land where its missionaries were guests. Even after the church officially abandoned polygamy with the 1890 Manifesto, appeals through American diplomatic channels enjoyed limited success, owing to opposition from the established German churches and the nefarious reputation that the Mormons had earned over the years.

When Swiss and German Mission President Hyrum Valentine exchanged periodic social engagements with Philip Holland, the American consul in Basel during the First World War, it represented one of the first attempts by a Mormon official overseas to forge a prolonged professional relationship with an American diplomat. The rapport they developed later helped a successor mission president, Angus Cannon, when he appealed to leaders of the American Expeditionary Forces for help in purchasing surplus military rations for postwar relief of beleaguered German Latter-day Saints.[67]

After the First World War ended and Germany adopted a democratic government, the Mormons began building friendships with the American diplomats who would intercede on their behalf when old German prejudices conflicted with the new Germany's legal code. When in 1925 the Swiss and German Mission divided into two separate entities, leaders of the new German-Austrian mission headquartered in Dresden developed a particularly close relationship with the American consul general. Arminius T. Haeberle, who served in that position for eleven years (1925–36), proved to be a valuable contact when the Mormons faced the challenge of dealing with the National Socialist government. The German-Austrian Mission leadership took an interest in consular affairs and apparently looked for ways to help the new American diplomat with mutually beneficial projects.

For example, in 1927, the missionaries staged a lecture and visual presentation at a municipal auditorium in Dresden, extolling the natural beauty of Utah and the American West, for which they charged admission and drew a handsome crowd. They donated the proceeds to the consul's fund "for the benefit of destitute Americans in Saxony."[68] Noting the success of this illustrated lecture, entitled "Utah, the Scenic Wonder of America and Home of the Mormons," a particularly talented bilingual American missionary named Arthur Gaeth scheduled this presentation at various places in eastern Germany. A notation from mission records in 1928 shows that Consul Haeberle, his wife, and "all seven members of the American consulate in Dresden" attended a subsequent presentation.[69]

Haeberle's influence helped the Mormons whenever they encountered difficulty with German civil authorities, such as in December 1927, when police in the city of Weißenfels in Prussian Saxony prohibited American missionaries from opening a ministry there. Consul Haeberle soon overcame police opposition. On another occasion, Haeberle intervened to counter the efforts of a German official who attempted to limit the stay of American missionaries in Germany. The German Consul in Montreal, from whom many Mormon missionaries obtained their visas, had issued documents of only one year's duration. When those approached expiration, Haeberle interceded with officials in Saxony to have the visas extended.[70]

Haeberle's influence also helped the Mormons interact with the German government when opportunities arose that allowed the faith to be presented favorably. The Dresden International Hygiene Exposition that opened in the spring of 1930 contained an exhibit run entirely by Mormon missionaries. It focused on the Word of Wisdom, the church code that prohibits smoking tobacco or drinking alcohol, and counsels against eating an overabundance of red meat.[71] The exhibition, replete with printed literature in English and German, took place inside the front entrance to the League of Nations Building in Dresden and lasted through the summer, stretching into the autumn. An average of five thousand people per day visited the Mormon exhibition, with a high of thirty thousand visitors on one single day. Missionaries handed out a quarter-million religious brochures. The degree of Haeberle's participation can be surmised by the following passage in one of the mission's quarterly reports: "Consul Haeberle, active in enlisting support and participation for the exposition, suggested that in his opinion there would be no more remarkable exhibit than one by our church, primarily about the Word of Wisdom. Through the intervention of these men, the directors of the exhibition extended the invitation in January to the church to present an exhibit."[72]

Consequently, when the American consulate in Dresden needed to draw upon the American expatriate community for its events, Haeberle knew he would find a willing group of volunteers from the local Mormon contingent. In February 1932, American diplomatic missions worldwide commemorated George Washington week, the two hundredth anniversary of the first American president's birth. Some 450 invitees attended the consulate's banquet at the Exhibition Building in Dresden. Mormons provided most of the musical entertainment, which included the services of a soloist who traveled 540 miles from his missionary station in East Prussia.[73]

Haeberle's assistance to the Mormon missionary efforts became so well known among the church hierarchy that U.S. Senator William H. King of Utah came to the consul's assistance during a congressional inquiry in 1928. A senate subcommittee investigated charges that Haeberle sold, for personal gain, a seized ship's cargo during his previous diplomatic assignment in Rio de Janeiro. King intervened and helped quash the investigation.[74]

The ability to forge relationships with diplomatic officials, and to call for their help during conflict with civil authorities, can be regarded as another stage in the Mormons' preparation to survive and prosper under the National Socialist regime. They learned valuable lessons under the Weimar democracy that helped markedly in dealing with the fascist government that followed. Being able to rely on the intercession of American diplomats helped convince officials of both Weimar and Nazi Germany that the Mormons had powerful friends within their own government who would intercede on their behalf when necessary.

In the Weimar World; Not of the Weimar World

Mormons are fond of quoting biblical scriptures that guide their spiritual outlook while they live in a secular world. At least five New Testament passages admonish the faithful who live "in the world" not to adopt the selfish, materialistic desires "of the world."[75] Such advice cautions young Mormon missionaries to live a somewhat cloistered life while preaching the gospel and working with ordinary congregants in a less-than-ideal spiritual environment. Because young LDS missionaries in Germany generally adhered to a strict code of missionary rules that discouraged temporal pleasures, mission records in Germany provide scant evidence of how Mormonism fit into the rich cultural fabric of the Weimar Republic.

For example, one finds little mention of artistic, architectural, or cultural innovations that defined the period. Missionaries and working-class German Mormons lived in simple dwellings in ordinary neighborhoods, and their workaday activities brought them into little contact with artistic or architectural refinement. Scant mention of stage plays or the cinematography of the period can be found in missionary journals or church publications. Missionaries were not expected to attend such events. Certainly, their conservative code of behavior and the limitations of the Word of Wisdom's dietary guidelines prevented firsthand appreciation of Berlin's cabaret nightlife. Albert Einstein and Max Weber held little intellectual appeal for young men who arrived in the mission field with a Utah high school education, and who spent their days among church members who were fortunate to have been educated at the *Realschule*. Although the aftereffects of the First World War permeated everyday life, the records contain no mention of popular literature that the war inspired, such as Erich Remarque's antiwar *All Quiet on the Western Front* or Ernst Jünger's militaristic *The Storm of Steel*.

Observations of economic life occur only slightly more frequently. For example, during the hyperinflation of 1923, the fact that missionaries carried hard currency in their pocketbooks "made them millionaires" in comparison to their German congregants. According to one missionary, "A dollar would buy them anything they needed for a week. While many Germans were freezing because they could not find means to buy coal, the elders could easily maintain a warm hall or meetinghouse. During that period, German money had no practical value at all, for between the time people received it and the time they spent it, even if it were only two hours later, it may have inflated markedly. Therefore, hundreds came to meetings to get warm and some joined the church, perhaps, in the hope it might bring them economic as well as spiritual salvation."[76]

Arthur Gaeth, an observer who served a prolonged mission in Germany, and who later became president of the German-speaking mission in Czechoslovakia, wrote with levity about missionaries who "decorated their rooms and the inside of trunks with German bank notes, using up several millions of marks worth," and who "were in a position to take a bus load of these people to town or to the neighboring restaurant, and for a dollar or two, feed them all and send them home contented for the time being . . . but unwittingly created conditions which later became difficult to rectify when times became normal again and people did not need to come to the meeting to get warm and be fed."[77]

Another young pair of missionaries learned a harsher lesson about the effect of hyperinflation. The young Americans decided to relocate to another apartment, and after giving their former landlady the required two weeks' notice, they moved out. The next day, they received a visit from homicide detectives representing the local police department who informed them that later in the afternoon of their departure their former landlady, a war widow, had committed suicide by sealing her apartment and turning on the gas. Apparently, the detectives explained, galloping inflation had depleted the once-substantial savings her husband had put aside for them before the war. Presumably, the loss of the young missionaries as paying tenants had been the final trigger in her act of despair.[78]

From the issuance of the *Rentenmark* that broke hyperinflation in 1923 until the advent of the Great Depression in 1929, economic issues disappear from records of the German missions. Instead, the chronology documents the mundane arrival of American elders, their assignment to new locations for proselyting work, the growth of church auxiliaries such as Boy Scout troops and corresponding Beehive chapters for young German girls, and the seemingly never-ending pace of baptisms, excommunications, confrontation with established churches, and emigration of Germans who could afford passage to the American Zion. When worldwide depression caught up with industrialized Germany shortly after the Wall Street crash of October 1929, the slowing arrival rates of American missionaries corresponded with reports of diminished financial contributions by members of German congregations suffering from horrific rates of unemployment.

Mission authorities, who did not understand the gravity of the economic crisis, initially attempted to shift the blame. At the end of 1929, three months into the depression, a report of the German-Austrian Mission blamed the decrease in tithing on "the large number of branches in charge of local brethren, where it requires time for the Saints to have the same feeling toward them as they did toward the American missionaries." The report nevertheless admitted that the membership suffered "from the unsettled economical [sic] condition of the country, and the great amount of unemployment and poverty resulting therefrom."[79] In January 1931, church officials in Salt Lake City cited the financial pressure the church was experiencing when they required congregations worldwide to enter into rental contracts for their meetinghouses, rather than approve new construction.[80]

At the beginning of 1931, the Swiss-German mission president told of one congregation in which only two male members remained employed. His report complained that "these conditions are directly affecting the attitudes of the people. In many places they are becoming more and more cynical and are less inclined to believe anything."[81] The 1932 year-end report of the Berlin-based German-Austrian Mission noted the third suicide of the year by a German member within the mission's boundaries.[82] Reports of suicides among Mormons seldom appeared, as church doctrine stressed the detrimental effect on one's eternal salvation that would result from the inability to repent of the sin of taking one's own life.

By 1932, on the eve of the Nazi takeover, one Swiss-German Mission's status report commented on "the serious problem of obtaining sufficient financial means to meet current demands," and blamed that on "ever-increasing unemployment and repeated reduction in government doles."[83] In 1932 in Switzerland, the church's women's auxiliary, the Relief Society, began collecting "clothing and other serviceable" supplies for distribution to beleaguered co-religionists in Germany. By December of that year, the same source cited "missionary shortage" as the rationale for closing several branches.[84] Not only was the Great Depression affecting the ability of German Mormons to pay tithes to support their local congregations, but the economy also hindered the ability of American parents to dispatch their sons overseas to minister to those congregants.

In his published research on Mormons in the Third Reich, historian Douglas Tobler has emphasized the apolitical nature of German Mormons, the majority of whom came from modest, working-class backgrounds. However, as much as they might have tried, any attempt to remain apart from politics seemed to elude ordinary Germans as the Nazi era approached. Especially after the 1932 national elections, in which Hitler's National Socialists captured thirty-eight percent of the vote and 230 seats in the Reichstag, politics appeared as an unwelcomed, uninvited, and unruly guest in modest German neighborhoods.

Berlin missionary Arthur Gaeth recalled thousands of Communist Party (KPD) members marching every other week on the *Frankfurterallee*, a main artery which ran through the eastern quarter of the city.[85] A missionary dispatch from Kassel in the state of Hesse reported that two policemen were shot dead and several spectators wounded during a KPD street demonstration.[86] Missionaries in Munich reported thousands of "Hitlerites" gathered to counter Communist Party demonstrators during May Day celebrations, and that a large contingent of police was mobilized to preserve order.[87] As a young child, Rudi Wobbe attended the St. Georg Mormon congregation in the Hamburg suburbs. He recalled regular street violence that accompanied the political upheavals during the waning years of the Weimar Republic: "One night my parents were standing in front of our courtyard talking with neighbors while we children were playing nearby. Above our heads was a display from the Communist Party, illuminated by a couple of spotlights. All of a sudden, a car with a group of Nazis came around the corner with brakes screeching. They . . . jumped in front of us and started beating up on the people standing there, even innocent bystanders. They didn't even stop for children. We got our share of whacks, too."

One month later, according to Wobbe's recollection, the violence turned deadly: "There was a torchlight parade on our street, about an hour long. The marchers were from the Social Democratic Party (SPD), but the Nazis had to interfere. They . . . stationed a machine gun on the roof. They started shooting the marchers from above, killing and injuring a number of them. The marchers scattered quickly, but a group of them raced up the stairs where the Nazis were, and a short battle ensued. Shortly thereafter, I saw the machine gun and several bodies lying on the roof. With the Nazis disposed of, the marchers regrouped and the demonstration continued."

Later, young Wobbe and his parents witnessed a gunfight in the street between Nazis and their political opponents. Afterward, his father counseled Rudi: "Son, don't ever get mixed up with these people, the Nazis.

They are bad people."[88] Rudi Wobbe apparently took to heart his father's opinion, although he violated the admonition against involvement. Years later, as an older adolescent, he engaged in uncharacteristic behavior for Mormons during the National Socialist period: he became a resister. Wobbe and three other teenagers constituted the Helmuth Hübener group, whose story unfolds in chapter 15 of this narrative.

Numerous other reports commenting on political conditions, and noting the activism of both communists and National Socialist adherents, appear in mission records—sandwiched between routine accounts of Scout jamborees, missionary transfers, and confrontations with Catholic and Lutheran ministers who remained intent on harassing Mormon missionary activity as they had always done.

As the calamity of Nazi rule approached, Mormons went about their affairs as usual. On January 31, 1933, the president of Zwickau District in the German-Austrian Mission convened a church court in Auerbach "to settle some trouble and gossip between members and friends of the church." That date marks a significant and ominous benchmark in German history, of which the young missionary was probably unaware. Adolf Hitler's first full day as chancellor seemed a faraway and irrelevant occurrence to the young American charged with resolving "difficulty of a childish nature" that nevertheless "was a decided menace to the welfare of the branch."[89] No surviving records document the result of the disciplinary hearing held that day. However, that a small American religious sect with approximately twelve thousand German members routinely carried on its business at the same time that eight hundred thousand card-carrying Nazi party members prepared for a seizure of power that would change history served as a testimony to the Latter-day Saints' inherent strength and potential vulnerability.

Mormons would survive their Third Reich experience relatively unscathed, while adherents of other new religions, such as Jehovah's Witnesses, would suffer incredible persecution. In doing so, however, the Church of Jesus Christ of Latter-day Saints would be challenged beyond its ability to adhere to its "in the world but not of the world" philosophy. Survival would demand definitive accommodationist, and in some cases collaborative, behavior that would prove to be problematic to Mormon authors who, in later years, wished to write faith-promoting historical accounts.

PART II

The Prewar Nazi Years, 1933–1939
A Forgotten History

4

The Mormon Battle Plan in the Third Reich

On a mild September day in 1933, a Nazi secret policeman visited the tranquil headquarters mansion of the German-Austrian Mission on Händelallee, a tree-lined boulevard in central Berlin.[1] As a gentle autumn breeze rustled leaves in the Tiergarten, the picturesque city park across the street, Mission President Oliver Budge engaged in cordial conversation with the Gestapo agent—who inquired about the Mormons' attitude toward the National Socialist government. Budge assured him that his co-religionists "were living in keeping with their claims, namely, to place members of the church subject to Kings, Presidents, Rulers, Magistrates, in obeying, honoring, and sustaining the laws of the land."[2]

Those words correspond almost exactly with the text of Joseph Smith's Twelfth Article of Faith, one of thirteen catechismal statements pronounced in 1842 as a response to a Chicago newspaper's request for a concise statement of Mormonism's foundational beliefs.[3] The Twelfth Article constitutes the Latter-day Saints' equivalent of the New Testament's admonition, found in the Gospels of Matthew, Mark, and Luke, for Christians to "render unto Caesar that which is Caesar's."[4] Used in conjunction with Section 134 of the Doctrine and Covenants, which defines the LDS Church's relationship with civil government,[5] the Twelfth Article of Faith provided a doctrinal basis for Budge to assure the Gestapo agent of the Mormons' willingness to obey the law—even in a godless state like Nazi Germany.[6]

The next day, Budge addressed a multipage letter to the Gestapo's infamous Prinz-Albrecht-Strasse address, the citadel of torture that housed adjacent command posts of Heinrich Himmler's SS and Reinhard Heydrich's SD (*Sicherheitsdienst*, the security service).[7] One passage pointed out a Mormon belief that coincided with an aspect of National Socialist dogma. Budge said, "It is expected that every eligible member of this Church marry and live the first great commandment—'multiply to replenish the earth,'" a statement that comported with early-Nazi period natalist policies.[8] Budge was stressing the Mormons' historic preference for large families, which corresponded with natalist policies common to several European countries after the First World War, but which the Nazis strove to exceed.[9]

Other paragraphs in Budge's letter stressed the self-reliance of American missionaries and the care taken not to burden German members with missionary support. He emphasized the benefit to the German economy derived from spending by the missionaries: "Considerable amounts of money come in from America every year, [. . .] spent by the missionaries of this Church for their traveling, board, and living expense. Not a cent is received by these missionaries from the mission, but they're supported by themselves or by their parents in America."

Budge emphasized his missionary service as a young man during the 1890s, his "nearly 40 years" spent studying the German people and their culture, and his appreciation of the country's natural beauty and the industry of its citizenry: "I have been a friend and a supporter of the German people in their righteous endeavors. I have seen this country at its best and again at its worst. And throughout it all I can say that the Germans possess a personal pride that is seldom found in other countries. They're full of vitality and ambition and are workers of the first class. . . . Their personal appearance is kept up to the highest degree, clothes pressed, shoes polished, hair combed . . . and those who desire to live the good life are wholesome to look upon."

When Budge addressed the Mormons' neutrality in politics and obedience to civil authority, he wrote a twentieth-century corollary to the Twelfth Article of Faith: "[Mormons] are taught, especially, to be able to class themselves with the best citizens of the country, and to support, in the full sense of the word, the ordinances and laws of the town, the state, and the country in which they live. The authorities of our Church have no advice to give regarding party politics . . . we teach that the present party in power, and the laws governing the country, be supported by the members of the church."

Never missing an opportunity to proselytize, even to the Gestapo, Budge finished his written appeal for Nazi approval by enclosing a number of printed cards containing the Thirteen Articles of Faith, and several recent copies of *Der Stern*, the church's German-language periodical distributed in Germany, Switzerland, and Austria. He noted several articles that the Gestapo might be interested in reading.[10]

Another Sect Adopts a Markedly Different, and Deadly, Approach

Budge's letter, and the approach he took toward the Nazi secret police, contrasted markedly with a totally different kind of letter written by another American-based religious body to the National Socialist government. On October 7, 1934, every Jehovah's Witness congregation in the country sent the same, exactly worded written message to the central government. Germany's Jehovah's Witnesses collectively notified the Nazis that "there is a direct conflict between your law and God's law.... We have no interest in political affairs, but are wholly devoted to God's Kingdom under Christ his King. We will do no injury or harm to anyone. We would delight to dwell in peace and do good to all men, as we have opportunity, but since your government and its officers continue to attempt to force us to disobey the highest law of the universe, we are compelled to now give you notice that we, by His Grace, obey Jehovah God and fully trust him to deliver us from all oppression and oppressors."[11]

The letter codified the Jehovah's Witnesses' previously informal practice of refusing to render the Hitler salute to individuals or to the swastika flag. It effectively served notice that they would decline service in the paramilitary Nazi labor corps and conscription into the German armed forces. Witnesses would continue to abstain from voting in national elections.

Mission President Budge's memoirs express the belief that his September 8, 1933, letter to the Gestapo "influenced the government to recognize our [Mormon] Church as a Land Church."[12] By contrast, the Jehovah's Witness Statement of Principles, written eleven months later, had exactly

The Prewar Nazi Years, 1933–1939

the opposite effect. The Witnesses' rigid doctrinal adherence allowed no flexibility that could have forged the kind of compromises with National Socialism that the Mormons would achieve. Thus, in the words of Staffordshire University historian Christine Elizabeth King, the Witnesses threw themselves "into a fully pitched battle with authorities . . . and [resulting in] a campaign of total persecution, designed to destroy them completely."[13]

Unlike the Mormons, Germany's Jehovah's Witnesses suffered tremendously. The government criminalized the conduct of Jehovah's Witness religious services and missionary work. Witnesses lost civil service jobs and employment in positions that were dependent on good standing within the Nazi Labor Front. Of an estimated twenty thousand German members, almost half served terms in prisons or concentration camps; in the latter, they wore purple triangles. Some 2,500 to 5,000, according to different sources, died during incarceration from hunger, exhaustion, exposure, or abuse—or after release as a result of injuries received or illness contracted. More than two hundred tried by Nazi tribunals were subsequently executed.[14] The burden of caring for Jehovah's Witness children became so great on the German state that, at one point, judges who pronounced sentences on couples alternated the terms of imprisonment for the mother and father so that they could care for their children. Later, SS officers forcibly adopted Jehovah's Witnesses children who bore acceptable Aryan phenotypes.[15]

All the while, few Witnesses availed themselves of a standing offer from the government that was unnecessary for a cooperating sect such as the Mormons: If any Jehovah's Witness signed a pledge renouncing his religious beliefs, that person could be released from confinement immediately. Instead, believers continued their church activities and missionary work within prison walls or concentration camp fences, attempting to convert other prisoners and even the guards. In Buchenwald, they set up an underground printing press to produce religious pamphlets. They refused to attempt to escape or to take hostile action against their captors, to the point that they became the camps' most trusted prisoners.[16] Their nonviolent nature gave rise to the legend that a particular concentration camp commandant would consent to be shaved only by a Jehovah's Witness barber, the only class of prisoner he would allow to hold a straight razor to his neck.[17] Outside of confinement, Witnesses continued the dangerous practice of smuggling their banned literature into Germany from Switzerland, and they attempted to win converts under the vigilant observation of the Nazi police apparatus. Their attitude caused *Reichsführer-SS* Heinrich Himmler to speak of the "unshakable faith" of Jehovah's Witnesses. He said that SS men should adopt the same faith in Adolf Hitler.[18] As historian Christine King observed: "The real reason for the clash between [the Jehovah's Witnesses] and the Nazi state lies not in the areas of practical concern, propaganda, refusal to fight, vote or give the salute, but in *"a clash of two totalitarian systems"* (my emphasis).[19]

The term "totalitarian" seems excessive when used in a twentieth-century religious context, when congregants enjoyed the freedom to disassociate themselves from churches at will. If one substitutes the word "authoritarian," King's views are particularly relevant when a third illiberal system, Mormonism, enters consideration. In her scholarship that compares the response of small "new religions" to the rise of the Nazi state, King theorized that the Mormons and the Nazis shared a common *Weltanschauung*, a conjunction of worldviews.[20] Within their ecclesiastical leadership, the Latter-day Saints were every bit as authoritarian and intolerant of internal dissent among ordinary members as were the National Socialists regarding rebellion within their ranks.

However, unlike the Witnesses, whose leaders were constrained by immutable dogma, the Mormons' hierarchical leadership allowed designated prelates, the mission presidents, a greater degree of flexibility to meet contemporary challenges. This freedom of action allowed these skilled American leaders to construct a plan that enabled the Mormons not only to survive National Socialism, but also to prosper during this challenging period to a much greater extent than other small religious denominations that were banned or persecuted by the National Socialist government.[21]

Such a strategy worked because the tenets of Mormonism, unlike those of the Jehovah's Witness faith, contained no doctrinal proscriptions that would inevitably cause the Latter-day Saints to clash with the Nazis. Jehovah's Witnesses were not pacifists, *per se*, but instead considered themselves to be enlisted in God's army, a position that forbade taking up arms for civil governments. By contrast, nothing in LDS doctrine prohibited service in Germany's armed forces; Mormons had fought proudly for the Kaiser during the First World War. Patriotic pronouncements, including saluting the flag, were acceptable and actually encouraged in Mormon society. That did not change for German Mormons when the black, red, and gold tricolor gave way to a black swastika on a white circle, centered in a field of bright red. Thus, in the face of intractable insistence by the Nazis, the Latter-day Saints could compromise regarding a few lesser traditions of their faith. Those included striking references to Israel from hymnals, prayers, and lesson manuals, and the suspension of Boy Scouting activities in favor of mandatory Hitler Youth membership.[22]

Merely surviving the Nazis was not sufficient. In the course of living in Hitler's world, the common *Weltanschauung* the Mormons shared with the Nazis compelled the Latter-day Saints to pursue a strategy that promised greater rewards. The Mormons sought to appease the Nazis to a degree that exceeded what was necessary for their survival as individuals and as a church. Two other American sectarian groups, the Christian Scientists and the Seventh-day Adventists, did only what was necessary to survive. Christian Scientists accepted a ban on collective worship; Adventists willingly acquiesced when the government removed its Saturday work exemption for civil service employees and military servicemen.[23] A third American sect, the Jehovah's Witnesses, resisted. The Mormons, by contrast, exploited National Socialism for the benefit of their church whenever a commonality of interest, such as genealogical research or sports, presented itself.

By the time Hitler assumed power in 1933, the Mormons had been in Germany for eighty-two years. Yet the LDS Church exhibited its greatest degree of conformity with German civil authority during the Nazi period. That is understandable in one respect. The penalties for disobedience to the Nazi government were much more severe than what the Mormons faced in Imperial or Weimar Germany. Simply put, Hitler or any of his higher-level minions could have banished American Mormons from Germany and confined German Mormons to concentration camps. Those sanctions were impossible in Germany's fractured federal system before the First World War or the constitutional democracy that followed. After having flaunted civil authority at home and abroad during the polygamy era, the Mormons dusted off the ninety-one-year-old Twelfth Article of Faith in 1933 under the totalitarian Nazis, thereby illustrating a flexible concept of duty to country. The Mormons chose to obey the law when the law prescribed penalties severe enough to mandate obedience, regardless of the nature of that law or how such obedience reflected on the character of the church. With regard to moral ambiguity, this argues—more than any example such as manual wording, genealogy, or sports—that historian Christine King was an astute observer of both LDS and Nazi outlook when she said both sides shared a conjunction of worldviews.

A Campaign for Survival Becomes an Opportunity

The Mormons began their campaign to survive the Nazis almost immediately upon the ascension of Adolf Hitler to the chancellorship of Germany on January 30, 1933, but steps taken during the last three years of the Weimar Republic laid important groundwork for that effort. Records of both the German-Austrian Mission and the Swiss-German Mission indicate that the American mission presidents, the senior ecclesiastical leaders of the LDS Church in Germany, were hardly cloistered religious prelates. They did not isolate themselves from civil affairs. Instead, their reports to superiors in Salt Lake City indicated that they were keen observers of the Nazis' rising political fortunes. Those early letters and memoranda expressed angst regarding the violence-prone politics of both the National Socialists and the Communists, and the consequences of eventual political domination by either of those extreme political parties. If either the Nazis or the Communists prevailed, the mission presidents worried, the new extremist government might eliminate missionary work and ecclesiastical control by Americans. No written record suggests apprehension that the German LDS Church would be dissolved. The mission presidents feared loss of their supervisory authority.

Obviously mindful of the election results in September 1930, when the Nazis finished second in the voting and won 107 seats in the Reichstag, the Swiss-German Mission's 1930 annual report informed superiors in Salt Lake City that "There are frequent Communistic and Nationalistic demonstrations in Germany that often result in street battles and bloodshed. Should the Hitlerites (Nationalists) win out and put their projected program into effect, all preaching and teaching by other than natives might cease in Germany, which might mean the expulsion of American missionaries."[24]

Two years later, with twenty percent of the work force unemployed, the Nazis captured a plurality of Reichstag seats in the summertime elections. The Swiss-German Mission's 1932 report noted that the Nazis had achieved a decided advantage over the Communists: "During the year, Germany has been in a very agitated and uncertain political situation.... The National Socialists, under the leadership of Adolf Hitler, are generally gaining ground over rival parties."[25]

Reports dispatched to Utah also reflected awareness of significant events that occurred after Hitler rose to power. After the Reichstag fire in late February 1933 and the Nazis' achievement of a parliamentary majority after a mid-March election, Hitler pushed through a set of decrees and laws that suspended numerous individual rights and civil liberties guaranteed under the Weimar Constitution.[26] Commenting on State President Paul von Hindenburg's Reichstag Fire Decree and the new Reichstag's Enabling Law, a report of the Swiss-German mission told church leaders in Salt Lake City: "Hitler soon did away with the forms of republican government which had been introduced at the close of the World War. Radical changes were undertaken on every hand. Governmental institutions and systems, as old as Germany itself, were changed overnight. Almost before the people knew it, the republican Constitution had been chucked into the relic-chest, and fascism took the government reins. Government by decree rather than by constitutional rights was introduced."[27]

When Hindenburg died seventeen months later, the same mission's report to the LDS hierarchy said: "At 9 A.M. on the morning of August 2nd, the German President, Paul von Hindenburg, died, leaving the nation entirely in the control of Adolf Hitler, [the] dictatorially minded Chancellor. The date which denotes the outbreak of the World War, also marks the end of the German Republic and the beginning of the dictatorial regime."[28]

Mindful of the perceived threat that the Nazis presented to the conduct of their missionary work and church activity before Hitler came to power, and the constitutional rights he curtailed afterward, the American Mormon leadership in Germany began to change its style of ecclesiastical governance. Two factors—the rising degree of political uncertainty in Germany and the shortage of American missionaries caused by the Great Depression—prompted the American mission leadership to appoint native Germans to positions of congregational leadership that had formerly been held by young American elders. On December 31, 1930, only two months after Mission President Oliver Budge had put down the congregational rebellion in Breslau caused by the members' desire for local leadership, the year-end report of the German-Austrian mission admitted: "We are placing branches in the hands of local brethren whenever possible. We have some difficulty in training the brethren to be conservative and not misuse their authority given them. It will only be a matter of time before the branches will be much better taken care of under local brethren, and besides, they understand their own people better than we, the elders from Utah."[29]

That constituted a profound shift of opinion for the American leadership, and undoubtedly provoked a degree of internal discomfort for American missionaries who aspired to fill the leadership positions that would be turned over to German members. Arthur Gaeth, an American missionary in Germany and later president of the Czechoslovakian mission, who served overseas for almost a decade during the Weimar period, described the aspirations of ambitious young Americans. They strove to be promoted from an ordinary proselyting position "to branch president, then district president, and then to positions of responsibility in the mission home such as leadership in auxiliary organizations, and then mission secretary."[30]

As late as 1934, the advancement of native Germans to positions of responsibility within the mission was still being hindered by an American conception of a stereotypically authoritarian German personality. In his year-end report for 1934, Swiss-German Mission President Francis Salzner, a native German who had immigrated to the United States, obtained naturalized citizenship, and later returned for missionary service, wrote: "We are putting every effort into the work of preparing our Saints to take over greater responsibilities. As fast as we can find men and women qualified to take over some part of the work we appoint them to a position. *The German way is to drive rather than to lead.* The spirit among the [American] elders is one of seriousness and humility" (my emphasis).[31]

Because the Great Depression hindered the ability of American parents to support their sons on overseas missions, it became inevitable that German believers would undertake more congregational responsibility

—regardless of the political situation. As membership grew while emigration slowed to a crawl during the later Weimar years and practically stopped during the Nazi period, more spiritually attuned German members became available to fill positions. The burgeoning population of the larger branches allowed the expansion of auxiliary leadership positions, such as Sunday school teachers, clerks, and youth leaders.[32] In September 1932, the Swiss-German Mission reported filling thirty-seven vacant positions that had occurred in the previous three months with German branch members. Even though all but four of those were lower-level auxiliary positions, the experience gained by native Germans provided credentials that qualified them to fill the important branch (parish) and district (diocesan) presidency positions that soon followed.[33] Within months of the Nazi assumption of power in 1933, the American mission presidents realized that when a Gestapo agent called upon the leader of a German Mormon congregation, the church would fare better if he talked to an older, more mature German member, rather than a fresh-faced American lad in his early twenties. However, that process took time. In the Swiss-German Mission, the complete replacement of American missionaries as district presidents occurred under the mission presidency of Philemon M. Kelly, who served in that position from 1935 through 1937.[34]

A great deal of work remained to be done by the mission presidents and higher-level officials in Salt Lake City to ensure that Mormonism would survive the Third Reich. Those closest to the threat in 1933, Mission Presidents Oliver Budge in Berlin and Francis Salzner in Basel, coordinated their efforts through messages and periodic personal meetings.[35] Within two months of Hitler's assumption of power, Budge issued "Circular Letter #2" to the elders of the German-Austrian Mission, which warned against expressions of political opinion: "By this country's officials and citizens we have been and are still being treated with respect. You are hereby notified to refrain from discussing or giving your opinion concerning the political situation, either in private or in public. You are also warned against writing anything whatsoever concerning politics or concerning the present situation in any of your local or foreign correspondence, including letters to your parents or friends. Any one of you who fails to take this advice *will* have occasion to *regret it*" (emphasis in original).[36]

Salzer, based in Basel, Switzerland, made a more public appeal to his missionaries and congregants in the western portion of Germany in a July issue of *Der Stern*, in which he included the text of a letter he had written to city officials in Darmstadt. He was responding to a magistrate's request for information about the Mormons' attitude toward the civil government after a missionary had been temporarily banned. As did Budge in his "Circular Letter #2," Salzner urged American missionaries and German church members to refrain from expressing political opinions.[37]

Several months afterward, Budge convened a meeting of the German-Austrian Mission Association. This was a group of German Latter-day Saints whose government-recognized *Verein* allowed the Mormons to conduct financial transactions and own property in Germany. According to the minutes, Budge "instructed those present as to the attitude of the Church toward the government." No detail of Budge's remarks survive in the records, but it is likely that the American mission president instructed his German charges to remain silent and apolitical.

When the government found something objectionable in a Mormon publication or exhibit, the mission presidents did not hesitate to withdraw or modify the offending material. Early in 1934, two "police officers" called at German-Austrian Mission headquarters in Berlin. They had come to confiscate all stocks of the missionary pamphlet, "Signs of the Great Apostasy." Budge surrendered every copy he had and promised that the balance of the tracts would be withdrawn from the field. Shortly thereafter, the government notified the mission office to recall another pamphlet, "Divine Authority." Subsequent investigation revealed that neither brochure contained language offensive to the Nazis. Instead, the police were acting on a complaint from an association of local ministers, who found the wording spiritually offensive.[38] Officials of the Swiss-German Mission also voluntarily recalled the same pamphlets.[39] During the Weimar period, the Mormons would have ignored the protests of rival pastors, and would have contested the authority of police who acted on behalf of sectarian opponents.

On other occasions, the Mormons policed themselves when the wording of church hymns or religious instructional material threatened to offend the Nazis. According to one missionary, mission presidents instructed congregations not to sing certain songs in the church hymnal, such as "Israel, Israel, God is Calling" or "Hope of Israel." Nor should sermons include references to the Lost Tribes of Israel or other topics that could be construed as relating to Judaism.[40] When the Relief Society, the women's auxiliary organization, published a manual that contained a lesson entitled, "Christ and the Gathering of Israel," the mission office instructed all local leaders to "cut these pages out and paste the adjoining two together." According to the wording of the accompanying memorandum, "It is our belief that any subject even remotely connected with the Jewish race would be better unexpressed in Germany today."[41]

5

Genealogy
Promoting a Common Worldview on Earth and in the Afterlife

When Joseph Smith formulated the tenets of Mormon theology during his early adulthood, he enjoyed one advantage over the framers of primitive Christianity. He understood the doctrinal disagreements that provoked hotly debated theological arguments among Christians on the early-nineteenth-century American frontier. He sought to imbed in his new sect's dogma the answers to some of the questions that must have confronted the circuit-riding preachers and itinerant evangelists who crisscrossed western New York's "Burned-Over District" during his childhood. Two of those spiritual mysteries directly influenced the foundational theology of nascent Mormonism: First, could those who had never heard the message of Christ's redeeming sacrifice go to heaven? Second, must a believer be baptized in order to achieve salvation?

His answers to those queries help define Mormonism's theological uniqueness. They also later played an important role, one hundred years after the church's founding, in the Latter-day Saints' relationship with the German government during National Socialism. By exploiting a common interest in genealogical research, the Mormons discovered another tool by which they could find common ground with the Nazi worldview. For some Latter-day Saints, however, including the religion editors of the church-owned daily in Salt Lake City, the *Deseret News*, that was not sufficient. They had to make it clear that their co-religionists in Nazi Germany were enjoying a better reception than other American sectarians, and demonstratively better treatment than Germany's Jews.[1]

Mormons and Nazis were enthusiastic genealogists, but each group conducted its archival research for markedly different reasons. Born during the Second Great Awakening, in part an American revolt against Calvinism's salvation of the elect, Mormonism taught that any believer could enter heaven after a life of faith and good works, but only after having been baptized by immersion. Joseph Smith's innovation accounted for righteous souls who never had the opportunity to learn of Jesus Christ. They could hear the gospel preached in the afterlife, in a place called "spirit paradise." Having adopted the Christian faith after death, the converted could then proceed to heaven. One more problem challenged Smith's groundbreaking theology: How could a dead person enter the waters of baptism? Smith's imagination, which biographer Fawn Brodie said, "spilled over like a spring freshet," provided the answer.[2] Living Mormons could perform "saving ordinances" by proxy, that is, baptisms for the dead, in the Holy Temple.[3] Only one obstacle remained: identifying those deceased spirits still waiting in spirit paradise for someone to do their temple baptism.[4] Genealogical research solved that problem.[5]

Germans living under Hitler's governance became interested in genealogy for totally different reasons. Salvation from National Socialist damnation lay in proving one's biological purity, free of "racial pollution" or the "corrupting blood" of Jews or others whom Hitler considered to be inferior. Of course, some Germans did not require certification from a genealogist or reference librarian to merit exclusion from Nazi society. The "Rhineland Bastards," products of unions between German women and black French occupation soldiers after the First World War, bore distinguishing pigmentation.[6] Others became the focus of the Nazi racial machinery as well. In 1936, the government opened an "Office to Combat the Gypsy Nuisance," which maintained a national data database on Roma and Sinti. Thousands of Gypsies were eventually deported to concentration camps, where they wore black triangles, denoting "work shy," or green triangles as common criminals.[7] But for other Germans seeking to prove they were not Jews, genealogical research promised redemption.

That need for pure ancestral lineage manifested itself shortly after Hitler became chancellor. On April 7, 1933, the Law for the Restoration of the Professional Civil Service disqualified non-Aryans, effectively Jews, from civil service employment. A series of laws that followed barred Jewish practitioners from most of the liberal professions. Jews employed in industrial trades also lost their jobs when their labor unions fell victim to the "coordination," *Gleichschaltung*, or co-option by the Nazi Labor Front.

If there had been a trade group for professional genealogists, however, its membership would have been delighted with the business provided by passage of the 1935 Nuremberg Laws. One statute outlawed "racial pollution," that is, marriage or sexual relationships between Aryans and Jews. Another required a medical examination and counseling before marriage—ostensibly to prohibit miscegenation by Aryans.[8] A third law limited German citizenship to those having no Jewish grandparents, and classified others as "subjects," effectively depriving a segment of native-born Germans of their citizenship. This statute classified a "full Jew" as someone who had three or four Jewish grandparents. Others were designated as mixed-breeds, *Mischlings*, of the first degree if they had two Jewish grandparents, or of the second degree for having one Jewish grandparent.[9] With regard to genealogical research, historian Klaus P. Fischer wrote that the Nuremberg laws "produced a bureaucratic nightmare because [they] involved scores of 'family researchers' hunting down uncertain records. The determination of who was a *Mischling*, nevertheless, was of vital importance because it could mean life or death once the decision had been made to exterminate the Jews."[10]

When the Mormons brought their genealogical research capabilities to the mission field and taught those techniques to the Germans they converted, they intended to enable deceased co-religionists to go to heaven as a reward for a lifetime of faithful, righteous living. Instead, Latter-day Saints stumbled into a life-or-death situation where their skills in the archives could be used to identify "racially inferior" members or to condemn a German congregant of bizarre new kinds of crime: racial betrayal or racial dishonor, *Rassenverrat* or *Rassenschande*.

Latter-day Saints began conducting family history research in the United States shortly after the church's founding in the early nineteenth century. The first evidence of Mormon genealogical inquiry in Germany, however, surfaced during the Weimar Republic.[11] The LDS Church experienced strong membership growth during the period of economic prosperity between the end of hyperinflation and the onset of the Great Depression. As congregations grew in the larger cities, more members could be directed toward duties in the church "auxiliary" organizations, such as Sunday schools, youth activities, and genealogical classes. By 1928, eight German LDS districts (dioceses) had established genealogical societies to promote research within their ecclesiastical boundaries.[12] Nevertheless, the growth of church-sponsored genealogical work in Weimar Germany remained proportional to the growth of other auxiliary organizations: Boy Scouts, Beehives and Gleaner Girls for teenage girls, M Men for older teenage boys, the Mutual Improvement Association for all adolescents, various priesthood "quorums" for men, and the Relief Society for women. Completing one's pedigree chart during the relatively stable Weimar period received more emphasis than it did in the unstable days of Imperial Germany, when the missionaries leading Mormon congregations were always in danger of being expelled from town, rendering leaderless the Germans they directed. Before the Nazis, however, a "calling" or church job to help other members research their genealogy was no more important than any other church auxiliary duty.

After Hitler came to power, priorities changed. When *Deseret News* religion writer Fay Ollerton visited the German-Austrian Mission early in the autumn of 1933, she noted that one of the mission's stalwart young elders had been appointed to serve, in conjunction with his other duties, as a mission-wide genealogy supervisor. "[He] goes from branch to branch with a great Book of Remembrance—*Buch der Erinnerung*—persuading German Saints to keep their family records."[13] By the end of the year, the number of LDS genealogical societies in the Swiss-German mission had multiplied to thirty-five. Some 575 members from that mission, which at the time numbered slightly more than 6,500 people, were engaged in genealogical research as a church calling by the end of Hitler's first year as chancellor. That mission's year-end report noted that 15,217 names had been forwarded to Salt Lake City for temple ordinances. Those names appeared on 339 pedigree charts, 5,224 family group records, and 1,008 sealing sheets. The same report noted that a native German, presumably one of unquestionable racial heritage, has been chosen as the Swiss-German Mission's genealogical leader, the first such mission-wide appointment in that mission's history.[14]

It could be asserted that the Mormons, in that first year of Nazi rule, adapted a customary church practice to the toxic racial environment in which they suddenly and unexpectedly found themselves living. In doing so, they arguably protected themselves from one of the most onerous policies promulgated by Germany's new fanatical dictator. When the church-owned *Deseret News* published its second story that year about how the Mormons were faring under Hitler, the author and editors of "Mormonism in the New Germany" demonstrated no hesitation in pointing out which group suffered at the expense of the Latter-day Saints' good fortune:

> Many of those who felt the greatest anxiety about being able to carry on their religious activities are finding that at least one branch of their church work has received its greatest boon since Germany's adoption of Hitlerism. It was always difficult for the genealogical workers to get into the archives of the recognized churches to trace back family records. When the pastor learned of the intention, access was often denied. Now, due to the importance given to the racial question, and the almost *necessity of proving that one's grandmother was not a Jewess*, the old record books have been dusted off and stand ready and waiting for use. No questions are asked. In fact, some of the Saints, instead of being refused by the pastors have now received letters of encouragement complimenting them for their patriotism (my emphasis).[15]

As the Mormons continued to use an aspect of their unique theology to comply with National Socialist dogma, it became more difficult to resist being drawn into a deepening abyss. In January 1934, one of the Swiss-German mission's genealogical lay leaders accepted an invitation to speak before a group of Social Darwinists, one that had existed for years before the formation of the Nazi Party. Walter Pohlsander, a member of the Hanover district, appeared before the German Society for Racial Hygiene, *Deutsche Gesellschaft für Rassenhygiene*, which had begun agitating in 1905 for selective reproduction and enforced sterilization.[16] Pohlsander spoke on the topic of "Pedigree Seeking" and explained the genealogical program of the LDS Church. According to the mission records, he "succeeded in creating great interest for our cause."[17] An enthusiastic Mormon with no discernible academic credentials, Pohlsander probably did not realize that he was addressing a group that owed its beginnings to professors and other members of the academic community who had embraced a bad idea. By the time the Mormon genealogical leader spoke in January 1934, he was addressing a group that had become infested by Nazis who embraced many unconscionable ideas.[18]

Both missions cooperated in February 1934 to publish the first German-language guide to Mormon genealogical practices. *A Practical Guide for Genealogical and Temple Work* (*Praktischer Führer für Genealogie und Tempelarbeit*) prescribed research methodologies and contained specific instructions for completing each of the approved church genealogical forms.[19] In the Swiss-German Mission, President Francis Salzner delivered the same Sunday sermon at four different district conferences, held on successive weekends in March before assembled congregations, in Hanover, Nuremberg, Bern, and the Ruhr. His topic, "Three Generations," stressed the need to prepare one's genealogical pedigree chart to include all four grandparents.[20]

As Salzner delivered his sermon, urging his fellow Mormons to put their genealogical research into writing, it was becoming more important in Nazi Germany to record a formal certification of one's ancestry. A statement of religious affiliation, signed by one's pastor or priest, may have been sufficient to prove the absence of Jewish heritage shortly after the Civil Service Law of 1933 passed. Even before adoption of the Nuremberg Laws of 1935, the Nazis were constructing a byzantine labyrinth of new racial laws and regulations. According to Eric Ehrenreich, a fellow at the U.S. Holocaust Memorial Museum, the twelve years of National Socialism saw adoption of "approximately two thousand statutes, ordinances, and regulations establishing legal rights on the basis of 'racial' status."[21]

This caused a potential problem for the state bureaucracy that would have to certify compliance with the bewildering volume of new race laws. Civil servants, worried that they would be inundated with requests for assistance with genealogical research, devised a tool that required German citizens to do most of the work. Members of the Reich Foundation of Civil Registrars developed the *Ahnenpass*, a small multipage, pocket-sized, folded document that resembled a passport. Applicants would fill in their own ancestral religious lineage, tracing back the required number of generations. For most trades or professions in Nazi Germany, being free of Jewish heritage for three generations was sufficient. Then, the applicant would take the completed *Ahnenpass* to a registrar of civil records, or to a custodian of church records, who would verify the accuracy of the primary documentation and then affix an official seal.²² For Germans fortunate to be free of Jewish heritage, the *Ahnenpass* acted as a type of internal visa, allowing them to navigate life in Nazi Germany without suspicion of being a racial alien.

No record found in the LDS Church historical archives documents that Mormon genealogists or ecclesiastical leaders ever certified an *Ahnenpass*. However, if congregants heeded Mission President Salzner's advice to prepare their genealogical records in a format that would be accepted by the state, they may have had experiences similar to at least one member's. According to one account, "a Mormon official was arrested and charged with being Jewish." Interviewed after the war, he recalled the incident: "I had to prove that I was an Aryan. I only needed to show the investigating officers my lines for three generations. Were they surprised when I showed them my family group sheets going back eight generations! I passed with flying colors."²³

By late 1934, it became apparent that genealogy had assumed a position of greater importance within the organization of Mormon districts and branches in Germany. Regardless of whether a congregation enjoyed sufficient numerical strength to fill all open positions in its auxiliary organizations, finding capable genealogical volunteers became a priority. During the Weimar period, a single teacher of genealogical methods might be appointed for a congregation. By 1935, branch and district presidents were appointing complete genealogical staffs, to include a president, two counselors, and a secretary, even at the branch (congregational) level.²⁴ The year-end report of the Swiss-German Mission said, "the members are showing an increasing interest in genealogical work. This mission is now one of the leaders in sending genealogical work to America."²⁵

A new method of motivating German members to perform ancestral research surfaced in the form of "genealogical conventions." In the Weimar District (diocese) in the autumn of 1934, fifty-two members attended the first LDS Church convention solely devoted to genealogical research held in Germany, one of several venues within the German-Austrian mission where such conventions occurred.²⁶ By 1936, genealogical conventions were occurring on the branch (congregation) level. In Breslau, Gleiwitz, Hindenburg, the Silesian city of Leignitz, and the Saxon city of Waldenburg, all congregations within each district held genealogical conferences during the month of September 1936.²⁷ Editors of *Der Stern*, the

German-language church periodical, devoted their entire September 1, 1936, issue to the subject of genealogy. Three weeks later, on September 20, the Swiss-German mission coordinated "Genealogical Sunday," requiring each congregation within that mission's jurisdiction to devote the weekly sacrament meeting (main service) to the subject of researching one's family tree.[28]

By 1938, Mormons in Germany were experimenting with new methods in order to convince members to research more names for posthumous temple ordinances. Those innovations included genealogical youth activities and discounted prices for family record forms. The October 15, 1938, issue of *Der Stern* said: "Genealogy is gaining more and more attention. Therefore, more time is to be made available which we will try to find by means of starting genealogy research classes in the Mutual, for the Senior classes, the M Men and the Gleaners. The meeting is to be conducted under the direction of the Mutual, however the class time is used for genealogical work. . . . It is the intention of the mission officers to make the program attractive to the youth of the church."

In order to make the required materials more attractive for purchase, the article announced: "Surely, no one has an excuse for staying inactive in this work, while other thousands are going forward enthusiastically, especially since the cost of genealogical supplies has been cut considerably. The price for family group sheets and pedigree charts has been cut by a third, the prices of books cut by a fourth."[29]

In February 1938, the director of the Genealogical Society of Utah, the LDS Church's nonprofit corporation established in 1894 to preserve vital records and encourage genealogical research, embarked on a European tour. James M. Kirkham came to assess the degree of difficulty that faced Latter-day Saints in conducting genealogical research in various countries.[30] When he got to Germany, he liked what he saw. His subsequent article in the *Deseret News* said:

> Mr. Hitler, through government agencies, is helping the Germans to find their ancestors. . . . Many magazines are published in different parts of Germany in the interest of genealogy. Space in nearly all of the papers is allowed a person who is seeking an ancestor. Also, over the radio, notice is given for persons seeking the information they wanted. Because of the great interest in genealogy among the

Genealogy

Germans, there seemed to be a desire for one person to help the other with their [*sic*] problems. To prove that he is a pure blood German for at least four generations or back to 1800 is the desire of each resident.

The remainder of Kirkham's article spanned four columns of the Friday afternoon Church Section and included two large, three-column-wide pictures.[31] It praised the technological progress made by the German government with regard to photographic reproduction of parish and civil records on thirty-five millimeter, fireproof film. It described a forerunner of the microfilm viewer, which allowed researchers to enlarge filmed images for easier reading. Then it expressed appreciation for the "vast amount of genealogical research" being conducted and "made available to persons of German descent."[32]

Such verbiage provokes discomfort in today's reader, especially in light of how the Third Reich ultimately used the workaday labor of ordinary Germans to foster its murderous agenda. Legions of clerks who coordinated railroad schedules for boxcars of Jews shipped to Auschwitz gave rise to the term "desk genocide," *Schreibtischtäter*. Philosopher Hannah Arendt characterized this kind of remote, detached, bloodless contribution to the machinery of murder as the "banality of evil."[33] Likewise, the thousands of Germans who studiously researched their ancestral lines in musty church archives or well-lighted municipal libraries, even if they did so in the fervent hope of proving they were *not* Jews, deserve appropriate scrutiny. How did their assiduous efforts to save themselves facilitate the fate, in the years that followed, of those who could not produce a "racially pure" pedigree chart? In the scholarly debates that classify Germans who lived during the Third Reich as perpetrators, victims, or bystanders, how should history look upon those who devoted countless hours to genealogical research?

For the Mormons, their religious obligation to perform the same genealogical duties presented a complicating factor. Author Gilbert Scharffs dismissed the connection between Mormon and Nazi genealogical research as "probably only a coincidence."[34] For the ordinary congregant who sat on the back pew, Scharffs' argument could have a limited degree of merit. For Mission President Salzner, however, a native German who was serving his second tour of duty as a missionary after having immigrated to the United States, the convergence of God's work and Hitler's work must have been more apparent. He did not preach four consecutive weekly sermons in 1934, exhorting his congregants to complete their three-generation genealogical records, exclusively as an appeal to save the souls of deceased ancestors. He was in a position to know more, and to appreciate the racial connotations of the government's mandate.

Regarding the way the LDS Church-owned *Deseret News* reported on the faith's activity in Nazi Germany, the best critique was a contemporary one. It came in 1939 from the pen of Fawn McKay Brodie, who enjoyed a unique vantage point. She was the daughter of Swiss-Austrian Mission President Thomas E. McKay, who at that time was serving his third mission among the German-speaking congregations in Europe. Her brother, Thomas, Jr., had recently returned from a mission in Nazi Germany. A former boyfriend, Dilworth Jensen, had served a mission in Germany when Hitler rose to power. In the late 1930s, Fawn corresponded regularly with her mother, the "mission matron," who like Fawn was undergoing a crisis of faith. According to Brodie's biographer, Newell Bringhurst, when Fawn's mother returned from the Swiss-Austrian Mission, her daughter considered her mother to be "a thoroughgoing heretic."[35] Presumably, the mother's letters to Fawn from the mission field did not sugarcoat the Mormons' relationship with the Nazis.[36]

Brodie had the advantage of another informed perspective. Against her parents' wishes, she had married a secular Jewish scholar she met at the University of Chicago, where she earned a master's degree in English. Bernard Brodie was a specialist in international relations. His observations, and the couple's circle of intellectual friends, ensured that Fawn kept abreast of the latest developments in Hitler's Germany.[37] In a letter to her uncle, Dean Brimhall, in which she accused the church-owned Salt Lake City daily newspaper of "falling over backwards" not to offend Nazi Germany, she added:

> Aside from the fact that the missions are not prospering and the church can ill afford persecution at this moment, I think there are other reasons why the *Deseret News* does not publish editorials about refugees. Of course, there is the latent anti-Semitism that exists in every area as provincial as Utah and which is not dispelled by the church doctrine that we are all 'of the blood of Israel.' Add

to this the fact that the persecution of the Jews has made 80 million people 'genealogy minded'—so much so that according to a recent campus acquaintance, a former Berlin lawyer, genealogy is the first subject for conversation in Germany. I can just hear the good brethren in the Genealogical Society at home saying, 'Of course, the persecution of the Jews is terrible, but God moves in mysterious ways, his wonders to perform.'[38]

Boasts regarding the Mormons' genealogical research, and how it protected the Latter-day Saints from being misidentified as Jews, disappear from the archival records and the pages of church-sponsored newspapers after *Kristallnacht* on November 9–10, 1938. It may have taken this horrific nationwide pogrom to stoke Mormon consciences. Enjoyable hours spent in the company of fellow church members, combing through dusty archival records, may have been regarded differently after "the night of broken glass." Likewise, writers, editors, and readers of the *Deseret News* may have finally been shocked into awareness of what was going on in Nazi Germany. Perhaps Mormons on both sides of the Atlantic then began to take another view of genealogical research in Hitler's Reich.

6

Mormon Basketball Diplomacy in Hitler's Reich

One Friday afternoon in late January 1936, readers of Salt Lake City's *Deseret News* encountered an unusual, sports-themed picture in the weekly Church Section. The six-column photograph showed two groups of athletes lined up in a military-style formation. A basketball lay positioned on the ground between each team. The squad of eight young men in the foreground, dressed in white athletic shirts, shorts, and sneakers, stood upright at the position of attention, their right arms extended rigidly forward and upward at a forty-five degree angle, hands and fingers straight with a bit of palm showing underneath. The team was rendering the Hitler salute. In the accompanying article that discussed innovative ways to preach the gospel of Mormonism, the writer declared: "In Germany Herr Hitler has sought the services of the Elders to teach basketball to the teams he hopes will achieve a Nordic victory at the Olympic games to be held this year in Berlin."[1]

With that brazen declaration, the Mormons interjected themselves into the most controversial sports story of the year, one replete with impassioned moral arguments that had international diplomatic reverberations. Subscribers to the *Deseret News*, the largest general-circulation, broadsheet, daily newspaper operated as a wholly owned subsidiary of a religious denomination west of the Mississippi River, were familiar with that debate.[2] Only weeks before, readers followed a blow-by-blow description of the Amateur Athletic Union's (AAU's) December meeting in New York City. Two articles, which appeared in the *Deseret News* several days apart, defined the issue: Would the United States send athletic teams to the Olympic Games in Germany?[3] The opposition, led by New York City Mayor Fiorello LaGuardia, Walter White of the NAACP, and William Green, President of the AFL, received widespread publicity in wire-service news articles transmitted across the country. The AAU meeting itself pitted the pro-boycott forces of Judge Jeremiah T. Mahoney, president of the AAU, against the anti-boycott side headed by American Olympic Committee Chairman Avery Brundage.[4] When Brundage's forces won the decisive showdown, it forced Mahoney's resignation as head of the AAU. That proved to be a decisive blow against an international effort to boycott the games of the eleventh Olympiad in protest of Hitler's treatment of Germany's Jews."[5]

Probably no Mormon attended that pivotal AAU meeting in New York, nor does any account record LDS attitudes regarding the proposed Olympic boycott. Because German-Americans enthusiastically supported American participation in the 1936 Olympics, it is almost certain that their cousins in the Mormon Culture Region did so also.[6] In subsequent days, no letters to the editor protesting the brash pictorial rendering of the Hitler salute appeared in the *Deseret News*, nor did any condemnation of the appeal for a "Nordic victory." If the article and accompanying picture had any effect on the readership, it probably stoked pride in the church's unconventional attempts to win converts.

Mormon missionaries played a small but significant role in the German national basketball team's 1936 Olympic efforts. It was not enough to help a hopelessly overmatched team win even a single game, but it helped Mormons win friends among government officials and assert that the American-based sect was no foe of National Socialism. Young elders introduced basketball fundamentals to some of the athletes who had been picked to play on the German team before a professional coach could be hired. Four missionaries kept the official score books for the first round of Olympic basketball play.

The roots of Germany's desire to host the Olympic Games, and the origin of the Mormons' infatuation with basketball, both lie in the beginning of the twentieth century. Imperial Germany had anxiously sought to host an Olympiad since the Athens games in 1896 marked the beginning of the modern Olympic movement. Shortly after the Stockholm Olympics in 1912, the IOC awarded the 1916 games to Germany. Germany greeted the news with such enthusiasm that it completed the Olympic track and field stadium three years early. However, the First World War caused cancellation of the sixth Olympiad, and lingering Allied bitterness disqualified Germany from participating in the 1920 games in Antwerp and the 1924 games in Paris. Finally, in the chaos that prevailed during the waning months of the Weimar Republic in 1932, the persistence of a few of the original organizers succeeded when the IOC awarded the 1936 games to Germany.[7] The winter games would be held in January in the Bavarian municipality of Garmisch-Partenkirchen and the summer games in August in Berlin. Defenders of the IOC later maintained that the international body awarded the games to a struggling democracy, and would not have done so if it could have anticipated the Nazis seizure of power and Hitler's exploitation of the games as a showcase for Aryan supremacy."[8]

As a political candidate in 1932, Hitler had criticized the German Olympic effort as "an invention of Jews and Freemasons" and "a play inspired by Judaism which cannot possibly be put on in a Reich ruled by National Socialists."[9] After he assumed power in early 1933, however, he made the Berlin Olympics a centerpiece of propaganda for German fascism and a weapon against the Jews. The Nazis not only purged Jews from the civil service and the liberal professions, but also from Germany's sporting community. Germany's national teams dismissed their Jewish athletes, making them ineligible for Olympic competition, but the ban eventually excluded Jews from the lowest level of recreational activity.[10]

On April 1, 1933, on the same day that the Nazis launched a nationwide boycott of Jewish-owned businesses, the German boxing federation announced that Jewish pugilists and referees would no longer be allowed in the ring.[11] In June, the ministry of education proclaimed that Jewish children could no longer enter gymnasiums or enroll in recreational organizations. By July, municipalities in Germany were closing swimming pools to Jews and prohibiting their employment as lifeguards.[12]

The first few decades of the twentieth century also saw the Mormons begin a basketball tradition that has remained a distinct part of life in LDS Church youth organizations through the present time. Less than two decades after the inventor of basketball, Dr. James Naismith, tacked two peach baskets to gymnasium walls in Springfield, Massachusetts in 1891, the Mormons adopted basketball as a youth activity and subsequently as a proselytizing tool. The effect of that decision can still be observed one hundred years later, when almost every Mormon "stake center" in North America has a large multi-use auditorium that includes basketball goals and floor markings. In 1931, when many of the young missionaries who eventually served in Nazi Germany were preparing to go overseas, the all-church basketball tournament in Salt Lake City drew eight thousand players.[13]

Mormon missionaries may have brought basketball with them to Germany as a way to blow off steam during rare opportunities for recreation. They soon found it to be a tool that would help them meet groups of potential converts where access would otherwise have been difficult or impossible, such as university campuses and military posts. In early August 1935, two elders, William Skidmore and Heber Hawkes, accepted an invitation to instruct "a select group of students in basketball" at a university in Neustrelitz. The training session lasted for several weeks, during which the missionaries "were treated with much respect," but found that their students had no interest in religious matters. "Churches are for the soul-saving aspect of life," their students told them, "and the state should develop youth without interference from churches."[14] That same month, Skidmore and another elder, David M. Morrell, visited several military posts, where they were welcomed as basketball instructors but not religious missionaries. They were not allowed to address *Wehrmacht* soldiers on spiritual topics.[15] Several months later in the city of Gera, town officials invited a group of missionaries to play a challenge game against a local team. Unlike their experiences on military posts and at the university, the elders were allowed to hold a post-game "illustrated lecture," after which "tracts were passed out; the mayor of the city helping to pass them out."[16]

At some point between the late summer of 1935 and January 1936, the Mormons agreed to furnish rudimentary basketball instruction to the German Olympic team. The catalyst seems to have been the Germans' realization that it would have to field an Olympic team in an unfamiliar sport, with a limited budget to fund the teaching of basic basketball skills. Basketball had appeared in the 1904 Olympics in St. Louis and again in the 1932 games in Los Angeles as a "display sport," an event that the host country can stage in order to call attention to emerging local sports, but in which medals won do not count in the official standings.[17] Basketball exhibitions, but not full-fledged competition, occurred as part of the 1924 games in Paris and the 1928 games in Amsterdam. In 1936, however, basketball became a regular Olympic medal sport, and the German hosts felt obligated to field a team to compete in every event. The problem was that almost no one in Germany knew anything about the game, except for a few foreigners attending German universities and the Mormon missionaries.

According to Professor Arnd Krueger of the *Institut für Sportwissenschaften* at the University of Göttingen, the Germans met the challenge by designating the second-string national handball team, not to be confused with American handball, as their Olympic basketball squad. The decision was theoretically sound. The handball players were accomplished athletes. Eight of the ten who eventually played in the Olympics had been students at either the Army Sports School at Wünsdorf or the Air Force Sports School at Spandau. However, they were not considered talented enough to make the Olympic team in their own sport. In fact, handball was not a German priority in the games. It was governed as a neglected subsection of the German track and field federation. Since the Germans had no expectations for Olympic glory in handball, no decision maker feared criticism for diverting second-line players from one unimportant sport to another.[18]

The Germans eventually hired a professional coach. Hermann Niebuhr had learned basketball as a teacher at a German secondary school in Istanbul, where he associated with American faculty members who coached the game. However, budget considerations left no money for player development prior to the beginning of Niebuhr's contract.[19] When the team assembled in eastern Germany in the autumn of 1935, probably at the army post in Wünsdorf or the air force base in Brandenburg, a group of Mormon elders greeted them. It was the task of the missionaries not to save the German players' souls, but instead to teach a group of handball players how to dribble, pass, and shoot before meeting their new basketball coach. Vinton M. Merrill, one of those basketball tutors, recalled the development of the German Olympic players that he "coached": "A bunch of broken down missionaries beat the Germans handily at first, but as time went on, they got better and better. After a while, they got so good that they could take the ball away from us easily. They were in superb physical condition." Merrill said that after the training camp, he and his fellow missionaries played weekly games against the German team, some of them at the Olympic venue.[20]

A short entry in the German-Austrian Mission Manuscript Histories in August 1936 comments on the beginning of the Olympic Games, the enthusiasm of the opening-day crowd, and the participation of one Mormon athlete, a student at Brigham Young University who occupied a spot on the American track and field team. It also notes briefly the role of four young American missionaries, some of whom had participated in teaching basic basketball skills to the German Olympic team: "Four of the Mormon missionaries were asked to be basketball officials in the basketball arena and were given official coats and badges to be worn at this time. They were Vinton M. Merrill, Charles A. Perschon, Jerome J. Christensen, and Edward G. Judd."[21]

One author misread that passage and overstated the role of those "officials." In modern basketball vernacular, an official is usually a referee. Thus, it is not surprising that Gilbert Scharffs, in *Mormonism in Germany*, said the missionaries were Olympic basketball referees.[22] In actuality, referees from the International Basketball Federation officiated the games. Instead, the four Mormons were the designated keepers of the official scorebooks, which recorded the outcome of the game and tracked each player's points and fouls. They served in that capacity only for the games of the first and second rounds on August 7 and 8, after which other scorers worked the remaining games. Undoubtedly, as a result of the missionaries' efforts to prepare the German team, four American missionaries were invited to offer their services as scorers. However, the official box score of each game recorded each young man's nationality as "German."[23]

The Mormons' experience with the 1936 Olympic basketball competition serves as an example of their tendency to explore all avenues of common interest with Germany's National Socialist government, with no regard to overarching international issues. By the time the Summer Olympics began, Germany's exclusion of its Jewish population from both athletic competition and most rights of citizenship had become well known. The Olympic boycott movement had failed, but its circumstances were familiar to anyone who read a general-circulation daily newspaper. Mormon missionaries in Berlin during that era saw anti-Semitic signs and banners disappear during the three weeks of the eleventh Olympiad in August 1936. Then, the same elders undoubtedly noticed the reemergence of that signage after foreign visitors departed.[24] No evidence suggests that even one German associated with the basketball effort converted to Mormonism. Thus, as a missionary effort, it did not succeed. However, it served as one more reminder that, in addition to "obeying, honoring, and sustaining the law," as the Twelfth Article of Faith pledged, this American sect would also support the Nazi system that imposed an onerous legal system.

7

Boy Scouting
The Mormons' Only Unconditional Surrender to the Nazis

Six months after the beginning of the Second World War, on March 4, 1940, the ocean liner SS *Washington* docked in New York Harbor after a fourteen-day voyage from Genoa.[1] A *New York Times* reporter interviewed several arriving passengers, including French and British diplomats, an international banker, and the last Mormon missionaries to evacuate Europe. A former Swiss-Austrian Mission president who became the senior LDS prelate in Europe after the war began, Thomas E. McKay, spoke with the journalist as he disembarked with his wife, daughter, and four young missionaries.

McKay expressed regret for having to leave Europe, where he had served three Mormon missions, two as a mission president. Then he summarized how his co-religionists had been received by Hitler's regime: "The Mormons have never been molested in Germany," McKay told the reporter. He continued, "We couldn't ask for better treatment. The only way the Nazis have affected our work is that our Boy Scout movement has been curtailed by the Hitler Youth movement."[2]

McKay's comment regarding the suspension of Boy Scout activities, which had occurred some six years earlier in 1934, focused on the only unconditional Mormon surrender to the Nazis. His disappointment was understandable to anyone who knew the special role that Scouting played in Mormonism during the first decades of the twentieth century. As the activities arm of the Aaronic Priesthood, Scouting performed a role unmatched in other church denominations that sponsored troops.[3] Attainment of merit badges and promotion in Scouting rank marked significant mileposts in a Mormon boy's advancement toward ordination in the senior Melchizedek Priesthood. In the LDS view, the lessons in sacrifice and endurance learned on hikes and wilderness campouts were building blocks for successful missionary service and adult church leadership. Boy Scouting was not an optional activity once a faithful Latter-day Saint lad reached the age of twelve; it was a boot camp, albeit an enjoyable one, that drilled the future shock troops of Mormonism.

The Boy Scout issue illuminates one important aspect of the survival strategy employed by skilled American mission presidents to protect the congregations they considered vulnerable and the missionary program they treasured. When Mormons decided to contest a Nazi decision, they usually did so locally.[4] They were cautious regarding which issues they allowed to reach authorities above the *Gau* level. Mormons decided to forego an appeal to save their Scouting program that would have to be made to the higher echelons of the of the National Socialist government. Because scout troops across Germany were being absorbed by the Hitler Youth, they knew they would lose this battle.[5] Mission presidents also terminated the German Scouting movement because any kind of compromise forged with the Hitler Youth would have surrendered control of a church-based program to outsiders.

By contrast, the Mormons maintained their traditional female youth organizations because challenges posed on behalf of the Nazi girls' organizations never escalated beyond the local level, and because LDS adult leaders could maintain control.[6] When a *Gauleiter* or other official ordered the cessation of local Beehive or Gleaner Girl activity, the Mormons obediently suspended meetings of the contested local youth organization.[7] Then they quietly worked behind the scenes, or in some cases tactfully appealed to the official's immediate supervisor, in order to mitigate the sanction.

The Mormons also became skilled at not drawing Nazi attention to the youth programs that survived. Unlike the Girl Scouts or Campfire Girls, who wore uniforms, and the *Bund deutscher Mädel* (League of German Girls), who wore Hitler Youth uniforms, the LDS girls' programs did not prescribe military attire. Unlike the Boy Scouts, other Mormon youth programs did not affiliate with an international organization, and thus did not provoke Nazi suspicions of foreign interference. Local congregational leaders also took care to comply with the exact wording of an official's banning order without exceeding its specifications. In 1938, for example, police in Zwickau forbade the local district's Mutual Improvement Association (MIA) from holding an Easter commemoration, ostensibly a dramatic production that would be open to the public.[8] However, the order did not prohibit the boys and girls who belonged to the MIA chapter from meeting together for other customary activities, which the Zwickau youngsters presumably continued doing. As a last resort, Mormon congregations learned how to disguise youth activities. In October 1938, the East German Mission replaced separate MIA meetings with an "Evening Hour" program. All auxiliary organizations, for adults as well as for juveniles, met at the church meetinghouse at one time.[9] With so many adults in the building, the gathering must have resembled regular congregational worship, which the Nazis never banned.

Nevertheless, the disappearance of church-controlled Scout troops, and the mandatory attendance at Hitler Youth activities required by the Nazi state, caused significant angst among Germany's Mormons. In order to understand why Scouting was so important, it is necessary to examine the roots of LDS Church–sanctioned youth activity in Utah during the first years of the twentieth century. Scouting in Utah evolved from the Mutual Improvement Association, founded through the direction of Brigham Young in 1875 as an educational and cultural association for adolescents. Over the next decades, it developed a wide-ranging but physically sedentary program of intellectual activities and spiritual guidance for Mormon adolescents. Church-wide competitions occurred in poetry reading, debate, public speaking, and other subjects.[10]

In 1911, a well-developed MIA syllabus of instruction, which contained discussions about contemporary political and socials issues, underwent a strong challenge from a former speaker of Utah's state house of representatives. Thomas Hull complained to the church's ruling triumvirate, the First Presidency, that a number of those lessons promoted socialism. Brigham Young University historian Thomas Alexander wrote that Hull might have been concerned about lesson plans having to do with public ownership of utilities, compulsory arbitration, higher wages, and women's suffrage.[11] Hull's complaint, which caused a major rewriting of the MIA curriculum, may have also contributed to momentum within the organization for expansion into more physical youth activities. In 1908, the MIA had adopted basketball as a church-wide youth activity. In the next few years, the MIA added gymnastics and track meets to the agenda.[12] Scouting, with its emphasis on hiking, camping, and other rugged outdoor skills, seemed to be another candidate that fit the new model.

The first step toward Mormon involvement in Scouting, however, occurred in England, where Lieutenant General Robert Baden-Powell held the first Boy Scout campout in 1907.[13] In 1910, the Boy Scouts of America (BSA) emerged under the guidance of Chicago publisher William Boyce.[14] Just one year later, the LDS church leadership started a derivative of that organization, the MIA Scouts.[15] For the remainder of the next decade, while Scouting became increasingly popular in Utah, church leaders debated the degree to which Mormon troops would affiliate with the national council of the BSA. John H. Taylor, a member of the MIA General Board, wrote: "At first the Church hesitated about this affiliation because it was not sure how far the National organization would take over the leadership of the boy. No program was of sufficient importance if it in any way interfered with the relationship between the boy and his Church."[16]

According to Alexander, the potential loss of power to appoint scoutmasters drove the leadership's initial reluctance. Heber J. Grant, who became prophet, seer, and revelator in 1918, feared "losing control to men who believed in smoking and drinking."[17] One of those obstacles—drinking—disappeared in 1919 with the ratification of the Eighteenth Amendment to the U.S. Constitution, which instituted Prohibition, and the other—smoking—ceased to be an issue in 1921 when Utah's legislature adopted a short-lived ban on tobacco sales.[18]

Shortly thereafter, assured of church control of their own Scouting troops, the name MIA Scouts disappeared when all LDS Church troops joined the national organization.[19] In the late 1920s, the leadership designated Boy Scouting as the "activity program for the deacons and teachers of the Aaronic Priesthood."[20] Because of emphasis by the church's ecclesiastical leadership, Scouting in the Mormon Culture Region took on the sense of a religious obligation, rather than a voluntary activity. In 1926, one in three teenage boys in Utah belonged to a Scout troop. The national average that year was one in five.[21]

Although the beginnings of Scouting in the English-speaking world can be traced definitively to Baden-Powell's campout on Brownsea Island in 1907, the origins of German Scouting are obscured in the evolution of the *Wandervogel* movement in the last decade of the nineteenth century. Conceived by middle-class youth who sought temporary escape from the rigidity of Wilhelmine society, *Wandervogel* groups staged hiking expeditions that lasted as long a month—adventures such as traversing the Harz and Bavarian mountain ranges and trekking along the banks of the Rhine River. Illinois State University scholar Lawrence D. Walker found several characteristics of *Wandervogel* groups that the scouting movement later emulated. Members of each faction, called a *Gruppe* or *Horde*, numbered from as few as seven or eight to a maximum in the twenties. Most established a *Nest* or *Heim*, a clubhouse of sort that served as both an escapist refuge and a place for planning future adventures. In the case of Scouting, that functioned as a place to store the troop's flags, emblems, and streamers. Ages ranged from twelve to nineteen, except in the case of young adults who undertook university studies and formed on-campus chapters. Finally, *Wandervogel* leadership tended to be young, often only two or three years older than the average age of each member of the *Heim*.[22]

Boy Scouting in Germany, the *Pfadfinder* (Path Finder) movement, emerged in 1909 when Dr. Alexander Lion, a physician and Bavarian Army veteran, spent several days in London with Baden-Powell, founder of the Boy Scouts. Shortly thereafter, he published *Das Pfadfinderbuch*, the first German-language Scouting manual. Lion founded the *Pfadfinder* organization in 1910, and by 1914 it had attracted as many as eighty thousand members. As Walker notes, it maintained a separate identity from the *Wandervogel* in the prewar period: "Youth led the *Wandervogel*; adults led the scouts. The *Wandervogel* concentrated on rambles; the scouts on woodcraft and paramilitary training. The *Wandervogel* wore bizarre clothing and strolled; the scouts wore uniforms and marched."[23]

Young veterans of the prewar *Wandervogel* and *Pfadfinder* movements returned after the First World War to find expanding opportunities for German young people to affiliate with a variety of organizations. According to the Reich Board of German Youth Associations, 4.3 million young people, out of a total of nine million, associated with some kind of youth organization in the mid-1920s. Some 1.6 million youth joined a sports club and 1.2 million belonged to a church youth group. The freewheeling days of the *Wandervogel*, during which young people ran their own organization, had disappeared. University of Essen historian Detlev Peukert wrote, "Both in [their] aims and the way [they were] run," Weimar Republic youth organizations were "largely controlled from the outside," meaning that they were directed by adults.[24] That included *Pfadfinder* troops, which divided mostly into rival sponsorship groups by the Catholic and Evangelical/Protestant Churches. The nature of German Scouting had changed, however, to amalgamate the handicraft and paramilitary aspects of the prewar *Pfadfinder* organizations with the hiking and camping activities of the *Wandervogel*.

This was the situation confronted by Swiss and German Mission President Fred Tadje in 1924 when he founded the LDS Church's Scouting program in Germany. He based the system of Scout ranks and merit badges upon the American model, but borrowed the German name *Pfadfinder*. In 1927, the Mormons changed that name to the LDS Boy Scouts.[25] Participation in Scouting appeared to grow steadily.

Although German Mormons apparently embraced Scouting enthusiastically, one problem remained. The German LDS Boy Scouts lacked affiliation with the national Scouting movement, and thus could not take part in meetings and jamborees alongside the German *Pfadfinder* organizations sponsored by the mainline churches. The dilemma seemed similar to the one the church hierarchy confronted less than a decade earlier, when it debated amalgamating the American Scout troop organizations with the Boy Scouts of America. Mormons feared losing control. Given the religious nature of Mormon Scouting, the American mission presidents could not tolerate the thought of Mormon Scoutmasters taking directives from senior Scout executives of another faith. The mission presidents sought a twofold solution: First, find a German Scouting organization with no ties to an established church, but with existing bonds to the national Boy Scout movement. Second, gain control of it.

On November 6, 1928, President Hyrum Valentine of the German-Austrian Mission, accompanied by LDS Scouting leaders from both German missions, met in Leipzig with Otto Stollbert, whom the mission records describe as "a representative of the Späher Bund of Scouting." They agreed to a merger between the LDS Boy Scouts and Stollbert's organization, which was not affiliated with either the Catholic or Protestant *Pfadfinder* movement. They synchronized the details of membership, such as registration procedures and age limits. They standardized the ritualistic and symbolic aspects of Scouting: the pledge, oath of allegiance, rank structure, and design of merit badges. When the meeting approached its end, the new "Baden-Powell Council," as one Mormon Scout official called it, elected its leadership. Herr Stollbert, who had entered the meeting as an equal, representing his own Scouting council, found himself relegated to drafting a constitution for the new organization, to be known in Germany as the *Deutscher Scoutverbund*, the German Scouting Association.[26] Valentine, who ostensibly had come to Leipzig to ride the coattails of an established German Scouting council to achieve national and international recognition for his Mormon Boy Scouts, emerged as Council President. That did not occur by happenstance. As Steven E. Carter of Henderson State University wrote, "By 1930, the Mormon Church had become a primary sponsor of the German Scout Association."[27] Mission presidents in Germany wanted access to national Scouting events while maintaining rigid control of their organizations. They were willing to pay for the privilege.

Less than one month later, on December 3, Stollbert and the Mormons met again, this time in Hamburg. According to mission records, "A representative of the international Scouting organization" accompanied the Späher Bund leader, along with delegates who represented "various Scout and *Pfadfinder* organizations in Germany."[28] Apparently, these were delegates from other small, unaffiliated German Scouting organizations who perhaps were attracted by offers of Mormon financial support. Some dissention within the German Scouting community arose from this meeting, which probably originated from those *Pfadfinder* organizations that attended the second meeting but chose not to affiliate with the new council. Negative articles appeared in several newspapers, which the mission records attribute to "various large *Pfadfinder* organizations in Germany."[29] Nevertheless, the February 3, 1929, issue of *Der Stern*, the German-language Mormon periodical, published a picture of officials signing the *Deutscher Scoutverbund* agreement. The accompanying article said the new organization had received international recognition. On March 3, an *Amtsgericht*, a local district court in Dresden, registered the new Scouting council as a legal organization under Weimar Republic statutes.[30] The Mormons had joined the German Boy Scouting movement on their own terms.

The Prewar Nazi Years, 1933–1939

For Mormon Boy Scouting in Germany, the last years of Weimar democracy served as a prolonged Indian summer: campouts in the Harz Mountains, international Scouting jamborees in England, and steady growth in membership numbers. More than six hundred boys belonged to the scout troops affiliated with the Berlin-based German-Austrian mission in 1930.[31] Many more participated in troops sponsored by the Swiss-German mission. A Scouting superintendent reported the existence of forty-four troops in both missions.[32] Scouting engendered great enthusiasm among teenagers and adults alike. One boy, presumably a member of an outlying congregation that did not have a troop, rode a bicycle for 1,000 kilometers in order to reach the site of a camping trip.[33] A visiting official from the Salt Lake City hierarchy, Oscar A. Kirkham, extolled the virtues of Scouting before an assemblage of three hundred Mormons in Berlin. He wore an Indian costume with a feathered headdress.[34]

As the economic calamity of the Great Depression worsened, the blustery winds of a National Socialist winter threatened. While Mormon Scout troops patrolled the wilds, Hitler Youth joined brown-shirted adults demonstrating in Germany's cities. Hitler appointed a dynamic young follower to lead the Hitler Youth in 1931. The *Führer's* equivalent of a "scoutmaster" was a handsome and fair-haired but ethically challenged young man who joined the Nazi Party at age seventeen and then became the Reich Youth Leader, the *Reichsjugendführer*, at twenty-four. Baldur von Schirach was hardly a street brawler; he had descended from an aristocratic background. His father was a German army officer turned theater director. His mother was an American whose lineage included two signers of the Declaration of Independence. Young Baldur did not speak German until the age of five, but by the time he completed German language studies at the University of Munich, he had mastered the vocabulary of virulent anti-Semitism. He devoured the works of Adolf Bartels and Houston Stewart Chamberlain, and he read Henry Ford's *The International Jew*. He met Hitler though his wife, the daughter of the *Führer's* personal photographer, and became part of the Nazi inner circle early in the Party's history. Prior to his assignment to lead the Hitler Youth, Schirach devoted boundless energy to organizing university students.[35]

When Hitler rose to power in January 1933, Schirach launched his own version of *Gleichschaltung*, the forced consolidation of German youth groups, with the characteristic energy of a recently appointed Scout patrol leader. His purpose was simple: to destroy anything that remained of the German Youth Movement, *Die deutsche Jugendbewegung*, that started with the *Wandervogel* in the late nineteenth century, and included all other youth groups that followed.[36] A combination of Schirach's infectious enthusiasm, the ruthlessness of Nazi officialdom, and the ambitions of *Reichsbishop* Ludwig Müller led to the forced rolling of all Protestant youth groups in Germany into the Hitler Youth on December 19, 1933. That included all *Pfadfinder* troops. Hitler's Concordat with the Catholic Church made absorption of Catholic youth groups more difficult, but the irresistible Nazi force caused eventual capitulation to occur in stages. By November 1936, the St. Georg *Pfadfinderschaft*, the Scouting subdivision of the main Catholic youth organization, had changed its name and suspended its Scout troop organizations.[37]

By the time that the Nazis exerted pressure on the Mormons to disband their Scouting program, the heady days of frolicking on campouts and basking in adult approval at merit badge ceremonies appeared to be as fleeting as were the memories of Weimar democracy. As P. D. Stachura of the University of Stirling wrote: "In the widespread euphoria which accompanied Hitler's accession to power, tens of thousands of new members swept into the NSDAP and the SA. German youth were not immune to the prevailing atmosphere with the result that the most immediate consequence of the *Machtergreifung* in the youth sector was the overnight expansion of the HJ [the *Hitlerjugend*, or Hitler Youth]."[38]

The Mormon historical records assiduously avoid documenting the number of members who enrolled in Nazi auxiliary organizations such as the SA or Hitler Youth. Likewise, individual Mormons, like their fellow Germans who lived through the National Socialist period, are reluctant to volunteer their recollections of a brown shirt–clad adolescence or young adulthood. Yet enough data seeps through those filters to suggest that when the Mormons finally surrendered their cherished Scouting program to the HJ, the majority of Mormon boys donned khaki shirts adorned with different badges and accoutrements.

In an article that appeared in the *Deseret News* in October 1933, religion writer Fay Ollerton noted, "Some of the brethren now wear the brown uniform, and others have fallen away."[39] As Steven E. Carter observes, "Many Mormon youngsters joined the Hitler Youth. Some became active participants in the Nazi organization and fondly recalled the experience."[40] Brigham Young University scholars Douglas F. Tobler and Alan F. Keele wrote, "The women's auxiliary of the Party and the Hitler Youth were regarded by some [German members] as secular equivalents to the Church's Relief Society, MIA, and Scouting programs."[41] Jared H. B. Kobs, who moved to Utah after the Second World War, recalled several years spent in the Hitler Youth's auxiliary for ten- to fourteen-year olds, the *Deutches Jungvolk*. He added that he was able to avoid participation in the older auxiliary, the *Hitlerjugend*, because of an approved vocational apprenticeship.[42] Likewise, Karl-Heinz Schnibbe was expelled from the Hitler Youth and Rudi Wobbe quit. Their disparaging testimonies of the HJ were atypical; they later became involved with the Helmuth Hübener group of resisters.[43]

Enrollment numbers found in LDS Church historical records indicate a decline in Scouting membership concomitant with rising interest in the HJ after the Nazi seizure of power. In 1930, the German-Austrian mission reported an enrollment of six hundred boys in its Scouting organization. That number would not have included the Scouting enrollment of the Swiss-German Mission, in which ninety percent of the members were German citizens. Arthur Gaeth, that mission's first Scouting superintendent, recalled the existence of forty-four troops in both missions.[44] By April 1934, when Mormon Scouting ended, the mission records reported a combined enrollment of 150, and in addition "about 100 boys [were] doing Scout work, but they were not registered."[45]

The Mormons successfully delayed the inevitable in 1933 when Protestant *Pfadfinder* troops dissolved. A notation in December of that year said: "The Hitler Jugen [sic], a youth's organization sponsored by the national government of Germany, has influenced quite a number of our boys to join them. The permanent continuation of our Boy Scout organization in Germany does not look good."[46]

The end came over a period of two months during the spring of 1934. On March 2, a Mormon scoutmaster in Freiberg, Saxony, Erich Kleinert, received a letter inquiring about the Boy Scout program from the Nazi youth leader for Saxony. After his response, the district president in Dresden, Robert Hoehle, received correspondence from another Saxon Nazi youth official, dated March 13:

> As I am informed you are the District President of the LDS Boy Scouts, a group of path finders, which is neither approved nor registered by the Youth Leader of the German Empire. I request, therefore, an immediate explanation of from what source you claim authorization for your organization, and to what extent you belong to another organization. At the same time, I would like to have a list of all existing troops in Saxony with the names of the troop leaders, not later than the sixth of the month, because, as already mentioned, I have nothing in my files concerning your organization.... [signed] Heil Hitler! The Youth Leader of the Saxony Free State, G. Gorschig.

The district president responded promptly, after which Herr Gorschig replied:

> I am well informed about the work and organization of the LDS Boy Scouts of Germany. I consider it of no value to allow groups to exist in Saxony that are functioning, to a certain degree, in the work that really belongs in the scope of the 'Hitler Jugend' and thereby disturb the latter more or less. I, therefore, inform you that the further existence of the LDS Boy Scouts in Saxony is not desired, and ask for notification before the 11th [of April] as to what time the groups in Saxony expect to be dissolved, or when you will be willing to transfer your members over to the Hitler Youth. After the uniting of the entire German youth in the Hitler Youth it is an absurdity to allow small sects to exist for any particular reason.... [signed] Heil Hitler! The Youth Leader of the Free State of Saxony, G. Gorschig.

The Mormon Scouting leadership in Saxony took its case to the mission office in Berlin. Helmuth Plath, who served as the German-Austrian Mission's scouting superintendent, wrote a letter of appeal to Gorschig's supervisor in the Hitler Youth but received no response. The mission office did, however, receive a visit from "an officer of the secret service." At that point, mission officials became concerned that the Nazis could seize the church's property. The decision was made. On April 21, 1934, the mission issued a "circular letter" announcing the discountenance of all Scouting activity at the end of the month.

On April 28, the German-Austrian Mission dispatched a letter to the "Youth Leader of the German Empire" in Berlin.[47] Baldur von Schirach may not have seen the correspondence, but if he did, it would have been regarded as one more small win in a year of victories for the Hitler Youth. "Coordination" of youth groups in Nazi Germany had resulted in the casualty of another small, independent organization amid burgeoning enrollment in the HJ. In the year 1934, when the Mormons gave up their small scouting organization, Hitler Youth membership increased by sixty-four percent over the previous year, to a total enrollment of 3,577,565.[48]

The Mormons' one-sentence surrender revealed capitulation in more than one respect: "In compliance with the wish of the German Youth Leaders, the German Scout Organization was dissolved April 30, 1934. . . . [signed] With the German salutation, Helmuth Plath, Chairman."[49]

In surrendering its Scouting program to the Hitler Youth, the church gave up a valued part of its youth activity program. More importantly, it realized there were some battles that could be fought in Nazi Germany, but others that required tactical surrender in the interest of strategic survival.

8

The *Führer's* Chosen People?
The Mormons' Hitler Myth

Almost exactly a year and a half after Adolf Hitler came to power, on a summer day in 1934, Senator Elbert Thomas of Utah visited the American Embassy in Berlin. Thomas, a former college professor, member of the Senate Foreign Relations Committee, and a Democrat, was enjoying a triumphant second year of his own. In the November 1932 elections, he had ridden Franklin Roosevelt's political tidal wave that swept the Democratic Party into a commanding congressional majority and swept out, in the case of Utah, Senator Reed Smoot, a Mormon Apostle and three-decade GOP senatorial veteran. Thomas's 1934 visit to Berlin was not a government-funded junket; he was traveling in Germany on the strength of his academic credentials. Before the election, Thomas's accomplishments as a professor of history and political science at the University of Utah had won him an Oberlaender Fellowship, in recognition of a distinguished career that also included the teaching of Latin, Greek, and Japanese culture and civilization. A five-year Mormon mission to Japan at the turn of the twentieth century had taught Thomas to speak fluent Japanese.

The United States Ambassador to Germany, William E. Dodd, was an accomplished scholar in his own right. He earned his Ph.D. from the University of Leipzig and subsequently taught American history for thirty-three years at Randolph Macon College and the University of Chicago. He published a biography of Thomas Jefferson in German. When the two distinguished former professors sat down to talk that Tuesday at the American embassy on Pariser Platz, the ambassador seemed surprised about the senator's concerns. Dodd wrote: "I was favorably impressed, although it is hard for me to understand how a man of intellectual distinction can be interested in Mormon missionary work. There are a number of Mormons in Germany and Hitler has not dissolved their organizations or expelled their active preachers. There are other than religious aspects to Hitler's let-up on the Mormons."[1]

When Dodd wrote in his diary, it had been only three months since the Mormons agreed to suspend their Boy Scout activities, a development that the ambassador may not have known about. Other than the Scouting ban, Latter-day Saints had little justification for complaint. Dodd's observations about Hitler's "let-up on the Mormons" probably resulted from his dealings with other small American religious sects in Germany who, unlike the Mormons, were indeed experiencing varying degrees of Nazi persecution. Christine King referred to Dodd's work on behalf of Christian Scientists, a denomination with roots in the United States, which eventually saw the Nazis ban its congregational worship.[2] Dodd had received visits from prominent Christian Scientists, including Viscount Waldorf Astor, in September 1933 after the arrest of church members in Thuringia. By the summer of 1934, Seventh-day Adventists, headquartered in Washington, D.C., had also experienced the temporary banning of church meetings in various German municipalities.[3] The Jehovah's Witnesses, based in Brooklyn, were already undergoing severe persecution. Many of their members had lost their jobs, and some were in jail because they refused military service and would not salute the Nazi flag. Thus, when Senator Thomas expressed concern regarding Mormon missionary work, Ambassador Dodd was perplexed. The Nazis were treating Thomas's Latter-day Saints better than any other small sectarian group with foreign origins. Dodd wondered why.

Others, including many rank-and-file Latter-day Saints, also wondered why the Mormons seemed to be enjoying a respite from persecution. The perceived "let-up" had little to do with Hitler; the Mormons had given the Nazis little reason to find fault. That did not stop many German Mormons from embracing contrived connections between the *Führer* and their church, and between many Nazi policies and Mormon customs. Most Germans, including Latter-day Saints, embraced what historian Ian Kershaw called the "Hitler Myth." Kershaw defined that fallacy as a series of artificial images, cultivated by propaganda, that resulted in the *Führer's* widespread adulation by the German populace.[4] Mormons managed to customize their own version of the Hitler Myth, which fancifully connected Mormon and Nazi ritual.

In 1896, the Mormon prophet, Wilford Woodruff, had changed the church's monthly fast day to the first Sunday of each month. Members would abstain from eating two meals and donate the money saved, called a "fast offering," to the church's charity fund.[5] Missionaries brought this custom with them to Germany. In October 1933, as part of the Nazis' Winter Relief program, the *Winterhilfswerk*, the government urged Germans to eat a simple meal on the second Sunday of each month. Newspapers published recipes and bookstores sold cookbooks devoted to "One-Pot Sunday," *Eintopfsonntag*. Nazi block and precinct captains went door to door to collect the money that families saved, the difference between the cost of stew and more elaborate fare. Presumably, when greeted at the door by enthusiastic gentlemen wearing swastika lapel pins or armbands, few householders found themselves unable to produce the fifty *Pfennigs* as expected.[6] From time to time, Hitler appeared at a public feeding for the needy, "humbled" himself by consuming the unpretentious cuisine, and then consented to be photographed by the "surprised" newspaper cameraman who had "coincidently" been assigned to that location. As historian Klaus P. Fischer stated, "Joseph Goebbels was the undisputed master of exploiting genuine benevolent impulses for ulterior, political ends."[7]

Among German Mormons and their American missionaries, a widespread belief quickly developed that Hitler had originated his welfare scheme by emulating the LDS Fast Sunday.[8] The Mormons' weekly *Millennial Star*, published in London, pounced upon the story by reporting that the Mormons' custom "may have either directly or indirectly [been] the inspiration and the model for the new scheme adopted by the German government—perhaps not."[9] By the time the *Deseret News* recounted the story, all doubt had evaporated:

> A friend of the Church in Danzig tells of how a number of his Nazi friends were trying to high-pressure him into getting on the bandwagon under the Swastika. Their trump card to show the originality and political genius of the Hitler party was the brilliant method they have undertaken to put over the charity drive for this winter. To them it was phenomenal; to the friend, however, it was just

another application of the effective method that has been used in the Mormon Church for decades. The Nazis have introduced Fast Sunday. . . . On this day a meal consisting of a one-bowl portion is all there is to be eaten and the price of a meal is expected to be donated to the winter charity fund.[10]

Sometimes the idea came from the top; in this case, at least one mission president embraced the myth. Roy A. Welker, president of the Berlin-based German-Austrian Mission from 1934 to 1937, told an oral history interviewer late in his life: "My personal opinion was that Hitler was very much impressed with the LDS faith and church and its practices, and I've always felt that this fast day he established, that's what it amounted to, and the contributions for aiding the poor and so forth, he borrowed from the church."[11] According to a privately published biography of Roy Welker, written by his eldest daughter Rhoda, "The whole Welker family believed that Hitler had acquired this idea from the Mormons."[12]

The same way of thinking led many Mormons to assume a connection between the propagandized image of Hitler as a non-drinking, non-smoking advocate of clean living and the Mormons' health code, the Word of Wisdom. The latter originated in 1833 when Joseph Smith lived in Kirtland, Ohio, and taught a spiritual adult-education course he called the School of the Prophets, ostensibly to train missionaries and future church leaders. Classes met in an upstairs room of a dry goods store owned by one of his bishops, Newel K. Whitney, where Smith lived at the time. The gathered men would smoke, chew, and spit tobacco, without ashtrays or spittoons, during Smith's lessons. According to Brigham Young's account, Emma Smith, the Prophet's first wife, complained about having to clean the filthy floor. Smith himself experienced some discomfort from "a cloud of tobacco smoke" during lectures.[13] The experience caused Smith to issue a "revelation" from God, classified as Section 89 of the Doctrine and Covenants, that prohibits the consumption of alcohol, tobacco, and "hot drinks," and additionally, urges moderation in the consumption of red meat. Although the Word of Wisdom underwent a period of interpretation and inconsistent enforcement during the nineteenth century, by the time the Mormons began attracting a flood of new converts during the Weimar Republic years, it clearly prohibited alcohol consumption in the beer-friendly nation of Germany.[14]

Although Hitler indeed consumed little alcohol and did not smoke, his image as a vegetarian teetotaler was carefully crafted propaganda used, in the words of Ian Kershaw, to evoke the image of a *"Führer* without sin."[15] Such a cultivated reputation was one element in an effort to portray Hitler as the sober, well-intentioned, moderate leader of a Nazi state that took extreme actions. It helps to explain why Hitler's personal popularity remained elevated when Germans' opinion of the Nazi Party began to decline. Although Hitler did not allow himself to be seen drinking, he never avoided association with the trappings of alcohol that make up every-day German life, and which devout Mormons avoided by the early twentieth century. Faithful Latter-day Saints would not be seen in a tavern, but Hitler gave one of his most famous speeches at the *Bürgerbräukeller* beer hall in Munich in 1923. After the Beer Hall Putsch that followed, and Hitler's subsequent trial and conviction for treason, authorities at Landsberg Prison allowed Hitler to maintain stocks of wine in his cell.[16] Hitler served copious amounts of alcohol at dinners with Party officials and visiting dignitaries.

Regardless of how Hitler's teetotaler image was framed, the Latter-day Saints seemed anxious to draw upon it as another parallel between Hitlerism and Mormonism. The same *Deseret News* article that proclaimed the Mormon Fast Sunday as the model for the Nazi Winter Relief campaign also told its readers that: "There is another noticeable trend in the Mormon direction. It is a very well known fact that Hitler observes a form of living which Mormons term the Word of Wisdom. He will not take alcohol, does not smoke, and is very strict about his diet, insisting on plain and wholesome foods, largely vegetarian. A specimen of physical endurance, Hitler can easily take his place alongside the athletes who are usually taken as classic examples."

Then, including Propaganda Minister Joseph Goebbels as another physical specimen to be admired, the article continues: "These two colorful leaders of the new Germany, in their gigantic struggle for political supremacy, have needed capable bodies and clear brains and have trained like athletes. Their very popularity is making intemperance more unpopular. The fact that they are worshiped may be one big reason for a growing dislike for smoking and drinking in Germany today. Posters from youth organizations fighting the use of tobacco actually appeared on the street."[17]

The absurd comparison of Hitler to a trained athlete illustrated how the *Deseret News* regarded fact versus fairy tale. The same held true for the highest LDS officials in Germany at the time. In his work on the Mormons in Nazi Germany, Steven E. Carter maintains that at least one American mission president (probably Welker) expressed the view that the Word of Wisdom and Hitler's abstinence from alcohol and tobacco were related.[18]

In such an atmosphere, it was inevitable that some believers would imagine a closer church connection with the *Führer*, to the point that one popular rumor said that Hitler "so admired the Mormon hierarchical structure that he patterned his party after it."[19] Others believed Hitler "had attended the funeral of an LDS Church member in his native Austria."[20] Some believed Hitler was a "secret Mormon."[21] In the 1980s, a Latter-day Saint from Hamburg told BYU researchers about a picture taken of him surrounded by his church friends in the 1930s. The mustached man in the middle of the picture was Hitler, the gentleman claimed. Another popular rumor maintained that during the First World War, when Hitler served as an army messenger with the rank of corporal, a friend and fellow solider saved his life. That friend was a Mormon, and his actions on the battlefield that day convinced Hitler to be favorably disposed toward Mormonism.[22] One Mormon missionary during the Weimar period claimed to have personally encountered Hitler and preached the Gospel to him.[23] Other beliefs surfaced as a result of actions taken by church leaders to elevate the LDS Church's profile with the Nazi government. In 1935, missionaries mailed copies of the Book of Mormon and several other religious texts to Hitler and other high-level officials of the Nazi Party.[24] To some, this was justification to proclaim that Hitler had read the Book of Mormon.[25]

Others have sought a more reasoned explanation for German Mormons' early infatuation with Hitler. In his work on the LDS Church during the Weimar Republic, BYU graduate student Jeffery L. Anderson connected LDS social attitudes with the misguided perception that Hitler was cleaning up ethical decay in Germany. "Mormons were also pleased with Hitler's attempts to institute what they perceived to be a higher morality in Germany. Prostitutes and homosexuals were arrested, and many of the decadent cabarets, for which Weimar Berlin was famous, were closed or closely monitored."[26]

Reports of sexual misconduct seem to have been the impetus for the only high-level contact between Hitler and a Mormon Church official. In 1936, the wife of German-Austrian Mission President Roy Welker became concerned about lax moral standards in the *Bund deutscher Mädel* (BDM), the League of German Girls, in which many Mormon youth participated. In her official capacity as the overseer of all LDS women's organizations in the mission, Elizabeth Hoge Welker received reports, one from as far away as a church member in England, about sexual promiscuity in Nazi youth camps.[27]

Indeed, Elizabeth Welker had a legitimate basis for concern, given the widespread rumors that emerged concerning the eighth annual Nazi Party Congress at Nuremberg in the summer of 1936. Some one hundred thousand German youth participated in that year's glitzy festival of Nazism, paradoxically named the "Rally for Honor," *Reichsparteitag der Ehre*, to commemorate the German remilitarization of the Rhineland.[28] Welker undoubtedly saw nothing honorable in accounts that nine hundred young women, ages fifteen though eighteen, returned home pregnant. When the official investigation failed to establish paternity in four hundred of those cases, societal reverberations within Germany were surprisingly strong for a police state.[29]

Elizabeth Welker's bold move resulted in meeting Adolf Hitler and the National Socialist Women's Leader, *Reichsfrauenführerin* Gertrud Scholtz-Klink. According to a private family history published by Welker's daughter, and the recollections of Roy Welker during an oral history interview late in his life, Elizabeth Welker used an intermediary to deliver her protest to the Nazi Women's League. She questioned the competency of adult supervisors at BDM camps, as well as the moral underpinnings of the organization.[30] Her brash approach could have been ignored, or conceivably it could have brought the Mormons attention they did not desire, the kind that could have triggered recriminations.

Instead, Elizabeth Welker received a polite response, followed by an invitation to meet with two of Scholtz-Klink's underlings at the offices of the National Socialist Women's League, the *Nationalsozialistische Frauenschaft*. Records of the German-Austrian Mission say Welker conversed with "Mrs. Daniels," who referred Welker to a subsequent meeting with a superior, "Dr. Unger."[31] A separate document, the Welker family's biography, describes two unnamed Nazi women with whom Welker met, "one who had received schooling in New York and another who as a linguist who spoke several languages fluently."[32] At Welker's invitation, "Mrs. Daniels" attended a lecture on "Utah and the Mormons." Subsequently, on September 30, 1936, Elizabeth Welker and her daughter Rhoda met again with both women at the *NS-Frauenschaft* headquarters where they give the Nazi women copies of two German-language church publications, "The Aims and Ideals of Relief Society Work" and "Hand Book of the Bee Hives."[33] The meetings led Elizabeth Welker to visit a Hitler Youth girls' camp. One morning, a black government limousine arrived at the mission office, accompanied by "two Nazi soldiers in full uniform in the front seat" and an English-speaking female representative who acted as Welker's tour guide. Elizabeth Welker not only satisfied herself regarding the moral suitability of the BDM camp, but she also took the opportunity to lecture her tour guide regarding the danger of the lady's smoking habit.[34]

For reasons not conclusively explained by surviving source material, Elizabeth Welker's outing to the BDM camp resulted in several subsequent trips in the company of Hitler and Scholtz-Klink.[35] In each case, she rode in the government limousine to Hitler Youth rallies with the *Führer* and the Nazi Women's Leader. According to Roy Welker, his wife Elizabeth was "face to face with Hitler quite a lot." Not much direct communication ensued, as Hitler did not speak English and Elizabeth Welker's command of German at the time was limited. However, Roy Welker notes that Scholtz-Klink spoke excellent English. "She seemed to take a notation to Mother," Roy Welker told historian Richard L. Jensen, "and that helped us a great deal." Welker also said: "When Mother got involved with this national women's organization, and was indirectly involved with Hitler, it was a great relief to us, I tell you. Things went along very well. We didn't have any trouble to speak of."[36]

Adoration for a job well done greeted Roy and Elizabeth Welker upon their return to Utah in 1937. When a *Salt Lake Tribune* reporter interviewed Roy Welker in Salt Lake City, the former mission president unashamedly proclaimed: "Jews are safer in Germany today than in many other parts of the world."[37] Perhaps Welker had fallen victim to a myth promulgated shortly after adoption of the Nuremberg Race Laws in 1935 deprived Jews of their German citizenship. As historian Saul Friedländer wrote, many Germans, including many Jews, initially believed that the "subject" status granted to Germany's Jewish population provided a degree of protection as an officially recognized national minority.[38] They naively hoped that the law would stop street attacks by Nazi thugs and Nazi Party–proclaimed boycotts of Jewish businesses. This belief quickly dissipated among Germany's Jews, as no protected status developed, and by 1937 only an observer as obtuse as the former German-Austrian mission president could utter such things with a straight face. Roy Welker went on to explain: "It is true that the Nazis are working to segregate the Jews, but they are treated well otherwise. Nazi dislike of Jews and hatred of communism are at the root of most propaganda against the nation."[39]

Roy Welker subsequently told a packed Salt Lake Tabernacle audience at the LDS Church's 1937 Semiannual General Conference in Salt Lake City that: "Mr. Hitler has learned of us and has said that the Mormon people are doing the German government no harm and he wants them left alone."[40] Roy Welker allowed his version of the Hitler Myth, augmented with a brimming tablespoon of Goebbels's propaganda, to narcotize his view of Nazi Germany. Elizabeth Welker simply allowed herself to be bamboozled by Gertrud Scholtz-Klink and her minions. She told the same *Salt Lake Tribune* reporter that Mormon women's organizations in Germany enjoyed "excellent cooperation from the Nazi women's division," which she described as "a combination Red Cross and diversified activities organization."[41]

Then, in an article written for the Mormon youth magazine, *Improvement Era*, Elizabeth Welker pontificated on the self-sufficiency and healthy living of German adolescent females, ostensibly in comparison with what she might have seen as the consumer-driven culture that engulfed spoiled American teenagers. The article mixes homey admonitions regarding sensible nutrition and modest dress with disquieting references to German racial superiority. "If [a German girl] goes to town," Welker wrote, "she carries a sandwich, not a sweet and not an ice." With regard to clothing, Welker lauded the choice of shoes that "permit her to walk ten miles a day," woolen sweaters rather than silk, and "underclothing [that] has a purpose, and that purpose is not to be seen."

Then, in the same tone, Welker praised the German girl who knows, "To build a superior race, she is doing all in her power to build a strong, vigorous body." The article then discussed the dating habits of German teenagers, and the priority placed upon selecting ethnically proper and physically attractive breeding stock for the next generation of German children: "I have read 'when a German youth comes to court a German girl he finds her pedigree chart hung in the front hall,' but long before he comes to call he has looked her over as a possible mother for his children, and unless she measures up to his ideal of a perfect body, he does not call. Motherhood is the ideal of this entire people." Welker concluded her article with a salute to the young German woman whose "wholesome outlook on life" propels a determination to "do her full part to develop a 'superior race.'"[42]

By the time the Welkers returned from Germany in 1937, the Mormons' strategy of exploiting commonalities with National Socialism would have pleased its architects, Oliver Budge and Francis Salzner, the early–Nazi era mission presidents. However, the last few years of the Mormons' American missionary effort in Nazi Germany, 1938–39, would require a degree of expertise that exceeded the capabilities of relatively unsophisticated leaders such as Roy and Elizabeth Welker. To ensure that Hitler's "let-up" on the Mormons continued, the church enlisted the services of other skilled intermediaries. They include a former American ambassador and undersecretary of state who dealt regularly with Hitler's *Reichsbank* chairman, a former United States senator who wrote a racially charged German-language article, a "Heil Hitler" bellowing mission president, and even a Prophet of God who preached the Gospel while standing in front of a large swastika.

Max Reschke (*right*) with his father, Theodor, in 1938. Max, a branch president from Hanover, saved a Jewish couple from Kristallnacht and protected Polish and Russian slave laborers during the war. He unsuccessfully tried to hide another Jewish man from the Nazis. Reschke remains an unsung Mormon hero because his courageous exploits did not comport with his church's accommodationist policy toward the Third Reich. Also, his family limited his postwar memorialization, probably because of his extramarital relationships that led to excommunication. (Courtesy Phil Reschke)

The Mormons practiced "basketball diplomacy" in the Third Reich. What started as an effort to gain access to previously forbidden proselyting venues, military bases and university campuses, evolved into an opportunity to train the 1936 German Olympic team in rudimentary basketball skills. In January of that year, the *Deseret News* ran a six-column picture in its weekly Church Section, showing a basketball team rendering the Hitler salute. This occurred in the midst of an international campaign to boycott Hitler's showcase Olympic Games, to protest how Jews were being treated in Nazi Germany. Articles describing the boycott effort appeared in the church-owned newspaper's news columns, but the religion section never eschewed Nazi symbolism. (Image from *Deseret News*, January 25, 1936)

Mormon youth, deprived of cherished church-sponsored Boy Scout troops, found other avenues for uniformed activity. Willie Ludwig of Essen (*left*) appears as a member of the Jungvolk, the Hitler Youth organization for boys ten through fourteen. Clemens Hegewald of Freiberg (*right*), shown in his Wehrmacht uniform, witnessed his brothers blend mandatory Sunday Nazi activities with Mormon Church services. His brothers would rush to church—where they would pass the sacrament in their Hitler Youth uniforms, with swastika armbands and a leather belt across their chests. They discarded only their swastika-emblazoned daggers when performing this sacred ceremony. (Courtesy Inge B. Ludwig and Heinz Hegewald)

By 1938, the year before the Second World War started, German Mormon branches—buttressed by restrictions on emigration and the appointment of native Germans to replace missionaries as congregational leaders—had grown sufficiently to allow their survival without American supervision. As this Relief Society Mother's Day picture from 1938 shows, the LDS Church in Germany retained significant American trappings. Lorenzo Snow, the fifth Mormon prophet, seer, and revelator, appears in the framed picture on the left. The founder of the Mormon Church, Joseph Smith, is in the framed picture on the right. German artist Heinrich Hofmann's depiction of Jesus Christ is in the center. (Courtesy Brigham Young University, Religious Studies Center)

Converting to Mormonism in Germany often resulted in being ostracized by family who worshiped in the Catholic or Protestant tradition, and cultural estrangement from friends who drank alcohol, coffee, and tea. When Nazi Germany's laws halted the high rate of immigration to Utah that German Mormons had enjoyed during the Weimar Republic, socialization activities—such as this Oder River trip by the Stettin Branch in 1938—became a critical component of life in the German congregations. (Courtesy Brigham Young University, Religious Studies Center)

Mormon Apostle Joseph Fielding Smith (*left*), his wife Jessie Ella Evans Smith, and East German Mission President Alfred C. Rees visit a small German congregation in the weeks prior to the outbreak of the Second World War. Smith was one of many high-ranking Mormon officials who visited Germany, and Rees's appointment as mission president demonstrated the importance that the Mormon hierarchy placed on sending politically astute and linguistically proficient mission presidents to develop relations with officials of the Third Reich. Rees developed high-level contacts in Nazi officialdom, which he used to attain preferential seating at Hitler's speeches and rallies, and to publish an article in the *Völkischer Beobachter* favorably comparing Mormonism and Nazism. (Courtesy Brigham Young University, Religious Studies Center)

Thomas E. McKay—paradoxically the father of Fawn Brodie, who was later excommunicated for writing an unflattering biography of Joseph Smith—was an example of the well-qualified mission presidents dispatched to the Third Reich in the prewar Nazi years. McKay served three missions in the German-speaking lands, two as a mission president. Designated to open the new Frankfurt-based mission in 1937, McKay instead found himself relegated to the Swiss-Austrian mission because of an old banning order in Imperial Germany. Because the Mormon strategy emphasized obedience to Nazi authority, it would not have been prudent to install a previously expelled prelate in the position. (Courtesy Utah State Historical Society)

The prophet, seer, and revelator Heber J. Grant visits German Mormons on his European tour in 1937. During a stop in Frankfurt in July, he spoke to an assembly of eight hundred Mormons. A picture of that event ran in the LDS Church–owned *Deseret News*, showing Grant seated below a large swastika banner. Most accounts of Grant's European tour do not include his unscheduled return to Hamburg in August, where he helped referee a squabble between mission presidents Alfred C. Rees and Philemon M. Kelly, concerning who would take command of the Berlin-based mission. (Courtesy Brigham Young University, Religious Studies Center)

Young American LDS missionaries worked with little Nazi government constraint during the peacetime years of the Third Reich, 1933–39. Some served as ecclesiastical leaders for their German congregations, but by this time native German Mormons had been installed in most local leadership positions. Nevertheless, the missionaries made themselves useful in the local branches, such as in this 1939 photograph where (*from left*) Paul Nichols, George Blake, Myron Seamons, and John Wesche built a rostrum for the Durlach Branch near Karlsruhe. (Courtesy George R. Blake)

J. Reuben Clark, Jr., as an undersecretary of state during the Coolidge administration in 1928. While serving as second-in-command of the LDS Church in the 1930s, Clark visited Nazi Germany twice to negotiate with Nazi finance minister Hjalmar Schacht on behalf of small American bondholders. In doing so, he served notice to the German government that Mormons enjoyed influential connections in American political circles. Late in the prewar period, Clark, who left a trail of anti-Semitic writings, denied desperate pleas by Austrian Mormon converts from Judaism who sought the church's help is escaping Hitler's persecution after the Anschluss. (Courtesy Utah State Historical Society)

Senator Elbert D. Thomas of Utah spent ten weeks touring Germany in 1934, the year after Adolf Hitler became chancellor. He did not like what he saw. His subsequent efforts to facilitate Jewish immigration to the United States encountered opposition from within his own Democratic Party—based on prevailing anti-immigration sentiment during the Great Depression. But his presence in Germany served to buttress the Mormons' strategy for surviving and prospering during the Third Reich. Like similar visits by well-connected Mormons, it sent the Nazis a message: unlike other small foreign religions, the Mormons had powerful friends in the American government who would take note of how their co-religionists were treated. (Courtesy Utah State Historical Society)

The Mormons' accommodating stance toward the Third Reich owes part of its impetus to the large German-American immigrant population of the Mormon Culture Region. In this late-1930s photograph, Utahns commemorate the twenty-one German prisoners of war who died in captivity during the First World War at Fort Douglas in Salt Lake City. One man, second from the right in the first row, wears two Iron Cross decorations from World War I. Another man wears the uniform of the German-American Bund, a pro-Nazi organization that thrived in the United States before the Second World War. Swastikas adorn flags and wreaths. (Courtesy Hans E. Kindt)

Signs such as this—"Jews are not allowed"—appeared commonly in Nazi Germany. Arthur Zander, the congregational leader in St. Georg, a downtown district of Hamburg, posted a similar sign on his branch's meetinghouse in order to deny entry to Salomon Schwarz, a Jewish convert to Mormonism from another small congregation who would visit Zander's branch for choir practice. (Courtesy George R. Blake)

The United States and Germany maintained amiable relations during the prewar National Socialist years. When the West German Mission held a conference in the downtown Frankfurt district of Römerberg on May 27, 1939, only four months before the Second World War began, the city fathers honored the occasion by flying American and Nazi flags from city hall. (Courtesy George R. Blake)

Karl Herbert Klopfer, president of the East German Mission, speaks to a congregational meeting in Schneidemühl in 1940. The inscription on the wall reads, "The glory of God is intelligence," a passage from Section 93 of the Doctrine and Covenants. Klopfer assumed leadership of the Berlin-based mission after the American missionaries evacuated. Subsequently drafted into the Wehrmacht, he died in a Soviet prisoner of war camp in 1945. In the Mormon collective memory of the Third Reich, marked by battlefield and home-front suffering, Klopfer serves as an important memory beacon. All German Mormons, the mythos proclaims, were victims of the Second World War. (Courtesy Hans E. Kindt)

All Mormon weddings in Nazi Germany were "civil" ceremonies in Mormon parlance: they occurred outside of the Holy Temple. Europe's first LDS temple did not open until 1955, in Bern, Switzerland. When Helga Abel and Horst Schwermer exchanged marriage vows on August 30, 1941, they first did so at church. Then, complying with the law, they married again at Spandau city hall. A portrait of Adolf Hitler adorns their wedding photograph, which was not an unusual sight in the Third Reich. (Courtesy Joshua Schwermer)

Rudi Wobbe, Helmuth Hübener, and Karl-Heinz Schnibbe in 1941, one year before the Gestapo arrested them for distributing anti-Nazi handbills in Hamburg neighborhoods. Red-robed Nazi judges condemned Hübener to the guillotine and sentenced his cohorts to prison terms. The Hübener story became a sensation in the mid-1970s, when a pair of BYU researchers inspired a campus playwright to produce a popular theatrical production that the Mormon hierarchy in Salt Lake City shut down. Mormon leaders were afraid it could offend German-American immigrants, inspire Mormon youth to rebel against dictators worldwide, and hurt LDS relations with the government of East Germany. (Courtesy Brigham Young University, Harold B. Lee Library, L. Tom Perry Special Collections)

The St. Georg Branch in Hamburg, dubbed the "high castle of Nazism" in the German Mormon Church by Hamburg District President Otto Berndt, seated seventh from the right on the second row. Branch President Arthur Zander, to Berndt's right, forced his congregants to listen to Adolf Hitler's radio speeches on Sundays, locking the door so that they could not leave, and once tried to replace meetinghouse pictures of Jesus Christ and Joseph Smith with one of Hitler. Hübener group co-conspirators Rudi Wobbe and Karl-Heinz Schnibbe are seated on the first row, fourth and fifth from the left. (Courtesy Brigham Young University, Harold B. Lee Library, L. Tom Perry Special Collections)

Helmuth Hübener liked everything American. He honed his English skills in conversation with the American missionaries, sang American songs, and dressed in the latest styles from overseas. He did not like the Nazi supporters in his congregation, who were led by Branch President Arthur Zander, First Counselor Franz Jacobi, and several other nefarious characters: a few congregants who played in the brown-shirted SA "storm trooper" band and one Mormon who had joined the black-shirted SS Death's Head brigades that eventually manned the extermination camps. (Courtesy Brigham Young University, Harold B. Lee Library, L. Tom Perry Special Collections)

The Federal Republic of Germany renamed parts of the old Hamburg city hall, which functioned as a Gestapo interrogation and torture facility during the Second World War. It contained the infamous "Hall of Mirrors," where Helmuth Hübener and other members of his resistance group suffered a relentless inquisition by secret policemen determined to discover the nonexistent adults behind their plot. Two of the survivors, Karl-Heinz Schnibbe and Rudi Wobbe, returned to their hometown in 1985 to receive accolades for their courage and dedicate a second Helmuth Hübener-Haus. The original building, pictured above, is now a home for old-age pensioners. (Photo by David Conley Nelson)

Helmuth-Hübener-Weg in present-day suburban Hamburg. In 1976, Mormon Church officials suspended continued performances of a commemorative play at BYU that lionized the young German resister. They feared that glorifying Hübener's defiance of authority would endanger Mormons in East Germany. BYU professors insisted that, on the contrary, officials of the German Democratic Republic would never equate an anti-fascist with an anti-communist—and that the best way to court favor in Germany would be to stage the production there, where Hübener's exploits were well known on both sides of the Iron Curtain. The Church allowed production of the play to resume in 1992, after the fall of the Berlin Wall and the Soviet Union. (Photo by David Conley Nelson)

Thomas S. Monson, then the Second Counselor in the First Presidency of the Mormon Church, shakes hands with Erich Honecker of the German Democratic Republic in 1988, celebrating a reciprocal exchange of Mormon missionaries between West Germany and the communist East. Monson began his church service as a 22-year-old bishop of a Salt Lake City ward comprised of German immigrants. During his years as an Apostle, he was the Mormons' emissary to German Latter-day Saints who resided behind the Iron Curtain during the Cold War. Monson suspended subsequent performances of a popular Helmuth Hübener theatrical play on the BYU campus, and froze publication of Hübener research by BYU scholars. As the currently serving Church President, Monson has chosen a former German citizen, Dieter Uchtdorf, as a member of the ruling three-man Mormon troika, the First Presidency. (Image from *Deseret News*, November 4, 1988)

9

A Countervailing Myth
Nazi Persecution of the Mormons

In April 1933 a "uniformed Nazi" assaulted two American Mormon missionaries, P. Blair Ellsworth and Preston C. Allen, while they were walking door-to-door, seeking converts in the small town of Hindenburg, located near Stendal in the Saxony-Anhalt district of northern Germany. The assailant, either an SA "storm trooper" or an older Hitler Youth, swung his belt and hit Elder Ellsworth with the buckle. The attack severely lacerated Ellsworth's scalp. When the perpetrator and his two victims arrived at the police station, and later when they appeared in court, the Mormon missionaries declined to press charges. After consultation with their mission president, they decided it was "better not to arouse trouble." The magistrate ordered the Nazi thug to apologize. He refused but received no penalty for either the assault or for violating the court's order.[1]

This incident marks the only instance recorded in official Mormon mission records of an unprovoked physical attack on representatives of the LDS Church by anyone connected with the National Socialist government or Nazi Party auxiliary organizations.[2] The belt-whipping assault, which appears in the writings of author Gilbert Scharffs and Henderson State University historian Steven Carter, has become part of the lore that involves the Mormons in Nazi Germany.[3] Together with the celebrated case of resister Helmuth Hübener and a few other incidents that occurred during wartime, it buttresses the myth that the Mormons were persecuted in Nazi Germany, a belief that has existed only in the postwar era. Quite to the contrary, the Mormon strategy of exploiting congruencies

Nazi Germany after the Anschluss and Czechoslovakian Crisis, on the eve of the Second World War, 1939. Map by John Gilkes.

with National Socialism made life as Latter-day Saints in Nazi Germany as tolerable as it was for other Christians who owed allegiances to both a church and the state.

From January 1933, when Hitler became Chancellor, until August 1939, when the American missionaries evacuated before the Second World War, the mission historical records document 112 particular cases of interaction between the Mormons and either the government or clerics. Only six of those chronicled instances involved hostile actions by clerical opponents, although it is likely that some police or Gestapo investigations of the Mormons were initiated by complaints from mainline churches. During Imperial Germany and the Weimar Republic, most opposition to the Latter-day Saints emanated from priests or ministers. In Nazi Germany, those Catholic and Protestant ministers had their own problems with the state.

Freed of most ecclesiastical opposition, the Mormons could concentrate on challenges posed by the Nazis. Most confrontations with the government were innocuous; on thirty-one occasions, local police or Gestapo agents merely requested information, examined a congregation's financial records, or seized reading material. In all cases except for a few banned pamphlets, the confiscated items were returned. During the prewar Nazi period, brown-shirted hooligans or police interrupted Mormon worship services or private devotionals on only three occasions. The government periodically suspended youth activities on the grounds that they interfered with the prerogative of the Hitler Youth, but this occurred on a local basis and was usually temporary. Nazis never banned congregational worship. Nine missionaries or German members were taken into custody, but only two victims spent more than three nights in confinement. One American missionary endured three weeks in a municipal jail, and three non-Jewish German members went to concentration camps but were later released. Most arrested missionaries or local church members were released the same day when police investigations or judicial proceedings found them to be free of wrongdoing. Often, their alleged infractions had little to do with their church work, but instead reflected individual transgressions, either real or perceived.

For example, in March 1935, police in the Silesian town of Liegnitz arrested and jailed American missionary Daniel H. Lehmann and his German companion, Hans W. Schultz. Someone had accused them of stealing Winter Relief cards from the doorways of houses. A judge heard their testimony that day, dismissed the charges, and authorized continued missionary work. That same month, American missionary James H. Riley, Jr., and his German cohort, Erich Heismann, ran afoul of the authorities while taking photographs of a coal mine near Beuthen in Lower Silesia. Police accused them of "being American spies," put them in separate jail cells, and thoroughly searched their living quarters. Later that day, the two missionaries "left the police station in good standing, but not before they had preached the Gospel to the officers."[4]

One month later, a Berlin-based missionary assigned to the headquarters of the German-Austrian Mission was visiting friends in the East Prussian city of Lötzen. On the morning of April 3, 1935, Lawrence A. Sessions set out on foot toward the town of Odoyen, where he intended to preach the Gospel for a period of ten days. En route, he encountered a contingent of soldiers engaged in marksmanship practice. When his accent revealed him to be an American, he was arrested, searched, and accused of being a spy. The soldiers subsequently released him, but not before they gave him instructions to leave East Prussia within forty-eight hours. Military officers seized his camera and exposed the film before they returned it to him.[5]

In each of these cases, the missionaries' clerical affiliation played no role in their difficulties with civilian or military authorities. Timing, especially with regard to the incidents involving the coal mine and the military exercises, seems to have been much more important. In early 1935, Germany was in the process of unshackling itself from limitations imposed by the Treaty of Versailles. In January, Germany regained possession of the Saar Valley after winning an overwhelming vote in a plebiscite. On successive weekends in March, Hitler announced steps in remilitarizing Germany that defied the Treaty. On March 8, he proclaimed that Germany would once again have an air force. Then, one week later on March 16, he instituted military conscription and announced plans to expand the *Wehrmacht* to thirty-six divisions with a total strength of 550,000 troops. The Treaty of Versailles had disbanded the air force and limited the German army to one hundred thousand soldiers. In June 1935, Joachim von Ribbentrop, upon whom Hitler had recently bestowed the title of Reich Minister Ambassador-Plenipotentiary at Large, negotiated an agreement with Great Britain that began German naval rearmament.[6]

In the months leading up to Hitler's remilitarization of the Rhineland in March 1936, the pressure to maintain military secrecy and guard key parts of the infrastructure must have profoundly affected military officers.

In such a climate of anxiety, it would not have been unusual to suspect malevolent intentions from young English-speaking foreigners who appeared suddenly in the midst of remote, rural military maneuvers, or who were observed photographing mining operations. The Mormon elders who stumbled into such trouble were fortunate to have encountered civil policemen and military officers, rather than hotheaded, brown-shirted thugs who may have reacted less judiciously.

The Mormons successfully navigated Nazi Germany's bureaucratic labyrinth because members, missionaries, and mission presidents learned how to deal with the different levels of government authority they encountered. George R. Blake was a promising undergraduate scholar at BYU in 1937 when one of his professors suggested that language skills acquired from a German mission would help him in graduate school. He described how astute missionaries would seek approval from a sympathetic bureaucrat: "We were interacting with minor officials in the government all the time. They turned out to be of two kinds. There were those of the old German bureaucracy, the civil servants who had trained in school and had a fine tradition of efficiency prior to the ascent of the Nazis. Superimposed on them was a group of Nazi officials who were usually their inferiors in terms of education or understanding, but their superiors in terms of authority and power [that] was used with arrogance and lack of civility. . . . We would try to get past that [Nazi] rung."[7]

Patience and persistence indeed prevailed when negotiating to overturn onerous, low-level decisions that limited congregational activity or missionary proselytizing. In June 1936, Elders Vergil Stucki and Norville Fluckiger arrived in the Schleswig-Holstein town of Neumünster "to open a new field of labor." When they applied to the local police for permission to live there, as all missionaries had been required to do for decades, their application was rejected on the grounds that "polygamy is not allowed in Germany." The official who denied their residence permit nevertheless helped the two missionaries file an appeal of his decision to a regional office in Kiel.[8] On July 9, a "representative of the secret police" informed the two missionaries that their appeal had been granted conditionally. The Mormons could establish a congregation in Neumünster

A Countervailing Myth

but only church members could attend services. Prospective converts could not be invited.

The Mormons found this compromise unacceptable, as presumably only a few members lived in town and the new congregation was intended to act as a magnet to attract converts. Nevertheless, the small Neumünster branch began its meetings under the imposed restrictions. On two consecutive Sundays, the Gestapo agent who delivered the notice of their appeal attended the services "with his assistant, apparently to . . . make sure those in attendance were members."[9] Having satisfied the local secret police with their willingness to comply, the two American missionaries, Stucki and Fluckiger, accompanied by a German citizen, Elder August A. Dittmer, arranged a meeting in August 1937 at the regional Gestapo headquarters in Kiel. There, they pleaded their case to be allowed to host prospective converts at Sunday church services. They learned that such a dispensation would have to be granted by the national office in Berlin. By October, the dispute had not yet been settled, as another Neumünster-based missionary wrote a letter to the Gestapo, asking once again to be allowed to invite guests to church services.

At this point the archival trail goes cold. No final resolution to the dispute in Neumünster can be found in the historical records of the Mormon missions, nor is one necessary to illustrate an important point. Several years after the Nazi assumption of power, the Mormons were not afraid to interact with the Gestapo, military authorities, or local police whenever the government imposed a policy that disrupted their ecclesiastical activities. Nor were the Mormons afraid to disobey in carefully calculated situations. In fact, selective defiance of local government leaders continued to occur and emanated, at times, from the level of the mission president. When German-Austrian Mission President Roy Welker, who supervised Mormon missionary work in the eastern half of Germany, returned to the United States in 1937, he told a General Conference audience in the Salt Lake Tabernacle: "We played strongly upon our Twelfth Article of Faith, declaring that we meant it when we said that we believe in sustaining and upholding the government." Then he said: "There [was] a law in Germany that the small religious denominations should not scatter their literature from door to door. We debated for a long time whether we should stop tracting, but we had been tracting; in most places we had never ceased tracting, and we felt that inasmuch as we had been doing it we could continue, and we did continue. And in only a few places were prevented from tracting."[10]

In other words, the Mormons told everyone they obeyed the law, even when they did not. Another incident illustrates how the Mormons pushed the limits of legal compliance. In the state of Baden-Württemberg in southwestern Germany near Stuttgart, an unspecified number of missionaries went before a judge in April 1935, charged with violating the law by "passing out tracts" in the towns of Mannheim and Pforzheim. The judge sentenced each to their choice of a twenty *Reichsmark* (RM 20) fine or five days in jail. Police searched the missionaries' rooms and confiscated pamphlets and other reading material. A note in the mission records commented: "We hope they read it all." The mission office paid the elders' fines and arranged a compromise. The missionaries would continue to proselytize, going door to door, but would issue personal invitations to meetings rather than distribute literature.[11] Based on Welker's remarks in Salt Lake City in 1937, that restriction applied only in that judge's jurisdiction. Elsewhere, they continued passing out leaflets in defiance of the law. The Mormons believed in "obeying and sustaining the law" as long as it did not conflict with their church duties. If that kind of conflict arose, they abided by restrictions only to the extent that they could avoid significant consequences for disobedience.

The unfortunate reality of life in a police state, however, made unintentional violations and thoughtless behavior as hazardous as deliberate disobedience. The situation became more complicated when pettiness or enmity led to denunciations by fellow Germans motivated more by spite than genuine interest in national security. In a country of approximately sixty-six million inhabitants, the existence of only twenty thousand Gestapo agents limited the investigative power of the secret police.[12] Historian Eric A. Johnson of Central Michigan University described the propensity for Germans to fill the void by reporting each other for perceived political crimes during the Third Reich: "Because average citizens were so often willing to keep watch over and denounce fellow citizens whenever they stepped out of line, and many times when they had not stepped out of line, relatively few secret police officers were needed to control a German population that was quite ready and able to control itself."[13]

Mormons were not targets of the Third Reich, as were Jews and Jehovah's Witnesses. Nevertheless, an inadvertent mistake reported by a third party could result in government reprisal, especially because of the church's connections with foreign missionaries and leadership. Such was the case in April 1935, when an anonymous source in Stuttgart reported an ordinary German LDS member for making a "hostile remark" regarding the government. The Swiss-German Mission's historical documents did not record the member's fate, but police summoned and admonished American missionaries against making political statements. The branch president, Erwin Ruf, underwent police questioning about an allegation that he had accepted a tithing payment from an unemployed member. Probably, the police confused the Mormon system of voluntary tithing with the Protestant and Catholic "church tax," which would not have been assessed on an unemployed parishioner. As the mission's report stated, "It was obvious that someone in that city was endeavoring to make trouble for the Church."[14]

The magnitude of governmental reaction to a provocation often depended on which branch of Nazi Germany's security apparatus dealt with the case. A serious set of consequences resulted from a well-intentioned local effort to communicate with Mormon members of Germany's armed forces. In January 1937, a district (diocesan) youth leader asked for the mailing addresses of all young Mormon men from Hamburg who had enlisted in the military. This request triggered a virulent reaction, probably not from the understaffed Gestapo or the local criminal police, but instead most likely from military counterintelligence. Since the Latter-day Saints were an American-based religious denomination, officers suspected foreign espionage.[15] Police arrested and jailed Hermann Noack, a German citizen. The mission records state that he was charged with "high treason" and subjected to "treatment as one of the worst criminals." Apparently, his attempt to mail copies of *Der Stern* and a church youth newsletter, *Geh Voran*, was characterized as "betraying Germany by sending military secrets and information to foreign points." After Noack spent three nights in jail, authorities released him to home confinement, monitored his mail, and kept his family under surveillance. The inquiry expanded to the district president, Alwin Brey, whom the police summoned for "the severest questioning." Police fingerprinted and photographed Brey and then detained him for two days. They confiscated all of his church publications and records and forbade him from communicating with mission headquarters in Basel.[16]

The Prewar Nazi Years, 1933–1939

For the Mormon hierarchy, having its members jailed for carrying out church duties was unfortunate. Inability to communicate with underlings in the field posed a more serious problem: lack of control. By March 1937, although tensions had diminished somewhat, the mission office in Switzerland was still not receiving Hamburg's periodic financial and activity reports, which were required from all districts and branches. Mail sent to Brey and a missionary, Alphonse Pia, was arriving late and showed evidence of having been opened. Authorities kept Brey under surveillance and required him to report regularly on church activities. They ordered suspension of all youth meetings, a measure they eventually relaxed, along with a ban on communication with higher headquarters. Cooler heads finally realized that the youth leader's actions were religiously motivated.[17]

Reverberations from the incident appear to have been restricted to the Hamburg district. When Hitler invaded Austria in the *Anschluss* of March 1938, annexed the *Sudetenland* in October 1938, and subsequently occupied all of Czechoslovakia by March 1939, Mormon congregants across Germany wrote letters and sent packages to their fathers and sons in the *Wehrmacht* without fear of a Hamburg-style reprisal. Nevertheless, the Hamburg incident may have played an instrumental part in the Salt Lake City hierarchy's decision, announced in the summer of 1937, to place all German missions and ecclesiastical units under the control of mission presidents stationed on German territory.[18] At the end of 1937, before the *Anschluss*, the two German-speaking missions reorganized into three. Responsibility for Austria and Switzerland shifted to the new Swiss-Austrian mission headquartered in Basel, Switzerland. The West German Mission, based in Frankfurt am Main, and the East German Mission, headquartered in Berlin, exercised administrative control over Mormons in Germany.[19] Part of the justification may have stemmed from the reluctance of German authorities to allow Hamburg Mormons to seek guidance from an American mission president based in Switzerland.

Considering the Hamburg experience, the need to be careful with correspondence should have become apparent to everyone involved with the Mormon missions in Germany. However, a young elder who spent most of his missionary career in Switzerland did not heed that lesson when he transferred to duty in Germany. Alvin J. Schoenhals had developed a reputation for efficiency early in his missionary service, and as a result he had been rewarded with an administrative position in the Swiss-German Mission headquarters in Basel. An observer of world affairs, he became accustomed to expressing his disapproval of the Nazi regime in his letters dispatched from Switzerland to his family in Utah. Toward the end of his term in the mission field, as is customary with "office missionaries," he transferred to proselytizing duties, ostensibly in an effort to make a few conversions before he went home.[20] Unfortunately for Schoenhals, his failure to exercise behavioral discretion as a foreigner in the Nazi state provided him with a trove of unpleasant stories to tell in future years.

On June 14, 1937, Mission Secretary Stanford Bingham in Basel received an urgent letter from a young missionary in Nuremberg, an Elder Christensen, who reported that Schoenhals, his roommate, had been arrested and that police searched their apartment. Three other missionaries serving in the city tried without success to visit their companion in jail. Philemon Kelly, the mission president, contacted the American consul in Bern, who relayed the concern to his counterpart in Munich. Kelly then employed an attorney on the young missionary's behalf.[21]

Three days later, American diplomats reported that Schoenhals was being held for a violation of the "Law Against Malicious Attacks on the State and the Party and for Protection of the Party Uniform," a Nazi-era statute adopted in December 1934. The young missionary had written a letter home that had been intercepted and read by a postal censor before it left Germany. In the words of the American consul, "It would appear that Mr. Schoenhals has unwisely expressed opinions of internal political matters."[22] Kelly visited Schoenhals in jail. The young man apologized for the trouble he had caused the mission. At one point during the interview with his superior, he broke down crying, not for fear of his fate but instead because of shame for the trouble he caused.[23] After three weeks in jail, authorities released Schoenhals and expelled him from Germany. Fortunately for Schoenhals, his case had been referred to the state prosecutors, the *Staatsanwaltschaft*, rather than a brutal agency of the Nazi Party. He was imprisoned in a municipal jail, not a concentration camp.[24]

Another case illustrated the different treatment afforded American missionaries and their German congregants when they ran afoul of the Nazi state. Sometime in 1938, while serving in Schleswig-Holstein, Elders Royal V. Wolters and Allen Lute posed for photographs of themselves wearing a Nazi flag as a breechcloth. They waited until their transfer to Saarbrücken, a city on the border with France and one where political sensitiveness was heightened, to submit the undeveloped film for processing. They sent it to a German Mormon, Johann Kiefer, who owned a photography business.

No adverse consequences resulted from the first batch of photographs that Kiefer processed. However, after Wolters and Lute transferred to a third post, they showed the pictures to friends, who asked for copies. This time, when they mailed the negatives back to Kiefer to obtain more prints, the photographer's employees reported him to the authorities.[25] If the two American missionaries had still been based in Saarbrücken, they probably would have been arrested. However, the mission was able to rush the two puerile young men across the Swiss border before Gestapo agents caught them. According to Mission Secretary Donald M. Petty's account: "They traveled by rail towards Switzerland, and they would go so far on one type of train, so that they weren't on an express train that was going straight through. They finally reached the city of Basel, where the railroad station on one side of the border is German and the other side is Swiss. As they were hurrying through the station, these Gestapo agents were right behind them. As soon as they passed over to the Swiss side, the Gestapo stopped because it didn't want to go into Switzerland and cause problems there."[26]

Because Petty did not personally observe the chase scene, this possibly embellished narrative is more significant for its contribution to the folklore of Mormon missionary work in Germany. If one desires to make a case for persecution of the Mormons by the Nazis, stories like this reinforce the argument. Nevertheless, as the mission records reveal, "Quite some trouble was made of it," which necessitated the precautionary step of removing the Mormon missionaries from Saarbrücken temporarily. The German photographer, Johann Kiefer, did not fare so well. He was arrested and dispatched to a concentration camp.[27] The real significance of this case, as with several others during this period, is that the Nazi government focused on finding and punishing individual perpetrators and did not ban church activity because of occasional renegade activity by American missionaries or German Mormons.

Not every Mormon confrontation with the Nazi State resulted from either calculated disobedience, reasoned appeals of unfavorable decisions by lower-ranking bureaucrats, or inadvertent brushes with authority resulting from poor judgment. Sometimes the Mormons deliberately took on the government when they felt they could win a straightforward legal case. Parts of the Weimar Republic's judicial framework survived the Nazi seizure of power, so that a legal challenge could be mounted if the petitioner were not a Jew, a Gypsy, a Jehovah's Witness, or a member of another disfavored class. For German citizens and foreigners who maintained favorable relations with the Nazis, the government still provided forums where grievances could be adjudicated. Tax court was one of those places.

In January 1937, the government served the German-Austrian Mission in Berlin with a bill for delinquent taxes. The dispute involved the Mormons' contention that they enjoyed a tax-exempt status, as any other church would. The government maintained otherwise, contending that the Latter-day Saints operated in Germany through the medium of a *Verein*, a club or a society, which unlike a church would be required to pay taxes on its profits.[28] The Mormons had received their legal recognition as a *Verein* in 1923 after an unsuccessful attempt to convince the Weimar government to grant certification as a church. This status allowed the Latter-day Saints to rent and purchase property, establish savings and credit relationships with banks and businesses, and enter into legally binding contracts.[29]

The government served the German-Austrian Mission with a tax bill for approximately ten thousand *Reichsmarks* per year to cover the three years from 1934 through 1936. Obligations were due on tithing collection receipts, profits derived from the sale of publications, and taxes owed for church-owned buildings in Chemnitz and Selbongen. The exact state of the Mission's finances cannot be ascertained from surviving records. Nevertheless, the church undoubtedly collected a substantial amount of money. Mormons desiring to maintain good standing were urged to pay "ten percent of their increase annually,"[30] and Swiss-German Mission President Philemon Kelly maintained: "Our tithing is the highest in all European missions."[31] The German-Austrian Mission's tithing collections, which Kelly compared to his own mission, were very close to the value cited in Kelly's letter.

That constituted an inviting target for Germany's tax collectors, who struggled to provide revenue to offset considerable deficit spending that had occurred since onset of the Great Depression. When Hitler assumed power in 1933, Germany's unemployment rate stood at thirty percent. The government used Keynesian fiscal policy in response to the crisis. To create jobs, it built the *Autobahn* and undertook other large public works projects. Price controls and business-friendly Nazi labor unions limited price and wage inflation. However, large increases in military spending exacerbated the national debt. By 1936, German military spending exceeded ten percent of the gross national product, making it the highest in Europe.[32]

The Mormons had no intention of mitigating the German budget deficit. They reacted as most targets of the tax collector would under similar circumstances: they hired a tax law firm. Dr. Wirth, an American lawyer certified to practice in German courts, in partnership with a German attorney, Dr. Turnheim, approached the government. They negotiated a settlement on terms quite favorable to the Mormons. The government settled for RM 386 for the year 1934, no liability for 1935, and RM 680 for 1936. Furthermore, the Mormons agreed to pay only RM 170 per quarter in future years, plus thirty percent of the profit derived from selling publications and from the rental of church property. The German-Austrian Mission paid its lawyers RM 1,500 in fees. "It was a large sum," the mission reported to Salt Lake City headquarters, "but small in comparison to the amount the mission will save each year." Furthermore, the Mormons won their point regarding donations. They would pay no income tax on tithing because those donations were voluntary, not an assessment.[33]

The settlement apparently had other favorable consequences. In February 1938, East German Mission President Alfred C. Rees refused to pay a municipal tax assessed upon Mormon missionaries in the Brandenburg town of Guben. He submitted a written appeal and promptly received a favorable reply from a "taxing official" employed by the city government.[34]

The Mormons became so skilled in dealing with the various levels of bureaucracy in Nazi Germany that they learned to exploit glitches in the system—sometimes with humorous results. Six months after arriving in Germany, after having lived his entire life in Utah, American citizen George R. Blake was astonished to learn that he was being conscripted into the Germany army. A terse letter instructed him to appear immediately before the local military commandant in the Rhineland city

A Countervailing Myth

of Herne. He was two months past due in reporting for induction, the letter warned. Blake was worried because: "I didn't speak German well and understood it with difficulty." His missionary companion, who had been in Germany much longer, told him: "You let me handle it. You say nothing!"

Blake continued: "We went to the office, and I passed my summons to the officer, an army lieutenant. He looked at it and began immediately to chew me out.... After briskly telling me I was in jeopardy for having delayed, the lieutenant asked for my pass. I gave him my American passport, which was quite different from the German pass. He looked at it, became quite befuddled, and went in the back room. After a few minutes he came out very apologetic that he had made this outburst against an American. It was obvious that he was not himself a Nazi or he wouldn't have been embarrassed by the situation."[35]

Occasionally, Nazis were indeed embarrassed. A pair of young American Mormon missionaries extracted an apology from a boorish local SA leader after they reported him to a higher-ranking Nazi authority for an abuse of his power. In the Rhineland town of Bad Homburg, missionary Donald M. Petty had a modest sign painted that marked the rented meeting hall used for Sunday services. The local leader of an SA contingent objected, claiming the sign was too large. He filed a complaint with the police department, who advised the missionaries to seek a ruling from government authorities in Frankfurt regarding the sign's legality. Petty arranged a meeting with a Gestapo supervisor in Frankfurt, who received him politely. The official requested details about the sign and the storm trooper who complained. After assuring the secret police that the sign listed only the name of the congregation and its meeting times, Petty overheard the Gestapo supervisor's phone call to the local police in Bad Homburg. The agent said: "Call in this man who made the complaint and we'll send papers to you.... He is to be removed from the Party register and he'll no longer be in charge of the storm troopers in Bad Homburg, because he has exceeded his authority in making this complaint."

Later, the demoted SA leader came to the missionaries and pleaded for help, "Can you do anything to get me reinstated, because this position I had was the highest in town. My friends will make fun of me!" As Petty explained, because the man lost his party affiliation, he also lost his right to be promoted at work or to attain better jobs. Petty concluded: "It was a sad blow for him. I thought at the time, well maybe the Nazi Party does have glimmers of democracy in it, under certain conditions. It gave me a better feeling toward the Nazi officers in their official capacity, because if a person had a legitimate complaint, it could be resolved."[36]

Presumably, Petty's observations regarding incipient democracy in the Nazi Party did not include justice for Jews or other *Untermenschen*. His day-to-day missionary activity gave him no reason to be concerned about Germany's disfavored classes. Mormons did not seek converts among ethnic or religious minorities. The LDS proscription against ordaining blacks to the universal male priesthood, which was not lifted until 1978, prevented Elder Petty from proselytizing among nearby "Rhineland Bastards"—descendants of white German women and black African French occupation troops.[37] Not one mention of Gypsies appears in the historical records of the German mission. Mormons may have recognized the Jews as God's chosen people of the Old Testament, but that commission had expired. Mormons considered themselves to be God's new chosen people. They were the disciples of Joseph Smith's restored Gospel that cleansed Christianity from the "Great Apostasy" that occurred between the death of Christ and the Roman Emperor Constantine's adoption of Christianity.[38] Despite pronounced theological differences the Mormons had with mainstream Christianity, few distinguishing temporal attributes set German Mormons apart from other Germans. They behaved as ordinary citizens.

If a gang of Nazi hooligans interrupted their worship, as was the case in the Westphalian town of Minden in May 1933, Mormons maintained their composure, explained that they were conducting a devotional service, and watched the uniformed thugs leave.[39] When the police forbade door-to-door proselytizing in the Ruhr city of Bochum in January 1936, the missionaries instead conducted a secular educational seminar. They showed an audiovisual presentation about the scenic wonders of Utah, invited the police, made friends, and saw their privileges restored.[40] If authorities challenged the "Jewish nature" of certain religious pamphlets, as they did in September 1936 in Berlin, the Mormons destroyed the questionable material and replaced it with five freshly edited and newly printed tracts.[41] When members of the Forst Branch in Bavaria deliberated whether they should attend Sunday services or a Nazi procession in

A Countervailing Myth

their town on one Sabbath Day in 1933, their collective decision was a sensible one. Some of them went to church; others marched.[42]

The Mormons' reasoned response to provocation even won them some admirers among those who were least likely to express sympathy. Missionary Donald M. Petty, who had provoked the apology from the SA leader in Bad Homburg, recounted the experience of a colleague, an American missionary named Curtis who had served in Bremen. Curtis "became very friendly with" a Gestapo agent sent to monitor Mormon Sunday services: "The Gestapo man told Brother Curtis . . . that he knew the Church was true. He said however, "I can't join because of my position and because of the situation I'm in. I want you to know that my feelings are such that if I could join, I would join your church.""[43]

The Mormons were not persecuted in Nazi Germany. They felt the hot lash of Nazi disfavor only to the extent that other, ordinary Germans may have experienced harassment if they attracted attention or consorted with foreigners. Those incidents could have occurred in any secular or spiritual realm during the Third Reich. Considering the perceived divine nature of the Mormons' undertaking and their history of being persecuted, an occasional, nonlethal squabble with the Nazi state was a small price to pay in order to reap God's eventual glory. In the nineteenth century, because of the specter of polygamy, universal opposition by clerics, and hostility regarding the emigration of marriageable young women and draft-age men, Mormons seemed distinctly out of place in Germany. Weimar democracy gave constitutional rights to both the Mormons and their clerical antagonists, and the Mormons gained a grudging acceptance of their right to coexist in the shadow of the Catholics and Protestants. Under Nazi rule, when ecclesiastical opposition faded, Mormons finally became the kind of ordinary Germans that historian Eric Johnson described:

> Most Germans . . . slept soundly at night, worked productively by day and enjoyed their lives during the peacetime years of National Socialist rule. Why should they not have? The economy was improving, most were finding employment, and their country was regaining its pride and was still at peace. . . . They knew there was a strong police presence, a surfeit of laws placing limitations on personal freedom, and potential danger for those who refused to comply with Hitler's wishes. Many grumbled and complained

privately, but most found little difficulty in conforming. . . . Nazi terror posed no real threat to most ordinary Germans.[44]

During an oral history interview in 1992, former missionary George R. Blake still supported the Mormons' policy of accommodation and ingratiation with a ruthless Nazi state: "We indeed came to the understanding that as evil as it was the government guaranteed our safety on the streets, preserved order and guaranteed a supply of food and shelter. The basic wants and needs of people were being met and protected by the government even though it was the Nazi government. To that extent we could and did sustain the government."[45]

For that reason, no climate of fear existed among Mormons who lived under Nazi governance. By contrast, Christine Elizabeth King describes the plight of a Christian Scientist in Munich who buried her Bible and other religious material in the garden for fear of being discovered as a faith-healing practitioner. When she needed scriptural inspiration, she dug it up, read it, and then reburied it before her neighbors could denounce her to the Nazis.[46] When Mormons encountered problems with publications that could offend the Nazis, such as those that contained references to Judaism, they did not think to hide the material as contraband. Instead, they rewrote it and carried on.

10

God's *Oberführer*
The Mormon Mission President

Copenhagen's regal Palace Hotel, glimmering in its recently remodeled splendor, hosted a brash newcomer at the annual meeting of European Mormon mission presidents in May 1938.[1] Among the eleven middle-aged men who attended with their wives, the most popular discussion topic concerned an energetic, aggressive former businessman and political activist from Salt Lake City who had won his position as the Berlin-based East German Mission President in a power struggle with a rival missionary leader.[2] Before the conference began, Alfred C. Rees had intrigued but mystified his colleagues with a cryptic memorandum that claimed he had extracted "some important, unprecedented concessions from the German government," actions he "couldn't mention specifically" in writing but would discuss at the meeting.[3]

Franklin J. Murdock, the president of the Netherlands Mission in 1938, recalled that a number of his contemporaries expressed discomfort with reports of close collaboration between Rees and the government of the Third Reich. Some, mindful of the way the Nazis were regarded around the world, believed that such an unsavory association would sully the church's reputation. Others, thinking pragmatically, maintained that Hitler's government could not be trusted to live up to any bargain it struck with the Mormons. Rees appealed for his colleagues' patience and trust. Murdock, however, employed his own method for assessing Rees's devotion to Adolf Hitler. One morning, while the mission presidents were descending the long, ornate staircase in the Palace Hotel's lobby, Murdock stealthily positioned himself behind the Berlin mission leader.

Murdock recounted: "He didn't see me. I put my hand on his right shoulder quickly, and I said 'Heil Hitler!'" Murdock described Rees's sudden, startled reaction: "He swung around [and said] 'Heil Hitler!' showing that he was used to that, and that he would go along with that. I did it just jokingly, to scare him, you see. And after [he recovered], he said, 'Oh, you'd better be careful; I've got a weak heart.' . . . But I wanted to test him out, to see if you could get him, unsolicited and unbeknownst to him. How quickly he responded, 'Heil Hitler!' Of course, that wasn't the thing for an American to do unless you were in favor of the regime."[4]

Rees's colleagues had reason to suspect him of an unprecedented degree of collaboration with the Nazis; his reputation had preceded him. During twenty-three months as a mission president in Germany, Alfred C. Rees did more to affiliate the Mormon Church with the National Socialists than any predecessor prelate. He met with important business and state officials. He forged an agreement with Joseph Goebbels's propaganda ministry to purge daily newspapers of anti-Mormon articles, and arranged for his missionaries to publish positive accounts of the LDS Church in municipal newspapers throughout Germany.[5] When the most important Nazi party daily subsequently printed an article about the Mormons that Rees did not like, he arranged for the *Völkischer Beobachter* to publish an article he had written that drew numerous parallels between Mormonism and Nazism, and between Utah and Germany.[6] In the weeks before the outbreak of the Second World War, Rees's savvy media-relations skills prompted a Nazi-controlled radio station to broadcast a shortwave radio program on Mormon topics intended for a Utah audience.[7] His excellent command of the German language allowed him to cultivate business and government contacts that a speaker with less fluency could not have accomplished.[8] In the autumn of 1937, Rees and his wife traveled to the annual Nazi Party rally in Nuremberg, where they enjoyed torchlight parades, fireworks displays, and other spectacular swastika-themed pageantry in the company of local Mormon missionaries.[9] When Italian fascist dictator Benito Mussolini visited Berlin, Rees posed as a correspondent for the *Los Angeles Times* in order to receive a prominent viewing place.[10] Based on his response to his colleague's surprise prank in the Danish hotel, Rees presumably rendered the "Heil Hitler" greeting with shameless regularity.

With regard to promoting synergies between Mormonism and Nazism, Rees was undoubtedly the most energetic of all Mormon mission presidents, but he was not alone in his enthusiasm. Many others—LDS Church leaders, United States senators, diplomats, and American college professors—wrote key articles or strategically timed visits to cultivate favor with the Nazis. They staged a coordinated effort to show Hitler's government that powerful and influential Americans backed politically astute Mormon mission presidents, their enthusiastic American missionaries, and the loyal German members who loved their church. More than eighty years of contentious experiences with civil government and mainline church leaders had taught the LDS hierarchy to marshal its forces effectively in Germany.

When National Socialism became the latest surmountable challenge, the Salt Lake City leadership drew upon a small pool of linguistically skilled, experienced, educated, and spiritually committed men who were willing to uproot their families and interrupt their professional lives. Seven men, all married with children, answered the call to become mission presidents (see table 10.1). All had labored as church missionaries in German-speaking lands as young men. One had served two previous missions, the second time as a mission president. Six of the seven were college graduates; two of those, an oral surgeon and a physician, had graduated from professional schools. Three were educators; one of those had served in the state legislature. Another was a prominent newspaper executive and official of the Salt Lake City Chamber of Commerce. The only skilled tradesman in the group compensated for his lack of a college education with the cultural understanding that could only come from having been born and reared in Germany. If the young missionaries they directed were the shock troops of Mormonism who fought spiritual battles in Hitler's godless world, each mission president served as a divinely anointed *Oberführer*.

The Battle for the Berlin Mission Presidency

Philemon M. Kelly was an example of that kind of Mormon stalwart, albeit a less bombastic one than Alfred C. Rees. As a young man of

Table 10.1. Mission presidents during the prewar National Socialist period, 1933–1939

Mission President	Years of Service (as president)	Mission	Profession	Prior Mission Service
Oliver H. Budge	1930–34	German-Austrian	Oral surgeon	1896–98
Franz "Francis" Salzner	1931–35	Swiss-German	Carpenter	1896–98
Roy A. Welker	1934–37	German-Austrian	School prinicipal Religion teacher	1901–1904
Philemon M. Kelly	1935–37	Swiss-German	Physician	1900–1903
	1937	East German		
	1937–38	West German		
Alfred C. Rees	1937	West German	Newspaper executive	1899–1902
	1938–39	East German	Civic leader	
M. Douglas Wood	1938–39	West German	School principal	1925–27
Thomas E. McKay	1938	East German	State legislator	1900–1903
	1938–39	Swiss-Austrian	Utility commissioner	1909–12[a]
	1939–45	All German Missions	School administrator	

[a]Served as president of the Swiss and German mission from 1909–12.

twenty-three who was planning to study medicine, Kelly postponed his ambitions in order to answer his stake president's call to serve a three-year mission in Germany beginning in 1900. He proselytized mostly in the western half of the country and kept a diary that recorded numerous faith-inspiring experiences. Before he departed in 1903, he vowed to return to Germany as a mission president. He repeated that determination to his wife after the couple wed in 1905, and he continued to hold onto the dream throughout medical school at Northwestern University and for decades in private practice as a family physician and general surgeon in southern Idaho. At Christmas dinner in 1934, he "prophesied" to his guests that he would soon "preside over the German mission."[11]

One week later, a prophet of God called. After attending to his patients on New Year's Day 1935, Kelly left St. Anthony, Idaho, at six o'clock in the evening and drove all night on country roads, arriving in Salt Lake City at seven in the morning. Wearing a new suit for the first time, he called upon Heber J. Grant, the Mormons' prophet, seer, and revelator, who said: "Brother Kelly, I would like you to preside over the Swiss-German Mission." By February 27, Kelly had sold his house, furniture, and medical practice to another doctor for $6,500. With his only other assets being $2,250 in a passbook savings account, Kelly, his wife Sue, and his daughter Connie embarked aboard the ocean liner SS *Manhattan* on April 24, 1935. At a time when other middle-aged professionals were shoring up their personal finances in anticipation of retirement, fifty-eight-year-old Kelly was garnering spiritual capital.[12]

The first two years of his mission presidency established Kelly's reputation as a kind yet firm ecclesiastical leader, based in the tranquil sanctuary of Basel, Switzerland, who taught his missionaries in Germany to eschew politics in an effort to coexist with the Nazi state.[13] His handling of the Alvin Schoenhals case provides a textbook example of how to use German lawyers and American diplomats with patient persistence to mitigate the wrath of an offended dictatorship. The young missionary had spent three weeks in custody for criticizing the Nazi state in a letter intercepted by postal censors. Likewise, Kelly's serene perseverance helped the Mormons endure the subsequent crisis in Hamburg, when officials ordered the arrest of a German LDS leader because he asked to send church material to Mormons in the *Wehrmacht*. By the time that the Salt Lake City leadership decided to reorganize the missions in 1937, however, merely avoiding trouble with the Nazis had become secondary to reaping the benefits of a favorable, active relationship. Kelly's plodding, nonconfrontational approach was no longer the desired tactic for the mission president who would serve in Germany's capital city.

A power struggle ensued for control of the crown jewel of Mormonism in Hitler's Reich, the renamed East German Mission in Berlin. The events of autumn 1937 reveal a glimpse of rare dysfunction within the Latter-day Saints' ruling triumvirate, the First Presidency. For knowledgeable observers within the German-speaking missions, it also provided an unaccustomed opportunity to witness jealousy and competition between mission presidents. That Kelly first won the coveted Berlin position, and subsequently lost it to a more politically savvy and skilled Nazi conciliator, Alfred C. Rees, also bespeaks the importance that the Mormon hierarchy placed on church relations with Hitler's government. In the Mormon mission field of Nazi Germany, winning powerful friends trumped winning souls.

At some point in the late spring or early summer of 1937, the Salt Lake City leadership decided to expand the number of German-speaking missions from two to three. Part of that reasoning may have emanated from the difficulties in Hamburg that spring, when the Nazi government prohibited German citizens leading LDS congregations from communicating with the American mission president based in Switzerland. Although the church hierarchy was not ready to appoint anyone other than an American to lead its missions, the necessity for establishing the West German mission based in Frankfurt am Main became obvious. Another justification may have been the burgeoning number of German-speaking Latter-day Saints, who had become difficult to govern with only one mission president in Berlin and a second in Switzerland. German speakers in Switzerland, Austria, and Germany comprised the largest contingent of Latter-day Saints outside the United States during the 1930s. The Nazi government made it difficult for Aryans, especially skilled workers or young men eligible for military service, to emigrate from the Third Reich. That, combined with the Mormons' desire to discourage immigration to the American Zion, resulted in the migration of only ninety-one German-speaking Latter-day Saints from the German-speaking missions from 1933 to 1939.[14] With Roy Welker's term as president of the German-Austrian Mission ending in 1937, and Kelly embarking upon the third and customarily last year of his mission presidency, the Salt Lake City leadership faced the need to find extraordinarily skilled leaders to fill these critical positions.

One obviously qualified candidate was Thomas E. McKay, who had served two previous German-speaking missions, the latter as president of the Swiss and German Mission from 1909 to 1912. McKay also needed a job. According to biographer Newell Bringhurst, the "changing political environment in Utah" caused McKay to lose his long-term salaried position on the Utah Public Utilities Commission in the spring of 1937.[15] Fortunately, Thomas McKay enjoyed an advantageous connection: his brother David O. McKay, who as Second Counselor in the First Presidency occupied the third-ranking position in the Mormon Church. Unfortunately, once McKay arrived in Germany, destined to assume command of the West German Mission in Frankfurt, a matter from his past surfaced to disqualify him from missionary leadership in the Third Reich. According to Donald M. Petty, who was secretary of the Swiss-German Mission in the late 1930s, Thomas McKay "had been expelled from Germany years before; that ban was still recognized by the German government."[16] Instead, McKay took charge of the newly created Swiss-Austrian mission, headquartered in the familiar Mormon outpost of Basel.

That pitted the veteran Kelly against the newcomer Rees for the coveted position in Berlin. The runner-up would receive the consolation prize in Frankfurt. Kelly's incumbency as leader of the Swiss-German Mission gave him a natural advantage, one augmented by the visit of the prophet, seer, and revelator, Heber J. Grant, to Kelly's mission in late June and early July 1937. Grant, age eighty-one, was the last Mormon Church president to have practiced polygamy.[17] He was beginning a three-month tour of Europe, the highlight of which would be the centennial celebration of the British Mission's founding in 1837.[18] When Kelly met Grant and his entourage at the Basel train station on June 28, the two began to discuss the planned realignment of the German-speaking missions and the position in Berlin. Grant spent a week in Switzerland, during which he stayed for several days at the mission home in Basel. By the time Grant, Kelly, and European Mission President Richard Lyman addressed eight hundred German Mormons below a large swastika banner in Frankfurt on July 8, Kelly had secured his appointment to head the new mission in the Third Reich's capital.[19] "While on his trip to Europe and before Brother Rees arrived in Germany," Kelly's memoirs said, "President Grant requested President Kelly go to Berlin and preside over that mission, and President Rees to open up the West German Mission in Frankfurt."[20]

Kelly wasted no time in moving to Berlin. Kelly appears to have embraced the adage that defined possession as nine-tenths of the law. Ida May Davis Rees, in a diary entry dated August 6, wrote that when she and her husband Alfred C. Rees stepped out of a taxicab at the Händelstasse mission headquarters in Berlin, they found "President and Mrs. Kelly already installed in the office."[21] Kelly dispatched a press release in another effort to entrench himself in his new position. In early September, a notice appeared in the *St. Anthony News*, announcing that the town's favorite son "has been appointed head of the large German-Austrian Mission of the LDS Church in Europe."[22] Notations in mission records, which Kelly controlled at this time, identified his nemesis Alfred C. Rees as president "of the newly organized Germany-West Mission."[23]

Rees would not be intimidated into accepting a lesser assignment. His duty, as he described it to anyone who would listen, was not limited to supervising missionaries and church members. According to Donald M. Petty, secretary of the neighboring Swiss-German Mission, "Alfred C. Rees was sent to Berlin for the express purpose of establishing relationships with the central (Nazi) government."[24] Stanford H. Bingham, who later was Rees's secretary, said: "He was called and set apart . . . to work with the government as well as to be a mission president."[25] Ralph Mark Lindsey, who became Rees's mission secretary after Bingham, said of his president: "You could certainly tell from his every action that his main objective was to break down the dislike the Nazi regime would have against the church, and to permit us to work."[26]

Lack of coordination within the First Presidency had caused Grant to offer the Berlin job to Kelly while the prophet's assistants had another candidate in mind. Probably, First Counselor J. Reuben Clark, a retired ambassador and undersecretary of state, recruited Rees to represent the Mormons in the capital of Hitler's empire. Another member of the Mormons' ruling troika, Second Counselor David O. McKay, anointed Rees to his Berlin position. According to Ida Rees's diary, "Alf was set apart by President McKay to preside over part of the German Mission with headquarters in Berlin." That entry was dated June 21, 1937, after Grant had left Germany to visit the British Mission. The Rees family then sailed to Germany in the company of Thomas E. McKay, who was David O. McKay's brother. When they left, there was no confusion on the American side of the Atlantic as to who had been designated to serve in Berlin. A *Deseret News* article described Rees as the designated German Mormon mission leader "in the north," meaning Berlin.[27] A farewell editorial two weeks later contained the *Deseret News*' speculation that Rees would lead the "North German Mission."[28] The *Millennial Star*, published in London at the European Mission headquarters, said in its July 15 edition that Rees would preside over "the northern division" while McKay would govern in the south and Kelly would move to the Swiss-Austrian mission.[29]

Neither antagonist was willing to let go of Mormonism's brass ring in Nazi Germany. On August 13, 1937, two weeks after Kelly moved to Berlin and one week after Rees arrived, the LDS prophet, seer, and revelator interrupted his scheduled trip to northern Europe to referee a squabble between mission leaders. After visiting Mormons in Scandinavia, Grant had been enjoying a Boy Scout jamboree in the Netherlands when he made a sudden, unscheduled visit to Hamburg. Grant, Rees, Kelly, Thomas McKay, the Swiss-Austrian Mission President, and Richard R. Lyman, the European mission president, attended. What transpired at that meeting remains unclear, as the records of each existing German mission conflict. The German-Austrian Mission's manuscript histories reveal Kelly's confirmation as president of the East German Mission and Rees's assignment to head the West German contingent.[30] By contrast, the Swiss-German Mission's records stated that both Rees and Kelly would be stationed in Berlin pending the final determination of each mission president's jurisdiction.[31] It appears that the octogenarian Mormon prophet tired of mediating a conflict between a pair of petulant men in their sixties. He returned to his Dutch scout jamboree and left it to Lyman, his European mission president, to restore order at the top of the German missions.

Rees, having no intention of being exiled to Frankfurt, responded by establishing himself in Berlin and spending the mission's money. As someone who would hobnob with the Nazi officialdom in the Third Reich's capital city, he needed an impressive residence. The Mormons' headquarters mansion across the street from Berlin's tranquil Tiergarten city park was occupied. Ida Rees's journal describes their house hunt: "Such a hopeless task . . . we went into some awful holes and some houses that must have belonged to the very well to do. One had about six great rooms in heavy carved furniture, oriental rugs, a chest of solid silver, great silver pieces on the sideboard. *So was the home of a Jew; we would have to keep his housekeeper.* One place had a big zebra skin rug and a great lion skin rug with the big heads on. Some places had immense carved figures on the house fronts, great marble staircases with life size figures in armor or statues of iron and bronze" (my emphasis).

When Ida Rees attended her first church service in Germany, she "didn't understand one word of what was said" and "sang the American words to hymns." Although she did not comprehend German, she probably understood why a Jewish owner had to vacate his property. However, the need to employ his servant seemed to be a greater consideration than the owner's fate. A Mormon mission matron did not express concern for Jews in those days; such an intemperate observation could have hindered her husband's task. The Rees family eventually settled on a house on Kürfurstendamm, "a fashionable street, wide and busy," often referred to as the Champs Elysees of Berlin. Ida Rees said their new abode had "a marble hall and two rooms in the back opening on a court."[32] After one month, the family tired of this house and found another, which Ida described in her diary:

> We have a room with a big desk bookcase, washstand, grandfather clock, two beds with an oriental rug and hand-woven rug for covers, two stands, two easy chairs, a leather one with a lion's head looking over each shoulder as we sit in it, a big stove and a balcony —all in shabby genteel make up, and 13 oil pictures of ancestors on the walls, also three sets of large deer horns and an iron figure on horseback on the desk. In the hall are iron figures and in the dining room there are over thirty oil paintings on the walls, also an immense wild boar's head with tusks, a wild turkey, two large grouse, a grand piano, etc.[33]

By the middle of October 1937, undoubtedly in part because of the Rees family's extravagant lifestyle, it was becoming expensive and inefficient to maintain two mission presidents in Berlin. Stanford H. Bingham remembered that Kelly ran the day-to-day affairs of the German-Austrian Mission while Rees concentrated on relations with the government. Bingham wrote in his diary: "President Rees hasn't been here three months yet but already has spent nearly 2,600 *Reichsmarks*, almost one thousand dollars. Of course, I wouldn't go so far as to say it has been wasted, but let's not talk about it. That along with other expenses in the last few months has lowered the balance in the German-Austrian mission from about 20,000 *Reichsmarks* to 5,000. No one needs to be an accountant to see where this is heading, in the very near future, to help from the mother church, something we haven't done in many years. I'm just thankful that I won't be held accountable."[34]

Meanwhile, with Thomas E. McKay safely sequestered across the border in Basel but cognizant of the old banning order that prevented him from living in Germany, no progress was being made in establishing a Frankfurt-based mission to administer church units and missionary work in the western part of the country. On October 5, 1937, the three mission presidents—Rees, Kelly, and McKay—met in Frankfurt. The Swiss-German Mission's manuscript histories reported that the disagreement had been resolved. The three men determined the geographical boundaries and proper name of each mission. Kelly relented by agreeing to relinquish control over the Berlin mission and move to Frankfurt at the beginning of 1938.[35] Kelly's memoirs indicate, in contrast to the mission's report, that the dispute had not yet been settled. It became the task of Richard R. Lyman, president of the European mission in London, to resolve the issue by convincing Kelly to move to the less prestigious post.

In a series of letters in the autumn of 1937, Lyman employed a combination of flattery and a threat to Kelly's legacy if he did not accept the move. Over two consecutive days in early October, Lyman wrote three letters to Kelly. Lyman told Kelly that church authorities would never require him to move to Frankfurt, but that Kelly was the most qualified man for the job. He implored Kelly to do so, citing the satisfaction that previous presidents had achieved by opening a new mission. Finally, Lyman warned of the consequences for failure to move to Frankfurt: "You are the master of the situation. Let everyone know that it is your right and you may remain in Berlin if you so desire. You can certainly do this and you will be backed up by the President of the Church up to the point of your being released. Of course if the situation is not harmonious, the probabilities are, a release might come, as it did to President Joseph J. Cannon at the end of about 2 years and 9 months."[36]

In referring to a fellow mission president whose inability to achieve consensus with his peers caused his dismissal, Lyman warned Kelly regarding his legacy. Would he wish to be remembered as the spiritual leader who successfully presided over three German-speaking missions, and whose final assignment included opening a new field of labor? Or would Kelly's tarnished reputation be that of a president who was prematurely discharged from his assignment because he could not get along?

On October 21, 1937, Kelly fired one last salvo, a four-page "report" of his success in the Swiss-German Mission. It took the form of a line-by-line comparison of his mission's performance with that of the German-Austrian Mission under Roy Welker's stewardship. In six different categories—pamphlets distributed, gospel conversations (lessons taught), convert baptisms, total baptisms, tithing, and fast offerings (charitable donations)—his mission enjoyed a statistical advantage over Welker's. He devoted a page to his development of "priesthood quorums" within his mission. As a result, all fourteen districts (dioceses) within the Swiss-German Mission had been removed from the control of American missionaries and placed instead under "local supervision." Finally, Kelly emphasized that his call to become president of the Berlin-based mission had come from God's anointed representative on earth: "[On] July 7th, 1937, President Grant, in company with President Lyman, called me into the sitting room of the Basel Mission Home and said, 'President Kelly, how would you like to take charge of the mission with headquarters in Berlin? We would like to have you do so.' I assured them I would be pleased to meet their request and began the necessary preparations to direct the mission."[37]

In a joint letter to Lyman dated October 26, 1937, the three American mission presidents—Rees, Kelly, and McKay—agreed to let the First Presidency in Salt Lake City make the final assignment. They reported their agreement on the need for three German-speaking missions and boundary lines that defined each. They also stated their willingness "to accept such assignments, and to preside over such mission as the First Presidency may designate."[38] In other words, they could not agree on who should lead the Berlin mission and deferred to higher authority.

Finally, a prophet of God spoke. In a letter to Kelly dated November 3, 1937, the prophet, seer, and revelator, Heber J. Grant, stated: "While it is true that for some reason, justifiable no doubt, you were appointed to take charge of the Eastern German Mission just prior to the arrival of President Rees, the fact remains that President Rees is the only one of the three presidents of German missions who has been specifically set apart to preside over 'that division of the German-Austrian Mission with headquarters in Berlin.'"[39]

In the end, the prophet deferred to a liturgical "ordinance." Although Grant himself had asked Kelly to serve in the Berlin post, his underling, David O. McKay, had performed a "setting apart" ceremony, which involved the "laying on of hands" to commission Rees as the Berlin mission president. Nothing in Kelly's personal correspondence indicates that he realized Grant's ultimate decision was based on political reality, rather than a sacred anointing. When faced with his prophet's decision, Kelly obediently surrendered, but he relayed a different narrative to others. In subsequent correspondence to a friend in Idaho, Kelly said: "My competitor was so determined to remain in Berlin and this mission so needed help that I wrote the First Presidency, volunteering to establish this mission on a proper basis."[40]

On December 8, 1937, Kelly and his wife departed for a month-long trip to southern Europe and Palestine. Kelly had served in the coveted Berlin mission presidency for five months. He arrived in Frankfurt on January 6, 1938, and by January 22 he had signed a contract to rent a stately mansion as the new West German Mission's headquarters. It lay on Schaumainkai, a street on the banks of the Main River in the midst of Frankfurt's art galleries and in its museum district.[41]

Kelly remained on the job until early July 1938, when he departed for "two months of intensive study of medicine" in Vienna prior to his return to the United States. Kelly had the opportunity to view the Nazification of Austria from a first-hand perspective. Four months had transpired since Hitler launched the *Anschluss*, the German occupation of Austria, in March 1938. The chance to observe the Nazi conquest gave Kelly one final opportunity to influence LDS policy in the German-speaking missions. On August 20, 1938, having returned from Vienna, he met with Rees and his successor as president of the West German Mission, M. Douglas Wood. Kelly's impressions, and his subsequent personal report to the

First Presidency in Salt Lake City, may have materially affected another reorganization of the missions.[42] On September 28, the First Presidency directed, "in view of recent political changes," that all church units in Austria be detached from the Swiss-Austrian Mission and assigned to the West German Mission in Frankfurt. The remaining mission was renamed the Swiss Mission.[43] Thomas E. McKay's reorganized Swiss-Austrian Mission, established to meet the political conditions prevalent prior to the *Anschluss*, had lasted for ten months.

The Quintessential Political Mission President

Freed of the burden of having a competing mission president on his territory, Alfred C. Rees began his vigorous effort to ally the Mormon Church with the Nazi government. If Kelly was a shining example of a spiritual mission president, Rees's background made him the prototypical political president. The exercise of political influence had played an important role in his adult life. Rees began his working life as a printer's apprentice in the late nineteenth century before undergoing his formal education at BYU and the University of Utah. While a missionary in Switzerland at the turn of the century, he attended classes at the Université de Neuchâtel. After a brief period as a high school language teacher and principal, he pursued a career in newspaper circulation and advertising. Prior to his mission presidency, he was the advertising manager of the *Deseret News*. He was active in the Utah Manufacturers Association, an industrial trade group formed in the early 1920s, and its successor, Utah Associated Industries. He served the Salt Lake City Chamber of Commerce in various leadership positions and appeared in *Who's Who in American Business*.[44]

Rees's interest in conservative political causes developed concomitantly with his business experience. In 1923 he became a founding member of the Utah Taxpayers Association, a "watchdog" group whose first newsletter proclaimed "there is an incessant demand within the state for a reduction of taxes."[45] Newspaper articles that announced his appointment to the Berlin mission presidency, and the obituaries published after his death in 1941, proclaimed him to be an "expert on taxation."[46] He was: he opposed it. Rees was also an early proponent of rolling back the gains made by trade unionism in the 1920s. He served as chairman of the

Council of American Industries, a successor group to the American Plan Open Shop Conference—which proposed to outlaw contractual agreements that required employers to hire union members.[47]

His combination of conservative political activism and stalwart church service undoubtedly brought Rees to the attention of J. Reuben Clark, the Mormons' number-two man in the First Presidency. Both men had atypical backgrounds for the church positions they occupied, and they shared convergent political views that sometimes differed from their fellow Utahns. Rees became a mission president after a career of business management and political advocacy, rather than the traditional proving grounds—education or the liberal professions. Clark joined the First Presidency after a lifetime of private legal practice during Democratic administrations and State Department service when Republicans occupied the White House. Clark was only the second member in the history of LDS Church's ruling triumvirate, the First Presidency, who had not enjoyed a long career as a Mormon apostle.[48]

Rees, as an executive with the *Deseret News*, may have been aware that Clark was the author of an unsigned editorial that ran in the church-owned newspaper before the 1936 presidential election, in which the newspaper endorsed the candidacy of Republican Alf Landon against incumbent Democrat Franklin D. Roosevelt. According to historian D. Michael Quinn, after the editorial ran, 1,200 *Deseret News* readers cancelled their subscriptions.[49] Utah voted with forty-five other states in reelecting FDR in a landslide. Utahns in the 1930s were devoutly LDS in their religious leanings, but both Rees and Clark found themselves in the minority with regard to Depression-era national politics. If Clark drove Rees's selection as Berlin mission president, he was nominating a kindred political spirit.

Another ability made Rees attractive as Mormonism's most important mission leader. While other mission presidents, including Kelly, had acquired sufficient linguistic skill to function effectively in a German-speaking nation, Rees had developed a command of the language unmatched by his peers. While serving as a young missionary in Switzerland at the turn of the twentieth century, Rees authored a German-language history of the LDS Church. German ecclesiastical units used it as a textbook for decades. Just before Rees departed for Germany, the *Deseret News* wrote: "He has been a lifetime student of the German language and has completely mastered it in both writing and conversation."[50] Ralph

Mark Lindsey, Rees's personal secretary for eighteen months, said of his boss: "He spoke excellent German and was always practicing his umlauts. I can see him now, manipulating his lips and his mouth, so that he could better enunciate all of the German diphthongs." An entry in Ida Rees's diary said: "Men came to me and asked if Alf was born in Germany. They [said] that otherwise he could not speak so well."[51] Actually, Rees was trilingual. On another occasion, Rees had the opportunity to speak French at a banquet in Berlin, where he had been seated next to the speaker, a native Frenchman. "He could talk French there as well as German," Ida wrote.[52] When Rees took academic coursework at the Université de Neuchâtel at the turn of the twentieth century, he was studying at a French-language university.

Alfred Cornelius Rees was a driven man. Undaunted determination, combined with political acumen and linguistic skill, made him highly effective in his new position. "He was a man of small stature," said Lindsey, "but in reality he was a human dynamo . . . he would always speak his mind and speak it properly."[53] Another missionary, Sterling Ryser, characterized Rees as "a very dynamic, energetic, full-of-life, go get 'em-type of person. We got the impression that he was going to stir things up."[54] At first, that meant making contacts among Germany's industrial elite and influential foreign firms doing business in Germany—in much the same way Rees had functioned as a business executive, trade association leader, and chamber of commerce officer in Utah. An entry in Ida Rees's diary reflected a typical week's schedule for her husband: "Today Alf went to see Mr. Otto Haas of the Carl Schurz Foundation and before that [this week] he had conferences with Mr. Mann of Brown Brothers Harriman Co., the head of the American Institute, the head of foreign languages at the University of Berlin, the head of the foreign ministry in charge of relations with America. Yesterday, he met a minister of the Reichstag and was present at a businessmen's luncheon."[55]

Meetings with Nazi party officials also received a high priority. Ida Rees wrote of consultations Rees had with officials of the government ministry of religion. Her diary entries may have misspelled their names and furnished incomplete identification of their positions within the ministry. Nevertheless, the reader can understand the value that Alfred Rees placed on hobnobbing with any Nazi official who would grant him an interview:

Alf met with Dr. Stahn and Dr. Haupt of the church ministry who consented to give a written statement that he could use with the local police that they refer all controversies between them and the elders to Alf. Through the courtesy of Dr. Hausberger he met Dr. Böhmes [sic] who controls the press affairs. He surprised all of us with his cordiality and invited him to a meeting at the Adlon [Hotel] to be his guest and sit at his table. At this affair the diplomats will be present to hear Dr. Rosenberg, a distinguished member of the Nazi [Party], explain the aims and purposes of that organization. Dr. Böhmes asked Alf to explain to him what Mormonism is. Has the promise of a future introduction.[56]

If the "Dr. Rosenberg" that Alfred Rees arranged to hear was Alfred Rosenberg, he would have met a true Nazi ideologue. Rosenberg had been an important adviser to Adolf Hitler since the 1923 Munich Beer Hall Putsch, and he was one of the eminent "philosophers" of National Socialism. He was a leading proponent of racial pseudoscience, which he promulgated in writing and speeches. He embraced the *Protocols of the Learned Elders of Zion* and issued numerous anti-Semitic pamphlets of his own, including one as early as 1919, entitled *The Tracks of the Jew Throughout the Ages*. In 1934 he established "The Institute for the Investigation of the Jewish Question" and declared that "Germany will regard the Jewish question as solved only after the last Jew has left the Greater German living space." In reality, the "Institute" served as a base for looting Jewish art collections, books, and other intellectual treasures as Jews fled Germany during the prewar years.[57] What may have interested Rees the most was Rosenberg's position as editor of the *Völkischer Beobachter* in the late 1930s, the official Nazi Party daily newspaper that the Berlin mission president eventually influenced. Rees did not live long enough to learn the fate of some of the Nazis whose favor he courted on behalf of the Mormon Church. In 1946 Alfred Rosenberg was hanged as a war criminal at Nuremberg.

Alfred and Ida Rees also tried to attend as many public Nazi Party events as they could fit into their schedule, especially if a meeting with church congregations could be incorporated. When they went to the 1937 Party Congress at Nuremberg, Ida wrote about attending the: "biggest show: soldiers, cannon, tanks, horses, bands, airplanes, bridge builders, search lights, guns, bombs . . . all went through various maneuvers which lasted three to four hours and showed precision, exactitude, obedience, and strength to a marked degree."

Then, without skipping a line in her journal, she added: "In the evening, we went to the Relief Society and were introduced and spoke." In the afternoon, the Reeses had spent hours witnessing a military procession staged by a godless state at its annual, bombastic party rally, at which the swastika replaced the cross and the Nazis extolled their liturgy of blood and soil. That evening, they attended a meeting of the LDS Church's women's auxiliary and spoke of the sacrificial blood of Jesus Christ. In their diaries, articles, and correspondence, the Reeses never expressed the slightest degree of dissonance between the church they served and the state they wished to accommodate. The same lack of editorial comment characterized their encounters with anti-Semitism. At the same 1937 Nazi Party Congress, Ida's diary entry mentioned that one day they "visited a show depicting the contention that the Jews had caused all of the ills in the world." Without beginning a new paragraph, she described that night's fireworks extravaganza: "Beautiful but hard to [watch]" because of its intense brightness.[58] She made no comment regarding whether the anti-Semitic exhibit was hard to watch.

Alfred C. Rees particularly seemed to enjoy the pageantry that surrounded one of Hitler's speeches, especially during the September 1937 visit of Italian fascist dictator Benito Mussolini. Alfred and Ida waited for hours to get a glimpse of *Il Duce* and the *Führer* during a joint public appearance at Maifeld, a large open field adjacent to Berlin's Olympic stadium. "We tried to see Mussolini but the crowd was so great that after standing a long time we barely glimpsed his blue uniform," Ida Rees wrote.[59] That was understandable; the Reeses were competing with eight hundred thousand other Berliners to watch the two fascist despots exchange trite verbal pleasantries.[60] Alfred Rees had an easier time when Hitler and Mussolini spoke to a capacity crowd inside the same stadium that evening. Earlier in the year, Rees had written a religiously themed article for the *Los Angeles Times*. Based on that single piece of freelance journalism, Rees had obtained a press credential as a "stringer" or part-time correspondent for the newspaper. His secretary at the time, Stanford H. Bingham, wrote in his diary: "President Rees managed to get one ticket... to the big Olympic stadium to hear Hitler and Mussolini talk tonight. It was right in the front row, so he felt pretty proud of that."[61]

Once Philemon Kelly left Berlin in December 1937, Rees had to balance his quest to cultivate influential Nazi friends with the day-to-day responsibilities of running a mission that utilized more than one hundred American and German missionaries and served thousands of congregants. Although Rees proved to be a competent mission president and ecclesiastical leader, there was never any doubt that he focused more on winning influence than winning souls. According to Ralph Mark Lindsey, Rees's secretary after Bingham, "He held conferences that were fantastic... but in and around Berlin [the members] did not understand him. He did not attempt to go out and speak too frequently with the Saints in the local area."[62]

The description of Berlin's Nazified social scene and business climate contained in Ida Rees's diary provides an important suggestion as to why Alfred Rees fought so hard to obtain the Berlin posting. Frankfurt would never have provided the level of official recognition, the access to power brokers, or the excitement that could be felt in Berlin during those heady years of National Socialism before the Second World War. Also, Frankfurt would have never furnished the opportunity for Rees's most noteworthy achievement: the one-time cooption of the *Völkischer Beobachter*, Nazi Party's official daily newspaper, as a vehicle to promote Mormonism in the Third Reich.

Mormonism in the Devil's Broadsheet

In November 1938, the *Völkischer Beobachter* published a front-page article entitled "A State Within a State: The American Parallel to the Question of the Jews in Germany."[63] Based on an 1857 book by Moritz Busch, *Die Mormonen*, it told the story of the Mormons' expulsion from Missouri and Illinois in the 1830s and 40s from the perspective of the hostile residents and officials who ejected them.[64] Previous mission presidents would have dismissed the article as merely another anti-Mormon story in the German press, but Rees saw an opportunity. Although the article did not depict nineteenth-century Mormons in a positive light, German

Mormons of the twentieth century were not its target. Instead, the author panned American criticism of Germany for the way the Jews were being treated. If nineteenth-century Americans could drive out their "undesirable element," the Mormons, why shouldn't twentieth-century Germany be able to excise itself of the Jews? Rees may have seen a way to use the article as an opening to Goebbels's propaganda ministry, with which he had been trying to cultivate contacts.

According to the mission secretary, Ralph Mark Lindsey, Rees pointedly removed the words "Jews, Israel, Zion, a promised land, our relationship with the Jews, etc.," from existing Mormon pamphlets and presented the revised editions to the government for comparison and approval. He also maintained that Mormon congregations had stopped singing certain hymns that the Nazis found objectionable. Previous mission presidents would have removed such wording from tracts and hymnals as a defensive measure, after having received notification from the government. Rees, instead, took the offensive and presented the changes to the government, presumably as a united front against Judaism. According to Lindsey, Rees forged an agreement with the propaganda ministry: "President Rees was told that the Church would be given good press in the *Völkischer Beobachter* . . . Hitler's newspaper and mouthpiece for the Nazi government."[65]

Contrary to that promise, and to Rees's surprise and indignation, in April 1939 the *Völkischer Beobachter* ran an old-style anti-Mormon article, one based on polygamy that could have appeared in a nineteenth-century German newspaper. Rees saw it as an opportunity. Said Lindsey: "This infuriated President Rees, and he said: 'I'm going to make hay out of this article.' He donned his hat and coat and marched right out of the mission office . . . and down to the propaganda ministry. He confronted them with the article and reminded them that they had agreed not to print any more anti-Mormon articles in their newspaper. President Rees was told he could write an article complimentary to the Mormons, and that they would print it in the most desirable location in the newspaper, either on the last page of the first section or the first page of the second section."[66]

For someone who had no moral objection to writing an article about his church for publication in the largest circulation Nazi daily newspaper, this was an ideal opportunity. Rees authored "In the Land of the Mormons," which began with a flattering description of the Salt Lake Valley and the courageous Mormons who escaped persecution by settling there in the late 1840s. Rees then depicted the Mormons as "a practical people . . . who can appreciate what the German people have endured as they passed through their hardships." Rees played upon German resentment of the allied blockade after the First World War, postwar occupation, and the Treaty of Versailles. Using a misquoted passage from Psalm 23, he wrote, "The German people have gone through the shadow of the valley [*sic*] since the World War." Rees linked the Mormon health code with the German government's "bold declaration of war against the use of alcohol and tobacco by the youth of Germany."

In another passage, mindful of Nazi pro-natalist policies, he stated that the Mormon people "are universally opposed to birth control, which they view as a contributing factor to the destruction of any race." He cited the LDS tithing system, which he likened to "the German ideal: community welfare before personal welfare." He paid tribute to Karl Maeser, the German who served as the first president of Brigham Young University. He then reminded his readers that J. Reuben Clark, a former American diplomat and the Mormons' second-in-command, often visited Germany and met with government banking officials in the interest of foreign creditors.[67]

Rees's article filled a whole page in the April 14, 1939, edition of the *Völkischer Beobachter*. It contained an aerial photograph of downtown Salt Lake City, showing the Mormon Temple, the stately church-owned hotel, the Hotel Utah, and the LDS Church headquarters building. Other pictures featured a portrait of Brigham Young, a map of the states that comprised the Mormon Culture Region, a picturesque scene from the campus of Brigham Young University, and the impressively lit Salt Lake Temple at night.

In 1939, the *Völkischer Beobachter*'s daily circulation approached one million copies. That was not enough exposure for Rees. According to Lindsey, "We clipped and pasted the article, making it a multi-page, five-by-seven inch pamphlet." Rees then took the new brochure back to the *Völkischer Beobachter* office, "and convinced them to print thousands of copies without charge, which were used in our mission as well as the West German Mission, as an extremely valuable mission tool."[68] The pamphlet bore the masthead logo of the Nazi daily newspaper complete with a swastika surrounded by an oak wreath, clutched in the talons of an eagle with its wings spread. Above that *Parteiadler* symbol, in seventy-two-point type, the article's headline, "*Im Lande der Mormonen*," provided the enduring linkage between Mormonism and Nazism that Rees had so fervently sought.

When Alfred C. Rees first appeared at the mission presidents' conference in Copenhagen in May 1938, he could only speak in vague generalities about "important, unprecedented concessions" he had extracted from the Nazis. When he returned for the 1939 summer conference in Lucerne, Switzerland, he could boast not only of how his agreement with the propaganda ministry had resulted in the *Völkischer Beobachter* article, but also of articles written by his missionaries and placed in smaller newspapers in Germany.[69] In a newsletter sent to his missionaries, Rees had been able to write enthusiastically about such local efforts: "Many of us, who only a few weeks ago, thought it impossible or of little value to reach the public press, are now glowing with satisfaction and pride in the fact that we have 'met the enemy and he is ours.' Already a number of your splendid articles have appeared, and others are in the course of preparation. In this way, hundreds of thousands are going to hear something good of 'Mormonism.' If your request has not already come in for help on your article, may we await it in the next few days? We are tingling in anticipation of a 'newspaper article in every field.'"[70]

According to an entry in Ida Rees's diary dated May 1, 1938, two weeks after the *Völkischer Beobachter* article: "All of the mission is rejoicing over the page Alf finally got in the *Beobachter*. It has taken lots of patient and persistent work to finally get in there. About twenty papers in other towns have also printed articles which were furnished from the office here."[71]

For one missionary stationed in Germany, Rees's article was literally something to write home about. Paul H. Lambert wrote a letter to the editor of the *Deseret News*, which the newspaper published in its weekly Church Section: "Every Mormon missionary is fairly walking on air, head high" because of the article, the young man said.[72]

Some of Rees's colleagues remained skeptical. M. Douglas Wood, who replaced Philemon Kelly as president of the West German Mission in Frankfurt, disagreed with Rees's approach to the Nazis. Wood was a schoolteacher and principal who came from an intellectual environment. His wife, Evelyn Wood, would later become nationally prominent as the speed reading coach for John F. Kennedy, through her Evelyn Wood

Reading Dynamics program. At the 1939 mission presidents' conference in Lucerne, Franklin J. Murdock noted frequent disagreement between Rees and Wood: "I would notice that these two men would converse and that they were quite opposed to each other's viewpoint. They couldn't agree on some of the things that were going on." Wallace F. Toronto, president of the Czechoslovakian Mission, told Rees about difficulties faced by his congregants and missionaries when the *Wehrmacht* occupied the Sudetenland in September 1938, and again in March 1939 when the Germans overran the rest of Czechoslovakia. Murdock said: "Here was Brother Toronto who had two missionaries in jail for six months . . . and he gave us the inside information on why those missionaries were put in jail, and the tremendous effort that he and the American embassy had put forth to get these boys out of jail.[73] So, Brother Toronto would listen to President Rees and then he'd say, 'Well, I couldn't trust them. That's the way I understand it. You'd better be careful, President Rees!'"[74]

Although he emphasized winning influential Nazi friends over winning converts, Rees did not neglect his administrative duties as a mission president. He enforced church discipline on errant members and missionaries. In December 1938, Rees called a special meeting of the Berlin East Branch in order to "discuss with several members of the branch, who had been causing a disturbance, the necessity of sustaining and supporting the authorities."[75] Routine excommunications continued to occur, such as in March 1938 when Paul Max Burkardt of Dresden lost his membership "for immorality."[76] In order to appease Nazi sensitivities, Rees cautioned his missionaries not to wear "tokens, badges, school pins, or emblems of any description. We are not to display our connection with any organization or association, school club or society." He admonished missionaries to "put your Kodaks aside until further notice," ostensibly to avoid conflicts that could be caused by American citizens photographing German soldiers. Then, he broached a subject that would become sensitive in the LDS and other Christian churches in the latter decades of the twentieth century. "If you will open your Missionary Handbooks on page 19 and read line 22," Rees began, "you will note that the authorities have issued a special warning. We love the little ones; we can express that love to them without touching or fondling them, without putting them on our knees. Let us accept and follow these instructions literally and unfailingly. Hands off!"[77]

Alfred C. Rees can be considered the most successful of Mormon mission president of the Nazi era because of the different approach he took to church–state relations. Prior to his arrival, mission presidents tried to avoid contact with the higher echelons of Hitler's government. They preferred to deal with lower-level police and party officials, to exploit differences in local enforcement of national laws, and to take advantage of rivalries between civil service officials and the new Nazi bureaucracy. If a local police commissioner or *Gauleiter* made a decision unfavorable to the Latter-day Saints, his ruling might be appealed to the next level. If the Mormons were still unsuccessful, they would comply with the edict and wait for a change of officials. Then, they would try again. Rees, confident of his ability to interact with the highest levels of Nazi officialdom, overhauled this strategy. While he still dealt with city and regional officials on a case-by-case basis, he did not hesitate to appeal to the most senior official in the Nazi Party with whom he could be granted an audience. Joseph Goebbels's propaganda ministry and the editors of the national Nazi Party daily newspaper were merely his most successful targets.

11

J. Reuben Clark
Mormon Ambassador Plenipotentiary and His Entourage

When Nazi Germany's *Reichsbank* president Hjalmar Schacht seated himself across from a heavyset American lawyer in August 1937, the colorless but cunning German minister knew he faced a formidable adversary. One month before Great Britain and France appeased Hitler in Munich, the *Führer's* financial wizard negotiated carefully with a well-connected representative of Germany's American creditors. J. Reuben Clark, Jr., a former undersecretary of state and U.S. ambassador to Mexico, had come to Berlin on a dual mission. By day, the retiring president of the Foreign Bondholders Protective Council represented the fleeting hopes of desperate small investors, who saw their life savings imperiled by a worldwide depression and a swaggering Teutonic behemoth that threatened to cast off its debts. By night, as second-in-command of the Church of Jesus Christ of Latter-day Saints, Clark encouraged and cajoled German Mormons and their American missionaries, whose fervent belief in Christ's impending millennial reign drove their determination to proselytize in Hitler's thousand-year Reich.

Clark, as First Counselor in the church's three-man First Presidency, led a procession of well-connected Americans who made their interests in Mormonism known to the leaders of Nazi Germany. No other foreign-based "new religion" in Germany was able to parade such an all-star cast in front of the Third Reich's powerbrokers. Politicians, church officers, and university administrators came to Germany from the Mormon Culture Region bearing the same tidings. For Latter-day Saints, their message was direct: Obey civil authority; one can be a good Latter-day Saint and a good citizen of Nazi Germany. For Hitler's government, their message was implied: Mormons are no threat to the Nazi rule, but they have powerful connections. Clark's legal, professional, and spiritual background made him the ideal emissary for this task.

One of Clark's biographers, Frank Fox, characterized the Utah farm boy turned international lawyer and statesman as a Mormon "stranger in Babylon."[1] Clark entered Columbia University Law School in 1903. At that time, many of his co-religionists regarded American territory east of the Wasatch Front as a godless republic that had murdered the prophet Joseph Smith. In 1906, in the midst of the U.S. Senate's confirmation battle regarding the seating of Mormon Apostle Reed Smoot, Clark joined Philander Knox's State Department as an assistant solicitor. By 1910, he had risen to the position of solicitor of state. Upon Democrat Woodrow Wilson's presidential inauguration in 1913, Clark, a partisan Republican, entered private law practice. Eventually, he established offices in New York, Washington, D.C., and Salt Lake City.

Clark then embarked upon a series of multiyear arbitrations with foreign governments that qualified him to represent the interests of America's foreign bondholders—and to confront Hjalmar Schacht—two decades later. As State Department solicitor during the Taft administration, Clark conducted an arbitration that eventually settled accumulated claims between the United States and Great Britain valued at more than ten billion dollars. Some dated back as far as the War of 1812. After the change of presidential administrations, as a lawyer in private practice, he became chief counsel for the American side. Following service as a major in the judge advocate general's office during World War I, Clark assumed responsibility for an arbitration board that tackled a stickier mess—American claims resulting from the Mexican Revolution of 1910–17.

In 1926, Clark's experience with the Mexican-American Claims Commission led to his appointment as Ambassador Dwight Morrow's legal advisor at the embassy in Mexico City. Clark's yearlong stint as undersecretary of state began in 1928, just in time to pen the document for which he is best known among diplomatic historians. The "Memorandum on the Monroe Doctrine" served as a necessary precursor to Senate ratification of the Kellogg-Briand Pact. It freed the Coolidge administration from military obligations in accordance with the Roosevelt Corollary to the Monroe Doctrine.² Earlier, Clark had written another historically significant but lesser-known paper, "Right to Protect Citizens in Foreign Countries by Landing Forces," in his capacity as solicitor of state in 1912. Drafted to justify William Howard Taft's desire to send troops south of the border during the first years of the Mexican Revolution, an intervention that would not take place until Woodrow Wilson's administration, it became a standard reference for subsequent presidents—including John F. Kennedy, who consulted it during the Cuban Missile Crisis the year after Clark's death.³

Clark's experience as a lawyer in government service and private practice, as undersecretary of state, and later as Herbert Hoover's ambassador to Mexico, constituted an attractive resume that impressed both the ruling triumvirate of the LDS Church and FDR's new administration, which kept a campaign promise by chartering the Foreign Bondholders Protective Council. The Mormon Church had never before sought the services of such a well-connected and experienced civil servant to fill a top leadership position. When Roosevelt's election in 1932 swept Republican political appointees out of office, Church President Heber J. Grant saw an unprecedented opportunity to enlist Clark for the task of modernizing church governance. As historian D. Michael Quinn wrote: "Clark drew upon his secular background to introduce outside research, position papers, and extended discussion" into a previously informal church decision-making process.⁴ For legions of beleaguered American small bondholders, J. Reuben Clark represented their last, desperate hope of recouping investments precipitously made during the helter-skelter, deregulated financial climate of the Roaring Twenties. Grant allowed Clark to split his time between professionalizing church administrative procedures in Salt Lake City and attending to the needs of the nation's small investors from the Council's Washington, D.C., office.

As one who would deal with high-level officials of the German finance ministry, and visit Germany periodically, Clark was positioned to watch over and attend to the needs of the Mormon missions in Germany. Clark visited Germany twice during the Nazi period, in August 1937 and June 1938, but his interaction with Germany's government extended back to 1934 when Hjalmar Schacht threatened that Germany would repudiate its foreign debt.⁵ It was the responsibility of more prominent American diplomats, such as Ambassador William E. Dodd, to advocate the interests of Wall Street, particularly the investment banks that had loaned hundreds of millions to Germany as part of the Dawes and Young rescue plans.[6] It was up to J. Reuben Clark to protect the millions of Main Street investors who had unwisely risked less substantial sums, often their meager life savings, to purchase financial instruments with nebulous prospects for profitability—such as Weimar Republic municipal swimming pool bonds.[7] The Council's constant advocacy on behalf of America's small investors made J. Reuben Clark a familiar name in the German ministry of finance. That not only warned the Nazis that the Mormons had powerful friends in America, but it also provided more tangible benefits.

Clark was able to help the Mormon hierarchy fight a *Reichsbank* decision in October 1934, when the Germans suddenly revoked a privilege enjoyed by parents in the Mormon Culture Region who had been able to finance their sons' missions by purchasing German currency at a discounted rate.[8] When the American Express Company notified the German Mormon missions that American parents could no longer purchase "Registered *Reichsmarks*," the First Presidency in Salt Lake City appealed to its colleague who was temporarily situated on the East Coast, attending to the bondholders' interests.[9] Clark used his contacts in the State Department to effect a solution. He urged Grant to write to Secretary of State Cordell Hull, and he informed the appropriate undersecretary that Grant's appeal was on its way.[10] Hull subsequently instructed Ambassador William E. Dodd to intervene.[11] In June 1935, the secretary of state informed Grant that the American influence with the *Reichsbank* had prevailed. The parents of American Mormon missionaries could, once again, purchase German Marks at a thirty-three percent discount.[12] Throughout the process, Clark corresponded with his old colleagues in the State Department, who made sure that the church's request was taken seriously and that the paperwork flowed efficiently.[13]

J. Reuben Clark's memorandum of his August 5, 1937, meeting with Hjalmar Schacht reveals no mention of Clark's interest in the German Mormon Church. Instead, Schacht assured Clark that Germany desired to pay its foreign obligations, provided that a new trade agreement between his country and the United States could be negotiated—one that would include most favored nation status and advantageous terms for debt payment. In addition to the August 5, 1937, meeting, Clark held several other conferences regarding bonded indebtedness with important

German officials, such as Rudolf Brinkmann, a state secretary in the ministry of economic affairs, and Karl Blessing, a *Reichsbank* executive board member.[14] While Clark focused on convincing his German hosts to pay their financial obligations, he could not lose sight of other visiting Americans who served as his rivals in the debt collection process. Representatives of large investment banks, such as Henry Mann of National City Bank, argued for the Wall Street contingent of Germany's foreign creditors, whose proposed solution to Germany's debt problems would not have necessarily coincided with Main Street's. For example, Clark argued strongly with Schacht and Blessing that Germany should settle its bonded indebtedness prior to seeking a trade agreement with the United States.[15] The larger banks, unconcerned with an ordinary American who may have risked several thousand dollars during the helter-skelter investment environment of the 1920s, would have profited from a more expeditiously negotiated trade treaty.

Clark did not have to discuss religion with any of these officials in order to advance the cause of Mormonism in Nazi Germany. When he was not admonishing his German hosts to pay their debts, or watching closely the actions of rival debt collectors, Clark found the time to preach the gospel of obedience to German Mormons and their American missionaries. While in Berlin, Clark spoke at two different Mormon Sunday sacrament meetings conducted at the Central and Moabit Branches. His message was the same at each: According to the mission's records, "He stressed the necessity of harmony among the Germany Saints and the admonition to remain in this goodly land and build up the Kingdom of God."[16] In other words, German Mormons should forget about immigrating to the American Zion, and instead build a Mormon Zion in Nazi Germany. Like America's bondholders, the Mormon Church had equity in Nazi Germany that its leadership did not want to write off.

Clark returned to Nazi Germany the next June, and on this occasion he divided his time equally between bondholder and church business. He conferred with U.S. Ambassador William E. Dodd at the American embassy. He held meetings with Rudolf Brinkmann from the German ministry of economic affairs and spoke with *Reichsbank* Chairman Hjalmar Schacht by telephone.[17] Germany, aggressively building its military might and pursuing a bombastic, expansionist foreign policy, had shown little desire to settle its foreign debts. This was the summer between the

Anschluss, Germany's forceful occupation of Austria in March 1938, and the Munich Conference the following September, when Great Britain and France capitulated to Hitler and allowed the German occupation of the Czechoslovakian Sudetenland. Thus, Clark set about preparing Germany's Mormons to survive on their own while making sure that if war came, the American missionaries would evacuate in an orderly fashion. The lessons of the First World War, when Mission President Hyrum Valentine had to make a hazardous trip into wartime Germany carrying a suitcase stuffed with cash to fund the evacuation of his missionaries, were not lost on this astute lawyer, diplomat, and prelate.

On the evening of June 25, 1938, Clark assembled the mission presidents from Berlin, Frankfurt, Prague, Amsterdam, and Basel. After dinner at the stately Kaiserhof Hotel on Wilhelmplatz, they gathered for Clark's briefing.[18] Clark discussed an evacuation plan that would dispatch the missionaries to temporary safe havens in nonbelligerent countries should war break out. He chose the Netherlands, Switzerland, and Denmark as staging points, from which the missionaries would proceed to port cities for their transatlantic passage to the United States.

That evacuation plan received an early test, an event that missionaries later called the "fire drill evacuation."[19] On September 13, 1938, after a provocative speech by Adolf Hitler, the Czechoslovakian government declared martial law to quell civil disorder in the rapidly escalating dispute with Germany over the Sudetenland. The next day, the State Department issued an advisory that urged all Americans to leave the potential war zone. Clark, back in the United States and monitoring the crisis with the help of his former State Department colleagues, was probably a driving force behind the First Presidency's telegram that ordered all missionaries in Germany, Czechoslovakia, and Austria to evacuate.[20] In Berlin, Mission President Alfred C. Rees received notification of the church hierarchy's decision through the American embassy.[21]

On September 15, 1938, as British Prime Minister Neville Chamberlain met Hitler in Berchtesgaden, Americans began leaving the German-speaking missions. Those assigned to the Berlin-based East German Mission went to Copenhagen, where Mission President Mark B. Graff had arranged housing.[22] Some twenty-four elders from the Frankfurt-based West German Mission also went to Copenhagen. The remaining forty-one sought refuge in the Netherlands, where Mission President Franklin J. Murdock provided accommodations in The Hague.[23] Czechoslovakian Mission personnel went to Basel where they received lodging from Swiss-Austrian Mission President Thomas E. McKay.[24] Most remained in their countries of refuge until the end of September, when Chamberlain proclaimed on the steps of 10 Downing Street: "Peace for our time."[25]

The next day, as Hitler's troops marched into the Sudetenland, the Mormon hierarchy began to sound the all-clear signal. By October 4, all missionaries assigned to the West German Mission had returned to their posts.[26] One day later, all missionaries from the East German Mission were back after almost three weeks in Copenhagen.[27] In their absence, church business had transpired routinely. Acting East German Mission President Herbert Klopfer, substituting for Alfred C. Rees, conducted a district conference in Schneidemühl. Local German priesthood leaders successfully ran weekend conferences in the Chemnitz Central and Mittweida branches and in the Berlin-East branch. In the West German Mission, Frederick L. Biehl of the Ruhr District reported to mission headquarters in Frankfurt, ready to assume the mission presidency as the designated replacement for M. Douglas Wood, if the Americans did not return.

Some returning missionaries encountered a skeptical reception from their German congregants. "We were criticized rather roundly by some of the members for being babies and having to leave," said Ralph Mark Lindsey. He said the German members did not understand that the American State Department could no longer guarantee their safety in Germany and that church authorities in Salt Lake City, such as J. Reuben Clark, had made the decision.[28] Part of that resentment may have resulted from the patriotic feelings expressed by German members. "Upon our return," Donald M. Petty said, "there was this feeling of jubilation among the Germans as a whole because of their success in negotiating the Sudeten 'Anschluss.'"[29]

J. Reuben Clark had come to Germany twice, each time with a dual agenda. Although his pursuit of relief for America's small bondholders had met with disappointment, his advocacy of his Mormon co-religionists produced unqualified success. Although Clark once expressed the fear that Mormon missionaries would be "thrown into concentration camps," no such concerns prompted an early withdrawal from Hitler's Reich.[30] As soon as it became clear that the missionaries would not be caught in a battle zone, Clark approved their redeployment to their German bases—from where they did not budge until Clark's former State Department colleagues warned him that war was imminent five days before the *Wehrmacht* invaded Poland on September 1, 1939.

An appreciation for the Mormons' successful campaign to accommodate and ingratiate themselves with the Nazi government can best be attained by comparing Clark's success in Germany with that of a rival American sectarian leader who visited the Third Reich. In June 1933, five months after Hitler assumed power, the leader of the Jehovah's Witnesses, Joseph Franklin Rutherford, visited Berlin. He assembled a convention of seven thousand Witnesses who unanimously adopted a defiant document they called "A Declaration of Facts." The Witnesses sent copies to every official, high- or low-ranking, in the government whom they could identify, and they had more than two and one-half million copies printed. Reaction was swift and virulent, and Rutherford became *persona non grata* in Germany while his German co-religionists suffered immense persecution.[31]

By contrast, when the Mormons' J. Reuben Clark traveled to Germany in 1937 and 1938, he expeditiously cleared customs because of his diplomatic passport—a perquisite from his State Department days.[32] He was equally welcome in the offices of the American ambassador and the *Reichsbank* chairman. Representatives of the world's largest investment banks and brokerage houses respected him as a worthy competitor. At the end of a day's meetings, he was free to use the American embassy transcription equipment to record the memoranda of his meetings.[33] Management of the Kaiserhof Hotel, the upper floors of which served as Nazi Party headquarters in 1932–33 and which Hitler frequented afterward, was happy to accept his dinner reservation and rent a room that he used to meet with mission presidents.[34] He was welcome to speak at any assembly of the German Mormon Church without interference from, but undoubtedly with the knowledge of, the Gestapo and the civil police. He, like others in the parade of Mormon Church and American government officials who visited Nazi Germany, were welcome guests of the state. It respected his influence.

J. Reuben Clark

The Prophet, the Swastika, and the Mormon Entourage in Nazi Germany

The prophet, seer, and revelator Heber J. Grant was also an appreciated visitor when he spoke to an assembly of eight hundred Mormons in front of a large swastika banner at a rented banquet hall in Frankfurt on July 8, 1937. The building belonged to the National Socialist Teacher's League, the *Nationalsozialistische Lehrerbund*. Like any meeting place available for rental in Nazi Germany, it came equipped with a large national flag, this one red with a black swastika in the center of a white circle. Prudent tenants did not take down Nazi flags during this period in German history, although the German Mormons probably would not have been motivated to do so. Grant spoke of spiritual topics but encouraged the faithful to pray and be persistent in their daily work.[35] The message was consistent with others delivered to Latter-day Saints outside of the United States during the Great Depression. Work hard, obey the law of the land, and build up the church at home rather than emigrating. One year earlier in Berlin, on May 30, 1936, approximately seven hundred of the faithful had heard European Mission President Joseph F. Merrill speak to a combined assemblage of the boys' and girls' church youth groups, the Mutual Improvement Association. Likewise, Merrill had spoken in front of a large swastika flag.[36]

On both occasions, the Mormon-owned Salt Lake City daily newspaper, the *Deseret News*, ran prominent pictures of the speakers at the rostrum with the Nazi flag in the background. The message was abundantly clear: At a time when the same newspaper was publishing wire service articles describing the plight of Jews in Hitler's regime, the church-controlled general circulation newspaper had no reservations about associating Mormonism's spiritual message with Nazism's stark symbolism. If the prophet or another esteemed church leader appeared in a picture, it presumably mitigated the potentially objectionable message sent by including the banner of Hitler's party.

Two veterans of the United States Senate, Reed Smoot and his successor, Elbert Thomas, also left their marks on the Mormons' effort in Nazi Germany. One wrote a German-language article, under the guise of spiritual guidance, that urged his fellow believers to participate in an important activity that exploited a common interest of the LDS Church and the Nazi state. The other, visiting Germany on an academic fellowship earned during his years as a university professor, toured the country talking to as many influential people as he could and showed the flag of Mormonism in a swastika-bannered nation, but also gathering information that would profoundly affect his opinion later.

On March 1, 1935, the LDS bimonthly periodical, *Der Stern*, contained an article written by Reed Smoot, "A Friend of Germany," in which the Mormon apostle who served five senatorial terms seemed to pontificate mostly on spiritual themes. Embedded within his message, a religiously aware Mormon could detect familiar verbiage that encouraged genealogical research—which was also a priority among the Nazis. In quoting from the Old Testament book of Malachi (4:6), Smoot cited a verse that Mormons interpret differently from Jews and mainline Christians. When Smoot urged his readers to follow the admonition of the prophet Elijah, "to turn the hearts of the children to their fathers and the hearts of the fathers to their children," he was urging his co-religionists to do the family history research necessary to fill our their pedigree charts and family group records.[37] When Smoot said, "in the Temples of the Latter-day Saints and among this people, the decrees of the Gospels regarding the sanctity of the living and the dead will be carried out," he was exhorting German Mormons to submit the results of their ancestral research to the Holy Temple so that deceased relatives could receive the ordinances of salvation.[38] In case a spiritual neophyte did not understand those hints, he also stated, bluntly, "that the Prophet Elijah has come shortly after the opening of this last dispensation of the Gospels about one hundred years ago and that in connection to this coming the number of genealogists who are seeking their forefathers has risen to 100,000."[39] This referred to the founding of the LDS Church in 1830 and Joseph Smith's subsequent emphasis on genealogical research and temple ordinances.

Having stated his message in scriptural terms familiar to his LDS readers, Smoot faced one additional problem. The Nazis who read the article, who valued genealogical research for different reasons, probably would not comprehend his spiritual code language. Smoot solved that problem by introducing an appeal to German resentment regarding the settlement of the First World War, plus a bit of old-fashioned anti-Semitism, into his biographical profile that accompanied the article. It described the former senator's "unremitting and energetic [work] for the freeing of Germany from the unjust demands of the Versailles Treaty." Smoot continued: "France was acting like the Jew, Shylock, in demanding the last pound of flesh . . . of Germany."[40]

Smoot's appeal for German Mormons to do their genealogical research occurred more than a year and a half after Hitler's rubber-stamp Reichstag disqualified Jews from civil service employment, but several months prior to adoption of the 1935 Nuremberg Race Laws that stripped Germany's Jewish population of its citizenship. It transpired in the midst of what historian Eric Ehrenreich identified as the adoption of a plethora of new racial laws, numbering more than two thousand.[41] It appeared in the official German-language newspaper of the Mormon missions one full year after Swiss-German Mission President Francis Salzner delivered four consecutive weekly sermons at various district conferences on the topic of "Three Generations," an appeal for his congregants to perform and submit the results of their genealogical research.[42]

Before Smoot's successor, Senator Elbert Thomas, toured Germany in 1934 on an Oberlander fellowship, he had spoken with Franklin D. Roosevelt. The president urged Thomas to use the ten-week trip, which was his reward for a distinguished academic career at the University of Utah prior to his Senate election, as a fact-finding mission. "We are doing just what President Roosevelt told us to do," wrote his wife, Edna Harker Thomas, "meet and talk with the educated people." Although the notes Edna Thomas made during their trip lack detail, they reflect the seriousness with which Elbert Thomas undertook his assignment.

By the end of his first week in Berlin, Thomas had spoken not only with U.S. Ambassador William E. Dodd, but also with academic and political colleagues on the Saar issue, women's rights, and "religious questions." On his third day in Germany, Thomas "called upon a German Jew, Dr. Newman."[43] He made the rounds of local Mormon congregations, spoke during services, conferred with German-Austrian Mission President Oliver Budge, and took young missionaries to dinner. However, unlike some other prominent Mormons who visited the Third Reich, Thomas appears to have pursued additional interests. The seriousness with which he approached his study of Nazi Germany is evident by the travelogue provided by Edna Thomas's notes. When in Dresden, they visited the International Hygiene Exposition, at which the Mormon missionaries had staged an exhibit on the Word of Wisdom, the LDS health code, in

1930. By the time Thomas visited in 1934, the Nazis had transformed the museum into a propaganda exhibition for its racial policies and for the promotion of eugenics. Elbert and Edna also toured men's and women's labor camps run by the *Reichsarbeitsdienst*, the Nazi Labor Front, and noted comparisons with the New Deal's Civilian Conservation Corps.[44]

Thomas visited hospitals, spoke at the American Chamber of Commerce, consulted with the U.S. consul generals in the other German cities he visited, and conferred with academic colleagues at the University of Heidelberg. When they saw Hitler at the Oberammergau Passion Play in the Bavarian mountains, Edna Thomas noted the sighting in her diary. But the couple did not exhibit the fascination with the *Führer* that Albert C. Rees demonstrated several years later in Berlin.[45] In fact, once Elbert Thomas returned to the United States in late September 1934, he became a rare Mormon critic of the Third Reich. While in Germany, at the time the Third Reich was intensifying its crackdown on another American sect, the Jehovah's Witnesses, Senator Elbert Thomas—like J. Reuben Clark—served as a reminder that powerful and influential Americans backed the Mormons.

PART III

Beacons of Mormon Memory in Nazi Germany

12

The Second World War and Its Aftermath

One Sunday morning in December 1943, while serving as a *Wehrmacht* occupation soldier in Denmark, Karl Herbert Klopfer felt an overwhelming desire to attend Mormon religious services—but he did not know where the local branch met. Dressed in his full military uniform, he walked the streets of the Jutland peninsula town of Esbjerg, humming an LDS hymn loudly enough to attract attention. A young girl approached and asked if he were a Mormon. Klopfer accepted the youth's invitation to follow her to sacrament meeting, where he surrendered his gun belt to the branch president at the door. Invited to address the small congregation, he avoided the use of German—as he perceived that his co-religionists loathed the language of the invaders. Instead, he delivered a spiritual message in English, which another congregant translated into Danish. His remarks struck sympathetic chords with the small LDS congregation. Klopfer told of how he had lost his home, the Mormon mission headquarters across from Berlin's Tiergarten Park, and all of his possessions to Allied bombing raids. But he was grateful that his family had been spared. He professed his love for his fellow Mormons and his belief in Joseph Smith's "restored" gospel of Jesus Christ.[1]

Karl Herbert Klopfer is a memory beacon. He typifies the kind of German Mormon who is treasured in the collective wartime memory of the faithful, when Latter-day Saints became combatants, survivors, and victims. As the president of the Mormons' East German Mission during the Second World War, he presents a stark contrast to his American predecessors. Unlike Alfred C. Rees, who aggressively sold Mormonism to Nazi officials, Klopfer gained privileges for the church without lofty pretentiousness. After being drafted into the German Army in February 1940, while serving as a paymaster with the rank of a non-commissioned officer, Klopfer convinced his superiors to grant him a private room with a telephone line. From Fürstenwalde military base east of Berlin, Klopfer ran the affairs of the mission by phone and through weekend visits to Berlin until he deployed abroad in 1943.[2]

Before the war, Klopfer was a well-loved, faithful, full-time employee of the Berlin-based Mormon mission. A skilled English and French linguist, Klopfer often received the flattering praise of his fellow countrymen, who complimented him on his command of German. His English skills were so proficient that Germans often thought he was an American who had acquired a remarkable fluency in German. When Klopfer was reported missing in action on the Russian front late in the war, German Mormons reacted with sadness. They recalled that he—like so many others among them—had missed his chance to avoid the war by emigrating. In 1928, Klopfer had intended to migrate to Utah, but postponed his plans when German-Austrian Mission President Hyrum Valentine called him to serve a mission.[3] Then he fell in love and eventually, after a four-year courtship by correspondence, married a girl he had met on his mission. After Hitler took power, going to America became impossible, as the law prohibited emigration by a military-age Aryan male. He instead served as a trusted confidant and translator for the American mission presidents based in Berlin. After the war, the Salt Lake City Mormon leadership tried to learn the fate of its favorite German son.[4] It was not until 1948 that Klopfer's widow learned that her husband had died of starvation in Russian captivity in March 1945.[5]

Klopfer's installation as a Mormon memory beacon occurred during the last decade of the twentieth century, when the church's collective memory of the Nazi epoch shifted. After November 1989, when the Berlin Wall fell and the reunification of Germany began, Latter-day Saints no longer felt compelled to restrain their writing of church history in consideration of the German-speaking Mormons who lived behind the Iron Curtain. As European communism began to fall, so did the Mormon Church's reluctance to glorify many dutiful former *Wehrmacht* soldiers. In June 1990, the church-owned *Deseret News*, through its full-color Saturday religious supplement, the *Church News*, introduced Karl Herbert

Klopfer as an example of a righteous Latter-day Saint who bravely fought and died for Germany in the Second World War. "Enemy Soldier in the Pulpit," written by Klopfer's son, emphasized the danger that the East German Mission President accepted when he worshiped in uniform with Danish civilians and relinquished his pistol to the congregational leader. Rather than engage in outright defiance against Hitler and overtly violate the Twelfth Article of Faith, as did Helmuth Hübener and his co-conspirators, Klopfer obediently answered the call of his country while maintaining service to his church. The faith-promoting article also emphasized that religious ties trumped wartime enmity. Said one Danish Mormon who was in attendance that Sunday morning in Jutland, "It was wonderful to see a man in the uniform we hated speak with so much love for us."[6]

Beacons of Memory: The Prewar Evacuation of American Missionaries

For most combatants in Europe, the Second World War began on September 1, 1939, when Hitler's army invaded Poland. For Mormons in Germany, the war effectively started one week earlier on August 23. From his office in Salt Lake City, connected by phone to his former State Department colleagues in Washington, D.C., First Counselor J. Reuben Clark monitored shocking events happening half a world away. The Mormons' second-in-command, a former undersecretary of state and ambassador, listened with apprehension to reports of a bilateral treaty being signed in Moscow. For the veteran diplomat and keen observer of international affairs, the Molotov-Ribbentrop pact between the Soviet Union and Germany could mean only one thing: war was inevitable. The unlikely alliance of a fascist and a communist state meant that Germany and the Soviet Union would divide the spoils. Several hours later, the First Presidency ordered all missionaries in Europe to evacuate.[7]

Having practiced the evacuation drill one year before, in the midst of the Sudetenland crisis, the elders who staffed the two German missions were well prepared to leave. Missionaries from the Berlin-based East German Mission began boarding trains. Within two days, all had arrived safely in Copenhagen. Joseph Fielding Smith, a member of the Quorum of the Twelve who was traveling in Germany at the time, supervised arrangements in Denmark. Within weeks, he dispatched the young Americans across the Atlantic from various European ports. Alfred C. Rees had returned to Utah one week prior to the evacuation because of ill health.[8] Despite the fact that his designated replacement, acting East German Mission President Thomas E. McKay, was in Basel, Switzerland, when Clark's telegram arrived on August 24, 1939, the mass exodus from the Berlin-based mission occurred without incident.[9]

That was not the case with the evacuation of American missionaries from the West German Mission in Frankfurt, which by 1939 also included the mission districts in Austria. Shortly after Mission President M. Douglas Wood's elders began traveling north, the Dutch government limited entry by foreigners. Relying on its experience during the First World War, when The Netherlands had absorbed a flow of refugees that had taxed resources, Dutch officials denied passage to any noncitizen who did not have adequate funds and proof of onward passage. Later, a few days before the war began, Dutch officials closed their border altogether. The Netherlands LDS Mission in The Hague had been designated as a primary staging area for missionaries, as it had been during the September 1938 "fire drill" evacuation. The Mormon evacuation plan had called for missionaries to receive their steamship tickets at their staging areas; thus, when they could not show evidence of a ticket out of the country, the Dutch border authorities denied them entry.

Traveling in small groups and running short of funds, many missionaries had to improvise. A German law that prohibited taking more than ten marks out of the country aggravated the missionaries' financial situation. Many, expecting the same kind of routine, uninterrupted journey they had enjoyed one year earlier, had made last-minute expenditures on souvenirs and consumer goods in order to comply with the currency export law. When thirty-one young elders did not report on schedule to their designated rendezvous points, Mission President Wood assigned a senior missionary, Norman George Seibold, to search for the missing young Americans amid the confusion of a country mobilizing for war, and to provide funds for their travel to alternative destinations—such as Denmark. He dispatched Seibold with a wad of cash and a handful of steamship tickets to roam German border cities and rail depots, looking for stranded comrades.

Another group of missionaries, detained by Dutch authorities at the border, managed to communicate by telephone with the mission president in The Hague. Franklin J. Murdock sent a young elder, John Robert Kest, with funds that would allow the detained missionaries to make other travel arrangements. Kest arrived at the border, only to find that the young Mormons he sought had been deported back into Germany. On impulse, Kest decided to pursue them into Germany in spite of the fact that he did not have a visa to enter the country. Despite a confrontation with German authorities, during which Kest was searched and ordered to leave the country—instructions he disobeyed—he located the missionaries he sought at a hotel.[10]

Although most of the missionaries found their way out of Germany without assistance, later accounts described their chance encounters with Seibold and Kest as "miraculous." Seibold and Kest became memory beacons in the scholarly and popular literature of the missionary withdrawal from the Third Reich. The evacuation of Mormon missionaries became an important nexus for the research of BYU professor of religious education David F. Boone, who wrote his master's thesis on the subject and has published several articles and a book chapter on the missionary evacuation.[11]

The evacuation also inspired a faithful Mormon freelance writer, Terry Montague, to undertake a research project that resulted in the publication of a 148-page, softcover book, *Mine Angels Round About*—based entirely on the few days of confusion that resulted from the Dutch government's decision to limit passage through its territory. In the late 1970s and early 80s, the author searched extensively for veterans of the West German Mission evacuation. She interviewed a few who lived close to her home in rural Idaho and many who lived in Utah, and queried others as far away as Israel and New Zealand.[12] The result was a faith-promoting chronicle of escape from the rapidly tightening clutches of war; every obstacle in their path generated an opportunity for God to intervene miraculously.

When Mission President M. Douglas Wood first learned of the evacuation order, he was in Hanover, a six-hour drive from mission headquarters in Frankfurt. Wishing to fly instead, Wood received discouraging news from his hotel desk clerk, who said all flights were booked and that airline tickets must be reserved weeks in advance. Miraculously, according to Montague's chronicle, Wood was able to obtain the last two seats on an airline flight leaving that afternoon.[13] When Emma Rosenhan, one of the few single female American missionaries assigned to the Frankfurt-based Mormon mission, learned she must evacuate, her German branch president was "inspired" to advise her to purchase a ticket for trans-channel passage to London. Thus, when she arrived at the Dutch border, her onward ticket allowed her entry into The Netherlands that her male missionary companions were denied.[14] Missionaries sent to search for stranded colleagues in crowded, chaotic train stations, according to Montague, seemed to sense when they should sing or whistle the first few notes of well-known church songs, such as "Do What is Right." That attracted the attention of colleagues who would not have otherwise met their rescuers.[15]

Although Montague's book primarily serves the needs of faithful readers seeking religious inspiration, the oral history interviews she conducted produced two important historical insights into the days that preceded the onset of the Second World War. Both occurred in train stations. The first revealed the pandemonium that accompanied the mobilization of Germany's army for war and the rush of civilians to escape the hostilities. Mormon missionaries pushed and shoved their way onto overcrowded trains that offered standing-room-only accommodations to passengers, some of whom—because of age or infirmity—found themselves trampled or crushed. Taxi drivers, railroad porters, and restaurateurs engaged in price gouging, and helpless passengers found themselves at the mercy of ill-tempered soldiers who used the power of their uniform to enforce their own boarding priorities. Often, passengers would travel in cattle-car conditions from one town to the next, perhaps only twenty miles away, only to be evicted from the train when authorities commandeered it for military transport. Confusion reigned among the deposed passengers when no official at the *Bahnhof* could predict the arrival of the next train headed north, or whether space would be available.[16]

In a tragic series of historical vignettes, Montague's missionaries described the desperate plight of many Jews who tried to escape the Third Reich at the last minute by using the German rail system. Missionary Frank Knutti remembered a conversation with a small Jewish boy, who told him that his family had been traveling for days, trying to escape Germany—but had been repeatedly turned away at border crossings with Germany's neighboring countries. They would try Denmark next, but it would be their last hope.[17] On the Dutch border that adjoins the Rhineland city of Emmerich, missionaries negotiating their way into The Netherlands observed the plight of several Jewish families seeking freedom from Hitler's empire: "The Jews were hysterical; they argued loudly and many wept, but the guards refused to allow them to leave the train. One Jewish man, his wife and children looking on in despair, got down on his hands and knees, clasping a Dutch guard's feet, and pleaded in vain that the guard take mercy on his family, but to no avail."[18]

In the city of Rheine in Westphalia, missionaries Richard Poll and Burt Horsley encountered an eighteen-year-old Jewish woman, the daughter of a wealthy foreign banker. Despite her possession of a valid Swiss passport and sufficient funds, she could not buy a ticket out of Germany. Stationmasters refused to sell tickets to a Jew. The missionaries agreed to help her but were stunned by her proposed solution. She asked one of them to marry her, arguing that the Germans would never refuse passage to the wife of an American citizen. She offered to pay handsomely for this special favor. When each missionary incredulously refused, she proposed another harebrained solution. The three of them would buy a car with her funds and they would run a border checkpoint at high speed. Finally, Poll and Horsley suggested a more sensible alternative. They went to the ticket window, and with her funds purchased rail passage for her, along with a ferryboat ticket to England. Grateful, she departed.[19]

Compared to the plight of Jews trying to escape the Nazis, the evacuating Mormon missionaries were never in danger. The greatest threat they encountered was a shortage of funds. If they had remained in Germany after the onset of hostilities, there is no evidence that they would have been in immediate peril. The United States did not enter the war for more than two years after Germany's invasion of Poland. Undoubtedly, American citizens were able to leave Germany after the war broke out. The greatest impediment was obtaining reservations on sold-out transatlantic ocean liners, not antagonism by the German government. Nevertheless, the relative ease with which Mormon missionaries were able to book steamship passage back to the United States became another reason to credit God's favorable intervention. J. Reuben Clark, predominantly responsible for triggering the evacuation plan, did not hesitate to thank divine providence for the success of the endeavor. Speaking in April 1940 at a church general conference, he said: "The whole group was moved from the disturbed areas in Europe to the United States. . . . The entire group was evacuated from Europe . . . when tens of thousands of Americans were besieging the ticket offices of the great steamship companies for passage, and the Elders had no reservations. Every time a group was ready to embark there was available the necessary space, even though efforts to reserve space a few hours beforehand failed."[20]

The success of the Mormon missionary evacuation from Europe at the onset of the Second World War can be attributed to fastidious planning, a successful rehearsal during the Sudetenland crisis, and disciplined execution. Its only hitch resulted from the failure to study the history of Holland's reaction to the flood of refugees that besieged its borders during the First World War, and the inability to anticipate that the Dutch would limit passage when war threatened again. Nevertheless, the evacuation was an overall success. Rather than relying on divine intervention, Mormons followed the counsel of St. Augustine—later incorporated into the Catechism of the Catholic Church—which Latter-day Saints subsequently attributed to Brigham Young: "Pray as if everything depends on the Lord, but work as if everything depends on you."

Battlefield Beacons: Courageous and Faithful Mormon *Wehrmacht* Soldiers

In the first decade of the twenty-first century, Jared Kobs was the kind neighbor every resident of suburban Salt Lake City cherished. A retired furniture upholsterer and salesman, and a veteran of the Second World War, Kobs kept a neatly manicured lawn and a garden planted with colorful flowers. He spoke cheerfully to his neighbors and doted over his seventeen grandchildren. Visitors to his house in Sandy, Utah, were struck by the bicultural humor of this German-American immigrant. On his front porch, readable from the sidewalk, was mounted a nameplate: *The Kobsens*. In German, many nouns take their plural forms by adding the suffix, "en." In English, most add the letter "s."[21] The linguistically hybrid sign announced to passersby that Jared Kobs belonged to two worlds, one American and one German.[22] The nexus was Jared's membership in the Mormon Church, where the collective memories of the Second World

War cast no aspersion on a veteran who fought valiantly and unashamedly for Adolf Hitler's Nazi Germany.

In the pecking order among former soldiers in Utah, an American veteran of the Normandy D-Day invasion or the Battle of the Bulge enjoys no advantage over a combat veteran who served the enemy. At sacrament meeting or stake conference, America's World War II combatants share an equal degree of respect with *Wehrmacht* veterans like Kobs, who courageously sought to relieve Field Marshal Friedrich von Paulus' encircled Sixth Army at the Battle of Stalingrad.[23] These faithful German Army veterans hold ecclesial rank in the Mormon priesthood comparable to that of U.S. Army veterans. The immigration of hundreds of German Latter-day Saints after the war added this particular demographic to the Mormon Culture Region.

Jared Heinz Bruno Kobs is a memory beacon. He appears in the work of author Frederick Kempe, whose book *Father/Land* set out to examine inherited guilt for the Holocaust among the postwar generations of Germans. The book's plot took a surprising twist when Kempe discovered a particularly reprehensible Nazi criminal in his own Mormon family tree, Erich Krause, who ran a "wild" concentration camp in Berlin.[24] Kempe found himself confronted by the same inherited guilt that beset German descendants of the Nazis. For Kempe, his uncle Jared was, by contrast, one of the good Germans from the wartime era—apolitical but cognizant of the role that ordinary Germans played in supporting the Nazi regime. Jared told his nephew that his fellow Germans of that era seldom opposed Hitler, and that members of his own family were members of the Nazi Party, to which they owed their employment.[25] Likewise, in correspondence with the author of this study, Kobs was blunt: "I don't think I liked the government in Germany but I had to obey the law and shut up!"[26]

When two BYU scholars, Robert C. Freeman and Jon R. Felt, began to research their book, *Saints at War*, they found in Kobs a faith-inspiring example of a teenage German soldier sent into combat with miniature copies of the New Testament and the Book of Mormon sewn into his uniform jacket. Jared's mother had stitched them into the lining, positioned to cover her son's heart.[27]

Kobs is a Mormon memory beacon because he was not only a good German soldier but also a good man. He took shelter from the Russian winter in peasants' houses, shared in the household chores, treated the owners kindly, and never inspired fear that he would rape their daughters.[28] The most important aspect of Kobs's story is that he remained a faithful Latter-day Saint throughout his years of wartime tribulation and afterward, reconnecting with the church after his release from a POW camp in 1947. Later, he immigrated to the American Zion and became a patriotic American, but he never questioned the church leadership's role in accommodating itself with Hitler's regime during the prewar period. More than half a century later, he still had no doubts. Said Kobs in a letter to the author in 2005: "Latter-day Saints should support the government!" With that letter, Kobs enclosed a photocopy of a 2004 LDS Church Sunday school lesson manual. Entitled "The Teachings of Heber J. Grant," it stressed compliance with the Twelfth Article of Faith and Section 134 of the Doctrine and Covenants.[29]

Kobs was not the first German combatant in the Second World War to become a Mormon memory beacon. However, in the days before the Iron Curtain fell, faithful Latter-day Saint authors were careful about commemorating the battlefield bravery of Mormon soldiers who fought honorably for a fascist cause. One of the first examples was a self-published book by Frederick H. Barth, born in Romania, who became a naturalized German citizen prior to the outbreak of war in 1939. Barth's autobiography, *Guided and Guarded*, released in 1981, received an unusual degree of approval by the Mormon hierarchy of the time. Mormon Apostle Howard W. Hunter, who later became the prophet, seer, and revelator for a brief period before his death in 1995, wrote the foreword. Barth had become acquainted with Hunter because of Barth's full-time church employment as an Eastern European genealogical research specialist, one of the few LDS Church employees at the time who was fluent in Romanian.

Barth's story was a relatively safe one to recount at a time when the LDS Church was still negotiating with the government of the communist German Democratic Republic on behalf of Mormons who lived in East Germany. Barth had not been born in Germany, nor was he a member of the Mormon Church when he served in Hitler's military forces during the war. His conversion to Mormonism began in 1953 when two female missionaries rang his doorbell in Stuttgart. The bulk of his account, however, concentrates on the close calls and perceived divine intervention that spared his life during the war. For example, one night shortly after

Barth had joined a *Luftwaffe* communications unit in 1941, he was not in his barracks, having received permission to make a phone call. Suddenly, in the mobilization for war with the Soviet Union, his unit received a deployment order that it executed within in a matter of minutes. When Barth returned to the barracks, he found his rucksack, rifle, and gas mask in the middle of the floor. His comrades were already gone. Rather than being sent to catch up with his unit, Barth received a posting to another outfit. He later learned that all of the men in his platoon had been killed in combat, except one who survived with an amputated leg.[30]

On another occasion, after having been deployed to the Russian front, Barth received a transfer when officials took belated action on an application he had filed for an intelligence specialist's position many months previously. Barth spent the next two years decoding messages for the ministry of aviation in Berlin. Meanwhile, his former *Luftwaffe* communications unit suffered heavy casualties inflicted by the Soviet Army and Russian winter.[31] The pattern is familiar to readers of faith-promoting Mormon chronicles. God intervened at the last moment to preserve one of his faithful servants—in this case, someone who would render obedient service in the years to come. Barth wrote: "I began to recognize that some supernatural power was at work preserving my life and influencing my circumstances."[32] The divine intervention in his life became clear to him in the 1950s, when after his conversion to Mormonism he decided to immigrate to Utah and subsequently found his linguistic skills in demand at church headquarters. God preserved him as a Nazi soldier in order to do divine work after the war.

Although published testimonies like Barth's were rare until after the demise of European communism, two forces conjoined afterward to facilitate the recognition of faithful Latter-day Saints who had fought for the Third Reich. First, German Mormons living in the former German Democratic Republic became citizens of the Federal Republic of Germany. Thus, the LDS Church leadership no longer worried about the effect of glorifying fascist warriors in resolutely anti-fascist, communist East Germany. Second, the nostalgia that surfaced in the western world for the aging veterans of the Second World War propelled an effort to recognize Mormon members of America's "Greatest Generation." BYU scholars Robert C. Freeman and Dennis Wright answered that demand by founding the Saints at War Project, a research effort that has produced more than three thousand contacts, and many detailed interviews, with Mormon veterans of the Second World War, Korea, and Vietnam. One byproduct of their work was the publication of *German Saints at War*, an unapologetically faith-promoting effort issued by Cedar Fort Media, a purveyor of Mormon spiritual publications.

It features no Nazi-saluting devotees of Hitler. Instead, Hitler's soldiers in *German Saints at War* pull the trigger sparingly but seldom encounter trouble with their superiors because they lack enthusiasm for war. Instead, miraculous series of events spare their lives, allowing them to live while the less faithful perish. They all survive the war in order to serve the church as obedient members in the postwar years, thereby becoming memory beacons. Eugene Dautel, for example, was a nineteen-year-old draftee into an army medical unit who received an untimely transfer to an infantry battalion. However, just before deployment to the front lines, he experienced an allergic reaction to an inoculation, which allowed him to be transferred back to his original medical unit. The very next day, every member of the infantry platoon was killed or seriously wounded on their first day on the battlefield. The miracles did not stop there. Toward the end of the war, Dautel deserted his unit, survived an artillery barrage that killed many others, and then suffered the pangs of conscience—which compelled him to return to his outfit. An officer told him he would be shot, a common fate encountered by deserting *Wehrmacht* soldiers toward the end of the war. However, the officer then became pensive, reconsidered, and stamped Dautel's orders to allow him to return to his unit. Said the author: "Once more the blessing was answered." Dautel's postwar actions also followed the faith-promoting paradigm. He married his Mormon sweetheart, became a branch president in the early 1950s, and subsequently immigrated to the American Zion.[33]

The remaining stories trace the same pattern. Wilhelm Krisch was a member of one of the first *Wehrmacht* units to cross into the Soviet Union when Hitler launched Operation Barbarossa in the summer of 1941. During one battlefield engagement, he sought refuge from an artillery attack with a group of other German soldiers. Fate intervened in his favor. In Krisch's words, "I ran only a few steps toward the men, when a soft, quiet voice called me by name, telling me I should go back." Krisch obeyed the "spiritual prompting," and as soon as he found a different hiding place, an artillery shell exploded in the middle of his first intended refuge. His comrades were either killed or seriously wounded.[34]

The most unusual story involved a young Mormon assigned as an administrative clerk to a *Luftwaffe* colonel who ran a training school for aircraft mechanics. Oskar Starke developed a close friendship with his commanding officer, who seemed to take an unusual interest in the young man's career, promoting the young Mormon regularly through the ranks from private to sergeant. One day, when Starke surreptitiously read the colonel's private journal, he learned that he was being groomed to fill two positions. The colonel wanted his young clerk to attend officer candidate school and then marry his half-*Mischling* daughter. The diary contained a compelling story of the colonel's marriage to a Jewish woman during the pre-Nazi period, the birth of their daughter, and his subsequent abandonment of his wife after Hitler took power. Starke was interested in neither of the colonel's propositions, as he was engaged to a Mormon girl from his hometown of Plauen. He had no desire to marry a girl he had never met, one who did not share his religious beliefs, nor did he want to become a military officer in a war that he knew his country was losing. Through fastidious prayer and contemplation, according to the narrative, Starke convinced the colonel to sign papers that allowed him to marry his fiancée.[35] That only occurred after the colonel had refused to grant permission for his clerk to marry each day for one week. The reader can thus conclude that God protected this observant young LDS man by providing him with a relatively safe wartime assignment, during which he proved his spiritual mettle by remaining determined to marry within his faith.

Beacons of the Home Front: Women, Children, the Elderly, and Evacuees

As the Second Counselor in the presidency of the East German Mission in 1944, Paul Langheinrich was the second-ranking ecclesiastical leader for German Mormons who lived within the boundaries of the Berlin-based mission. Mission President Herbert Klopfer had been deployed to the Russian front as a junior officer in the *Wehrmacht*. Too old for military conscription, Langheinrich and First Counselor Richard Ranglack remained. They cared for home-front Mormons who were losing their houses and apartments to a relentless Allied aerial bombing campaign, their husbands and fathers to the battlefield, and many of their children to evacuation from cities imperiled by air raids.

Langheinrich assumed another responsibility. Employed by a company that provided heating services to railway stations, he obtained access to three different government radios and a telephone line. That allowed him to furnish a unique air raid early-warning system to alert fellow Latter-day Saints. When a military radio announced that enemy bombers were on their way to a particular city, Langheinrich telephoned specially designated Mormon contacts in that locality. The church's early-warning network often got the word to members in the endangered city sooner than the government's civil defense warning system. In Berlin, Langheinrich monitored the local police radio network, which efficiently reported the addresses of newly bombed-out houses and apartment buildings. Langheinrich maintained a list of Berlin church members. When he learned that a member's residence had been bombed, he quickly dispatched church members to render assistance.[36]

The Mormon mutual assistance network in Germany functioned well despite wartime travel restrictions, the disruption of peacetime telephone and telegraph capabilities, and the deployment of so many male priesthood leaders to the front lines. The solution, in the latter case, was the intervention of women whose natural leadership abilities had been suppressed or conveniently managed by male ecclesiastical leaders during less troubled times. When East German mission leaders, Ranglack and Langheinrich, decided to establish clothing distribution centers for needy church members, they found three vacant buildings, each in a rural location that made them unlikely targets for destruction by aerial bombing. The first was located in northeastern Germany on a railway line near the obscure village of Kruez. The second was at Neuzage, near the university city of Cottbus in Brandenburg. The third was at Neuwürschnitz, near the Erzgebirge in Saxony.

The two male leaders of the East German Mission located and rented the warehouses but they tasked Mormon women with stocking the shelves. Despite the shortage of consumer goods in a wartime economy, clothing losses in the bombing campaigns, frequent Nazi winter relief drives, and special appeals to send clothing to ill-equipped, beleaguered

German troops suffering in subzero temperatures on the Russian front, the "sisters" of the mission performed in excess of expectations. Within six weeks, all three storehouses were filled to capacity and the leadership had to request that members make no more donations.[37]

Women played an ever-increasing wartime role in performing official church business. Some, faced with a shortage of men in the branches, even took on traditional male duties by performing unauthorized liturgical ordinances restricted to the all-male Mormon priesthood. That commenced as early as the 1938 "fire drill evacuation" during the Sudetenland crisis. According to Donald M. Petty, when missionaries returned from a three-week absence, they found a few isolated cases in which women had blessed (consecrated) and distributed the sacrament (Eucharist).[38] Otto Berndt, president of the Hamburg District, recalled that during the war, he assigned women to the traditional male job of collecting fast offerings—a duty they performed assiduously. As a result, Berndt said, German Mormons remained faithful wartime tithe payers. At the end of the war, he turned over the entire cache of donated money to the mission office in Frankfurt.[39] Mormon women also assumed responsibility for maintaining an informal church congregational barter system.[40]

LDS wives and mothers also assumed the role of protecting their families from the threat of violence perpetrated by invading enemy troops. As the Red Army advanced toward Berlin, stories of Russian soldiers raping German civilians in the eastern states became prevalent in Berlin. Faced with the dual threat of Allied bombing and physical violence by Soviet troops, German women coined the cynical expression: "Better a Russian (rapist) on the belly than an American (bomb) on the head." Mormon women, at least in the faith-promoting stories that have emanated since the war, saw no humor in such remarks. Roger Minert, a professor of family history at BYU, interviewed a number of LDS survivors of the Red Army's advance on Berlin. Rape was a threat they were determined to escape. Although no records provide the number of Mormon women assaulted by Red Army soldiers, author Anthony Beevor stated that two Berlin hospitals estimated the local rape victims to number between 95,000 and 130,000.[41] One LDS mother successfully disguised her seventeen-year-old daughter as an old woman in order to protect her from marauding and raping Soviet occupation soldiers.[42] Others sent their daughters to live with relatives in the countryside.

The records of the East German Mission do contain accounts of Mormons raped during forced evacuations from East Prussia: "Women and girls, some just approaching adolescence, have been repeatedly ravished. One of the mothers was forced at the point of a gun to watch her daughter being ravished by a group of ten soldiers. Another girl, not yet twelve years old, has been raped several times. One of the sisters, whose husband was snatched out of his sick bed and deported to Siberia, was ravished three times in one night, resulting in the birth of a little Russian baby boy for whom she is now caring along with her other two children."[43]

For women caring for children and elderly family members, shelter became the next problem. Otto Berndt estimated that sixty to seventy percent of Hamburg's Mormons lost their homes as a result of the horrific Allied aerial attacks in 1943, when the British Royal Air Force bombed by night and the American Army Air Force wreaked havoc by day. Only one Hamburg District branch meetinghouse, the rented Masonic Temple in Altona, survived the bombardment. By the end of the war, Hamburg's Mormons were traveling on foot from all over the devastated city and its distant suburbs to attended services in Altona. Despite the hardships imposed by lack of shelter and a ruined public transit system, the city's Mormons were able to operate their youth organization, the Mutual Improvement Association, throughout the war without interruption.[44]

Berlin's Mormons had an additional problem. Not only did they have to provide shelter for bombed-out church members from their own city, but they also inherited the responsibility for accommodating German-speaking Latter-day Saints fleeing the relentlessly advancing Soviets from the East. In 1944, after one summer evening in which thirty-five Mormon families lost their homes to bombing of the former Prussian capital of Königsberg, Langheinrich wrote the city's Mormon district president, advising Königsberg's Latter-day Saint population to relocate. Because of Allied bombardment, Berlin was considered too dangerous to be a place of refuge, but it did serve as a way station for German-speaking Mormons being relocated to the towns of Zwickau and Erzgebirge in Saxony—where LDS families opened their homes to their fleeing co-religionists.[45]

The problem of finding temporary shelter for the refugees arriving in Berlin had been compounded in 1943 when the Berlin mission headquarters was destroyed in an air raid. The circumstances surrounding that attack provided another beacon in the collective memory of LDS wartime experiences. Mission President Herbert Klopfer, on leave from his military duties, tried to visit the stately building across from Berlin's Tiergarten Park one evening but found himself locked out. Shortly after he left the premises, in search of his keys, enemy bombers raided the neighborhood, leaving much of the Hansaviertel suburb of Berlin in flames and ruins. As postwar Mormon lore recounts, the Lord preserved Klopfer's life by causing him to forget his keys.[46]

After the destruction of the mission home on Händelallee, Langheinrich moved all mission operations to his Berlin apartment. The limited space available would have proven inadequate for quartering evacuees in comparison to the former mission headquarters—except for the fact that many other tenants had chosen to abandon their flats. Believing that their apartments would never survive the Allied bombing campaign, many of Langheinrich's neighbors handed over their keys and gave the Mormon leader permission to shelter refugees in their apartments. The building became the temporary refuge for evacuee Mormons from the east. Some thirty-seven church members took shelter there at one time, while they awaited placement with Mormon families in Saxony. Another problem surfaced when the newcomers learned that they needed Berlin ration cards. That required the short-staffed church leadership to accompany the refugees to their appointments with rationing authorities, to attest to their temporary residency in Berlin. Meanwhile, individual memory beacons continued to appear in the personage of Mormons who unselfishly shared scarce food with the needy transients. According to one account, a teenage girl, Ingrid Bendler, rode a bicycle "under fire" to Langheinrich's apartment complex, bringing much needed margarine and cocoa to the hungry evacuees.[47]

The larger German cities proved no safer than the evacuated abodes of the eastern territories. Many Mormons who worked in essential industries continued to risk death by remaining in targeted metropolitan areas. Some worked exhausting day shifts, only to have their limited nighttime rest interrupted by air raid alerts. One Latter-day Saint later recalled that the prevailing attitude of defenseless civilians was that "today may be my last." The physical and emotional strain of taking shelter each time the air raid sirens sounded began to wear on the populace. Langheinrich wrote that during the war years he had sought refuge in the air raid shelters a total of 395 times. The pressure was especially intense on the elderly. According to one account: "Eventually, the old and the weak, upon hearing the siren, pleaded to be left behind, resigning themselves to possible death rather than use up the strength of the younger people in carrying them to the shelters."[48]

Others were able to escape the threat of death that rained down from the skies. Some had relatives in rural Germany, where they could wait out the war in relative tranquility. A few with financial means paid to have their children placed in boarding schools or with families in small towns that were of no strategic interest to Allied aerial targeting planners. Max Reschke, an upper-level manager in a Hanover pharmaceutical manufacturing plant, could afford to send his eleven-year-old son, Horst, to a private school for well-connected German children in Austria in 1941 and 1942. Then, Max found Horst a suitable family with which to live in the medieval town of Hildesheim, located thirty kilometers southeast of Hanover. Even the relative safety of the countryside did not offer absolute protection, however. Once, when Horst was a passenger on a local train that he rode to school, the cars came under a strafing attack by an Allied dive bomber. A bullet penetrated his friend's school satchel, positioned over the boy's head on the luggage rack, and lodged in the boy's books.[49] If the machine gun round had found its mark in the child's body, presumably this story would not have found its way into the trove of miraculous Mormon wartime accounts.

Wolfsgrün: A Beacon of German-Mormon Self-Help

The postwar period witnessed the continued diaspora of both German-speaking people from former German territories in the East, and of ethnic Germans from countries that the Third Reich had occupied. Understandably, many fled the advancing Soviet forces while the war raged, but even after the cessation of hostilities the migration continued because of forced expulsions. Altogether, some twelve to fourteen million German speakers, either *Reichsdeutsche* (German nationals) or *Volksdeutsche* (ethnic Germans) fled or were compelled to leave their homes between 1944 and 1950.[50] Many died along the way because of exposure, starvation, or violence.

Although Mormons fled along with other German speakers, relatively few perished. Their collective behavior while en route, sharing their limited provisions, preserved many lives. Some pushed their possessions in handcarts and wheelbarrows, which many saw as emblematic of the Mormon "handcart migration" across the Great Plains from Iowa City, Iowa, to Utah almost one hundred years earlier.[51] East German Mission leaders sheltered them upon arrival in Berlin. The Langheinrich apartments became a way station where, according to an American occupation soldier who once served as secretary of the German-Austrian Mission: "They received clean clothing from the mission's reserve stock. They were seated around a long table and fed hot soup and nourishing food. Then the weary newcomers were allowed to sleep for as long as they wished. Then they were given a train ticket."[52]

The rail ticket took evacuees to the Saxon village of Wolfsgrün, situated several miles from the larger town of Eibenstock. There, a large manor house situated on a hill served as their refuge. From 1945 to 1947, the Latter-day Saints ran a home for displaced Mormons that housed as many as ninety-nine families.

How the East German Mission leadership obtained the property has become another beacon of memory in Mormon history and folklore. For many generations prior to the Second World War, the property belonged to the family of a turn-of-the-century industrialist named C. G. Bretschneider, who made his fortune in the paper industry. Between 1898 and 1902, Bretschneider constructed a large house that resembled a castle, complete with many bedrooms, an expansive dining hall, and a main portal that led to a grandiose reception area. He built the house amid a meticulously landscaped park with pathways, ponds, and lush, grassy lawns. During the National Socialist period, Bretschneider encountered financial difficulties because of his refusal to court favor with the Nazis. Presumably, he would not join the Party. Eventually, the owner lost the property to the state, probably because of the inability to pay property or business taxes.[53] The large manor house became the property of the Nazi Party social welfare organization, the *Nationalsozialistische Volkswohlfahrt* (NSV), who used it as a home for young mothers.[54]

The NSV, formed in Berlin in 1931 by a Nazi municipal counselor named Erich Hilgenfeldt, began with modest goals, to help Party members weather the economic difficulties brought on by the worldwide depression that hit Germany particularly hard. After the Nazis came to power, it absorbed various church and secular relief agencies, such as the German Red Cross. With sixteen million members in 1942, it became the second-largest Party auxiliary organization.[55] Its programs to aid expectant mothers became known for their maternity and childcare workers, referred to as the "brown sisters"—in contrast to the "blue sisters," Catholic nuns who had run many of Germany's pre-Nazi homes for unwed mothers.[56] Ostensibly, the brown sisters had no objection to Hitler's lascivious natalist policies, which cast no moral aspersion on women who wished to "give Hitler a baby" by engaging in premarital relations.

After the war, when the East German Mission leaders began looking for a place of refuge for its refugee members, the former Nazi property at Wolfsgrün was available. As the Mormons maintained good relations with the Soviet occupying authorities, the Red Army military commandant at Eibenstock granted permission for the Mormons to move in on the same day that the request was made, September 3, 1945.[57] Because of the way that Donald C. Corbett worded his report, however, others have mischaracterized the use of the Wolfsgrün property during the Nazi regime. Corbett said: "During the Hitler period, it had been used as a convalescent home for mothers."[58] That prompted one historian to write: "Paul Langheinrich and Arnold Schmidt, a branch president from Krese, secured a former *Lebensborn* home in Wolfsgrün south of Berlin for an LDS refugee camp."[59] Schmidt confirmed that the Wolfsgrün had indeed been used as an NSV facility for mothers, but the property does not appear on the list of SS *Lebensborn* maternity homes.[60] The *Lebensborn* program, according to differing historical accounts, served as either Heinrich Himmler's pet project to allow Aryan women to bear their "racially pure" out-of-wedlock children without shame—or as an SS stud farm where black-shirted Nazis could have sex with genealogically screened German women in order to produce a "master race." The *Lebensborn* project also became associated with the kidnapping of children from occupied countries, who were then adopted by SS families in Germany.[61]

Regardless of how the Nazis employed the Wolfsgrün facility during the war, afterward it continued to be embroiled in controversy. For the Soviet occupation forces, there was no problem with allowing a peaceful

German religious denomination to use a former fascist facility to shelter refugees. For officials of the local government, though, the prospect of importing displaced war victims to their town threatened to tax limited food supplies. Others worried that the outsiders might pose a threat to law and order. During the period in which the Mormons operated the refugee facility, feeding its occupants and staving off local opposition remained a constant challenge.

Because local officials denied the Wolfsgrün occupants "grocery cards," twice-weekly shopping trips for provisions had to be made to towns at least forty miles away. Occupants ground wheat into powder in order to make soup. During the winter of 1945–46, the residents ate nothing but carrots. When Arnold Schmidt's wife was able to convince a local farmer to sell her two pigs, Wolfsgrün's residents anticipated a feast. However, after the hogs had been slaughtered, police from Zwickau arrived and confiscated the meat. Schmidt managed to hide a pot of lard, on which the residents subsisted for many days. In the spring of 1946, the residents planted a vegetable garden, but even this task was complicated by a lack of shovels.[62]

Throughout the Mormons' stay at Wolfsgrün, they fought a constant battle against local authorities who were determined to close the facility. Between Christmas and New Year's Day of 1946, the police commissioner of Saxony appeared with a notice to vacate within five days. Later in January, the local mayor, accompanied by four policemen, arrived with an evacuation notice. Several weeks later, Saxon authorities in Dresden sent a message that demanded the Mormons vacate the premises, along with their assurances that the refugees would be accommodated elsewhere. Enjoying the continued support of the Soviet military governor, Schmidt refused to comply with these edicts. In February 1946, under pressure from Russian military authorities, local authorities granted "food cards" to the residents, which allowed them to shop locally.[63]

The Mormon refugee home in Wolfsgrün operated until July 1947. A combination of factors led to its closing.[64] Records of the East German mission indicate that government pressure to close the facility persisted throughout its twenty-two months of operation. Also, as food became more plentiful, complaints began to arise regarding the indolent work ethic of some of its residents. One report said residents had split into rival factions. Allegations of sexual improprieties arose.[65] As economic conditions improved in Germany and Mormon assistance began arriving from the United States, the residents of Wolfsgrün began to find homes elsewhere. Through the effort of the mission office in Berlin, the majority relocated to cities under the occupation of the western powers. The remainder found places to live in the eastern zone under Soviet jurisdiction. Some thirty residents chose homes in the vicinity of Wolfsgrün, which allowed a small LDS branch to function for years afterward.[66]

The Brightest Memory Beacon: Ezra Taft Benson and American War Relief

When *Wehrmacht* forces in Berlin surrendered to the Red Army on May 2, 1945, one nightmare ended for the city's civilian population, but another began. No more air raid sirens sounded and no more bombs or artillery rounds fell, but Germans found themselves unable to enjoy the nighttime tranquility because of hunger. Civil administration was in shambles, and supply distribution networks, intermittent and unreliable during the war, ceased to function altogether. Ration coupons were worthless in the stores that survived amid the rubble. There was nothing on the shelves and no deliveries were scheduled. The Red Army had provisions for itself but little to share with the civilian populace. Indeed, Soviet soldiers looted whatever German stocks they could find.[67] For three weeks, according to Donald C. Corbett, Berlin's Latter-day Saints shared among church members the meager supplies of food they had, and what they could obtain from farmers if they could make it past Russian sentries and into the countryside.

Then, the Russians began to establish food distribution centers that issued limited quantities of bread to the civilian population.[68] It was not enough. During the month of July, the average daily nutritional intake in Berlin was eight hundred calories per person, worse than a concentration camp diet that had been deliberately designed to starve prisoners to death.[69] By the end of the summer, the Allied military government established a meager ration of 1,550 calories per day as a basis for distributing limited food aid to Berlin's surviving population of more than three million people.[70] A British plan, "Operation Barleycorn," called for

German prisoners of war to work agricultural fields to bring in the summer harvest, but the operation failed when three continuous weeks of August rain ruined the German wheat crop.[71]

For Latter-day Saints, the situation began to improve when American servicemen arrived in Berlin. Missionaries who had served in Germany before the war and who were fluent in the language made a special effort to connect with their former congregants. On Sunday mornings, German Mormons tried to conduct sacrament meetings in darkened, bomb-damaged buildings without electricity or heat. Sometimes they received surprise visits from familiar faces dressed in U.S. Army olive and khaki. "*Ein Bruder?*" a famished, dispirited German Mormon might ask an unexpected visitor at his door.[72] The look of astonishment would turn to one of glee when a soldier from Utah arrived bearing a standard military mail package of eleven or twenty-two pounds, dispatched by a Berlin resident's American relative by way of a familiar missionary. Two former mission secretaries, Major Donald C. Corbett of the German-Austrian Mission and Major John R. Barnes of the West German Mission, using their privileges as commissioned officers, commandeered jeeps and other military vehicles in an attempt to deliver relief supplies to church members.[73]

The following winter was the worst that the German population had experienced since the Allied blockade at the end of the First World War, which had been designed to ensure cooperation with peace terms to be dictated at Versailles. The first winter after the Second World War was even harder because that conflict inflicted vast destruction on the home front. Having no coal or wood for their stoves, Germans went to bed at night and "tried to cover themselves with old newspapers and wrapping paper."[74] Food, fuel, and shelter were in short supply in March 1946, when Mormon Apostle Ezra Taft Benson arrived in Berlin to coordinate an extensive postwar relief effort. Latter-day Saints in the United States and Canada provided a year-long relief campaign for bombed-out and hungry Mormon victims of the war. Benson spent nine months in war-torn Europe that year, reorganizing the local church hierarchy and overseeing relief efforts for members.[75] Germany and the eastern territories where German-speaking Mormons resided received the preponderance of his attention. His speeches to German Mormons attracted overflow crowds, some of them in partially destroyed meetinghouses.[76]

Except for the small quantities of relief supplies provided on an individual basis by American soldiers, the first church-dispatched aid for Mormons arrived in Germany in June 1946 by way of Geneva, Switzerland. The Salt Lake City hierarchy enlisted the aid of the International Red Cross for its distribution, as the Red Cross enjoyed the cooperation of the military occupation authorities.[77] While the Mormon relief effort had to overcome bureaucratic obstacles in each zone of occupation, particular difficulties surfaced in the Soviet zone. Russian officials feared that American aid might affect the political attitude of the populace.[78] The Russians also insisted, for a time, that any relief supplies be distributed throughout the population and not reserved for church members.[79] A second shipment of American food and clothing arrived in Berlin in early October 1946. By this time, the reluctance of the Soviet occupation authorities had been overcome.[80] Canadian Mormon farmers in the western province of Alberta dispatched massive amounts of cracked wheat to Germany in three shipments in 1946 and 1947.[81] Mormon relief efforts in support of distressed German members continued through the summer of 1947, when currency reform in the western sector of Germany coincided with an economic recovery that allowed most German Latter-day Saints to become self-sufficient. Some forty-one freight carloads of clothing and ninety-nine freight carloads of food, with a total value of $1,232,000, found its way from North American Latter-day Saints to European Mormons in 1946–47. The total cost, including shipping and insurance, was $1,736,000.[82]

American Mormons, particularly those of German descent, aided their Teutonic countrymen in another way. The year 1948 saw the beginning of a substantial German Mormon migration to the United States. Through the year 1962, according to one estimate, 4,493 German Latter-day Saints immigrated to the Mormon Culture Region. Many received aid from relatives who had come to America before the war. This occurred despite the Mormon hierarchy's unwavering opposition to migration to the American Zion, a stance that had not changed since the 1920s. It happened in the midst of well-publicized LDS Church plans to construct its first Holy Temple in Europe in German-speaking Bern, Switzerland. That temple opened in 1955. Although German Mormons worshiped at the new temple enthusiastically, its establishment did not slow the rate of emigration.

The Second World War and Its Aftermath

Priorities: Mining Genealogical Records Amid Starvation

During the winter of 1945–46, while Berliners were subsisting on a diminished rations and heating fuel was in short supply, the leadership of the East German Mission found its time occupied with additional interests. Besides saving lives by feeding the hungry and sheltering the homeless, the mission leadership concerned itself with saving the souls of the dead. The traditional Mormon practice of baptizing deceased nonmembers into the LDS Church by proxy took on increased importance in light of the Second World War's carnage. There were many more dead souls to save. Less than a year had passed since liberating soldiers had exposed the horrors of Nazi gas chambers and crematoria to a shocked world. While destitute Germans, without coal or wood, wrapped themselves in paper at night to keep warm, Mormons sought other valuable papers to fuel their genealogical program. Aware that the Nazis' fastidious record keeping had produced bountiful quantities of family history information, the LDS leadership kept a watchful eye for caches of records scattered during the war.

On August 9, 1945, barely three months after Germany surrendered, Second Counselor Paul Langheinrich wrote the commander of Soviet occupation forces, seeking information and a blanket authorization to retain any genealogical records that the Mormons might obtain. He told Field Marshall Georgy Zhukov: "Through the *Reichsamt für Sippenforschung* (Department of Genealogical Research) Berlin, N.W.7, Schiffbauerdamm 26, many documents, pedigree charts, etc. were compiled. Films were also made of 50% of all German church records. *Of particular value is also a complete file that has been compiled of Jewish people.* All the records have been stored somewhere in a fire- and bomb-proof place, which is unknown to us. It must be in or near Berlin. These records are of no value to you. For us they are priceless" (my emphasis).[83]

He asked if the Red Army had any knowledge of such records. One week later, the Soviet commanding general, through his chief of staff, replied that the Russians had no knowledge or interest in genealogical records, but granted the Mormons permission to keep any that they might find. General Wasili Sokolowski wrote: "We know nothing of . . . German church records and files of the Jews, and do not know where they are at this time. If you find them, and the contents agree with this, we do not object if you take possession of these."[84]

Langheinrich had been a Nazi government-certified genealogist who conducted research on bloodlines at the University of Berlin in 1934. He subsequently turned down an offer to become a government lecturer on genealogical subjects, on the basis that he was not a member of the Nazi Party. Nevertheless, his government certification had given him access to all genealogical records in the Third Reich.[85] Regardless of the destitute condition of German Latter-day Saints during the first winter following the war, Langheinrich was determined to attend to the salvation of the dead in addition to the welfare of the living. In his correspondence with the Soviet authorities, he emphasized that: "None of us has ever been a member of the NSDAP [Nazi Party] or any of its departments."[86]

In February 1946, one month before Ezra Taft Benson arrived from Salt Lake City to coordinate the Mormon war relief drive, Langheinrich learned of the existence of a trove of genealogical records stored in a castle on a mountaintop in Thuringia. The records consisted of more than five thousand bound books of parish and civil registries covering the past several centuries, and thousands of thirty-five millimeter films in canisters—ostensibly recorded by the Nazis as part of their prewar genealogical research efforts to document non-Jewish blood lines. The collection contained many names of Jewish Germans obtained from the historical records of synagogues. The records were part of a larger store of artworks, gold, ancient scrolls, illustrated church books dating from the Middle Ages, and other treasures that Nazi authorities had hidden from the advancing Russian armies.[87]

The next step was to seek permission to expend church funds to retrieve the records. At the time, the two mission leaders could not write to Salt Lake City. Occupation authorities prohibited German civilians from communicating by mail with correspondents outside of the country. Instead, on a Sunday afternoon in February 1946, Langheinrich knocked on the door of Major Donald C. Corbett, who was serving on the staff of General Lucius D. Clay, the military governor of the American zone of occupation. Clay would later gain fame for his role in leading the Berlin Airlift of 1948–49. Corbett, a former secretary to the president of the German-Austrian mission, was the highest-ranking American Mormon that Langheinrich could find. Money was not a problem. Germans had remained regular tithe payers during the war, and the mission had more than one hundred thousand *Reichmarks* in cash, and a million more in a frozen bank account. Langheinrich estimated that shipping the records to Berlin would require three railroad cars at a cost of RM 1,500 per car. Enthused by the prospect of obtaining so many names for temple ordinances, but unsure of his authority to approve the expenditure of church funds, Corbett nevertheless granted permission for Langheinrich to finance the project.[88]

Years later, Corbett reported the retrieval of the records in an essay written for the LDS Church Historical Department. It contained several pages of perceived miraculous interventions that allowed the project to continue in the face of adverse weather, mechanical breakdown of equipment, and confrontations with Soviet soldiers. It also recounted the reaction of Mormon Apostle Ezra Taft Benson, who viewed the records on his trip to Berlin later that spring. Corbett described Benson's first visit to the new East German Mission headquarters building, a stately structure obtained from the occupation government at the paltry rent of four hundred marks per month. The expansive house had belonged to a high-ranking Nazi functionary who committed suicide in the waning days of the war. Benson toured a house stacked with items from its floor to the ceiling. Half of the material was war relief supplies. The other half was genealogical records. Benson was delighted to see both.[89]

One noteworthy aspect of the record retrieval project stands out in the accounts of the event. The presence of numerous Jewish records among those retrieved for genealogical research and subsequent temple baptisms is prominently noted in Corbett's report, in the East German Mission records, and in Langheinrich's correspondence with Red Army officials.[90] In a report that Langheinrich later wrote for the LDS Church Historical Department, he emphasized the importance of obtaining Jewish records, among the others. He recalled searching the basement of a destroyed Jewish synagogue in Berlin. He established contact with former employees of the Reich Genealogical Office in order to seek files of Jewish names. Describing the search for one particular quantity of records, the report described the "great regret we had to find out that a large part of the Jew [*sic*] file had been given to a paper mill."[91]

The Mormon Church's controversial practice of converting Jewish Holocaust victims by posthumous baptism became well known in the last decade of the twentieth century. The postwar records retrieval project in Thuringia and related searches for genealogical data in the rubble of Nazi Germany may have represented the first steps in that process. It presents an interesting contrast with the prewar actions of a church that strenuously tried to sever all ties with Jewish symbolism, and in fact refused to heed—at its highest levels of authority—the desperate pleas of a few Jewish converts to Mormonism for assistance in leaving the Nazi state. Saving their souls after death posed a more manageable solution.

Resumption of American Ecclesiastical Authority

For German Latter-day Saints, the historical period that marked the Second World War came to a close in November 1946 with the appointment of American mission presidents and the official resumption of Salt Lake City's ecclesiastical control over German Mormons. Walter Stover, a furniture sales magnate from Salt Lake City and a native German, assumed control over the Berlin-based East German Mission. Several months later, Jean Wunderlich, a prominent attorney from Los Angeles, took command of the Frankfurt-based West German Mission. Both men adhered to the same pattern that had proven successful for mission presidents in Germany during the first half of the twentieth century. Each man spoke fluent German and had served a mission in Germany as a youth. Each was married and had children. Both had achieved distinguished professional success prior to their calling as mission presidents, and had sacrificed financially in order to accept the church post. Each had served in the Mormon hierarchy at the ward (parish) and stake (diocesan) level and was familiar with church governance.

Wunderlich began restoring American authority by correcting deviations in Mormon liturgical practice that had crept into Sunday sacrament meetings during the war. He found that one branch had covered its sacrament (Eucharist) table with red cloth and distributed the sacrament water in a gold chalice. Other congregations had served the sacrament with a musical accompaniment, either a violin or an organ. In one case, the young men who served the sacred bread and water clicked their heels in unison, as if they were practicing a military drill. His message: "Let's get back to basics!"[92] Despite his admonishments, the Mormons of the

West German Mission apparently embraced their new American mission president with enthusiasm. His experience as an American attorney facilitated relations with Allied occupation officials.

By most accounts, Stover was also a well-loved leader of the Mormons in eastern Germany. However, his status as a former German citizen and a naturalized American caused periodic problems with military authorities in all zones of occupation.[93] As the mission historical records noted: "It should be stated, perhaps, that President Stover has not been very successful in his contacts with the military officials in Berlin. This is probably due to his German background which places him under some suspicion, and also because he has been investigated and is being watched by the Criminal Investigation [Division] of the U.S. Army, because of the unusually large quantity of goods and supplies brought with him from America."[94]

Officials initially denied permission for Stover's wife, Martha, to join him in Berlin.[95] He found it difficult to receive the military's permission to remain in Germany beyond the limit of his initial thirty-day travel authorization. At one point in the spring of 1947, he had to leave Germany for thirty days in order to gain eligibility to reenter.[96] Eventually, after the intercession of Mormon officials with the military chaplain corps leadership, he received permission to dine at American military mess halls and purchase army gasoline.[97] Stover also had periodic run-ins with Soviet authorities and with the nascent government of the German Democratic Republic when it formed in 1949. When Stover received permission to visit Latter-day Saints in the Soviet zone of occupation, that authorization was given verbally but never put into writing, which caused difficulties with border guards and policemen.[98] On one occasion, Soviet authorities arrested Stover.[99]

For German Latter-day Saints who lived behind the Iron Curtain, greater results emerged under the informal direction of Walter Krause, a native German lay leader who was more successful in convincing GDR officials that Mormons could simultaneously owe allegiance to an American church and a communist government. Unlike Stover, Krause had never immigrated to the United States. As late as the 1970s, when Salt Lake City–based Mormon officials could only visit East Germany in conjunction with the annual Leipzig Trade Fair, Krause cultivated a degree of trust with GDR officials that allowed him to travel to Salt Lake City for periodic church general conferences. Nevertheless, the Mormon hierarchy had difficulty accepting the premise that mission leadership could be entrusted to anyone who had not undergone a spiritual apprenticeship in the American Zion. Walter Krause was never appointed to be a mission president.[100] Despite the fact that native Germans acquitted themselves in an outstanding manner in the crucible of wartime leadership, when both world wars ended, the Salt Lake City hierarchy dispatched American replacements. It seemed as if the task of accommodating an authoritarian religious denomination with an equally rigid German civil government could only be entrusted, in both Nazi Germany and communist East Germany, to Americans.

13

Forgotten Heroes and Rediscovered Villains

Max Reschke, whose heroism in saving a Jewish couple on *Kristallnacht* begins this narrative, never imagined that he would become a Mormon saving angel amid the godless reprobates of Nazi Germany, or that his co-religionists would find discomfort in the memory of his valor. In the decades that followed his spontaneous acts of courage that saved lives but violated the Mormons' cooperative strategy, his church and even his family struggled with how to tell the story of his nonconformist courage. After a period of resistance, Latter-day Saints have embraced the puerile wartime courage of the Helmuth Hübener group of adolescent resisters. Books, plays, DVDs, and websites laud the trio of LDS boys, and one non-Mormon, who saved nobody but whose anti-Nazi rebellion cost their teenage leader his life.

Yet Reschke's bold defiance remains practically unknown, in part because of the conflicts between his public and personal life that make his memorialization difficult. In his public persona, he was a prestigious industrial leader who fought the Nazis behind the scenes. In his private life, he was a spiritually revered branch president turned excommunicated adulterer. Faithful historians, and even his loving children, have not sought Reschke's public recognition as the flawed hero to whom at least four people owed their lives. Such a task may have involved revealing more of their church's stance toward the Nazis, and more of Reschke's private failings, than believing writers and his family were willing to do.

For most of his life, Max Reschke was the consummate conformist, albeit one with a conscience. A German patriot as a young man, he needed his father's signature to allow underage enlistment in the Kaiser's army during the First World War. His battlefield service, as painfully described in his diary, included the trauma of killing an enemy soldier whom he had stared in the face before he pulled the trigger. Max was sixteen years old when he took a human life in the service of his country. When a different kind of militancy gripped Germany later in Reschke's life, he reacted by saving lives at the risk of being considered traitorous.

The peaceful interlude between the tragedy of war and the catastrophe of National Socialism revealed the kind of man that Reschke wished to be. Deliberate, well-thought-out decisions characterized his professional life, resulting in career advancement and financial prosperity. Upon discharge from the military, he embarked upon an apprenticeship that resulted in his certification as a journeyman metalworker at age nineteen. Thereafter, he found work in a number of mechanically related enterprises—as a boilermaker, a tractor and diesel engine mechanic, and finally as the lead mechanic at a manufacturing plant. His skill in dealing with machines and people qualified him to enter the supervisory ranks, where he eventually attained the second highest managerial position in a large pharmaceutical firm in Hanover. He loyally served Dr. Wolfgang Laves and his company, Laves-Arzneimittel GmbH, for twenty years.[1]

The same measured approach applied to his spiritual life. As a youngster, he rebelled against taking Lutheran religious classes. Only his father's desperate plea to the pastor, and a spanking applied to Max's bottom, allowed him to secure his confirmation. Thereafter, he put his religious life on hold until the relative maturity of his thirties led him to seek spiritual fulfillment. When Reschke and his second wife attended an LDS service in 1931, they did so as part of a methodical religious search that included the consideration of another denomination, the New Apostolic Church. After his Mormon baptism in June of that year, Reschke faithfully and unpretentiously served his new Latter-day Saint congregation in various callings until Philemon Kelly, president of the Swiss-German Mission, chose him to become the leader of the Hanover Branch in 1937.[2]

Reschke's patience wore thin during his dealings with the Nazis. In 1932, at the urging of a friend, Reschke attended one of Hitler's political speeches. Unimpressed by the bombastic message and the pompous messenger, he nevertheless decided to sign up for Nazi Party membership at the urging of a companion, who said it could help him professionally.

Noticing that the line to greet Hitler was shorter than the one at the enrollment table, he elected to meet the *Führer* first. "His hand felt like a wet sponge," Reschke remembered. "I had such a revolting feeling that I resolved on the spot never to have anything to do with that man or his party."[3]

Reschke obviously conveyed his sentiments to his Mormon congregation's Boy Scouts in early 1934 when the Hitler Youth took over the troop. Reschke watched his boys "tear the patches off of their [Scouting] uniforms, take down the troop flag and other insignia, soak everything in kerosene, and set fire to it." Unlike other Mormon boys of Scouting age, who embraced the Hitler Youth enthusiastically, Reschke's church troop staged the only protest it could get away with—burning their own uniforms. Later, when an adolescent Hitler Youth leader came to his door demanding the enrollment of Reschke's son, the father politely but firmly refused. Then the teenager made a mistake. He stuck his foot in the door and vowed he would not leave until Reschke sent his son to Hitler Youth meetings. Reschke's son recalled what happened next: "Max grabbed the startled young man by the scruff of his neck and the seat of his pants, carried him down two flights of stairs, and unceremoniously threw him on the lawn." For that assault, Reschke was arrested but soon freed.[4] In this and other confrontations with the Nazis, he could rely on the intercession of Laves, the influential Hanover industrialist and owner of the pharmaceutical firm that Reschke helped manage.[5]

Not every confrontation Reschke had with the Nazis resulted in an explosion of temper. Some required imperturbability and sangfroid. Reschke was an ardent Social Democrat who had been active in the metalworkers' union, but when the Nazis seized power, they outlawed all independent trade unions. When the Nazi Labor Front moved into Wolfgang Laves' factory, the boss and his trusted employee conferred. In order to mitigate the influence of the Nazis in his workplace, Laves was able to have Reschke appointed as shop steward. For several years, Reschke was the only non-Nazi shop steward who attended mandatory political indoctrination meetings in Berlin. His refusal to join the Party eventually resulted in his forced removal as the labor leader for his factory.[6]

Reschke responded with a plainspoken refusal whenever someone urged him to participate in a Nazi activity. His sober words often got him in trouble in a Germany that seemed to be inebriated with Hitler. To raise funds for the 1935 Nuremberg rallies, party hacks pestered everyone to purchase small tin badges. Reschke declined brusquely: "If the party wants to stage a congress, the affair ought to be paid for by its members, not its non-members. I am not a member of the party; therefore I'm not buying anything." For that verbal indiscretion, he faced a formal police hearing, charged with anti-party sentiments. He escaped with a reprimand. On another occasion, a plebiscite conducted in 1936 to ratify Hitler's decision to remilitarize the Rhineland, Reschke voted "no" with a Nazi observer looking over his shoulder. The poll watcher recorded an "unpatriotic act."[7] "In the end," wrote Max Reschke's son, Horst, "he became a figure so well known at the local Gestapo headquarters that when he was hauled in, he did not always have to go through the regular booking process."[8] At work, his secretary devised a euphemism to inform Reschke's family that he was once again in custody. She would dispatch a message to his home: Max was "out of town" again.[9]

Insubordinate words alone did not result in the greatest danger Reschke faced because of his defiance during the Nazi years. He bravely hid a local Jew, Kurt Lazarus, in his vacation cottage and then in his apartment, to prevent Lazarus's deportation to the ghettos in the 1940s. (Lazarus, a prominent Hanover banker, was a decorated German Army captain during the First World War, a status that he naively thought would save him when the Nazis came to power.) In retaliation for his defiance, authorities sent Reschke to a concentration camp outside of Hanover for a short period of time in 1941. Then, Reschke's status as an important manager in a critical local industry once again expedited his release.

Kurt and Kaete Lazarus were family friends of Lilly Reschke, Max's third wife. Lilly's mother, Sophie, had enjoyed long-term domestic service employment in the Lazarus home during the happier years before Hitler's ascension. "The Lazarus family showered [grandmother] with affection," wrote Max's son, Horst Reschke. "They had special names and expressions of endearment for her. Knowing of her loyalty and uprightness, they entrusted her [with] their funds, keys to their house, and their possessions."

The Reschke family did not forget Sophie's former employers once Hitler reduced the Jewish couple to the status of *Untermenschen*. When Kaete Lazarus was forced to wear a yellow star on her coat, Horst wrote, she would visit Max's house each week to exchange her coat for one that belonged to Max's wife, "so she could go to the beauty shop. With the star visible, the beauticians would have had to refuse service." The family also dispatched ten-year-old Horst to the Lazarus house with supplies. "My sister was under five and entitled to whole milk coupons," he wrote. He explained further, "The rest of us received only skim milk. She heard that Mrs. Lazarus was ill and sent me with the milk." Horst recalls being stopped by a policeman "who scolded me for going into the house with 'those Jews.'"

Horst also remembers the account of Sophie's last visit to Kaete Lazarus, after her former employer had been driven out into Hanover's ghetto: "Having forced her way past the SS guard into the cramped [ghetto] quarters in Hanover's old town, where the Jews had been taken just prior to their forced departure, Sophie was the last person in our family to see Mrs. Lazarus alive, and the picture of the misery and the sorry plight of all the good people, for whom she had such high regard, never left her."[10]

Kurt Lazarus escaped confinement in the Hanover ghetto where his wife had been dispatched. Lazarus, the college-educated banker, sought refuge with Reschke, a skilled tradesman. As a former German army officer, Lazarus accepted the hospitality of a former enlisted man. Both men had fought bravely for the Kaiser, but Hitler treated each of them so differently. Lazarus caused no trouble for the Reich, but as a Jew he hid from his countrymen and perished when caught. Reschke, as a member of a controversial American religious sect but the manager of an important company, openly defied the Nazis but survived his brushes with authority.

Horst Reschke viewed their relationship through a child's eyes and later wrote: "We had [Kurt Lazarus] live in our *Gardenlaube* on the edge of town. But one night, he came to our apartment, asking if we could take him in. The howling wind, the lonesome feeling, and the need to keep out of sight were too much for him. He stayed with us and we learned to love him. Eventually, a neighbor must have seen him. The Gestapo came in and took both him and my father."

Kurt Lazarus never reached a concentration camp. He died in the city of Hamelin's *Zuchthaus*, a maximum-security prison in which inmates performed backbreaking labor. The Germans deported Kaete Lazarus from the Hamburg ghetto to the horrific Section R ghetto for German Jews in Riga, Latvia. Inmates who survived the Riga ghetto were sent to a number of slave labor camps, particularly Kaiserwald and its satellites. No record documents the fate of Kaete Lazarus. Assumed to have perished, she remains officially listed as "missing." Max Reschke was sent to the Ahlem concentration camp near Hanover, but was soon released because of the intervention of highly placed friends.[11]

Max Reschke did not take risks solely for Jews. In late 1939, shortly after Germany invaded Poland, the Laves's pharmaceutical company received the services of a sixteen-year-old Polish slave laborer named Stanislaw. Reschke, whose West Prussian background provided him with a command of the Polish language, befriended the young man and once saved him from a dangerous confrontation with an enraged German police officer. Stanislaw survived the war, immigrated to the United States, took the name Stanley Blake, and served in the American military. He later exchanged correspondence with Max Reschke and his children.[12]

Reschke saved the life of a Russian prisoner of war, a Red Army captain and forward artillery spotter sent as a prisoner of war to Hanover for slave labor. In doing so, he defied the regulations prescribed for relationships between German civilians and military captives. Horst Reschke told the story of his father's rescue of "Nikolai" from a swarm of emaciated Soviet prisoners brought to their city: "He was a pathetic figure in rags, sitting there in our living room, an alien creature from another world. Max had been given permission to pick him out of a camp. Lilly (Max's wife) was aghast. She whispered to him that this could be a dangerous man, one who could slit their throats. . . . 'Don't be silly,' Max said, not keeping his voice down at all. 'This is one poor, starving human being, and you don't have to talk in a whisper. He can't understand you anyway.'"

Had Reschke possessed an ordinary German's sense of obedience to the wartime regime, Nikolai would have been locked up in the company factory at night and furnished only with the bare essentials necessary to sustain life. Instead, on that first night in 1944, with fuel supplies running short in Germany, the Reschke family sacrificed its weekly bath in order to provide Nikolai with two tubs of hot water, "one for the first hard scrubbing and one for a nice, leisurely soaking-type bath." When Nikolai reappeared, clean, shaven, and dressed in Max's old clothes, Reschke again horrified the rest of his family by seating Nikolai at the family dinner table and compelling his children to introduce themselves to the stranger who spoke no German.

Forgotten Heroes and Rediscovered Villains

Over the weeks and months that followed, Reschke learned that Nikolai was an educated man, one who had earned a PhD, whose quick-witted change of clothing with a dead Red Army private—his radio operator—saved him the uncertain fate of having been captured in the uniform of an officer. Reschke used his influence with local authorities to allow Nikolai to be employed in the rubble-clearing operation of the Laves Company's bombed-out Hanover plant. Reschke was able to continue earning a living as the manager of Laves's satellite facilities that remained undamaged.

When American occupation forces arrived in Hanover, they found the ghastly remains of most of Nikolai's fellow Russian prisoners of war. SS troops had murdered them in the last days of the war. American soldiers went door to door, conscripting German residents to view the mass grave and to rebury the bodies. When a young American officer knocked on Max Reschke's door, Nikolai greeted him, introduced himself as a Russian army captain, and persuaded the American soldier to excuse his host family from the grisly detail. Against all advice, Nikolai subsequently made a harrowing trip back into Soviet-occupied territory after the war, seeking to determine the fate of his family. Having learned that they had died, and after escaping a brush with military police sent to arrest him, he eventually settled in Australia—where Max's son Horst traced him.[13]

Max Reschke's strongest character traits seemed to manifest themselves after an eruption of temper. For an otherwise tolerant, even-keeled man who was appalled by what the Nazis were doing to his country, the vilest provocation occurred on one of the worst days in German history. On the evening of November 9, 1938, the fatherland of Goethe, Schiller, Beethoven, Bach, and Einstein became a cradle of vandalism, abduction, arson, assault, and murder. *Kristallnacht*, framed as the spontaneous eruption of popular rage because of the murder of a diplomat in Paris, was instead a carefully choreographed act of domestic state terrorism against Germany's Jews. Conceived at the highest levels of a malicious Nazi state and carried out by legions of brown-shirted thugs, the "Night of the Broken Glass" left at least one thousand dead, many thousands more in concentration camps, businesses destroyed, synagogues burned to the ground, and quaint cobblestoned streets transformed into rivers of shattered glass.

If it had not been for a half dozen goose down pillows, Max Reschke would have been a bystander to this horrific event. Because his second wife, Wilma, had sent him on an errand to retrieve bedding she had left at a laundry one week before, Reschke joined a small group of brave non-Jewish Germans who courageously rescued Jews from the Nazis' murderous clutches. Reschke joined an even smaller group: he is probably the only such hero whose religious denomination has shunned commemorating his heroism. His faithful family still struggled—generations later—with how to appropriately memorialize his life on earth.

The Scheurenbergs, a Jewish couple who ran a small business in downtown Hanover, were not close family friends. When Max Reschke went to town on a pillow-fetching errand that tragic evening, he found a city in chaos. A uniformed SA hoodlum blocked the door to the Scheurenbergs' business. First politely and then brusquely, the plainspoken plant manager asked the brown shirt to step aside. "Nobody goes up to that Jewish pigsty!" the storm trooper replied.

Horst Reschke described what happened next: "Max's temper, which he normally kept under control, quickly flared. He warned the man that he'd better move on the count of three. . . . At the end of the count, Max applied some kind of judo grip, swung the brown-shirt over his head, and laid him out on the sidewalk."

Reschke found a horrific sight upstairs: pillow feathers and smashed furniture were scattered about. Human excrement had been rubbed into the furniture, on the windows, and onto the ceiling. There was no trace of the owners. Worrying about the consequences of his actions, Reschke fled before the unconscious Nazi thug could awake and spread the alarm.[14] Broken emotionally, he hurried home to tell his family what was happening.

Horst wrote: "My father came home, sat down and wept, [and] told us what was going on in the city. I was horrified to hear him tell about the destruction of the Jewish stores and homes and in particular the burning of the synagogue. The display windows of the Jewish businesses were being smashed by hordes of people. The Jewish people were being herded through the streets, some of them in their nightclothes."[15]

Then, the shock of what he had seen and the fear of retribution for his assault on the storm trooper began to fade. A sense of duty regarding unfinished business shocked him to a sudden realization: "I forgot to check on the Scheurenbergs!" he told his startled family. Against Wilma's pleadings, he went back to town. Horst recounted what happened two hours later: "He came back with the bedraggled couple. He had found them at the end of a column of people being herded through the streets by armed guards. Calmly Max stepped up to a uniformed guard and, flipping his overcoat lapel in the manner of a plainclothes policeman to show his concealed badge, he said, pointing to the Scheurenbergs, 'I'll take these two.' 'Very well, Sir!' the guard said, saluting."[16]

Max Reschke put the Jewish couple in an automobile and embarked upon an odyssey of more than four hundred kilometers, through the troubled night toward the Swiss border. No record recounts the difficulty they may have encountered in crossing into Switzerland, which at the time was consumed with an internal political debate regarding Jewish refugees.[17] How the Scheurenbergs found temporary sanctuary, and the story of their immigration to Shanghai in the midst of the Second Sino-Japanese War, would have made a riveting narrative. The account of their return to Germany after the war to thank Max Reschke would have told a heartwarming story.[18] Except for one paragraph written in a privately published biography of Max Reschke, the remaining details of this heroic rescue remain untold.

One wonders why, in the midst of certain late-twentieth-century events that challenged the Mormon-Jewish relationship, a faithful LDS historian would not have undertaken a scholarly project to demonstrate that at least one Mormon, along with a scant number of other Christians, courageously saved Jews in Nazi Germany. In 1984, when BYU announced plans to build a satellite campus on Jerusalem's Mount Scopus, objections to potential Mormons proselytizing led to an investigation by the Knesset, Israel's parliament.[19] In 1995 Jewish leaders condemned the Mormon practice of posthumously baptizing Jewish victims of the Holocaust, a controversy that continues to percolate each time more posthumous baptisms are discovered.[20] In the context of either of these events, the story of Max Reschke would have argued against the contention that Mormons disrespected Jews and their faith.

One prominent LDS scholar, historian Douglas Tobler, learned of Reschke's courageous exploits, but devoted only one paragraph of a scholarly article, entitled "The Jews, the Mormons, and the Holocaust," to the story. Tobler had heard about Reschke from one of Max's grandsons, who had enrolled in his BYU history class.[21] After writing five sentences about Reschke in a thirty-three-page article, Tobler concluded: "The full story of Reschke's heroism is yet to be told."[22] At least two other scholars with roots in the Mormon Culture Region had incidental knowledge of Reschke's heroism. In the mid-1990s, University of Utah professor Ronald Smelser hosted Horst Reschke during his university's workshop on the Holocaust. In the context of arguing that not all Germans approved of Hitler's methods, Max Reschke's son told his father's story.[23] In an extensive "selective chronology," included as an appendix to D. Michael Quinn's two-volume study entitled *The Mormon Hierarchy*, published in 1997, the former BYU historian summarizes Reschke's heroism in nine lines of eight-point type.[24]

It was left to Reschke's four children by his second marriage, all of whom immigrated to the United States during the postwar period, to tell their father's story. Max Reschke also immigrated but never recounted his own narrative in his new country. He died on May 3, 1971, at the age of seventy-two. Only Horst, the second-oldest child, left written remembrances that are available to the historical researcher. Even those are hard to access. The best consists of a well-written, privately published, professionally bound, illustrated, 164-page paperback book that he distributed to family and friends. *Max: A West Prussian Odyssey* is available only in a few municipal libraries in the United States that have presumably acquired copies through donation by the original owners. Horst Reschke also authored a few articles for obscure genealogical magazines that mentioned his father.

Max Reschke qualifies for induction into *Yad Vashem's* Righteous Among the Nations, an official recognition by the State of Israel of non-Jews who rescued Jews from death at the hands of the Nazis. However, induction requires sworn eyewitness testimony. That would have been available in past decades, but the trail of evidence has now gone cold. The Jewish couple he rescued, the Scheurenbergs, has not been heard from since they visited Germany after the war to thank Max. Horst's accounts do not contain their given names, and it is unlikely they are still alive. Horst died in 2011 and was predeceased by his younger brother, Dieter. Horst's older sister, Ursula, who witnessed the drama unfold in the Reschke living room on *Kristallnacht*, would be eighty-six years old in 2015.

Wilma, Max's second wife who begged him not to go back into Hanover on *Kristallnacht*, and Lilly, his third spouse who came to America with the family, are both dead.

According to Rabbi Mordecai Paldiel, a former director of the Department of the Righteous for *Yad Vashem*, no known Latter-day Saint numbers among the 23,788 Righteous Among the Nations from forty-five countries.[25] The LDS Church, after having pursued its policy of accommodation and ingratiation that put its members on the wrong side of history, could use a hero—if only to illustrate that sometimes a lone believer's conscience trumps the collective wisdom of a religious hierarchy. Before he died in 2011, Horst Reschke declined assistance in attaining this special degree of recognition for his father. He stated that simple family modesty prevented him from seeking *Yad Vashem's* recognition of Max Reschke.[26] That may be true, but an important clue Horst Reschke included in his book suggests consideration of an additional motive.

To use his son's words, Max Reschke was "a ladies' man." He married three times. The divorce from Ida, his first wife, was amicable despite Max's philandering—according to Horst's account. Max and Ida remained friends after nine years of marriage that produced no children. When the couple divorced in June 1929, the woman whom Max would take as his second wife, Wilma, was already pregnant with the couple's first child, a daughter they named Ursula. She was born in late 1929, just a few months after Max and Wilma wed in September. According to Horst, Wilma attended Max and Ida's divorce proceeding, and two months later Ida was cheerfully on hand to see Max marry Wilma.[27]

Max and Wilma stayed married for twelve years. She gave him two sons and two daughters. She bore the brunt of the pressure when Max would run afoul of the Nazis and be hauled off to Gestapo headquarters. She was at home on *Kristallnacht*, and begged Max not to go back into the dangerous streets. Their domestic life was not tranquil. Apparently, Max fought a two-front war, one at work against the Nazis and another at home in a stressful marriage. When they divorced in 1941, the separation was not amicable. They fought for custody and, for a while, each cared for two of the children. Eventually, they settled the custody issue when they sent the children to the countryside to escape the wartime bombing of Hanover.[28]

Max's third wife, Lilly, had been a trusted friend of the family who had provided childcare and cooking for years. Apparently, their friendship began while Reschke was still married to Wilma, his second wife, and was probably a factor in the breakup. After the divorce but before Max and Lilly married at the end of January 1942, Max became involved with a fourth woman. In September 1942, Paula Golombeck gave birth to Max's son Klaus. Lilly forgave Max for his indiscretion and acquiesced to his support of his illegitimate child, but they did not tell the rest of Max's children about young Klaus for ten years. At some point after the couple immigrated to the United States along with Max's four children by his second marriage, Klaus, Max's love child, joined them.

In the early 1940s, Max Reschke's philandering attracted the attention of the Mormon Church authorities. With Wilma, his second wife and the mother of his first four children, he had joined the LDS Church—a fact that was not lost on the elders who sat on the "church court." During their marriage, Reschke served as branch president, a position in which he was expected to maintain the highest standards of morality. Following the example left by the departed American mission presidents, the LDS district leadership convened a disciplinary tribunal and excommunicated Reschke for adultery. Stubborn as ever, Max refused to attend the proceedings.[29]

For Max Reschke, the Nazi government and the Mormon Church each presented rigid systems that required unyielding submission and threatened drastic consequences for disobedience. He defied both of them, risking physical death in one case and spiritual damnation in another. During the period in his life when he saved the Scheurenberg couple from the horrors of *Kristallnacht*, surreptitiously driving them across the Swiss border, he was stealthily defying his church's proscription against marital infidelity. When he sheltered Kurt Lazarus from deportation and sent milk to Kaete Lazarus in the Hamburg ghetto, he was beginning a third marriage while awaiting the birth of his girlfriend's love child. When he saved the life of a Russian prisoner of war in 1944, Reschke was a man without the promise of eternal salvation, having been damned through the loss of his church membership.

Many heroes are, in reality, flawed human beings who compensate for weaknesses in one facet of their lives by excelling in another. Max Reschke pushed the extremes of that paradigm with his unbridled courage and consistent philandering. He successfully saved lives without hesitation but struggled to save his marriages. In the eyes of faithful Mormon historians, and especially those of his children, the opportunity to memorialize Max Reschke for his admirable heroism may have been offset by the task of explaining his failure to adhere to church moral standards. It was, perhaps, too great a burden.

Erich Krause: An Unwelcomed Mormon Memory Beacon

When *Wall Street Journal* journalist Frederick Kempe decided in the 1990s to write a book about contemporary Germany's "inherited guilt" for the sins of Nazism, he thought he would rely on contacts he established during years of reporting from central Europe. Kempe, a lapsed Mormon whose German father arrived in Utah early enough to fight for the United States Army in the Second World War, was confident that he would be able to conduct his research as a detached, dispassionate observer. Instead, an old trunk that contained family journals became the first step on an investigative trail that led to a startling realization. If guilt for the crimes of Hitler were a heritable commodity, Kempe himself would be subject to such an unsettling bequest of culpability.

By sleuthing in the close-knit German community that settled in the Mormon Culture Region before and after the Third Reich, Kempe discovered that a distant relative he had never met, the German Mormon who married his great aunt, had been an especially cruel and sadistic Nazi torturer and murderer. Through research conducted in the archives of the Federal Republic's prosecutor, and in the recently opened archives of the East German secret police, the reporter learned the ghastly details of his distant relative's offenses. He also discovered that the LDS Church, through its American mission president sent to reestablish Zion's authority in Germany after the war, loaned bail money and pleaded for the accused's pre-trial release when West German prosecutors charged the perpetrator with crimes against humanity.

Erich Krause murdered dozens and tortured hundreds as the brownshirted commandant of a "wild" concentration camp in Berlin during the early days of the regime. Then, as a military policeman in the eastern theatre during the war, he sent correspondence home stamped with the postmarks of a town known to have housed a prominent Jewish ghetto that served as a way station for the Final Solution's gas chambers and crematoria. Having joined the Mormon Church in 1923 and the SA in 1928, Krause validated, in an extreme way, the concept that one could strive to serve both the Mormon Church and Nazi Party.

Krause also personified the German expatriate community's worst nightmare, even though he never immigrated to Utah. At crowded family reunions up and down the Wasatch Front in the latter half of the twentieth century, many spoke in whispers—in German and in German-accented English—about *their* special relative. That person could have been someone who performed small acts of kindness for beleaguered Jews. Conversely, the subject of those hushed tones could have been a relative who embraced Nazism a bit more enthusiastically than society can now comfortably forgive—considering how the war turned out. Few families could claim a hero as admirable as Max Reschke or a villain as evil as Erich Krause. The collective memory of the ghastly excesses of Nazi Germany, however, is contained not only on the European side of the Atlantic. It also is not limited to Germans who lived through the war and migrated afterward. As journalist Frederick Kempe discovered, those nightmares of memory can haunt the descendants of émigrés who left Germany before Hitler took power. Kempe's father arrived in time to fight for his new country in the war; his mother was born in the United States, but the great uncle left behind was the murderous Nazi.

When Erich Krause leapt out of the pages of Kempe's book in 1999, his unwelcomed arrival in Utah created a belated victim of Hitler's treachery. Inge, Erich Krause's daughter, knew the Second World War only from history books and the infrequent comments of her forward-looking parents. She was born in Germany in 1956. At seventeen, she realized the dream of many faithful LDS girls who were not fortunate enough to have been reared in the Mormon Culture Region. She immigrated to the United States in order to attend college in Utah, where she aspired to attain an education and find an "R.M."—a returned missionary to take her to the Holy Temple. Life's reality mitigated her dreams by the end of the twentieth century. Her celestial marriage had ended in earthly divorce. That had been her greatest sorrow, until that sickening, turn-of-the-century phone call from a half-brother with news of a new book that had just hit the shelves. It turned her life upside down.[30]

Forgotten Heroes and Rediscovered Villains

It was *Vati!* The loving father who had never spanked her, the hardest working genealogical researcher in her postwar German church congregation, and the man who fervently preached Joseph Smith's restored gospel from the podium during Sunday services—had suddenly become a monster. Inge's four siblings by her father's third marriage, solemnized in a 1955 civil ceremony and posthumously sealed in the Holy Temple, also took the news with difficulty. For one, it was an emotional shock that aggravated an already existing physical ailment. How does one deal with the news of a loving and ostensibly godly parent's hidden treachery, the cold-blooded killings and torture of human beings before he bequeathed life to his offspring?

Inge sought redemption by making a pilgrimage to a huge, multi-story, red-brick building on General-Pape-Strasse in Berlin's Tempelhof district.[31] Here, in the basement of a former police barracks, her father had directed a chamber of horrors that terrorized more than two thousand of the Nazi regime's alleged political opponents, mostly Communists and Social Democrats, between March and December 1933.[32] Inge found the structure locked, and only a small plaque noted its nefarious past. As she walked around the periphery, she may have conjured up images described in the state prosecutor's investigation. Erich Krause, holding the rank of SA *Obertruppenführer* and wearing a brown shirt with "red collar patches and two stars with a braid," reserved some of the worst treacherous excesses for himself. He beat prisoners with a rubber truncheon and an iron bar. He sliced open the soles of their feet and packed pepper into the wounds. He made other barefooted prisoners run outside on gravel. He gave one man a rope and told him to hang himself; presumably weary of the torture, the emotionally drained prisoner went into the lavatory and complied. Krause exercised prisoners to the point of exhaustion and extreme thirst, and then made them drink a concoction of wastewater and human feces. He told one prisoner that he was free to go, and then had him shot as an escapee on his way out. He staged "sporting nights," when his drunken SA companions made prisoners run a gauntlet of clubs and batons. A number of prisoners died of gunshot wounds, which he never inflicted in front of others—but he made other prisoners fall to their hands and knees and lick up the spilled blood with their tongues.[33]

On that walk around this citadel of horror, Inge may have recalled the language of postcards Krause dispatched to his second wife and her half-brothers when he was a staff sergeant in the military police. After the book came out, Inge's half-brother, Fridtjof, sent copies of those cards. Many of them contained admonitions to remain true to the family's Mormon faith, and for the children to take their Sunday school lessons seriously. The first *Feldpost* cards arrived from Poland, where Krause's MP unit had followed behind the September 1939 invasion. He also dispatched cards from France, Yugoslavia, and the Ukraine, as the *Wehrmacht* advanced relentlessly. Then the postmarks became more disturbing. In 1944 a card arrived from Lodz, the site of Poland's second-largest Jewish community after Warsaw. It was also the location of a ghetto from which Jews were dispatched to Auschwitz and Theresienstadt. As Fridtjof Krause said of his father: "One only chose the most trusted of Nazis to break up the ghettos."

Erich Krause returned to German society in 1949 after his release from Soviet postwar confinement. Soon after his arrival in Berlin, he began having violent family arguments that resulted in frequent beatings of his second wife and children. After a brush with East German authorities, he fled to West Berlin. In October 1950, one of his Pape Street victims recognized him and filed a report with the authorities. In December, West Berlin police arrested him, after which he spent a year in "investigative custody." After his release, his second marriage dissolved, but he was soon back in prison. In 1952 the Berlin State Court "charged him with murder, crimes against humanity, and applying torture and violence to gain confessions."[34]

Author Frederick Kempe consulted the recently released Stasi archives, as well as the records of the state court transcripts. Among the pages of revolting testimony against Erich Krause, the journalist found a sworn statement from Krause's first wife, Käthe Elsa Antonie Ziburski. Theirs was a marriage made in hell and destroyed on the altar of anti-Semitism. They met at the gravesite of the infamous brown-shirted martyr, Horst Wessel, where Erich was stationed as an SA honor guard. She had gone to the memorial to pay her respects to Hitler's most revered thug, accompanied by another storm trooper. Krause wooed her away, married her, impregnated her, and then later divorced her because his genealogical research revealed she had a Jewish ancestor.[35]

Another surprise stood out among the pages of vile evidence. The president of the Mormons' East German Mission, Walter Stover, attested to Krause's character in an effort to win his freedom. Stover, a native German, had joined the LDS Church in 1923, the same year in which Erich Krause converted. Stover moved to Utah in 1926, where he became a bedroom furniture manufacturer and advanced to the clerical rank of high priest—an ordination not normally performed in the German mission field. He also became a naturalized American citizen. Stover returned to Germany as a mission president in 1946 and served until 1951.[36] Early in Krause's confinement, Stover asked the court to release the accused to the custody of his family and offered the LDS Church as guarantor. Stover paid two thousand marks from church funds as bail.

Said Stover in his letter to the authorities: "Herr Krause is personally known to me as a member of our church. I am convinced that he will keep himself available to the court at any time and hasn't any intention to suppress evidence or leave Berlin." Stover continued his plea by citing Krause's six years in military service and five in Russian postwar confinement, which he termed "enough punishment for any man."[37]

Despite the seriousness of the charges against Krause, and the violent nature of his relationship with his family, the Mormon community in Berlin stood behind one of its own. According to Inge, who became Krause's first child by his third marriage but knew little about his Nazi background until Frederick Kempe's book, her father became very devout in his faith. When he was in jail, the members of his ward (congregation) would visit him regularly.[38] He was a stake genealogy leader and later advanced to the position of stake high councilman, a member of the governing board for a Mormon organization comparable to a diocese.[39]

Frederick Kempe, paraphrasing one of Krause's sons, summarized how the former storm trooper reconciled his faith in God and his faith in Hitler: "He felt very strongly about the church. Mormonism and National Socialism were his two greatest passions. Both worlds offered a man discipline and a doctrine of absolutes by which to lead his life. One required absolute faith in some superior being, and the other demanded absolute loyalty to a *Führer*."[40]

At the end of his trial, Erich Krause, faithful Mormon and ruthless killer, walked free. Prosecutors produced no eyewitness testimony to his murders. Anyone who had watched him kill seemed, conveniently, to have already died. With regard to the charges of nonlethal assault and torture, numerous witnesses testified to confirm his culpability. However, his defense team secured an acquittal based upon a five-year statute of limitations that applied to noncapital crimes.

Inge, as a daughter born eleven years after the war ended, never knew the man who appeared in a distant cousin's book, or even the one who emerged from a five-year legal proceeding the year before she was born. Inge saw a different man, one who seemed incapable of violence: "He never laid a hand on me or any of us." She recalled the worst punishment he ever inflicted on her. One evening when she was a young child, she threw a stack of papers out of their apartment's window. A policeman arrived in the middle of the night and instructed her father to clean up the mess. "So, the next day," Inge recalled, "my parents walked me to the police station so that the police could explain to me that it was not correct. That was scary."

On only one occasion during her childhood did the events of the past intrude on Inge: "I remember one time in the seventh grade our school was getting ready to go to a concentration camp to clean it up. It was going to be a field trip and I wanted to go. There was this terror on his face. I was not allowed to go. Just seeing his whole countenance change to absolute terror, I couldn't stand seeing that and respected it. Whatever that meant [at the time], I had no idea."[41]

During his lifetime, Erich Krause never gave his daughter an explanation. On one occasion when Inge was still an adolescent, she asked her father about his previous life. He refused to discuss it. "There will be a time," he promised. That time never came. The brutal Nazi killer turned placid family man died in August 1983, without ever having alluded to shocking news that his children would later learn from the pages of an unwelcomed book. If indeed he was sincere when he became religiously observant later in life, part of his reluctance may have had its roots in Mormon theology. In the LDS concept of redemption, premeditated murder cannot receive godly forgiveness while the perpetrator is still living. Heavenly Father can only grant that absolution in the afterlife, and presumably only if the sinner showed genuine repentance during his lifetime. Erich Krause could never promise his daughter that she would reap one of the unique benefits of Mormonism: a heavenly afterlife in which families are together forever.

Today, Inge clings to a single account of her father's life, one that gives her hope that they will meet again. It is based on information she learned by happenstance. In a chance encounter with one of her father's old friends after the publication of Frederick Kempe's book, Inge learned of a postwar conversation that occurred on a Berlin streetcar. A group of Krause's old friends recognized him: disheveled, unshaven, and wearing a dirty winter coat. They shouted: "Erich! Erich! Erich!" He hung his head and tried to ignore them; he wanted to cut all ties with his past. Finally, after their persistent beckoning, he reluctantly conversed. Erich Krause—storm trooper, killer, sadist, ghetto liquidator, loving father, and repentant Mormon—told his old companions, "I have served the wrong master."[42]

Horst Reschke, in contrast to Inge, had no doubt about his father's status in the afterlife. Eight years after Max Reschke's excommunication, the courageous lifesaver and serial philanderer was "re-baptized." That restored his Mormon Church membership. Several years later, after having moved with his third wife and the rest of his children to Utah, the family entered the Holy Temple to be sealed "for time and all eternity." That is the LDS ceremony that binds husbands to wives and children to parents on earth and in heaven. The son who so carefully controlled the memory of his father's exploits in this life was content to have his father's heroism recognized in another.

14

Mormons and Jews
An Inconvenient Association

Egon Engelbert Weiss was a Mormon of Jewish descent, a member of the Vienna Branch of the Swiss-Austrian Mission in 1938. Although few details of his life have survived, the historical record offers a reasonable synopsis of how he lived before and after Hitler's troops marched into Austria in March of that year. Jews had enjoyed full rights of citizenship in the Hapsburg Empire since a decree from Emperor Franz Joseph I in 1869. Under the Austrian Republic that emerged after the First World War, Mormons like Weiss peacefully coexisted with others, even though their small religious denomination numbered in the hundreds and exerted no political influence.

As a citizen of Jewish origin in the 1930s, Weiss probably could have been counted among Austria's intellectually and commercially privileged. Some sixty-two percent of Vienna's lawyers, forty-seven percent of its medical doctors, and twenty-nine percent of its university faculty were Jewish. According to the Nazis' own estimates, one-quarter of Vienna's businesses were owned or operated by Jews, including sixty percent of those in banking or "big industry."[1] When the Nazis took control of Austria, the Mormon mission leaders had one concern: how to configure the boundaries of the German-speaking missions to conform to the new political reality. "Brother Weiss," as his fellow Mormons called him, had more serious worries. Regardless of his devotion to Mormonism, his pedigree branded him with the indelible mark of Judaism.

After Austria became a member of the Third Reich, all of the dangers and indignities that Germany's Jews had experienced over the past five years hit the Austrian Jewish community like a sudden thunderclap. In just one day, when Jewish students were banned, Austrian universities lost forty percent of their students. Shortly after the *Anschluss*, Adolf Eichmann established the Central Office for Jewish Emigration in Vienna, which was in reality an agency to promote intimidation of Jews and pressure them to leave the Reich. For those Jews who remained, it later coordinated ghettoization and deportation to concentration camps. Its subsidiary agency, the Asset Transfer Office, stole Jewish possessions and "transferred" them to non-Jews. The horror of *Kristallnacht* did not stop at a former national border. In Egon Weiss's Vienna, paramilitary thugs burned forty-two synagogues, vandalized and looted 4,038 Jewish shops, and desecrated the city's Jewish cemeteries. If Weiss' residence was like most others occupied by Jews, he watched the mob destroy it.[2]

With no other recourse, Brother Weiss took a pen in hand and appealed to his Mormon co-religionists in the American Zion. On November 23, 1938, two weeks after *Kristallnacht*, he wrote to the First Presidency in Salt Lake City. Then he addressed eight additional letters to former missionaries in Utah and Idaho whom he had befriended when they served in the German-speaking missions.[3] Weiss complained that "Conditions are terrible for us Jewish people, and we have absolutely no hope of working at our learned trades. . . . It is simply that we must get away from here." Addressing the church presidency as "Dear Brother," he asked for help "to make the necessary affidavit to enable his family to escape to America."[4] Weiss assured his church leadership that his family had adequate financial support for the journey and to sustain itself upon arrival in the United States. "We can't enter the United States without having resident Americans vouching for our integrity and possible worth as future citizens." His letter closed, "Your brother in the Gospel."[5]

No available record reveals a response, but Jewish pleas for help addressed to the Mormon hierarchy ran into solid resistance from the second-ranking member of the LDS leadership triad, J. Reuben Clark. Clark dispatched boilerplate responses to most. Historian D. Michael Quinn, who wrote two biographies of Clark, summarized the language used by the Mormons' first counselor whenever such a plea came across his desk: "In regard to 'your interesting letter,' President Clark began his standard reply to desperate Jews in January 1939, 'we have so many requests of this sort from various persons, including members of the

Church, that we have found it necessary to ask to be excused from making the required guarantee.' His letter recommended that the petitioners, some of whom were LDS, contact Jewish organizations for help."[6]

The church's response to another lifelong Austrian Mormon of Jewish linage was not as perfunctory but it contained the same refusal. Richard Siebenschein, also of Vienna, wrote two letters, dated December 25 and 28, 1938, addressed directly to Heber J. Grant, with whom Siebenschein claimed to have shared an apartment "in the boarding house of Mrs. Parker" when both served as Mormon missionaries in Tokyo in 1901. Claiming that he wanted only an "affidavit as required by the law of the USA for entry into your country." Grant's former missionary companion pled: "We are not in trouble through no fault of our own, except our [Jewish] descendence."

This time, J. Reuben Clark responded with a chatty letter that detailed the present circumstances of each missionary with whom Siebenschein served in Japan at the turn of the twentieth century. He said President Grant was away from the city, but that the Prophet would be pleased to know Siebenschein remember him and had written. Then, in a startling switch of tone, Clark reverted to his form-letter verbiage, asking to be "excused" from providing such assistance because the church received "so many requests of this sort."[7]

The LDS Church thus erected a firewall between its resources and the Jews who needed them to leave Germany, even if they had converted to Mormonism. It did not, however, refrain from using its influence to seek diplomatic help for those not tainted by a Jewish heritage. Several months prior to the arrival of Weiss's plea, using a term made infamous by the Nazis, Clark requested the assistance of his former State Department colleagues in expediting the immigration to the United States of a Mormon couple. "She and her husband are *Aryan* natives and nationals of Switzerland," Clark implored (my emphasis). Subsequently, according to Quinn, Clark privately urged the State Department not to help Jewish children to leave Nazi Germany if their parents were trying to send them to the United States.[8] Thus, if a non-Jew needed assistance, the LDS hierarchy sometimes stood ready to help. If a Jew asked, it not only refused, but at least in one case also urged its government not to assist.

Clark explained his opposition to Jewish immigration in a letter to Allen Dulles, a prominent law partner in the New York firm of Sullivan

& Cromwell who later became the first civilian director of the Central Intelligence Agency. "I share all of the sentiments you expressed, both of sympathy for those who are in distress, and anxiety over the vast numbers of people who are coming to this country. We have had a tremendous meal of aliens in the last two or three years, and I am just a little bit afraid that we may have over-eaten a bit. I think, therefore, we should allow a little time for digestion to begin before eating very much more."[9]

That remark illustrates two important prejudices that Clark brought to the LDS leadership. As Quinn maintained, this prominent lawyer, statesman, and religious prelate subscribed to xenophobia and nativism, characteristics that he displayed early in life. In 1898, as valedictorian of the University of Utah's graduating class, Clark drew enthusiastic applause when he proclaimed, "America must cease to be the cesspool into which shall drain the foul sewage of Europe."[10]

Clark explained this admonition with bombastic, anti-immigrant rhetoric typical of early-twentieth-century progressivism: "Great tidal waves of foreign paupers are rolling in upon our shores. Time after time have these mountainous ocean swells, racing with a mighty imperative, crested and thrown far inland a continent's filth. . . . These great, undesirable elements have invaded our lands, are pillaging our homes, and threatening our lives. 'Tis time these thieves, anarchists, and assassins were excluded from our shores."[11]

Catholic immigrants, Italians and Irish, attracted Clark's disdain during this turn-of-the-century address. Later in life, his experience in the practice of law on the East Coast cultivated a new prejudice: a particularly virulent strain of anti-Semitism that remained in the forefront of his character for the remainder of his life. He dealt with Jews, both as clients and as legal opponents, during the years between his stints of State Department service. These contacts, established in the adversarial arena of the law when large amounts of money were at stake, led Clark to embrace the anti-Semitism that was a popular American vice at the time—one that saw Jews as both selfish and dishonest in their financial dealings.[12]

Another factor may have aggravated Clark's anti-Semitism. He lost two primary election campaigns, in 1922 and 1928, for the Republican senatorial nomination from Utah. Clark's victorious opponent was a Jewish mining magnate, Ernest Bamberger. Frank Fox, another Clark biographer, said that Bamberger "simply believed that public offices could be purchased, and in 1922 he decided to buy himself one." Bamberger organized a political money-raising machine called "The Order of the Sevens." Fox explained: "An inner ring of seven principals each recruited seven satellites, who in turn drafted seven of their own, and so on. The group held secret meetings and had a colorful ritual of recognition beginning with the question, 'Which way are you going?' and ending [with] the words 'Jere' and 'Miah' to form the name of an ancient prophet."[13] The fact that a Jewish candidate could defeat a Mormon favorite son in Utah seemed to cement another aspect of Clark's prejudice.[14] Not only were Jews corrupt in their financial dealings, he believed, but the way they conducted political affairs also suggested contempt for America's governing system.

Clark had built his foundation of anti-Semitism upon three pillars: his anti-immigrant nativism, a belief that Jews were financially dishonest, and a conviction that Jews placed their own interests over that of their country. He left a long written trail of evidence, both before and after the Second World War, to substantiate each facet of his prejudice. Presumably, Clark brought his biases with him when he visited the twentieth century's bastion of anti-Semitism, Nazi Germany, and negotiated with the financier who bankrolled Hitler's campaign against the Jews, Hjalmar Schacht.

Clark understood why Jews wished to leave Germany. The persecution of Jews in Hitler's Reich made headlines in the *Deseret News* daily newspaper that Clark helped to control editorially. In addition, his Mormon missionaries were keen observers. Young American elders walked streets littered with the shattered glass of Jewish businesses, conversed with Mormon congregants who had Jewish friends, and dispatched their observations to the mission president—who forwarded the information up the chain of command to Salt Lake City.

One of those reports could have come from Sterling Ryser, who served in the western part of Germany. In the months before *Kristallnacht*, he observed: "You could tell what was going to happen. It had a routine to it. A Jewish store would be selected. The first thing you would see is anti-Jewish slogans. The next step would be a broken-in front window. The next step would be a fire. Then you would see it all, all through the city and some of them were big stores. The thing was pretty obvious. As you know, they had some scandal sheets that they published that were all anti-Jewish propaganda. I have [saved] four or five of those someplace."[15]

When Jews decided to leave Germany, they often fled after forfeiting most of what they owned to a Nazi state that devised elaborate mechanisms to steal their wealth. This was obvious to Mormon missionaries who sent their reports up the ecclesiastical ladder, through their mission presidents, to J. Reuben Clark and his associates in the First Presidency.[16] Donald M. Petty, while waiting to board an ocean liner for the passage home, wanted to ensure that his luggage would not be forgotten: "Going through the warehouses in Hamburg when I wanted to check out my baggage, I saw these long extensive warehouses with these big wooden crates packed with household belongings, mostly of Jewish people, wanting to come to America. This was July of 1939, when there just wasn't enough time to send even part of it over."[17]

Clark's papers contain newspaper-clipping files classified by subject. One folder, marked "Jews," includes eleven articles written from 1939 to 1942.[18] All except two pertain to the migration of Jews from Germany to Palestine and the United States, and most were extensively underlined, indicating that he had read them carefully. Clark seemed especially interested in the May 1939 voyage of the SS *St. Louis*, which carried 937 German Jewish refugees on a futile voyage to Cuba, where they were supposed to wait for visas to enter the United States. Clark underlined words and phrases that raised his hackles, such as "powerful influences in the United States" that advocated for the refugees. Another article, written before the United States entered the Second World War, concerned Jews who had successfully landed in Cuba but had waited several years for entry visas. Heavy underlining in key passages of "Havana is the waiting room for America" may have demonstrated Clark's nativist sentiments.[19] Another article that drew Clark's attention featured a picture of a bearded man wearing a hat and a long coat, standing on the steps of the United States Capitol. It announced that for the first time an Orthodox Jewish rabbi had given the opening prayer for a session of the U.S. House of Representatives. Clark circled words "Orthodox rabbi." Clark also extensively marked on a four-column display advertisement that advocated the formation of a Jewish army in Palestine. His handwritten comment asked, "To whom would they owe allegiance?"[20]

In political speech, according to Quinn, Clark barely disguised his anti-Semitic xenophobia by using "code words" for Jews: "political émigrés, aliens, and alien émigrés," who were "boring termite-like into our national structure—financial, economic, social and political." Clark, whose rabid Republican partisanship increased in tenor the farther away from Salt Lake City that he spoke, saw a Jewish conspiracy behind the New Deal policies of Franklin D. Roosevelt. A typical anti-FDR speech contained Clark's quota of anti-Semitic imagery: "Alien émigrés, with their puppets in . . . key positions in administration, have secured the setting up in our Federal Government of a mass of governmental agencies —the alphabet bureaus."[21]

Clark also disliked Jews because he thought they were anti-democratic and displayed a propensity toward communism. He expressed these feelings to anyone who sought his opinion, regardless of his correspondent's status or position in society. In a long letter to Herbert Hoover in 1942, he blamed Jews for the Treaty of Versailles and "the present war." He added: "They are completely dominating the entire government policy at this time. They are brilliant, they are able, they are unscrupulous, and they are cruel. They are essentially revolutionary, but they are not statesmen. They, as a race, are sowing dragons teeth in this country. . . . The harvest which they will reap will be as dire, if not more so, than any they have reaped in any other country in the world."[22] To an ordinary Latter-day Saint in Idaho who forwarded the outline of a proposed theological book, Clark admonished: "There is nothing in their history which indicates that the Jewish race loves either free agency or liberty. 'Law and order' are not facts for Jews. . . . Whenever the Jew has power, he has been as oppressive as any race in history."[23]

According to Quinn, Clark considered some of the world's most dangerous political radicals to be Jews. The list of left-wing Jewish politicians and revolutionaries he loathed included Leon Trotsky and Vladimir Lenin of the Soviet Union, Karl Marx, Wilhelm and Karl Liebknecht, and Rosa Luxemburg of Germany, Leon Blum of France, and Americans such as anarchist Emma Goldman and Communist Party USA cofounder Benjamin Gitlow.[24] Apparently, Clark never saw a contradiction between his belief that Jews were dangerously communistic and his other anti-Semitic tenet, that Jews made too much money by exploiting the capitalist system with ruthless efficiency.

Clark often shared his anti-Semitism with a missionary's zeal. He was a devotee of the early-twentieth-century Russian secret police forgery, *The Protocols of the Learned Elders of Zion*, which purported to reveal a high-level Jewish plot to achieve world domination. From the time he accepted his governing position in the LDS Church in the early 1930s until his death in 1961, Clark distributed copies of the *Protocols* with the enthusiasm of a young elder handing out a tract.[25] He ordered batches at a time from the same printing house in Houston.[26] To Ernest L. Wilkinson, a Utah attorney who later became president of BYU, Clark recommended reading the *Protocols*, calling the contents "chilling . . . they will give you the shivers."[27] To Ezra Taft Benson, Dwight Eisenhower's secretary of agriculture and later the prophet, seer, and revelator of the Mormon Church, Clark referred to a point in the paper linking communism and Zionism, and recommended that Benson read the *Protocols*.[28]

Clark not only distributed anti-Semitic material, he was also a collector. His papers at BYU contain a file of brochures and articles that link Jews with anti-capitalist world revolution and communist domination. Most were dated after the Second World War. One picture shows men clothed in religious robes. Some are bearded. Others wear *yarmulkes*. All glare at the reader with hostile, penetrating stares. The caption reads: "Praying Jews. Yahweh, the god of the Jews, they invoke as follows: 'Let madness strike the non-Jewish councils, and disconcert their brains. Let their Leaders be madmen. Dethrone their kings by severe wars, and let fall on them Thy revenge. In Thy fury crush their heads against the ground.'"

Another pamphlet, headlined "Bolshevism Is Judaism," advises in all-capital letters that "The Jews are the children of the devil according to the Gospel of St. John 8:44. Therefore, for my country—against the Jewry." Another, entitled "The Letter," consists of six pages of single-spaced, typewritten names of Jewish governmental officials and diplomatic consular representatives in all European countries of the postwar Communist Bloc. It then lists prominent Jews in the British and American governments, and Jewish diplomats accredited to the United Nations. A tabloid entitled *Common Sense: America's Anti-Communist Newspaper* contains the masthead slogan, "All the News Kept Out of Print," featuring a seventy-two-point headline that proclaims, "UN—World Jewish Plan." The first sentence of the front-page article states: "The Jewish plan for world conquest and for ruling the world is now well underway."[29]

Clark often spoke in nuanced terms and moderated his anti-Semitism when addressing someone he did not know; he reserved his harshest comments about Jews for his friends, family, and close political and religious associates. He may have shown some restraint when speaking with his counterpart in the First Presidency, Second Counselor David O. McKay, who developed a reputation throughout his years of church service as a promoter of Mormon–Jewish relations. McKay, a moderate Republican and an internationalist on foreign policy, possibly mitigated some of Clark's more extreme rhetoric. McKay wielded little influence in the prewar years regarding the Mormons' decision not to accommodate its Jewish members, or any Jews, who wished to escape Nazi Germany. That also applied to charitable contributions. In 1940, when Utah's Jewish leaders asked the LDS Church to donate several hundred thousand dollars for the relief of European Jews, Clark led the opposition.[30]

Not all Mormons agreed with Clark, but those who did not were often ineffective. Two United States Senators from Utah, Elbert Thomas and William King, both Mormons and both Democrats, spoke out against Hitler's excesses prior to the Second World War. When Thomas returned from his ten-week fact-finding trip to Germany in the autumn of 1934, he was appalled at what he had seen in the Third Reich. He later introduced a resolution in the Senate Foreign Relations Committee that would have created a government agency to rescue refugees. In the midst of the Great Depression, federal action to allow foreign refugees into the United States was not politically popular. Thomas was unable to gain the support of Franklin D. Roosevelt. Finally, in 1944 after the reality of what the Nazis were doing to Europe's Jews became undeniable, the Senate created the War Refugees Board. By then it was too late. In 1940, King introduced a bill that would have opened the Territory of Alaska to Jewish refugee settlement, a proposal that received the endorsement of both the Interior and Labor Departments. The King-Havenner Bill never became law, in part because of anti-immigrant and anti-Semitic sentiments that prevailed in the United States at the time, and in part because of opposition from Alaskan interests.[31]

Despite Clark's anti-Semitism and the Mormons' refusal to help their Jewish converts escape Nazi Germany, one scholar who has studied the prejudices of Latter-day Saints does not consider the LDS Church to be theologically anti-Semitic. Sociologist Armand Mauss wrote, "The unique doctrine of Semitic identification" makes "Mormons less likely than any of the other denominations to hold secular anti-Jewish prejudices, such as that 'Jews cheat in business or are disloyal and unpatriotic.'"[32] The term "Semitic identification" refers to the main plot of the Book of Mormon, in which a family of six Jews sailed to the Americas after the fall of Babylon in the sixth century B.C. Descendants of this family became the American Indians, according to LDS beliefs. Mauss implies that Mormons exhibit another form of anti-Jewish prejudice: a spiritual anti-Semitism inherited from traditional Christianity. That pertains to the treatment of Jesus Christ by Jewish elders prior to his crucifixion and the subsequent failure of Jews to convert to Christianity.[33] But, according to Mauss, it does not carry over into day-to-day relations between Jews and Latter-day Saints in the Mormon Culture Region.

Mauss's analysis seems to be supported by the historically amicable relationship that Latter-day Saints enjoy with Utah's small but accomplished Jewish minority. Several Jewish businessmen served as directors of the Salt Lake City Chamber of commerce in the late nineteenth century. Utah was only the third state to elect a Jewish governor, Democrat Samuel Bamberger, in 1916. Salt Lake City elected a Jewish mayor, Louis Marcus, in 1932.[34] When Ernest Bamberger lost the 1938 general election to Senator William King, the Jewish Telegraph Agency's dispatch said: "Religious prejudice appears to have played very little, if any, part in the contest. No mention was made of it in the public prints."[35]

There is no trace of anti-Semitism in the writings of front-line Mormon missionaries, either before or during the Nazi period. Their failure to embrace and protect Jewish converts, who probably numbered no more than several dozen, seems to have been a pragmatic decision. German-speaking Mormons, the third-largest immigrant group that populated the Mormon Culture region, were predominantly descendant from Protestant or Catholic lineage. German Christians were much more important to the Mormons' objectives than the few Jews who found a home in the LDS Church. Steven Carter, using an unpublished paper authored by Douglas Tobler and Alan Keele, estimated that five to ten percent of German Mormons in the 1930s joined the Nazi Party.[36] Undoubtedly, more of them participated in Nazi auxiliary organizations that did not require party membership. Given the hatred of Jews that prevailed within the Nazi Party, it is not surprising that American Mormon missionaries found it convenient to tolerate, although not to endorse, their German members' prejudices.

It was up to individual Mormons to determine how they would treat their co-religionists of Jewish dissent. Anecdotal evidence is rather scarce, but what exists does not reflect favorably upon Mormons as their brother's keeper. Jared Kobs, who lived through the Nazi period as a child, discussed his uncle Theo, a grocer who felt sympathy for a Jewish family that could not shop in his store because of harassment from customers. Theo would leave bags of groceries at the couple's apartment door late at night, when nobody could see him befriending a Jew. Kobs also told the story of "a Jewish convert to his Mormon Church showing up each Sunday with his yellow star—until one of the fascist members of the congregation spoke out so strongly against him that he never returned. 'We couldn't stop what happened because of the pressure on us not to get involved.'"[37]

Douglas Tobler recounted an interview with an American missionary, Hyrum J. Smith, who invited a Jewish family to Sunday services at some point in 1936 or 1937. Smith said: "The boy was snubbed by the members. They told me that no Jew boy was going to take the sacrament and that Jews were not welcome in the meetings."[38]

Arthur Zander led the St. Georg Branch in Hamburg in 1938. He wore the gold swastika lapel pin given to those who joined the Nazi Party before March 1933.[39] "He was quite enthused about it," recalled Karl-Heinz Schnibbe, who as a youth was involved in the Helmuth Hübener gang of resisters. "He saw good in [the Nazi Party]. No more unemployment, the autobahn was constructed, and everyone had work under Adolf." Franz Jacobi, Zander's first counselor and also a Party devotee was, in Schnibbe's words, a "super Nazi." The two congregational leaders wanted to begin Sunday services with the Hitler salute, but found their enthusiasm overruled by the district president. Regardless of the Mormons' desire to coexist with the Nazis, altering the liturgical sequence of a sacrament meeting would never have been acceptable. However, when the *Führer* would speak over the airwaves, Zander would provide a radio and lock the doors so that nobody in the congregation could leave during the broadcast.[40] Church policy allowed a congregational leader, a bishop or a branch president, the latitude to change the starting time of church services. Although it was doubtful that the church elders intended to accommodate political oratory, Zander's rescheduling of worship services for Hitler's speeches was permissible.

According to Schnibbe, Zander and his assistant weren't the only enthusiastic National Socialists in the congregation: "In our branch, we had some who came in their SA uniforms to the meetings." Schnibbe did not think of his brown-shirted congregants as "the brutal, street fighter types." Many of the storm troopers who sat through Sunday services in St. Georg were musicians; they played in the local SA band.[41] Another local Mormon was a Nazi of a more dangerous variety, a black-shirted member of the *Totenkopfverbände*—the Death's Head SS that guarded concentration camps. It was an open secret in Schnibbe's congregation that this man had been involved in the cold-blooded murder on the street of a communist organizer.[42]

A conflict arose when Salomon Schwarz, a member of a smaller LDS congregation in Hamburg, wished to attend choir practice at St. Georg. According to his Mormon Church records, he was a full-fledged member, having been baptized on June 7, 1935. He held the Aaronic priesthood rank of teacher. On the other hand, according to the Nuremberg Race Laws adopted three months after his baptism, the government did not consider Schwarz to be a citizen worthy of associating with other Germans. Nazi bureaucrats mistakenly assigned him the status of a "full Jew," even though they classified his siblings as first-degree *Mischlinge*, "half-Jews." Schwarz considered himself to be neither, as he had never practiced his mother's Judaism, but the distinction eventually proved fatal.

Salomon was born in the Siberian city of Balagnsk. His mother was a Hungarian of Jewish descent whom Russian Army soldiers abducted during the First World War. One soldier raped and impregnated her. When Schwarz was two years old, his mother married a German prisoner of war. She had been able to buy Hermann Schwarz's freedom. By paying a bribe, the couple could live outside the walls of the POW camp. With the assistance of the German Red Cross, they resettled in Hamburg after Hermann Schwarz was released from his prisoner's status.[43] Hermann gave Solomon his surname and treated him like a son.

The entire family, including Salomon's three siblings, attended the Evangelical (Lutheran) Church in Hamburg before they eventually converted to Mormonism. Salomon Schwarz was an enthusiastic Latter-day Saint who participated in every activity his small branch offered.

According to his sister, Anna Marie Schwarz, "Whenever there was a church meeting of any kind, Salomon was there." Unfortunately, Arthur Zander, the St. Georg Branch president, thought the visitor who arrived for choir practice "looked Jewish." Zander did not want a Jew in the building. He badgered Schwarz for racial identity papers to prove that he was an Aryan. When Salomon could provide none, Zander erected a sign outside that announced Jews were not allowed to enter.

Few Mormon leaders in those days practiced Nazism with the relentless devotion of Arthur Zander. Alfred Schmidt, president of the Barmbek Branch, welcomed Salomon Schwarz back to his smaller Mormon congregation, but Schwarz's unfortunate experience with the St. Georg Branch president continued to prove troublesome. When on September 1, 1941, Reinhard Heydrich, chief of the Reich Main Security Office (SD), declared that all "full Jews" in Germany must wear a yellow Star of David, Schwarz no longer attended the services of any Mormon congregation. Instead, a group of his closest friends from the Barmbek congregation, led by the branch president's father, Walter Schmidt, risked punishment by visiting Salomon at home.[44]

With his friends in Barmbek praying and fasting for him, Salomon Schwarz left his apartment to lodge a personal appeal for reclassification as a half-Jew or first degree *Mischling*. If he had won his appeal, he would have been able to shed the Star of David, dispense with food coupons stamped with the letter "J," and return to church services. He made a fatal mistake on his journey; he did not wear his yellow star. His sister, Anna Marie Schwarz, said in a letter to Hübener group conspirator Rudi Wobbe: "One time when Salomon traveled to Berlin to go to the Ethnicity Office of the Reich, the whole branch prayed for him. Still, while he visited the Ethnicity Office, somebody denounced him to the Gestapo. I know and you know who denounced him. I don't want under any circumstances for his name to be revealed."[45]

Salomon Schwarz's appeal may have been successful. According to his sister, "On the seventeenth of July [1942], I received a communication, after making an inquiry, that the possibility existed that Salomon could be classified as a cross-breed first grade." However, it was too late. Anna Marie Schwarz continued: "At the same time, the denouncement took place. The Gestapo arrested Salomon. . . . The person who denounced him brought about some heavy consequences. . . . Had the denouncement not happened, Salomon could have been reclassified as a cross-breed."

For not wearing a yellow Star of David on his clothing, Schwarz spent three weeks in an "education camp." When released in August 1942, according to his sister, "He was a wreck. He often had fainting spells and heart problems." Life deteriorated after that. In September, still classified as a "full Jew," Salomon Schwarz entered the Hamburg ghetto. Walter Schmidt, the father of the Barmbek branch president, visited Schwarz in the ghetto on many occasions, despite warnings from the Gestapo and pleas from his own wife not to endanger himself. "Walter had it in his heart to help him," Anna Marie Schwarz said. On February 12, 1943, Salomon Schwarz left Hamburg in a packed railroad cattle car. His destination was Auschwitz, where he perished.[46]

Most German Mormon congregational leaders were neither as fanatically loyal to Hitler as Arthur Zander nor as faithful to their few Jewish members as Alfred and Walter Schmidt. Most decisions made by German LDS leaders and their American missionaries were based on carefully calculated assessments of risk. Missionary Donald M. Petty told of the limited assistance he was able to provide to a Jewish Mormon in Wuppertal, a city in the Rhineland. A man he referred to as "Brother Goldberg," a tailor by trade, was married to a German woman who was not Jewish. When Hitler came to power, Goldberg elected to live apart from his wife and child in order to protect them from harassment. From time to time, Petty and his missionary companion would visit Goldberg or his wife, acting as couriers to deliver small amounts of money and written messages. Goldberg never asked and presumably never expected anything more from the Mormon Church. He tried to escape from Germany by crossing the border on his own, was caught, and went to a concentration camp. He and his wife survived the Nazi regime, but their marriage did not. Petty explained the missionaries' reluctance to do more: "If we got too involved in their difficulties we were breaking our own rules. Our job was to proselyte the gospel. We were also endangering ourselves if we were caught helping or sympathizing."[47]

Likewise, the purveyors of memory—those who told their own stories of Mormonism in Nazi Germany and the faithful historians who published those accounts—exercised careful discretion. Joseph Dixon, who wrote the first scholarly article on the Mormons in the Third Reich in

1972, devoted only two sentences to an unnamed Latter-day Saint who tinkered daily with the machinery of murder. He was a mechanic at Auschwitz. Dixon euphemistically said that the man "install[ed] specialized machinery." That was code language for gas chambers and crematoria. Dixon dutifully noted that his subject—ostensibly guilt-ridden—had a nervous breakdown when he returned from Poland.[48] Likewise, when Alan Keele wrote an article for a BYU-sponsored scholarly magazine, he told the story of a Mormon who had enlisted in Hitler's elite, black-uniformed *Schutzstaffel*. Keele's subject became no ordinary purveyor of genocide. This SS man developed a conscience, based upon his prewar Mormon religious instruction. He elected to become a wartime deserter.[49] If these two cogs in Hitler's killing machine had been unrepentant, they probably would not have appeared in articles authored by believing scholars.

For German Jews who did not wait too long and had the money, it was possible to leave the country before the onset of the Second World War. In fact, Nazi policy officially encouraged emigration of Jews prior to October 1941, although the difficulty of fleeing after the war started was greatly intensified. Some thirty-six thousand Jews left Germany and Austria in 1938 and seventy-seven thousand followed in 1939. After *Kristallnacht*, the United Kingdom admitted an additional ten thousand Jewish refugees from Germany and Austria.[50] For Jews who had embraced another faith, like Egon Weiss, Richard Siebenschein, or Salomon Schwartz, another barrier presented itself. When Weiss and Siebenschein desired to become two of the four thousand Austrian Jews who emigrated after *Kristallnacht*, they could not count on the help of various Jewish relief agencies that provided a limited amount of funding. Even though a religious conversion did not exempt a German from the "tainted" blood of Judaism in Nazi Germany, conversion from Judaism would have made it harder to seek Jewish help.

Considering the few Jewish converts to Mormonism in Nazi Germany, and the desire of the Nazis to rid themselves of as many Jews as possible in the prewar period, it would have been relatively easy for the Mormon Church to help its own. Most pleas that reached Salt Lake City contained no appeals for funding or personal intervention with the government of Germany. Instead, they only asked for the issuance of legal affidavits attesting to the prospective émigré's moral character and financial wherewithal. Those were not requirements of the German government for an exit visa; instead, they were an American prerequisite for admission to a country still suffering from the anti-immigrant sentiment spawned by the Great Depression's unemployment. Such an effort, if conducted with the same degree of skilled diplomacy that J. Reuben Clark brought to his meetings with Hjalmar Schacht, could have become successful without endangering American missionaries or German congregants.

When Richard Siebenschein of Vienna wrote the second of his appeals to his old friend, Mormon Prophet Heber J. Grant, in December 1938, Siebenschein apparently understood the sensitivity of the request he was making. He asked, "in order to ease our mind and anxiety," that a cable with only the word "willing" be included in the text, "in case there is someone generous enough and willing to help us out of our plight." In this letter, Siebenschein hopefully enclosed two snapshots of himself with Grant and other LDS missionaries taken in Yokohama, Japan, in 1901.[51] His pathetic plea stood no chance of being fulfilled. Because of xenophobia and anti-Semitism at the highest level of the Mormon Church, its leadership chose to approach this challenge neither with the wisdom of Solomon nor the charity of Jesus Christ. Instead, the Mormon tactic resembled that of Pontius Pilate. When presented with this moral dilemma, the Mormon hierarchy washed its hands of the matter.

15

Helmuth Hübener
A Memory Beacon with a Dimmer Switch

On a crisp October evening in 1942, a fair-skinned, blue-eyed, seventeen-year-old boy—naked from the waist up—walked under guard into a darkened chamber at Berlin's Plötzensee Prison. Hands bound behind his back, he stared momentarily at a crucifix mounted on a black altar, illuminated by two flickering candles.[1] Then, cooperating completely with his jailers, he mounted a nineteenth-century guillotine.[2] When the state executioner severed the Hamburg native's head, carrying out a red-robed Nazi court's condemnation for high treason, he became the only Mormon executed for resistance to Adolf Hitler's regime. Perhaps more significantly, he claimed anti-fascist martyrdom as the religious equivalent of a stateless person. Ten days after the Gestapo arrested the young man for producing anti-Hitler tracts with a church-owned typewriter, the lad's congregational leader, an enthusiastic Nazi supporter, excommunicated Helmuth Hübener from the Church of Jesus Christ of Latter-day Saints.[3]

Helmuth Hübener is a memory beacon. His bright, redeeming light cuts through the murk of the Mormons' accommodating behavior in Nazi Germany. Principled and heroic, Helmuth presents a stark contrast to a mission president who rendered the "Heil Hitler" greeting, to a "mission matron" who rode with the *Führer* in a black Nazi limousine, and to a church hierarchy that hastily purged Semitic references from its liturgy and ignored the pleas of Mormonism's Jewish converts. But Hübener's memory beacon comes equipped with a dimmer switch that allows his commemorative light to be brightened or darkened according to the self-interest of the Salt Lake City church leadership.

In the early postwar period, the light of Hübener's memorialization shone dimly. Those traumatized by war sought refuge in forgetting and rebuilding. In the aftermath of the Second World War, many members of Hübener's St. Georg congregation immigrated to the American Zion. Those who stayed behind busied themselves with creating what became known as the *Wirtschaftswunder*, the postwar German Economic Miracle. In the process, German Mormons on both sides of the Atlantic tried to put their wartime recollections behind them. The memory of this brave and idealistic young man dimmed to the point of near extinguishment. Then, in the early 1960s, a Hamburg high school student, Ulrich Sander, tasked with researching local resisters, rediscovered the Hübener group.[4] His newspaper articles attracted the attention of novelist Günter Grass, who used the adolescent gang of four resisters as the inspiration for his 1969 novel, *örtlich betäubt*, and his 1970 play, *Davor*.[5] Neither Sander nor Grass is Mormon.

Grass's tale interested Alan F. Keele, a professor of Germanic languages at Mormon Church–owned BYU. Keele's research had focused on Grass, an author who used German memory of the Second World War as a foundation for his fiction. Together with a colleague in BYU's history department, Douglas F. Tobler, Keele began investigating the story of a Hamburg youth who listened to forbidden wartime broadcasts of the BBC and wrote seditious summations distributed by three friends, two of whom were fellow Mormons. At a faculty seminar in the early 1970s, Keele and Tobler approached their colleague Thomas Rogers, a professor of Russian who dabbled as an amateur playwright. Keele and Tobler suggested that Rogers, who had written several dramatic works performed on campus, produce a play based on Hübener's exploits.[6]

The ensuing stage performance was a resounding box office success—in fact, it was too successful for the comfort of the Mormon Church leadership. Rogers' play, *Huebener*, attracted capacity audiences during its extended run in the fall of 1976 and prompted newspaper reviews statewide.[7] The play's success motivated wealthy BYU alumni to offer sponsorship to stage the production in California. After a visit from a high-ranking member of the Salt Lake City Mormon leadership, however, the university banned future performances of Rogers' play and halted publication by Keele and Tobler. The story of why the church leadership suppressed the story of a genuine Mormon hero unfolds in the next chapter. First, it is necessary to introduce a young Mormon whose principled resistance to the Nazis contrasted with older co-religionists who invoked God's authority to justify cooperation with a government the lad despised.

The Evolution of a Young Revolutionary

Helmuth Hübener, conceived as the consequence of a single crime, died at the hands of a Nazi government so felonious that its crimes defy enumeration. In 1924, his mother succumbed to workplace blackmail by her corrupt foreman at the government mint in Hamburg. She had illegally provided metal blanks for the fraudulent stamping of *Pfennig* and *Reichsmark* coins that he pocketed. Sex was the price she paid for his silence.[8] The birth of a principled and highly intelligent young man was her reward.

Helmuth embraced his Mormon religious faith and excelled in school. Like most German students on the *Oberbau* or "honors track" at the *Realschule*, he took four years of English.[9] Unlike most, he mastered the language with diligent study and some help from the American missionaries.[10] He made excellent grades in a variety of academic and vocational subjects, including typing and shorthand, and especially embraced his coursework in history and political thought.[11] One of his partners in treason against the Nazi state, Karl-Heinz Schnibbe, called Helmuth "the professor."[12]

Like most boys growing up in Nazi Germany, Hübener was active in the Party's youth activities. "He was very well liked in the Hitler Youth," said Schnibbe.[13] Marie Sommerfeld, to whom Helmuth wrote a goodbye letter on the day he was executed, remembers that "Helmuth was quite enthused at the beginning" about the Hitler Youth.[14] Another co-conspirator, Rudi Wobbe, believed Helmuth "was not an ardent follower of Hitler," but instead "put up a smoke screen so others would not see his real convictions."[15] Regardless of how Hübener's attitudes evolved, he derived one tangible benefit from his experience in the Hitler Youth, an organization not known to encourage intellectual development. He wrote a prize-winning, pro-Nazi graduation thesis, "The War of the Plutocrats," at the conclusion of his studies in the spring of 1941.[16] His reward was a coveted civil service job. He worked for a government social welfare agency located at the Bieber-Haus, a prominent building in Hamburg. His employment gave him access to an extensive archive of books, some of which had been banned in Nazi Germany. Said Rudi Wobbe: "This allowed Helmuth to occasionally sneak out books for us to read."[17]

Helmuth Hübener's intelligence drove a confrontational personality that could annoy older Mormons.[18] "When he talked to the elders in the church, he asked them questions he knew they couldn't answer," Schnibbe recalled, and then explained, "He liked to embarrass them a bit."[19] Wobbe remembered that Helmuth would loan books to his friends and then quiz them on their reading: "He had a great depth for one so young and a remarkable ability to share his insights."[20] Hübener's dysfunctional family upbringing may have also fueled his nonconformist tendencies. His mother never married the corrupt supervisor who impregnated her. She had been divorced from the father of his two older half-brothers for many years when she instead married Hugo Hübener in 1939. Hugo, a low-ranking SA storm trooper, legally adopted Helmuth, probably at the urging of his mother.[21] But Helmuth could not stand his new father. Like an older half-brother, Gerhard Kunkel, Helmuth embraced his first opportunity to move away. When Kunkel went into the Nazi Labor Front, Helmuth moved into Gerhard's room in his maternal grandparents' apartment. They lived only one block away.[22] That proved to be a fateful decision, as the lack of supervision at his grandparents' house later provided a convenient opportunity for the Helmuth Hübener resistance group.

Hamburg's once-diverse political climate, straitjacketed under the Nazis, was probably on Helmuth Hübener's mind. He read extensively about political subjects and was just barely old enough to remember the turbulence of the last years of the Weimar Republic.[23] Helmuth's best friends, Rudi Wobbe and Karl-Heinz Schnibbe, came from families that had been active in Germany's Social Democratic Party. Wobbe, one year younger than Hübener, recalled the "torchlight parades . . . machine gun nests on building roofs . . . and men with revolvers stationed behind overturned cars" that marked the street violence that pitted National Socialists against the German Communist Party (KPD) in his neighborhood.[24] As a port city with a large maritime industry, Hamburg had been a stronghold for the KPD and its labor-organizing efforts. "Hamburg never did go completely over to the Nazis," said Karl-Heinz Schnibbe. "There were too many Communists and Social Democrats there." Marie Sommerfeld, a St. Georg congregant and Hübener family friend, recalled: "There were quite a few communists in the area."[25]

Sommerfeld also remembered that Helmuth's opinion of the Nazis began to change because of conflicts in the neighborhood and in church.[26] Wobbe related a street confrontation that Helmuth had with a Hitler Youth patrol: "Most of the time we liked to sing hymns but occasionally we would sing American songs, such as 'You Are My Sunshine' or 'Moonlight and Roses,' that the missionaries had taught us. One day a Hitler Youth patrol stopped us . . . and demanded to know why we were singing English songs. 'These are not English songs, but American,' Helmuth smarted off, 'and why shouldn't we sing them? It's not against the law! Talking about the law, what right do you have to harass German citizens on the street? You've not been given the authority of a policeman to question people!'"

The Hitler Youth group, confounded by Hübener's tirade, backed off. After they left, Helmuth continued: "That's the trouble with these people—put them in a uniform and they think they have the authority to bully people around. It doesn't matter whether they belong to the Hitler Youth, the SA, or the SS. . . . Our country is being run through threats, intimidation, and even brutal force! And something has to be done about this!"[27]

Events at Helmuth Hübener's St. Georg congregation of the Mormon Church also affected his evolving opinion of the Nazis. "The final straw for Hübener," said historian Douglas F. Tobler, "was that he saw Nazi ideas coming into the LDS Church."[28] Branch President Arthur Zander, who occasionally wore a suit coat with swastikas woven into the fabric,[29] overtly politicized a diverse group of congregants with his desire to render the Hitler salute during services and his insistence that congregants listen to Hitler's speeches on the radio.[30] When, as part of the broadcast, the Horst Wessel Song was played, Zander required the congregation to sing. According to Otto Berndt, Sr., who initially served as a congregational youth leader under Zander, the branch president would station spies around the room to report who was not singing in tribute to the Nazi martyr. "Zander was one hundred fifty percent for the Nazis," recalled Berndt.[31] Berndt maintained that District President Alwin Brey had installed Zander as branch president in 1938 because of his political beliefs, in order to facilitate good relations with the Nazi Party.[32]

Berndt remembered an incident that put him at odds with Zander and other pro-Nazi branch leaders, such as First Counselor Franz Jacobi. One year, near Christmas, the congregation rented additional rooms in the building where it held church meetings. During remodeling, a picture of Adolf Hitler appeared on the wall, replacing pictures of Jesus Christ and Mormon Church founder Joseph Smith. Berndt's temper exploded: "I couldn't stand it. I called one of the leaders in and said, 'I'll give you five minutes to take that picture down and hang the picture of Christ and the picture of Joseph Smith back up.' He said: 'Are you against the *Führer?*' I said, 'I have nothing against the *Führer*. . . . This is the Church of Jesus Christ of Latter-day Saints and *His* picture goes there! Joseph Smith founded this church and *his* picture goes there, not Adolf Hitler! Joseph Smith was born near this time [of year], and when we celebrate Christmas, we celebrate it for these two persons, and not for Adolf Hitler!'"[33]

The branch leaders took down Hitler's picture and restored the pictures of Christ and Joseph Smith, but they retaliated by dismissing Berndt from all of his "callings" or jobs in the congregation. Later, when Berndt returned from a period of military service, he became acting district president, Zander's supervisor. As "acting" president, he did not have the power to remove Zander, although he could veto individual decisions made by the branch president. Rudi Wobbe, one of the Hübener conspirators, remembered Zander as someone "who did a lot for the St. Georg Branch, but he was a dyed-in-the-wool Nazi."[34] Karl-Heinz Schnibbe, the other Hübener conspirator, called Zander "a dedicated branch president, a natural leader of young and old" who "took charge in the branch and made things happen," including "enlarging the branch house and installing a baptismal font" and "[making] certain there was always cake and hot chocolate for the volunteer workers."[35]

Those "natural" leadership skills manifested themselves when he cleansed his congregation of Jews and other "subversive" influences. Arthur Zander was the leader who erected the sign, "*Juden ist der Eintritt verboten,*" on the St. Georg meeting house door, a proscription aimed at Salomon Schwarz, the sole Mormon of Jewish heritage who visited.[36]

Zander also refused baptism to another man of partial Jewish lineage who desired to become a Mormon, Rudolph Kaufmann. Otto Berndt, who had the authority to override that decision as the acting president, baptized Kaufmann into the church.[37]

Zander, whose church typewriters Hübener eventually used to produce his anti-Hitler handbills, also saw to it that no enemy propaganda contaminated his congregation. Said Rudi Wobbe: "On her way to church one morning, an elderly sister stopped to pick up a leaflet dropped by [a] British [aircraft] onto the streets of Hamburg. When she arrived at church, she casually showed it to some of the other members. When [Zander] saw what she was doing, he ripped the leaflet from her hand and started shouting, 'If you ever bring enemy propaganda literature into this branch house again, I will see to it that you are brought to a concentration camp.'"[38]

Helmuth Hübener undoubtedly heard of this incident, as he was aware of most of what transpired and probably all of the gossip in his small Mormon congregation of less than two hundred. What happened to one of the branch's most devout members, sixty-six-year-old Heinrich Worbs, must have profoundly expedited sixteen-year-old Helmuth along his path from Nazi loyalist to resister. Worbs, who would stand air raid spotter duty with the younger boys in the congregation once the war started, made an intemperate remark on the streetcar one day in Hamburg in 1941.[39] Passing a newly dedicated monument to a martyred Nazi, the plainspoken Worbs said: "Another statue for one of those Nazi butchers!" Someone heard his remark and reported Worbs to the Gestapo. Rudi Wobbe described the consequences:

> The Gestapo immediately arrested him and shipped him to Neuengamme concentration camp. . . . They kept him for six months. After being released, he attended church meetings again, but we could hardly recognize him. He was a broken man, a shadow of his former self. Brother Otto Berndt took him under his wing and slowly nursed him back to where he could at least carry on a conversation. When Helmuth and I had a chance to question him privately, he told us he was not allowed to talk about [it]. He'd been forced to sign a paper that said he was simply there for educational purposes and that he had been treated well.[40]

Berndt was able to coax information from Worbs. While in the camp, Worbs had been treated, in Berndt's words, "worse than an animal." Worbs came back with a swollen mouth, missing all of its teeth. On several occasions, guards had chained him outside in winter temperatures, stripped naked, knee-deep in snow for periods of up to forty-eight hours. They positioned him so that water would drip on his hands, which would then freeze.[41] Periodically, a guard would appear with a rubber hose and sadistically beat Worbs' hands in order to remove the ice and "warm you up," as the guard would say. That broke his fingers.[42]

Six weeks later, Worbs died. The last weeks of his life were not pleasant. According to Rudi Wobbe: "What upset Helmuth and me the most was the way the other members of our congregation treated Brother Worbs upon his return. Rather than rally to his defense to comfort him, many turned a cold shoulder, refusing to speak to him. He was ostracized because he 'kicked against the pricks' by opposing the government. Many, I suspect, were afraid to be seen with him for fear the Nazis would suspect them as well."[43]

Helmuth Hübener kept no diary to record the evolution of his attitude regarding National Socialism. By the summer of 1941, based on comments he made to his close circle of young friends, it was becoming evident that he had adopted a rigidly anti-Nazi viewpoint. The young man who once wrote an honors thesis that extolled Nazi economic theory questioned aloud how Germany had the resources to win a war against the rest of the world. The numbers did not add up, he told Karl-Heinz Schnibbe. Before the *Wehrmacht* invaded the Soviet Union in June 1941, Hübener wondered how Germany would obtain access to the petroleum it needed to sustain combat.[44] After Hitler launched Operation Barbarossa, Hübener listened skeptically to the official news reports, which lauded the tremendous losses sustained by Soviet forces with scant mention of German casualties. He asked how a country of sixty-five million could defeat a combined enemy population of more than five hundred million.[45]

Hübener appeared confounded regarding a solution. To Rudi Wobbe, he quoted Napoleon: "Revolutions are rare, because human life is too short. Everyone thinks to himself, 'It will not profit me to upset the existing order, so why bother?'" He brooded over Heinrich Mann's assessment of the German people: They are too fatalistic to engage in revolution.[46]

Yet events during the summer of 1941 prompted Hübener to conduct what Alan Keele described as "a full fledged information resistance."⁴⁷

The Quixotic Anti-Goebbels

On September 1, 1939, the same day that Germany started the Second World War by invading Poland, Nazi Propaganda Minister Joseph Goebbels announced the "Extraordinary Radio Measures" decree. Listening to foreign radio stations became a crime punishable by imprisonment. Distributing information derived from foreign broadcasts carried a maximum penalty of death. To transmit its own propaganda to its citizens, Nazi Germany provided inexpensive, mass-produced, reflex-technology radio receivers with a limited selection of channels and a short reception range. The larger variety of the *Volksempfänger*, the people's receiver, sold for seventy-six marks. A smaller model, the DKE38, cost thirty-five marks. Germans derisively nicknamed it *Goebbels-Schnauze*, Goebbels's snout.⁴⁸

Helmuth Hübener was hungry for information that he could not glean from the Nazi puffery masquerading as news that came out of the *Volksempfänger*. Gerhard Kunkel, his half-brother who was five years older, unwittingly satisfied Helmuth's curiosity. While serving abroad in Reich Labor Service, Gerhard acquired a much more powerful radio. Unlike the German *Volksempfänger*—purposely designed to limit the listener's choice of broadcast stations—Kunkel's French Rola allowed the listener to tune in shortwave broadcasts. It provided a longer reception range and greater choice of stations, which is precisely what the Nazis wanted to deny to the German people. Kunkel stored his long-range radio in a locked closet at his grandparents' apartment before he departed for service in the *Wehrmacht*. At some point afterward, Helmuth committed the only real crime of his life: he broke into the cabinet.⁴⁹

Rudi Wobbe remembered that Hübener brought a radio to air raid spotter duty on December 31, 1940.⁵⁰ The next time one of his friends saw the radio was on June 22, 1941, a fateful day in the history of the Second World War. That evening, after his grandparents had gone to bed, sixteen-year-old Hübener welcomed seventeen-year-old Karl-Heinz Schnibbe—a friend since their days together in Mormon "primary," the church activity for children. With the Rola's volume turned low, Karl-Heinz watched Helmuth carefully turn the turning dial until, at precisely ten o'clock in the evening, the first four notes of Beethoven's Fifth Symphony cut through the annoying static. The musical pattern formed Morse code for letter "V," three dots and a dash. That symbolized Winston Churchill's "V for Victory." In perfect German, the announcer welcomed his listeners to the BBC's German-language news program. The broadcast led with the *Wehrmacht's* surprise invasion of the Soviet Union.[51]

Karl-Heinz listened, spellbound. It became obvious to him that this was not Helmuth's first time listening to forbidden enemy broadcasts. Several weeks later, his friend sprang another surprise. One night, after Schnibbe had listened to another broadcast, Helmuth pulled out a small, red, typewritten pamphlet—imprinted with an official Nazi Party stamp. Schnibbe read it in shocked silence. Entitled "Down with Hitler," the brochure used a pun to denounce the *Führer*. Helmuth modified the German word for "people's leader," *Volksführer* by adding a three-letter syllable in the middle. It became *Volksverführer*, the people's seducer. He also called Hitler the "people's corruptor" and the "people's traitor."[52]

Douglas F. Tobler, the BYU historian who researched Hübener in the 1970s, believed that the shocking German invasion of the Soviet Union and Helmuth's ability to hear alternative news and opinions not available through the Nazi-controlled media, served as the capstone to the young man's evolving revolutionary spirit. "As Helmuth Hübener listens to the BBC, he is immediately convinced they're telling the truth," Tobler said.[53] "The British provided much more detail," added BYU's Alan Keele.[54] As he continued to listen, Hübener noted that the BBC would discuss the losses of British troops, aircraft, and ships. The Nazi-controlled media never enumerated German battlefield losses.[55]

Within weeks, Hübener introduced another close boyhood friend from the Mormons' St. Georg congregation to the broadcasts, fifteen-year-old Rudi Wobbe. Wobbe lived in Rothenburgsort, a Hamburg neighborhood known in the Weimar Republic days for its communist leanings. Hübener wanted to sow his revolution on sympathetic ground. Wobbe also noticed the difference between the British and German versions of the news: "BBC London gave the casualties precisely for both sides—not at all like a typical German news report which sounded something like,

'Massive casualties were inflicted on the Russian Army, with relatively few losses of our own victorious troops.'" Then, just as Helmuth had done with the older Karl-Heinz Schnibbe, he initiated Rudi as a full-fledged conspirator. Wobbe said:

> He gave me a handbill, about one quarter of the size of a sheet of typing paper, and asked me to read it. Entitled, "Hitler the Murderer," . . . it talked about the murder of General von Schroeder, military commander of Serbia. I told him the pamphlet looked great, particularly because it was printed on red paper. "Then let's go to work," Helmuth replied. He handed me a stack of leaflets and said, "Put them in mailboxes, telephone booths, and other places—be inventive." I went [to an apartment building] and began dropping off the handbills in the mailboxes. . . . I covered about three apartment houses before my supply ran out. I distributed about thirty to thirty-five handbills that night.[56]

The following Sunday, using the Mormon meetinghouse as a rendezvous point, the trio of conspirators discussed their next steps. Hübener had prepared another series of pamphlets. Two took aim at German propaganda that accused the British of initiating bombing raids against civilian targets. "Hitler's Guilt" and "Hitler is the Sole Guilty One" maintained that before the Royal Air Force's strikes against German cities, the Luftwaffe had bombed Warsaw and Rotterdam, "where unarmed women and children, cripples and old men were killed." Another pamphlet, "Who is Lying?," compared the battlefield reports from German and British media regarding the Eastern front. German broadcasts claimed insignificant opposition from the Red Army as the *Wehrmacht* marched toward strategic objectives. The BBC reported pitched battles. Schnibbe and Wobbe surreptitiously distributed these pamphlets the following week. Said Wobbe: "I [found] that the Nazi Party had placed bulletin boards at the entrance of every apartment building in the area with the intriguing title of 'Bulletin Board of the N.S.D.A.P.' . . . I couldn't resist the challenge of placing our handbills on these boards."[57]

For Rudi and Karl-Heinz, working with Helmuth seemed to be an adventure, but they also had ideological motivation. Wobbe cited "the excitement of doing something secretive."[58] He recalled the days when he and Schnibbe had served as Hübener's lieutenants in an imaginary "Lord Lister Detective Agency," a name they took from a popular comic strip. Helmuth had membership cards printed. The boys would comb the newspaper's crime reports and try to guess who was guilty.[59] Although Schnibbe and Wobbe may have considered their pamphleteering to be an extension of such adventures, they also had their own grievances with the Third Reich. "What really upset me was when I was just about ready to join the Boy Scouts," Wobbe said in reaction to the abolition of Scouting as a Mormon Church youth activity in Germany. "Oh, I was dreaming about it," recalled Rudi.[60] Helmuth Hübener's motivation extended beyond the loss of Scouting, the activities arm of the Mormon Aaronic (junior) priesthood. He imagined his campaign as a precursor to revolution.

"Helmuth Hübener hoped to incite a mass uprising," said Alan F. Keele. "He was hoping that there would be a tidal wave of information flow." At age sixteen, Keele said, Helmuth "had emerged as a full-blown anti-Nazi."[61] Many pamphlets encouraged the reader to listen to the BBC. For the next eight months, three Mormon teenagers, ages fifteen, sixteen, and seventeen, waged a propaganda war with Joseph Goebbels. They fought that war with the unwitting assistance of the government they were trying to topple and the pro-Nazi church leaders they refused to appease.

Listening to forbidden foreign broadcasts on a powerful radio that his brother had acquired while in labor service for the Third Reich, Hübener would tune in to the BBC late at night after his grandparents had gone to bed. Most of the time he listened in German, but it is possible that he also listened to English-language broadcasts, as he was fluently bilingual. Skilled in shorthand that he learned at his state-funded school, he would make extensive notes. Then, using carbon paper and other materials obtained from his government job at the Bieber-Haus, he would type as many as five copies of a subversive pamphlet at a time.[62] Hamburg Nazi researcher Ulrich Sander claimed that Hübener would produce as many as sixty copies in such a fashion, retyping the original eleven times.[63]

Hübener obtained his church-owned typewriters, at first a portable and then a Remington desk model, from Branch President Arthur Zander, who had tasked Hübener with writing frontline soldiers. Helmuth, while trying to overthrow the Nazi regime that Zander loved, worked in a church "calling" as the clerk for Zander's ecclesiastical boss, District

President Otto Berndt. Berndt had given Helmuth a key to the building and to his office.[64] Then, after Hübener finished typing and stamping a swastika emblem on each pamphlet with the stamp he stole from his job at the Bieber-Haus, he would meet with his Mormon co-conspirators, Schnibbe and Wobbe. Karl-Heinz and Rudi would take public transportation to various places in Hamburg, looking for new and creative targets for their message.[65] Those who attended stage renditions of the Hübener story saw the boys crash a large hotel party and gain access to the coat closet. They stuffed anti-Nazi messages into the overcoat pockets of guests, some of whom may have been Nazi Party functionaries.[66]

The two couriers, Schnibbe and Wobbe, exercised a great deal of caution and periodically expressed reservations to Helmuth about the danger of what they were doing. Schnibbe said they would often read about people being caught and punished for violating the prohibition against listening to foreign broadcasts. "But I just had to know," Karl-Heinz said.[67] One evening, Schnibbe, his pockets filled with subversive pamphlets, encountered a police patrol that demanded to know why he was out so late. Suspecting that the Gestapo must be looking for the author of the seditious propaganda, he approached the policemen with trepidation, fearing that he would be searched. Instead, the police merely cautioned him to go home, as they expected an RAF bombing raid that night.[68] Schnibbe said: "I never took a leaflet home. I always carried matches with me. If I didn't get rid of all of [the pamphlets], I'd burn them."[69]

Helmuth never displayed a hint of fear; the other boys found his cockiness disarming. Once, Karl-Heinz expressed reservations about the danger involved in their project. They next time they saw each other at church, Helmuth loudly mocked him: "Karl, have they arrested you yet?" Horrified to hear his impetuous young friend say this in front of their fellow congregants, Karl-Heinz could only respond: "Would you just shut up?"[70]

Poet, Satirist, and Revolutionary

At some point during his eight-month tenure as a quixotic warrior of words against Joseph Goebbels's relentless propaganda machine, Hübener decided to expand his brochures to full-size paper. This allowed his transition from sloganeering to the authorship of full-fledged satirical essays, based in part on what he learned from the BBC and in part on his contempt for Adolf Hitler and his minions. He even wrote anti-Nazi poetry. One of his targets was Hermann Göring, supreme commander of the *Luftwaffe*, who had once boasted that, if Allied aircraft ever flew into German airspace, his fellow citizens could call him "Meier."

Hübener, knowing that his fellow Germans called air raid sirens, "Meier's Buglehorns,"[71] loved to poke fun at "Good old fat Hermann: Reichsmarshall. . . . Yes, he has something on the ball, this little rogue with the saucer eyes. A dazzling career, a pretty actress,[72] and a very ample salary that is not to be sneezed at, but no brains! When the RAF gets around to bombing Berlin, you can call me Meier he said at the beginning of the war. Today, the streets of Berlin show clear evidence of the British air offensive, yet Göring is still Göring, and he is glad that he is!"

Hübener cited Göring's wealth, referring to him "as a shrewd war profiteer and businessman, from his war factories."[73] Helmuth believed that Göring was the most corrupt of all Nazi leaders, several years before the Nuremberg tribunal revealed the extent to which Göring profited from the seizure of Jewish assets, including priceless art treasures.[74] At Hübener's trial in August 1942, the red-robed Nazi judges chuckled at the humor directed toward "fat old Hermann" during the reading of the anti-Göring handbill.[75]

Helmuth could be crude with his satire, but he could also write poetry. On December 20, 1941—only eleven days after Hitler declared war on the United States—the *Führer* appealed to the German people to donate items of winter clothing to beleaguered German soldiers on the Russian front, who were ill equipped to survive the winter cold.[76] In one of his many grave miscalculations, Hitler had thought that the Soviets would succumb to the same *blitzkrieg* tactics the *Wehrmacht* had employed in Western Europe. But the campaign was not over in three months. Helmuth responded with a doggerel poem: "I've Calculated for Everything."

> Poor "Joseph" stands at the microphone,
> Entirely unable to bring forth a tone.
> How am I going to convince the *Volk*
> that Hitler's figures aren't just a joke?

How could he have said—so embarrassing—
That he's calculated for everything.

What Joseph says sounds pretty slack;
Oh woe is us, alas, alack:
"It's winter now and bitter cold."
(Even chillier when you sit in a hole
'cause shooters always seem to freeze.)
Didn't Hitler calculate for these?

This handbill had several goals. First, Hübener wished to sow popular discord regarding Hitler's decision to attack the Soviet Union with the expectation that victory would be attained before the harsh Russian winter set in. Second, he wanted to provoke indignation that the government could not provide basic necessities for its soldiers, such as winter clothing.

"We're engaged in a battle, at the turning place
So everyone step up the wool-collection pace!"
That's what Goebbels begged for, and he also believed
That you'd follow his orders and be deceived.
That everything you own you would quietly give,
And keep nothing at all on which to live.

Yes, Hitler's the reason the people must share
From their meager belongings whatever they'll bear!
For Hitler's mistakes the *Volk* must now pay,
What good now is Russia, it's lost anyway.
And that Stalin now marches the victor in the war,
The *Führer* neglected to calculate for.

In response to Hitler's appeal, German civilians provided nearly seventy million articles of clothing for their freezing soldiers. Many of the articles donated were useless. They were women's sweaters, children's gloves and hats, and threadbare socks. Two years of clothing rationing limited what the home front could donate to the Russian front.[77] As the word spread among the civilian populace, undoubtedly because of letters sent home by soldiers, Hübener sought, as his third goal, to stoke mistrust of the entire wool collection effort as a front for Nazi profiteering:

"Time will tell whether the government cheated the people out of their woolens and furs only to graciously allow them back later on their ration cards. Time will tell!!!"[78]

The longer handbill format allowed Hübener to quote from Hamlet and William Tell, to list the German-language broadcast schedule for the BBC—including special programming for Wehrmacht troops, early shift workers, and early-retiring farmers—and to provide periodic comparisons of the tactical situation on all battlefronts. It also allowed the targeting of special audiences, such as boys in the Hitler Youth. He made two appeals to young men affected by a Hitler Youth policy that allowed confinement for disciplinary purposes. Boys given "weekend detention" could be fed bread and water diets. Longer "youth service arrest" could confine a Hitler Youth as young as fourteen to a standard jail cell for a maximum of ten days, for infractions as minor as insubordination or sloppy uniform preparation.[79] A sample handbill aimed at HJ members said: "So this is the Hitler Youth, praised far and wide. A compulsory organization of the first order for recruiting Nazi-enslaved national comrades. Hitler and his accomplices know that they must deprive you of your free will at the beginning, in order to make submissive, spineless creatures out of you. . . . 'You are the future of Germany,' they will tell you but then you are tyrannized and punished for any little offense."[80]

Hübener seemed fascinated with the flight of Rudolf Hess, Hitler's deputy Führer and the third-ranking Nazi behind Hitler and Göring, who fled Germany on the eve of the invasion of the Soviet Union. Hess flew solo to Scotland in an effort to negotiate an unauthorized peace treaty. Helmuth recounted the details of Hess's Christmas 1941 shortwave broadcast from captivity in Great Britain. He contrasted that message with previous holiday broadcasts Hess had made to the German people. In his latest broadcast, according to Hübener, Hess criticized the Gestapo, the invasion of Russia, and a perceived plot against his life that would have been carried out if he had remained in Germany.[81] In a shorter pamphlet, Hübener speculated that Hess left Germany because he did not agree with Hitler's plans to invade Russia or with the Führer's murderous desires.[82]

Other pamphlets decried the Japanese attack on Pearl Harbor, questioned the will of the Italian people to support Mussolini, and projected Germany's shortfall of critical petroleum supplies. Hübener saved his most intense vitriol for Adolf Hitler. Almost every pamphlet criticized the *Führer's* character and ability to lead the German people. In one publication devoted to a Hitler speech, Hübener called him a "false prophet" who utters many words but says little of substance.

> For nearly two hours the Führer continued this vacuous beating of his gums; for nearly two hours he blew one soap bubble after another. But still, despite this . . . and despite the numbers of propagandists, politicians or armchair politicians, and scribblers, who are also willing to trim to size this or that sentence, to garnish Hitler with glimmers of hope and calculated optimism, in order to make it palatable to the man on the street, Hitler has lost his halo. After the extraordinary prophesies of the past year, after dozens of futile promises of ultimate victory, scarcely anyone still believes in him and in his prophetic words.[83]

What Did Hübener *Not* Say?

In the twenty-nine pamphlets he authored, Helmuth Hübener did not mention Nazi anti-Semitism. In the documentary video released in 2002, *Truth & Conviction*, historian Douglas Tobler stated that Hübener "did not like the way the Nazis treated the Jews. It was a central component of his political beliefs." However, no documentation either supports or refutes Tobler's contention. Both of Helmuth's Mormon co-conspirators, Rudi Wobbe and Karl-Heinz Schnibbe, said they had been sickened by the treatment of Jews in Nazi Germany. Hübener expressed no opinion on the issue, at least in writing. More than likely, he had made a tactical decision. He understood Nazi anti-Semitism, as he also understood the unfortunate reality of anti-Semitism among many Germans of that era. He would win no converts to his cause by being sympathetic to Jews.

The Downfall of the Helmuth Hübener Group

At nine o'clock in the morning on February 4, 1942, a thirty-eight-year-old woman filed a complaint at Hamburg's Forty-Third Police Precinct.

Bertha Flögel, born in Altona and a resident of Hamburg, reported that earlier on that Wednesday morning she found a flyer when she entered a telephone booth to make a call. Because of the suspicious nature of the material, she promptly brought it to the police station. She told the investigating officer that she had no idea who had left it.[84]

For eight months, Helmuth Hübener, Karl Heinz-Schnibbe, and Rudi Wobbe produced and distributed more than one thousand copies of their seditious tracts. Each pamphlet bore the instruction: "This is a chain letter. . . . So pass it on!"[85] No evidence exists that any recipient forwarded the original or made a copy. Only "eight or nine" concerned citizens reported the illegal literature to the municipal police.[86] Nobody turned in a pamphlet to the Gestapo office in the Rothenburgsort district of Hamburg, where Wobbe had scattered so many anti-Nazi tracts in his home neighborhood, known for its communist sympathies.[87] But the brochures prompted no attempt to overthrow the government of Adolf Hitler. After nine years of the Nazi police state and two years of war, most readers had other priorities. Survival trumped initiative in wartime Nazi Germany.

The downfall of the Helmuth Hübener group began when its lead conspirator decided to recruit accomplices outside of his close circle of Mormon friends. In January 1942, the month in which Hübener turned seventeen, he approached Gerhard Düwer, a coworker at the government social services office in the Bieber-Haus. Düwer was also seventeen. According to the Reich attorney general's indictment, Hübener asked Düwer if he would like to join a "spy ring." He gave Düwer as many as fifteen copies of two different leaflets. Later in the month, Düwer tried to interest three friends in reading the anti-Hitler literature, but each refused.[88] His friends questioned Düwer's sanity, but they did not report him.

According to Rudi Wobbe, Hübener wanted Düwer to act as intermediary in recruiting another worker at the same office—Werner Kranz, who was fluent in French. Hübener did not speak French and needed someone to incite rebellion among French military prisoners of war at a camp near Hamburg.[89] On January 20, 1942, Hübener and Düwer approached Kranz and asked for help in translating a document. Initially, Kranz was receptive, but when he read the brochure, he brusquely refused. This reaction attracted the attention of the office informer, whose desk sat across the room. Heinrich Mohns was the designated *Betriebsobmann*, the Nazi Party shop steward and political overseer.[90]

After Hübener and his friend Düwer left, Mohns approached Kranz and asked what happened. The French speaker told him about the pamphlet. The shop steward instructed Kranz to approach Düwer and express a willingness to do the translation. Mohns wanted a copy of Hübener's subversive pamphlet to use as evidence. When Kranz complied, Düwer told him about the second pamphlet. Mohns, the Nazi shop steward, then approached Düwer and ordered him to turn over both seditious tracts. Düwer stalled for almost two weeks but eventually obeyed. The fourth conspirator in the Hübener group, Gerhard Düwer, gave Mohns two red, swastika-stamped tracts that criticized Adolf Hitler. It was Wednesday, February 4, 1942—the same day that Mrs. Bertha Flögel, as a patriotic citizen of Nazi Germany, reported the flyer she found in a telephone booth. The Nazi shop steward studied the pamphlets overnight. The next day, Mohns ensured that both Hübener and Düwer were in the building. Then he made a phone call.[91]

The Gestapo arrived ten minutes later.

Interrogation, Trial, Conviction, and Execution

That Sunday, February 8, 1942, Arthur Zander, a fervent supporter of the National Socialist German Workers' Party and the branch president of the St. Georg congregation of the Church of Jesus Christ of Latter-day Saints, stood at the pulpit. As Rudi Wobbe recalled:

> The branch president announced that he'd like everyone to stay seated after the service for a special meeting. It was then that he dropped the bomb. Helmuth Hübener, a member of the St. Georg branch, had been arrested a few days before by the Gestapo. He told us he didn't have any details but he knew it was for political reasons. He also said that as his branch clerk, Helmuth had been given the use of the meetinghouse typewriter to write servicemen in the field, but had misused that trust to write antigovernment propaganda, which had resulted in its confiscation.[92]

Karl-Heinz Schnibbe and Rudi Wobbe sat in the pews, stunned. The three boys had made an informal pact: If one of them were arrested, he would take the blame as the lone culprit.[93] So far, Helmuth Hübener, their smallish, non-athletic, intellectual friend had withstood Gestapo interrogation for almost three days.[94] The Gestapo had not been easy on Helmuth. After arresting Düwer and Hübener on Thursday, agents took each suspect to his respective home to search for incriminating evidence. Düwer, having stalled the Nazi shop steward, had ample time to purge his residence of all traces of the plot. Arrest had been a surprise to Hübener. When the agents arrived at his grandparents' apartment, they found the Rola radio and the church's Remington typewriter. Wound around the rubber platen, they discovered seven pages of paper with carbon paper inserted between each page. The essay's title read: "Who is Inciting Whom?"[95]

"He was terribly beaten up," Helmuth's mother Emma told a fellow congregant when her son arrived at the grandparents' apartment in the custody of Gestapo agents. He was not allowed to speak to his relatives in the short time that the agents searched the apartment.[96] Then, after retrieving the evidence of his guilt, the Gestapo had one overriding concern in subsequent interrogations: Who were the adults behind this enemy propaganda operation? The Nazi secret police could not believe that an adolescent could mastermind and execute such a sophisticated campaign. Foreign agents or domestic collaborators must have been involved. When Helmuth told the truth—that no adults from his church or employment had a role in the scheme—the Gestapo beat him. When he maintained that he was the lone perpetrator—which was a lie—he became the target of more savage violence.

The Gestapo kept carefully detailed records of its interrogations, written in chillingly euphemistic language. One report said: "Only after *lengthy remonstrations* and *explicit admonitions*, was Hübener moved to give a confession about the scope of his destructive activity."[97] Another chronicle of sadism said: "Responding to *assiduous persuasion*, he admitted to having distributed documents" (my emphasis).[98] After five days of torture, deliberately understated in the Gestapo's official documentation, Helmuth Hübener gave his tormentors the name of Karl-Heinz Schnibbe. Helmuth had kept his bargain for as long as he could.

The Gestapo then took Schnibbe into custody on Tuesday, February 10, 1942, at the job site where he worked as a painter. When the agents insisted that Schnibbe come with them, he told his colleague that he would be "back in a minute."[99] He returned seven years later.[100] Karl-Heinz then joined Helmuth in a daily routine of brutal interrogation at the infamous "hall of mirrors," the Gestapo's interrogation facility in the basement of the old Hamburg city hall. With walls painted white, excessively bright illumination, and uncomfortably hot temperatures, it served to make the Gestapo's suspects as miserable as possible while waiting their turn to be interrogated. It employed a full-time staff of sadistic inquisitors who, after a hard day of extracting information by inflicting cruelty, went home to their wives and children.[101] Then, in the evening, a police bus took the captives to the Gestapo's infamous "Kola-Fu" prison on the grounds of the Fuhlsbüttel concentration camp.[102] The concentration camp's prison supported the daytime interrogation at Gestapo headquarters by breaking down a prisoner's resistance. The nighttime regimen consisted of physical assault, exhausting exercise, poor nutrition, and sleep deprivation.[103] Nevertheless, Hübener and Schnibbe managed to avoid incriminating Rudi Wobbe for another eight days.[104]

In the search for adult instigators, the Gestapo turned its attention to the St. Georg Branch of the Mormons' Hamburg District. In Branch President Arthur Zander, it found a Party loyalist who seemed more concerned about retrieving the confiscated church typewriter than the fortunes of three lost sheep named Hübener, Schnibbe, and Wobbe. Because the Gestapo did not apprehend Wobbe until February 18, 1942, almost two weeks after it caught Helmuth Hübener, Wobbe observed the congregation's initial reactions to the arrest of his two friends. Opinions were mixed. Wobbe heard his church friends say:

> "Those poor boys, I wonder what made them do it?" and "Who else is behind this?" Someone else said, "How terrible getting arrested by the Gestapo—they do awful things to people!" Then, there were other voices, full of anger and hurt, such as, "How could they oppose a government that is installed of God?" Another asked, "Doesn't this violate the Twelfth Article of Faith which says we should be subject to our rulers and sustain the laws of the land?" Someone else spoke up and said, "They surely have broken the law. I hope they throw the book at them!"

One comment made a lasting impression: "This is treason, and they should be shot—if I had a gun I would shoot them myself!" The responsibility for those words, according to District President Otto Berndt, belonged to Branch President Arthur Zander. Berndt said Zander made that remark during sacrament meeting, the main Sunday worship service.[105] Others, including Rudi Wobbe, said First Counselor Franz Jacobi, who was also a member of the Nazi Party, might have been the one who advocated shooting Hübener.[106] Regardless who made that extreme statement, strong emotions permeated the St. Georg Branch on the first Sunday after Hübener's arrest. Many years later, Rudi Wobbe said that the St. Georg Branch was "the *Hochburg*," the high castle of Nazism in the Mormon Church in Germany.[107]

Zander had already taken two actions that influenced his flock. In his sermon, he preached "about the importance of keeping the laws of the land and supporting and sustaining the Führer who was ordained of God."[108] Three days earlier, without consulting with District President Otto Berndt, Zander excommunicated Helmuth Hübener from the Church of Jesus Christ of Latter-day Saints.[109] Otto Berndt said Zander might have performed the excommunication because he believed it would placate the Gestapo. But, added Berndt, "He did it behind my back."[110] According to Mormon theology, Zander had withdrawn the companionship of the Holy Ghost from Helmuth as he tried to survive the Gestapo's daily brutality. In removing Helmuth's name from the church membership rolls, and simultaneously defrocking him from the universal Mormon male priesthood, Arthur Zander had decreed that Helmuth Hübener's soul could not enter the Celestial Kingdom, the Mormon concept of Heaven.[111]

That was a steep price to pay for defaming Adolf Hitler, but apparently the Nazi Party was pleased with Zander's actions and with the attitude of his congregants. On February 24, 1942, nine days after Zander's excommunication of Hübener, the Hamburg district leader for the Nazi Party wrote to the Gestapo: "This [St. Georg Mormon] church congregation is legally recognized and stands on a firm footing with the present government."[112] One possible suspect within the Mormon leadership remained: Hamburg District President Otto Berndt. He had vetoed some of Zander's more egregious pro-Nazi manifestations, such as beginning Sunday services with the Hitler salute. Hugo Hübener, the SA *Rottenführer* who married Helmuth's mother, accused Berndt of being the plot's adult instigator. Berndt recalled that he "was a guest of the Gestapo" for a period of three days during the early weeks of the Hübener investigation. That description seems as euphemistic as the language that described the Gestapo's interrogations.

Nevertheless, Berndt was able to survive the questioning, an accomplishment that he attributed to divine intervention: "When I went to the police headquarters I prayed like I had never prayed before. When I entered the room and the questioning started, I felt that my spirit left my body and another spirit entered and took over my thinking. I was asked hundreds of questions in rapid succession and I, or I should say the spirit of the higher power that had possession of my body, was able to answer them all without hesitation. I felt very sure of myself."

Eventually, the Gestapo stopped looking for a nonexistent adult leader of the Helmuth Hübener gang. In seeking to try Hübener as an adult, and thus condemn him to death, the Reich attorney general argued that the defendant "in spite of his youth, already possessed a sufficient capacity of political discernment." The indictment cited the political sophistication that Hübener displayed in writing his pro-Nazi graduation thesis.[113] On February 28, 1942, having been convinced that the Hübener resistance gang was limited to the four conspirators, the torturous interrogations stopped.[114]

The Gestapo transferred Hübener, Schnibbe, Wobbe, and Düwer to the Hamburg "investigative prison" to await the bureaucratic process of indictment and subsequent trial. The five peaceful months spent at the city jail were a stark contrast to the bedlam of the previous weeks in the Gestapo's custody. "It was so quiet," recalled Karl-Heinz Schnibbe. "I thought I was on vacation. It was the first time I had slept in weeks." But the investigative prison had a maddening routine of its own. From March until the end of July, each young man stayed in an isolated cell with no companionship and nothing to read. During the day, prisoners could not lie down, but instead had to sit on a wobbly stool.[115]

In early August 1942, authorities loaded the four accused traitors onto a train for Berlin. On the eleventh of the month, they faced trial in the Third Reich's highest criminal tribunal, the *Volksgerichtshof*, the People's Court. Informally, Germans called it the "Blood Tribunal." The impressively decorated courtroom bespoke the power of the Nazi state. The participants sat on different levels, according to their legal status. The defendants sat in the floor's lowest recess, their attorneys positioned on raised platforms beside them. The prosecution's elevated rostrum stood across the room. In front, towering above all, sat three judges who had been appointed to the court by Hitler. They wore crimson robes and caps. Behind them on the paneled wall appeared the emblem of Hitler's state, the *Hoheitsadler*, a large eagle clutching in its talons a wreath encircling a swastika. Each judge's robe bore an embroidered rendition of the same symbol. The court's other officers, bailiffs and recorders, wore perfectly tailored black and brown uniforms of the SS and the SA. The state attorney general charged each defendant with high treason and aiding the enemy, in addition to violating the Extraordinary Radio Measures law.[116]

Each defendant had one attorney, chosen from a pool provided by the National Socialist Lawyers' League.[117] Wobbe quickly became convinced that his attorney was merely going through the motions. Their pretrial conference had consisted of one question. His lawyer, who had pledged loyalty to Adolf Hitler, asked if Rudi could volunteer any information not contained in the indictment. When the chief justice, a jurist named Fikeis, began to speak, Wobbe deduced that they would be convicted without a fair hearing.[118] Helmuth Hübener knew that also. Rather than argue for his acquittal, he engaged the judges in debate. One judge asked: "Young man, do you honestly believe Germany will lose the war?" Hübener responded: "Don't you?" Another asked: "Do you mean to tell me that the German broadcasts are wrong and the English ones are correct?" Helmuth answered, "Exactly." Astonished, Hübener's attorney turned to him and asked: "Are you nuts?"[119]

Hübener was not insane. Instead, in Wobbe's opinion, his friend was deliberately focusing all of the court's hostility on himself, diverting the judges' enmity away from the other defendants.[120] In the end, it did not matter. For three of the four young men, the judges awarded sentences more severe than the prosecutor requested. The attorney general requested a minimum of two years imprisonment for Gerhard Düwer and Karl-Heinz Schnibbe. Instead, Düwer received four years in a labor camp. Schnibbe, because he listened to the forbidden broadcasts in addition to distributing leaflets, got five years. The prosecutor recommended seven years for Wobbe, as he had distributed leaflets in the politically volatile communist neighborhoods; the judges awarded ten. Hübener received the maximum sentence, death, as the state had requested.[121] Helmuth's final exchange with the judge marked the last stage of his evolution as a revolutionary. Given the opportunity to speak at the end of the proceedings, Hübener negated any chance he may have had to receive post-conviction commutation. He told three red-robed justices: "I have to die now for no crime at all. Your turn is next!"[122]

At five minutes past one in the afternoon on October 27, 1942, the warden of Berlin's Plötzensee Prison informed Helmuth Hübener that Adolf Hitler had personally denied an appeal for clemency.[123] The warden allowed Helmuth to write letters, one to his mother, one to his maternal grandparents, and one to Marie Sommerfeld, an elderly friend of the family who cared for Helmuth as a child.[124] At 8:13 in the evening, Hübener walked into a converted prison tool shed that housed the guillotine. If the state executioner, Wilhelm Röttger, followed protocol that evening, he wore a top hat and tails. Eighteen seconds later, Röttger severed Helmuth's head, for which he was paid eighty marks in addition to his annual salary of three thousand marks.[125] Helmuth's body was sent to a medical school.[126] The next day, his mother learned of her son's death by reading one of the bright red posters erected throughout Hamburg to announce Helmuth Hübener's execution. It was her birthday.[127]

Before services the next Sunday at the St. Georg Branch, District President Otto Berndt pleaded with other members of the branch hierarchy not to mention Helmuth's death to the congregation. Those who cared already knew. Arthur Zander, who never missed a chance to urge adherence to the Twelfth Article of Faith in Nazi Germany, ignored the advice of his ecclesiastical superior. With Helmuth's mother in the audience, Zander announced the lad's execution from the pulpit.[128]

The Last Mormon Diaspora

Excommunication is not an unusual occurrence in the Church of Jesus Christ of Latter-day Saints. Since the denomination's founding in 1830, some of the more common justifications have included adultery or fornication, defiance of priesthood authority, and the failure to attend meetings. When St. Georg Branch President Arthur Zander scribbled on Helmuth Hübener's membership record on February 15, 1942, he probably noted the only excommunication in Mormon Church history for "intercepting and spreading foreign broadcast transmissions."[129]

In 1946, freed of both the Nazi government and Zander's branch presidency, Hamburg district president Otto Berndt saw his courage validated. A clerk wrote "excommunicated by mistake" on Hübener's membership record. Then, on January 24, 1948, by order of the prophet, seer, and revelator, George Albert Smith, the entry was made, "Decision of excommunication reversed by the First Presidency of the Church of Jesus Christ of Latter-day Saints, who ordered this notation placed upon the record of excommunication."[130] According to Gerhard Kunkel, Helmuth's half-brother, members offended by Zander's vigilante style of ecclesiastical justice took several extra steps, "just to make sure." They submitted Hübener's name for posthumous temple ordinances.[131] On January 7, 1948, Hübener was "baptized for the dead" in the Holy Temple. He received the "temple endowment" ordinance on June 8, 1948, after which he was ordained an elder in the senior Melchizedek Priesthood.[132]

Berndt probably felt a sense of redemption upon the nullification of the excommunication. Hübener's status in the afterlife was now secure, as was Berndt's legacy as someone who had battled Nazis in the church congregations he supervised. For three grueling days of Gestapo interrogation, Berndt had stubbornly refused to revoke the young man's membership.[133] On the other hand, the Gestapo had no difficulty convincing Zander to perform the excommunication. It is just as likely that terminating Hübener's membership was Zander's idea. Berndt's rift with the St. Georg Branch Nazis was also personal. Zander once called Berndt a communist because of his lack of enthusiasm for Hitler. Franz Jacobi, Zander's first counselor, once threatened to have Berndt sent to a concentration camp.[134]

Berndt had the last laugh. After the war, Ezra Taft Benson, who coordinated the LDS Church's relief effort in Germany, invited Berndt to serve a mission in Frankfurt.[135] Berndt's nemesis, Arthur Zander, was in a different position in 1946. He was in the United States, interned in a POW camp. At some point after Zander announced Hübener's execution from the pulpit in October 1942, he was drafted into the *Wehrmacht* and subsequently captured. Zander did not return to Germany until 1947.

In 1952, after Berndt's missionary service had been prolonged by a second assignment, he made a life-changing decision. At age forty-eight, he became one of more than four thousand who joined the postwar German Mormon diaspora to the American Zion. The LDS Church provided substantial postwar welfare aid to German members and continued to encourage its flock to remain at home and build a German Zion. Nevertheless, the desire to join family members and co-religionists in the Mormon Culture Region proved too strong for the church hierarchy to overcome. It was not by accident that the LDS Church built its first European temple in a German-speaking city. The Swiss Temple in Bern opened its doors in 1955, providing "sealing" rooms for couples to be joined in celestial marriage, "for time and all eternity." It did not stem the tide of German emigration.

"We were *commanded* to immigrate!" declared W. Herbert Klopfer, the son of the wartime East German Mission president.[136] The younger Klopfer, born in 1936, referred to an inherited outlook, dating from the nineteenth century, that compelled Mormons to "gather" in the American Zion. During the Roaring Twenties, despite official opposition from the Salt Lake City leadership and restrictive new American immigrations laws, a record number of Mormons left Germany for the Mormon Culture Region. The Great Depression stifled that flow. Then, the peacetime Nazi years (1933–39) brought new German laws that limited emigration by Aryans.

By the end of the Second World War, a smoldering desire to emigrate had been stoked into a flaming passion by the postwar economic conditions. German Mormons found sponsors among American missionaries who had proselytized among them.[137] They formed immigration clubs to share ideas and formulate migration strategies.[138] As table 15.1 shows, they migrated to the American Zion in record numbers. Relatives took out loans from American banks to fund ocean liner tickets; the new arrivals thankfully assumed those loans on the day they arrived.[139]

By the early 1950s, it did not matter if a prospective immigrant had been a Nazi. The governments of the United States and West Germany were growing weary of the denazification process. The Cold War's anxieties regarding communism replaced older concerns about fascism. In 1952, the same year that Otto Berndt immigrated to the United States, a former executive of a soap distribution company also joined the Mormon migration. Arthur Zander, who had marketed Persil laundry detergent at work while selling Hitlerism at church, had no trouble obtaining his *Persilschein*.[140] Time and changing priorities had scrubbed him clean of his Nazi past. Zander, his wife of twenty-one years, and his three sons,

Table 15.1. German-speaking Mormon immigration to the United States during the post–World War II era

	Douglas Alder's Method[a]				Gabriele Kindt's Method[b]
	Swiss Mission	West German Mission[c]	East German Mission	Total	Germany
1946	9	0	0	9	
1947	44	18	0	62	
1948	71	21	27	119	32
1949	97	71	12	179	91
1950	76	116	37	229	131
1951	54	250	74	378	290
1952	37	348	133	518	398
1953	55	265	247	567	583
1954	25	257	173	455	418
1955	37	59	151	247	288
1956	51	310	121	482	431
1957	112	201	224	537	339
1958	47	140	523	710	458
1959	—	—	—	—	215
1960	—	—	—	—	153
1961	—	—	—	—	292
1962	—	—	—	—	89
Total	715	2056	1722	4493	4208

[a]For the period covered, Douglas D. Alder relied upon the tabulations of emigration from the German-speaking missions found in the LDS Church–published bimonthly periodical, *Der Stern*. See Alder, "The German-Speaking Immigration to Utah, 1850–1950," Appendix F, 123. Alder completed his master's degree at the University of Utah in 1959; thus, the year 1958 is the last included in his tabulations.
[b]Gabriele B. Kindt, an undergraduate at Brigham Young University, used two sources that she compared for accuracy. Each year, branch and district clerks completed the LDS Church's Form E, the "Transcript of Records of Members," which it submitted to the mission president's office. Each mission then used the data on Form E to tabulate its Annual Mission Financial and Statistical Report, which it submitted to the church's headquarters in Salt Lake City. The German ecclesiastical units began using Form E after the arrival of the American mission presidents in 1947. After 1962, the LDS Church ceased using Form E, thus limiting the time frame of Kindt's study. See Kindt, "Statistical Study, 1945–62."
[c]The West German Mission included Austria during the period of Alder's study.

aged eighteen, eleven, and nine, embarked on a ship anchored in Hamburg harbor and sailed to the United States. Zander, who had embraced the Nazi Party in 1933 in order to "get ahead at work," was preparing to embark upon a new life in the country that helped topple the fascism he once advocated.[141]

In 1952, only three years after returning from a Soviet prisoner of war camp, Karl-Heinz Schnibbe spent the last of three indemnity payments, provided to German citizens persecuted by the Nazi regime, for a steamship ticket to the United States.[142] The next year, Rudi Wobbe, his wife, and two daughters made the same journey. Wobbe had been released from captivity in June 1945 and, like Berndt, served a mission for the Mormon Church afterward.[143] Helmuth Hübener's two half-brothers, Hans and Gerhard, also immigrated to Utah, as did Marie Sommerfeld, to whom Helmuth wrote from Plötzensee Prison on his last day of life. Schnibbe and Wobbe quickly found work in their respective trades, Karl-Heinz as a painter and Rudi as a machinist. Forty-five-year-old Zander, who had a managerial background but could speak little English, went to work for the Church of Jesus Christ of Latter-day Saints. He worked as a janitor at a local church meetinghouse, sweeping the floors in a venue similar to one where he had presided over as the highest ministerial authority.[144]

Utah welcomed its German immigrants of the post–World War II generation. All carried their hopes to the place where previous generations of foreign converts had entered Zion's ecclesiastical melting pot. Most gravitated initially to German-speaking LDS church units, which resembled the small branch and district structure they left behind. Once a month, there was a German-language devotional on Temple Square in central Salt Lake City. There were many social activities that the newly arrived immigrants could enjoy while speaking their native tongue. When Rudi Wobbe's wife went into labor with their third child, Rudi had to be summoned from rehearsals with his German-language theatrical troupe.[145]

Once the immigrants learned enough English, a fresh life beckoned. A new identity could be forged in the catacomb of wards and stakes, clerical units that underlaid city blocks and neighborhoods. One could live barely a mile from a neighbor who had been a National Socialist but never see him at church or conferences. Mormons do not shop for churches; one attends services in his *assigned* neighborhood ward. The

LDS identity trumped all previous allegiances. Only the most callous, or perhaps the most ignorant, of Mormon brothers and sisters wondered if a new neighbor had been a Nazi. On rare occasions when that pejorative word may have been mentioned, it could have clumsily and mistakenly been interchanged with the word "German." In Utah of the 1950s, all that really mattered was the new immigrant's willingness to work, congeniality, and of course, love for the "restored gospel" of Jesus Christ.

Arthur Zander, relegated to custodial duty at work, found his own version of the American Dream in his hobby. He promoted the game of soccer. He started several clubs, and in 1954, only two years after he arrived in Utah, he provided the impetus for the founding of the Utah High School Soccer Association. His obituary would later read that he introduced the sport to Brigham Young University. For twenty years he ran the Arthur Zander Soccer Equipment Store from the basement of his home, and later from a small shop in his backyard. In 1956, the German Soccer Association awarded him its "Silver Pin" in recognition of his efforts to promote the sport in his new country.[146] In the few years that had passed since his ship sailed past the Statue of Liberty, the former Nazi enthusiast had forged a new identity.

Zander's dream of blissful anonymity continued until professors from BYU began asking questions about a young man named Helmuth Hübener.

16

A Premature Curtain Call

Margetts Arena was not the main theater on the BYU campus in the mid-1970s. With a seating capacity of only 240, it served as a laboratory for thespians. In October 1976, because of an unusual dramatic presentation, it took center stage at the nation's largest religious university. Ticket demand for Thomas Rogers' *Huebener* caused students to stand "in long, serpentine lines . . . as generally happens only when tickets are sold for football, basketball, or rock concerts."[1] Ninety-eight percent of the university's students were members of the Mormon Church. Seventy-five percent came from Utah. The idea that a principled young Mormon their age fought the Nazis was a captivating idea, especially when he defied his Nazi-sympathizing branch president. The playwright, Thomas Rogers, said: "It gave them a heroic counterpart from their own century about whom, until then, few if any were even aware. We all need heroes with whom, in terms of our particular values and personal ideological commitment, we can identify. Helmuth Hübener did that for young Mormons."[2]

Huebener featured a cast of a dozen main characters and eighteen supporting actors who took the real-life names unearthed in Alan F. Keele's and Douglas F. Tobler's research. Two exceptions prevailed in the case of living Nazis; their names were changed to protect the culpable. First Counselor Franz Jacobi became Sandman; and Branch President Arthur Zander became Arnold Zoellner. Zander's pseudonym was so close to his real name that no doubt existed regarding his identity among those who knew him in the German immigrant community.

Playwrights write fiction. They assume no obligation to follow the historical record. Rogers adhered closely to most verifiable details, including the trademark of Gerhard Kunkel's French shortwave receiver. He departed from reality on a few of the bigger points. Rogers transformed the branch president into a morally complex character. When "Zoellner" repeatedly pontificated on the need to obey civil authority, or when he exchanged "Heil Hitler!" greetings with Helmuth's stepfather, the audience was free to feel contempt. But when Zoellner found an anti-Hitler tract mistakenly left in the church's duplicating machine, a reality that never confronted Arthur Zander, the audience felt sympathy for a church leader in the horns of a moral dilemma. In the play, Zoellner granted Hübener the confidentiality of the confessional when they debated whether the safety of the congregation justified collaboration with the Nazis. Then, when he announced Helmuth's excommunication from the pulpit at church services, and handed over Schnibbe and Wobbe to the Gestapo in front of the congregation—the audience was left to wonder. Did Zoellner betray Hübener to the Nazis, or was the branch president merely acting to protect his flock after the French-speaking employee turned in his office colleague?

Fiction can play a valuable role in teaching history, provided that it does not lead to distorted conclusions. The documents Tobler and Keele discovered, and the interviews they conducted, leave no doubt that the real branch president, Arthur Zander, would have never debated the moral righteousness of opposing the Nazis. According to all sources, he always put the party first and the church second. If Zander had found one of Helmuth's pamphlets, all evidence indicates that he would have gone straight to the Gestapo. There would have been no principled debate in the branch president's office.

As the attendees filed out of Margetts Arena, ushers offered them a handbill. It explained that no evidence existed that the real branch president was aware of Hübener's exploits until the boy's arrest. It also said the historical record revealed no attempt by the Gestapo to have Hübener excommunicated.[3] But a handbill could hardly offset the dramatic effect of the play's emotional words and stark images. Some older members of the audience had probably served as congregational leaders in the Mormon system of lay church governance. Presenting the branch president in a sympathetic light was reassuring to them.

The artistic license granted the playwright distorted Hübener's memory in another important way. Having the fictional Zoellner surrender

Hübener's co-conspirators to the Gestapo deprived Hübener and Karl-Heinz Schnibbe of recognition for their greatest feats of courage. Helmuth withstood torture for five days before being forced to name Schnibbe. Both boys underwent another week of horrific Gestapo interrogation before incriminating Rudi Wobbe.

More than five thousand attended during the play's three-week engagement, which had been extended by extra performances.[4] Statewide, newspapers ran laudatory reviews, including the LDS Church-owned *Deseret News*.[5] According to leading lady Margaret Blair Young, who played Helmuth's mother, the play *Huebener* became a "BYU event," with cast members receiving recognition on campus comparable to star athletes. The cast, ecstatic because of the reception they received, looked forward to taking the play on the road to California, one of ten offers Rogers had received to perform off campus.[6] Wealthy BYU alumni were ready to open their pockets to spread the gospel of a genuine Mormon hero who had fought the Nazis.[7]

Two honored guests attended and personally greeted the performers. Karl-Heinz Schnibbe saw the play three times. Rudi Wobbe came once. Schnibbe joked backstage with the young actors, teasing them about their fake German accents, which had been a mandate from director Ivan Crosland. Both Schnibbe and Wobbe figured prominently in the play's crowning moment: October 27, 1976, the thirty-fourth anniversary of Helmuth's beheading. At the curtain call, two graying men stood on the tiny, darkened theater's stage, each illuminated by a spotlight. A third beam exposed the naked floor between them, where Helmuth Hübener should have stood. The deafening applause slackened only when spectators reached to wipe tears from their eyes.[8]

Two additional spectators figured significantly in this thespian memorial, one who attended and another who watched with trepidation from afar. Thomas S. Monson, a member of the Quorum of the Twelve and a key player in the Mormons' efforts to normalize Zion's relations with communist East Germany—where many Latter-day Saints still lived—viewed a performance during the play's last week of production. He watched in the company of BYU President Dallin Oaks.[9] The other "spectator" resided forty-five minutes north of the Provo campus. Arthur Zander had been living a quiet and unremarkable life when two BYU faculty members, Tobler and Keele, arrived unannounced at his house one day and requested an interview. He had not responded to phone messages and postal inquiries.[10] They promised to tell his side of the story and treat him fairly. He responded courteously but refused to be interviewed. He said he would tell his side of the story one day.[11] If he ever spoke out, more than likely he did so through the confidential chain of authority that began with his ward bishop. At the top of that ecclesiastical rank structure stood Thomas S. Monson.

Monson was the Mormons' point man with regard to dealing with all German matters, from interaction with German-Americans at home to relations between Mormons and the East German government. He had been a rising star in the LDS Church since becoming a ward bishop, the pastor of a large Mormon congregation, at the unusually young age of twenty-two. His first assignment was a Salt Lake City ward with many German-American members, recent immigrants and descendants of Germans who had come to Utah in previous generations.[12] Monson made numerous friends. Thereafter the German-American community in Utah had the ear of a highly influential member of the Mormons' governing council.

The BYU production caused German immigrants, lulled into complacency by decades of assimilation into the Utah mainstream, to sit up and take notice. For a few like Zander, who had a past worth hiding, the play proved to be particularly disturbing. When the historians who tried to interview Zander were unsuccessful, they started questioning others. They talked to members of the Salt Lake City German-American community who knew Zander. According to what they learned, Zander's calm, courteous demeanor when confronted by Keele and Tobler changed in the presence of family and friends. Friends reported his irrational fear of retribution by B'nai B'rith, the Jewish Defense League, or some other imagined enemy.[13] According to Rudi Wobbe, who stayed in touch with his former branch president, Zander regarded Tobler and Keele as representatives of his fantasy "American Gestapo."[14]

Just prior to their penultimate performance in Provo, with visions of their California tour beckoning, the cast of *Huebener* gathered around director Ivan Crosland. He made a shocking announcement. As the actress who played Helmuth Hübener's mother, Margaret Blair Young, described it: "After Brother Monson's visit, the church said California was off limits. . . . The play, Crosland reported, would apparently summon too many memories in the German members and perhaps awaken old resentments. There could be problems. Our show was branded '*verboten*.'"

Old resentments were not quashed when the Margetts Arena darkened after *Huebener's* final curtain call. After Rudi Wobbe appeared on stage, and after he became the subject of newspaper and broadcast interviews, not all of the reviews were positive. He wrote: "I was surprised to receive a number of disturbing phone calls. I'd pick up the receiver and hear a voice say, '*Landsverräter*' (traitor). It became clear to me that the underground Nazi movement, led by German diehards, was alive and active, even in the remote mountain deserts of Utah. Obviously, the report of our story touched a nerve with these people."[15] He told the *Salt Lake Tribune* that following the BYU play, unidentified callers would shout: "You traitor, you Bolshevik." Then they would hang up. "So that tells me that there are still people around who are taken in by that Nazi jargon," Wobbe said. "I'm not afraid of these people . . . We must never forget."[16]

For various reasons, forgetting became a priority for the Mormon hierarchy in the mid-1970s. At some point prior to the 1976 *Huebener* play, an associate professor of history at Brigham Young University approached Thomas S. Monson in the Salt Lake City airport. Knowing Monson's interest in German Latter-day Saints, Douglas F. Tobler wanted to describe the exciting new research he was conducting. Tobler told Monson the story of Helmuth Hübener. Monson's response was not what Tobler expected. Instead of encouraging the young scholar, Monson asked to review any manuscript that Tobler and Alan Keele wrote before its submission for publication. In an interview in 2001, Tobler recalled that he had been "lathered up," the natural resentment that a scholar would feel when pressured to stifle promising research.[17] Keele remembered his colleague to have been "somewhat rattled" by having a member of the Quorum of the Twelve wanting to supervise his scholarship.[18]

After Monson viewed a performance of *Huebener* in the last week of its scheduled run, BYU President Dallin Oaks summoned Tobler, Keele, and Rogers to his office. There he ordered the "hold" on Hübener-related articles and books, and on subsequent performances of Rogers' play. Oaks forbade Rogers from allowing any other theater group to use his script. Keele and Tobler had already written the draft of a scholarly article and were in the process of negotiating with a journal. They were also working on the manuscript of a book. Oaks cited only the sensitivities of

German-American Mormons to the resurrection of the Hübener story, but said there were other reasons that he could not divulge.[19]

There were indeed other reasons, and they included a fundamental misunderstanding by the Mormon hierarchy about how the communist East German government would view a young anti-fascist who rebelled during the Nazi period. In 1968, Monson had become the Quorum of the Twelve's liaison with German Mormons living in East Germany. Although some church members had moved to West Germany and others had immigrated to the United States in the years following the Second World War, some 3,700 remained behind the Iron Curtain. During the Cold War, their status as members of an American-based church in the officially atheistic German Democratic Republic caused problems. It became impossible for the Salt Lake City hierarchy to maintain the customary chain of authority.

BYU religious historian Bruce Van Orden said that Monson, in addition to his experience working with German-Americans, had another qualification to be the Mormons' lead negotiator with the GDR. As the youngest member of a twelve-man governing gerontocracy, Monson was probably the only Mormon apostle "vigorous enough to endure the rigors of forty-eight hour visits behind the Iron Curtain."[20] East Germany in those days permitted a visiting American only a two-day visa. That was an improvement over the previous decades, when contact with East German Latter-day Saints could take place only once a year—when Mormon leaders accredited as trade representatives visited with the faithful at the internationally renowned Leipzig trade fair in March.[21]

Monson had another problem, one that emanated from within the Quorum of the Twelve. Ezra Taft Benson, formerly Dwight Eisenhower's Secretary of Agriculture, was an older Mormon apostle. Because of Benson's seniority among the Twelve, he was almost certain to ascend to the position of Prophet, Seer, and Revelator.[22] Benson was a supporter of the John Birch Society and an outspoken anti-communist. His "neo-McCarthyism," as historian D. Michael Quinn termed it, stood in stark contrast to the image that Monson and the East German Latter-day Saints wished to project. In dealing with the GDR, it was essential to stress that one could be a good Mormon and a good citizen of a socialist state.[23] Benson's frequent bombastic anti-communist tirades, combined with the less-frequent and less-vitriolic anti-communist pronouncements of Church President David O. McKay, made life difficult for East German Mormons.[24]

Tobler wrote: "LDS leader Walter Krause remembers how the anti-Communist speeches of President David O. McKay and Ezra Taft Benson were monitored in East Berlin. Police and government officials fattened their files with speech after speech that stigmatized 'godless Communism' as the incarnation of evil."[25]

When Richard Nixon initiated détente with Chinese and Soviet communist governments in 1971, a crack emerged in the East German section of the Iron Curtain. The LDS Church negotiated permission for a selected few East German Mormons to attend the 1973 regional conference in Munich, where new Church President Harold B. Lee dutifully admonished them to return to their homes in the GDR.[26] That same year, an East German LDS leader received permission to attend the church's General Conference in Salt Lake City.[27]

As the situation in East Germany was appearing to become slightly more favorable for the Mormons, other conflicts worldwide stoked the fears of the Salt Lake City leadership. When *Huebener* appeared on a Provo, Utah, stage in October 1976, it had been only several months since an Argentine military coup d'état overthrew the presidency of Isabel Perón. In the months that followed, the disappearance of many Peronist sympathizers and other opponents of the new military junta—including many young people—were making headlines as the "Dirty War" unfolded. It had also been only three years since right-wing Chilean dictator Augusto Pinochet had taken power in a coup d'état against socialist Salvador Allende. The Pinochet regime became notorious for its record of human rights abuses. Based on the political climate of the mid-1970s, an assistant to the Quorum of the Twelve, Joseph Wirthlin, feared the example that Helmuth Hübener might set for Mormon young people who lived in dictatorships worldwide.[28] He also opposed continued performances of the play and the publication of scholarly works that brought Helmuth Hübener into the spotlight. By the end of 1976, after a brief interlude of light, the heavy hand of the Mormon hierarchy had firmly rotated the dimmer switch of Helmuth Hübener's memory to the fully dark position.

Keele, Tobler, and Rogers had no choice but to comply with the edicts of the LDS leaders who controlled their continued employment. For the young students who performed *Huebener*, it was a bitter disappointment. Individual cast members threatened to form their own theatrical troupes and stage their own tour.[29] But rebellion is a short-lived phenomenon at BYU, where decisions from university administrators are met with the same reverence Mormons accord pronouncements from their church hierarchy, guidance they consider divinely inspired.

Rogers, hamstrung by the ban on releasing his own intellectual property, continued to provide encouragement to young playwrights who approached him with their own versions of the Hübener story. He read their scripts and advised them as to whether their own literary creations deviated sufficiently from his own.[30] Keele and Tobler used BYU President Dallin Oaks to negotiate with Monson and other members of the Twelve. It was difficult to make headway against what the two scholars saw as unreasonable fears.[31] Both understood that Helmuth Hübener's anti-fascist rebellion would never pose a threat to Erich Honecker's communist East German government. An independent Mormon intellectual journal wrote in 1984: "Sources inform *The Sunstone Review* that the most likely reason for the Church's concern was the fear that East German Saints would follow Hübener's example and engage in anti-communist activities. 'That would never happen,' retorts Keele. 'The fortunes of the Church in East Germany would not be disturbed by publicity concerning the Huebener Group because no East German would equate anti-fascism with anti-communism. It would not be misconstrued as an example of opposition to unpopular governments."[32]

Keele spent the last half of the 1970s arguing with the Mormon hierarchy, using Oaks as his intermediary, that Hübener's example would help, not hinder, the LDSs Church's private diplomacy with the GDR government. He once told Oaks that East Germany should be the next stop for Rogers' play. Helmuth Hübener was a well-known figure in the GDR's anti-fascist collective memory, Keele maintained, and his identification with the Mormons would only help the LDS Church in that communist country.[33]

In 1980, Oaks, a noted legal scholar, left BYU's presidency to become the chief justice of the Utah Supreme Court. Keele and Tobler decided they had waited long enough. They approached the editors of *BYU Studies*, a journal that publishes peer-reviewed academic articles that do not interest mainstream publications, such as scholarly treatments of Book of Mormon topics. According to Keele, the on-campus editors—themselves employees of the LDS university—initially expressed interest but then "got cold feet."[34] Tobler and Keele then submitted their article to *Sunstone*, an independently published, interdisciplinary Mormon scholarly magazine. "The Führer's New Clothes," which appeared in *Sunstone's* final 1980 edition, introduced the Mormon intellectual community to Helmuth Hübener.[35] The ten-page illustrated article summarized the young resister's bravery and set it in the context of Mormon accommodation with the Nazi state. One facet left over from the 1976 play manifested itself in their article. The two co-authors used Rogers' stage name, the mythical Arnold Zoellner, as a pseudonym for Helmuth Hübener's branch president. Thirty-five years after the fall of the Third Reich, authors and editors were still taking care of Arthur Zander, keeping him on its payroll and protecting him from unwanted notoriety with a pseudonym concocted by its scholars.

The Brightening but Filtered Light of Memory

On October 9, 1982, a surprise announcement from Salt Lake City provided a significant clue for solving the riddle of Mormon interference with the work of its scholars and playwrights. After four years of negotiation, the communist government of the German Democratic Republic agreed to allow the LDS Church to construct the first Holy Temple behind the Iron Curtain. For the Mormons, it ended years of difficult bureaucratic wrangling whenever East German Latter-day Saints wished to visit the Bern temple in Switzerland. For the GDR government, it provided a much-needed source of American money to bolster its hard currency reserves. The proposed temple in Freiberg, Saxony, received priority for expedited construction. The GDR government allowed the temple to tap into the Trans-Siberian Pipeline as an energy source. Groundbreaking for the Freiberg Temple occurred in April 1983. It opened in June 1985, which outpaced the construction schedule for the Frankfurt Temple in

West Germany. The Frankfurt Temple was announced earlier and finished later.[36]

The Freiberg Temple cannot, however, explain Mormon hierarchy's decision to suppress Tom Rogers' *Huebener* play in 1976. For the Salt Lake City leadership, the opportunity to build a temple in East Germany was a surprise. The issue surfaced two years after the play at BYU, in 1978, because of a suggestion by the GDR government. It took four years to complete the negotiations, longer than subsequently required to build the temple.

Tobler and Keele suffered no recrimination for publishing the Helmuth Hübener story without the permission of the LDS hierarchy in 1980. The university president who imposed the ban had taken a new job, reviewing judicial appeals in Salt Lake City. But four years later, in 1984, when a Salt Lake City attorney wished to have the *Huebener* play performed by his theater group, he found that playwright Thomas Rogers was still bound by the original proscription. Undaunted, David Anderson wrote his own script. "Huebener Against the Reich" debuted at Salt Lake City's Shire West Theater in February 1984 for a one-month engagement. Both of Salt Lake City's daily newspapers, the LDS-owned *Deseret News* and the family-owned *Tribune*, wrote articles in advance of the play.[37] However, only the *Tribune* reviewed Anderson's play.[38] When an official of the theater troupe inquired as to why the church-owned newspaper declined to review the play, he was told it was not an inadvertent omission. Instead, an "editorial decision" had been made.[39]

BYU's refusal to authorize release of the original script and the failure of the church-owned daily newspaper to review the play attracted the attention of an Associated Press writer based in Salt Lake City. Reporter David White began making inquiries, one of which led him to Thomas S. Monson, who was responsible for shutting down Rogers' BYU play and inspiring Oaks to place a "hold" on Hübener-related scholarship. Obviously irritated by what he considered to be the reporter's impertinent questioning, Monson snapped, "Who knows what was right or wrong then? I don't know what we accomplish by dredging these things up and trying to sort them out."[40] White's article—and Monson's quotation—appeared in newspapers worldwide, including the *New York Times* and the *Los Angeles Times*.[41]

Buttressed by the controversy over Mormon censorship of the previous version, Anderson's play received critical acclaim. Reviews written by wire service reporters appeared in major American daily newspapers. One ran in the *Times of London*.[42] Although the playwright was a BYU graduate, a veteran of the university's theater program, and presumably a faithful Mormon, he was under no obligation to adhere to the LDS Church's mandate to dim the light of Hübener's historical memory. While glorifying Hübener's bravery, his script nevertheless adhered to the pattern of protecting the pro-Nazi branch president. Arthur Zander, under the pseudonym of Ernst Schmal, played a minor part in Anderson's fictional account. He appeared in only one significant scene, in which a character representing Heinrich Worbs returned, delusional, from a concentration camp and interrupted a meeting. Instead, the role of the congregation's "super Nazi" fell to Zander's real-life first counselor, Franz Jacobi. Likewise, the playwright protected Jacobi by assigning his character a pseudonym. In one scene that does not correspond to the historical record, but which does conform to Mormon mythology in Germany during the Nazi period, the first counselor tries to convince Hübener that Adolf Hitler has read the Book of Mormon and is a righteous person.[43]

It is doubtful that Anderson, the playwright, knew Zander's name and the circumstances of his immigration to the United States. That information remained secure until one of Helmuth Hübener's co-conspirators, Karl-Heinz Schnibbe, decided to publish his own account. With the assistance of Tobler and Keele, Schnibbe produced a tightly written, 126-page narrative in 1984. *The Price* described Schnibbe's role in assisting Helmuth Hübener, his interrogation by the Gestapo, trial and imprisonment, subsequent wartime military service, and years as a prisoner of war in the Soviet Union.[44] Although the book broke little new ground, the publishers still sought a degree of Mormon Church approval.

Alan Keele recounted an incident that happened toward the end of the publication cycle. "Bookcraft [the publisher] was careful to test the opinions of the Church leaders. I learned that by accident when I was reading the proofs in a conference room all by myself. When I finished I noticed another folder on the otherwise empty tabletop and assumed it was more proofs. Opening it I found that [the publisher] had left his personal folder there, presumably by mistake. The first note in it which

I couldn't help seeing was a note to the effect that Bookcraft had been assured by their contact among the Twelve that there were no more objections to the publication of the book."[45]

By this point, the mid-1980s, the LDS Church probably realized that it could not stop enterprising members, including Hübener's fellow heroes, from telling the story. The Associated Press article that quoted Monson in an unfavorable light, and which revealed the extent of the church's censorship attempts, embarrassed the Mormon leadership. Tobler and Keele, confident that the church hierarchy's concerns had eased, assisted Schnibbe with writing his story. However, the publisher consulted the Mormon leadership because it knew that one word of public admonishment from a church leader in an article or General Conference speech would adversely affect sales of the book.

That kind of caution proved providential several years later, when the LDS hierarchy put the Sunstone Symposium in its crosshairs. For years, the Sunstone Foundation had hosted an annual interdisciplinary conference for Mormon academics and intellectuals. The Mormon leadership found some of the papers presented to be offensive. In 1989, Dallin Oaks, the BYU president who forbade the continued presentation of *Huebener* and curtailed Tobler and Keele's research, wrote an article in the LDS monthly magazine that cautioned Mormons against listening to "alternate voices" of opinion.[46] By this time, Oaks had left the Utah Supreme Court and had been called to fill a vacancy on the Quorum of the Twelve. Less than two years later, the Twelve released a "Statement on Symposia," which in conjunction with Oaks's admonition had a chilling effect on Sunstone.[47] Neither statement mentioned the organization, but attendance by spectators and participation by "faithful scholars," that is, BYU faculty members, dropped precipitously.[48] If the Mormon Church could not control the actions of those who wrote and performed, it still profoundly influenced those who attended or purchased books. With regard to Helmuth Hübener, it had been *Sunstone* magazine that broke Oaks's proscription in 1980.

It became even more difficult for the Mormon Church to dim the light of commemoration in 1985, when the Federal Republic of Germany honored Karl-Heinz Schnibbe and Rudi Wobbe at the dedication of the Helmuth Hübener Haus in Hamburg. Schnibbe and Wobbe returned to the basement of the old city hall, where the Gestapo had interrogated and tortured them, along with Helmuth. This time, pictures and other memorabilia honoring the small resistance group adorned the walls of the "hall of mirrors," where prisoners had once stood awaiting their appointment to be interrogated under torture. They also visited the prisons where they had been confined. On a very special Sunday morning, Wobbe gave the Sunday school and priesthood lessons at a Mormon congregation in Hamburg, the one that served a neighborhood where he had lived and spread Helmuth's anti-Nazi tracts. His lesson concerned the Twelfth Article of Faith. Wobbe explained it a bit differently, citing the Mormon Doctrine and Covenants, Section 134, verses two and five: "We believe that no government can exist in peace, except such laws are framed and held inviolate as will secure to each individual the free will and exercise of conscience. . . . We believe that all men are bound to sustain and uphold the respective governments in which they reside . . . however, holding sacred the freedom of conscience."[49]

A series of events in late 1988 and 1989 profoundly affected the commemoration of Helmuth Hübener's heroism. In October 1988, meetings between Thomas S. Monson, then the Second Counselor in the First Presidency, and German Democratic Republic State Council Chairman Erich Honecker, sealed an accord that had been negotiated during the previous months. They agreed on a reciprocal exchange of Mormon missionaries. Young Mormon elders from the West would be allowed to proselytize in East Germany. Young citizens of the GDR would be allowed to serve Mormon missions in the "free world." The official LDS Church monthly magazine, the *Ensign*, featured a two-page article and a large photo of Monson and Honecker shaking hands.[50] Although the two Germanys reunited before this reciprocal exchange of missionaries could be fully implemented, the agreement was a remarkable treaty between a western church and a Communist Bloc country.

Arthur Zander died on June 2, 1989, in a Salt Lake City hospital. In his last years, according to Rudi Wobbe, he maintained his intractability, refusing to admit any degree of culpability and "even tell[ing] his children lies about the past." Wobbe continued: "I don't want to judge him too harshly, as he probably repented in the meantime but he doesn't want to admit it. If he were a big enough man he would say, 'I made a mistake; I sure picked the wrong way to go, and I'm sorry about it,' and that would be the end of it. But no, the stubbornness!"[51]

A Premature Curtain Call

On November 10, 1989, the Berlin Wall fell, leading to the full political unification of Germany. By 1991, the Soviet Union had ceased to exist. With Arthur Zander dead and many of the Wasatch Front's old Nazis dying or losing their influence because of declining health, every justification the Mormon Church leadership had for dimming Hübener's historical memory had disappeared. The Mormons would soon open missions behind the former Iron Curtain. Military dictators had given way to constitutional governments in Argentina and Chile. The world was a quieter place, and LDS leaders could no longer fear that idealistic young Mormon youth would rebel, using Hübener as an inspiration.

For those who would commemorate Helmuth in this more tranquil atmosphere, however, old habits die hard. When a Mormon author, Neal Chandler, wrote a third commemorative play, published in *Sunstone Magazine* in December 1990, the protagonist, Karl Immer, appeared as a conflation of Arthur Zander and the district president, Otto Berndt. Immer, like Berndt, was not a Nazi Party member but had suffered Gestapo interrogation. In *Appeal to a Lower Court*, Immer was an aged man in the 1980s who convened a "church court" to consider his guilt for excommunicating Helmuth Hübener—whom the actors refer to by a pseudonym. As the court examines its evidence, it witnesses several flashbacks to the early 1940s, including one scene in which the branch president's wife urges him to excommunicate Hübener for the safety of their family. His colleagues in the branch's governing council urge Helmuth's excommunication for the good of the congregation. The play ends before the mythical 1980s court reaches a verdict on the branch president's guilt, but there is no doubt that he will be acquitted.[52]

Forty-eight years after the real Arthur Zander excommunicated Helmuth Hübener, and fourteen years after Thomas Rogers' first play, playwright Chandler was still presenting Zander in a sympathetic light. There was no need to protect a man who had died the year before. No evidence indicates that the LDS Church directly influenced Chandler, an independent author and playwright. Instead, his sympathy for Zander seemed to stem from an established precedent. Mormon authors are often reluctant to criticize the actions of someone who has served as an ecclesiastical leader in their church, no matter how he did his job. In the performance of their duties, those leaders supposedly receive divine guidance. Criticizing their actions is tantamount to criticizing God.

In 1992, the LDS Church made its amends to playwright Thomas Rogers for holding his tongue and not criticizing its censorship sixteen years earlier. BYU staged *Huebener*—not in the small, bandbox Margetts Arena but instead in the larger Pardoe Theater, the main performing arts arena on campus. Rogers celebrated the rehabilitation of his script by appearing on stage in the role of Helmuth Hübener's grandfather. The characters retained the same stage names they had used in 1976, including pseudonyms for the two Nazis, Arthur Zander and Franz Jacobi. The *Salt Lake Tribune* headlined its review, "BYU's *Huebener* Plays It Safe with Tough Play," reflecting the reviewer's skepticism. Said Nancy Melich, "Director [Ivan] Crosland has taken a safe, and not always interesting, approach in making sure that the LDS branch president, Zoellner, is presented sympathetically."[53] By 1992, the truth about Hübener's relationship with his branch president was known in the Mormon Culture Region, provoking criticism from those who saw a continued soft peddling of Zander's role.

Rudi Wobbe, who died in 1992, never lived to see the publication of his book, *Before the Blood Tribunal*. Death spared him from learning that his faith-promoting Mormon publisher, Covenant Communications, was still engaging in the shenanigans of memory. According to the *Salt Lake Tribune*'s reviewer, Paul Swenson: "Wobbe, who died of cancer a week after signing the contract for his book, might turn over in his grave if he knew that mention of [Hübener's] excommunication has disappeared from the manuscript. Co-author Jerry Borrowman (who said he learned of the omission from this reviewer) explained it was inadvertently dropped during editing."[54]

Ten years after the publication of *Before the Blood Tribunal*, Borrowman and Covenant Communications released a second edition of the same text, renamed *Three Against Hitler*. It was a verbatim reprint.[55] The first omission may have been an inadvertent editing mistake; the second proved that it was not. By 1992, both Arthur Zander and his wife Charlotte were dead. There was nothing to protect except the pride of the Mormon Church, which was not well served by Covenant Communications' refusal to acknowledge that Arthur Zander had excommunicated Helmuth Hübener.

In 1995 the University of Illinois Press published a scholarly monograph on Helmuth Hübener. *When Truth Was Treason* appeared two decades after BYU censored its researchers and playwrights. By this time, Keele had broken his research partnership with Tobler and recruited another BYU historian, Blair Holmes, as his coauthor.[56] Their book told the story from the viewpoint of Karl-Heinz Schnibbe, with whom Keele and Tobler had collaborated in producing a shorter, popular book, *The Price*, eleven years earlier. *When Truth Was Treason* contained a trove of primary documents mined from the Hamburg municipal and Gestapo archives. It also enlightened the reader with extensive footnotes that expounded on the narrative.

In 2002, two BYU graduates, Rick McFarland and Matt Whitaker, combined to produce an eighty minute documentary, *Truth & Conviction*, which told the story of Helmuth Hübener. Alan Keele, Douglas Tobler, and several other BYU faculty members narrated, but the strength of the video was the appearance of Nobel Prize winning author Günter Grass, who used Hübener's imagery in several of his literary and dramatic works. The original Hübener researcher, Ulrich Sander, appeared on screen to explain how he uncovered the story and wrote newspaper articles that attracted Grass's attention. Karl-Heinz Schnibbe, in his seventies, also narrated. The producers filmed part of the documentary on location in Hamburg. They recorded video images of Helmuth's old office at the Bieber-Haus, where his shop steward called the Gestapo, and the old city hall where the conspirators underwent interrogation and torture. They skillfully recreated images of Hübener's pamphlets, and included an original Rola radio receiver and Remington typewriter like the one the young Mormon used to create his seditious pamphlets. The producers did not hide Zander's Nazi Party affinity and some of his more egregious acts, such as compelling members to listen to Hitler's speeches. They did advance the theory that Zander excommunicated Hübener to protect the rest of the congregation from Gestapo reprisal. The producers left one character out of the script. Gerhard Düwer, a non-Mormon conspirator, apparently had no useful role in this faith-promoting production.

Because Covenant Communications, a publisher on Mormon subjects, would distribute the documentary, the producers took precautions to assure that powerful LDS interests were not offended, and that the product would sell to faithful buyers who would not want their church to be criticized. They invited Arthur Zander's children to view the documentary before they released it. One final visitor put the Mormon hierarchy's stamp of approval on the work. The producers invited Boyd K. Packer, acting president of the Quorum of the Twelve, to screen the video. Packer sanctioned the documentary and suggested its title, which the producers were happy to accept.[57]

Hübener commemoration took an unfortunate downturn in 2003, when Richard Lloyd Dewey wrote *Hübener vs. Hitler*, a book that targeted faithful Mormon audiences. He wrote an inspiring narrative that never challenged the judgment of LDS church leaders, but also did not let small factual inaccuracies interfere with the plot. Its first edition contained so many mistakes that Dewey hired *When Truth Was Treason* coauthor Blair Holmes to proofread a second edition in 2004, which has presumably sold well in the Mormon Culture Region.

Hübener vs. Hitler, published in Provo, Utah, by a previously unknown enterprise called the Academic Research Foundation, mimicked a scholarly monograph.[58] Its dust jacket billed it as "Volume 1 in the Faith in Conflict Series." There have been no subsequent volumes. Its endnote section could have been several pages shorter if the author had been familiar with shortened, subsequent citation notation. Dewey was careful not to besmirch the character of Hübener's Nazi branch president or any other Mormon who held Party membership. It dealt with Hübener's excommunication as an unfortunate necessity that was reversed after the war. It described Arthur Zander's American life as "active in the Church, having raised a family also active, even stalwart, in the faith."[59]

The entry of a profit-focused ersatz historian into the effort to commemorate Helmuth Hübener could have been expected as the Mormon Church permitted its faithful members to brighten the young hero's historical memory. Unfortunately, as Dewey attempted to make money from Helmuth's sacrifice, another regrettable aspect of the American market economy surfaced. The entrepreneur began to buy out the competition. Midway through the first decade of the twenty-first century, Dewey purchased the rights to the only scholarly monograph on Hübener, *When Truth Was Treason*, from the University of Illinois Press. Then he bought all unsold copies of Holmes and Keele's work.[60] When one performs an on-line query for that book, search engines now reveal the book's publishers as both the University of Illinois Press and the scholarly sounding Academic Research Foundation. This paradoxical development occurred in the same university town, Provo, Utah, where Mormon leaders once banned their scholars from publishing research on Helmuth Hübener.

Since the LDS Church no longer considered the Hübener story to be *verboten*, it was not surprising that faithful storytellers would attempt to profit from it. Michael O. Tunnell, in *Brothers in Valor*, filled that requirement with a fast-moving children's narrative in 2001. Latter-day Saint readers did not need to read the author's biographical sketch, which revealed that he lived in Orem, Utah, and was the father of four and grandfather of six, in order to suspect that he shared their faith. He also demonstrated fluency in Mormon parlance, including the details of LDS church youth organizations. Like his co-religionists, however, he struggled to find an acceptable accommodation between respect for church leaders and Arthur Zander's overt Nazism. Tunnell told his young readers about Zander's deplorable treatment of Emma Hasse, whom the branch president threatened with a concentration camp sentence for taking an air-dropped enemy propaganda leaflet to church. But in his relationship with Hübener, Zander came across as a kind, fatherly figure, who gently admonishes Helmuth and his friends: "'You're good boys,' he said, looking straight at Helmuth. 'Listen to me. Read *German* books. Listen to *German* music. Play *German* games.' 'But our church is American,' Helmuth said. 'It's God's church, not America's,'[Zander replied.] 'Our church leaders want us to be good citizens wherever we live. That means doing what our *Führer* asks, and he's asked us to be German through and through.'"[61]

Perhaps in consideration of LDS parents who would read from the storybook at bedtime, the author did not mention Zander's excommunication of Hübener in the narrative. Instead, Tunnell reserved those details for the afterword, where he was careful to state that church leaders revoked Zander's action after the war.

At the turn of the twenty-first century, Hübener's story began to attract the attention of secular children's authors. Hübener appeared as one of seventeen young subjects in Robin K. Berson's *Young Heroes of World History*, published in 1999, which equated Helmuth's courage with that of Chai Ling, a young woman who led the Tiananmen Square revolt in China.[62] One non-Mormon children's author also wrote a Hübener book, and in doing so she pushed the young man's religious beliefs into the background. When Susan Campbell Bartoletti published *The Boy*

Who Dared in 2008, she told his story through flashbacks while Helmuth awaited the executioner in Plötzensee Prison.[63] Using a fiction writer's license, she placed a younger Helmuth at the scene of historical events that led to the rise of Hitler, such as street riots between Nazis and communists. She also concentrated on the young man's relationship with his mother. Given the way that religious interests have manipulated the focus of Helmuth's commemorative light in the past, the novelist's secular approach was refreshing. Expectedly, one leery reviewer noted that, "The character is Mormon. But LDS parents may find the book not faith promoting."[64]

Hübener in the Context of Other Resisters

Overt resistance to the regime of Adolf Hitler was a rare occurrence in Nazi Germany. The risks were too great and the price when caught was too high. In his search for valor among his countrymen, historian Detlev Peukert broadened the definition of a resister to include "nonconformist everyday behavior," such as listening to foreign broadcasts or telling anti-Hitler jokes in trusted circles of friends. Withdrawal of enthusiasm in the workplace or voluntary changing of jobs also played a role in the limited range of protest available to the ordinary citizen of Nazi Germany.[65] Likewise, for young people, the most popular paths of resistance took them away from direct confrontation with the Nazis. Refusing to join the Hitler Youth or not participating devotedly probably constituted the most widespread avenue of protest. Others pursued escapist activities such as the Edelweiss Pirate patrols that hiked in the countryside in the spirit of the turn-of-the-century *Wandervogel* movement. Occasionally, the Edelweiss Pirates would confront and fight with a Hitler Youth group when they crossed paths in the wilderness, but this was an uncommon occurrence. Nonconformist young people, especially upper-middle-class city residents, also gathered in the "swing movement," which held covert dances and other social gatherings to the accompaniment of American and English music.[66]

For young people like Helmuth Hübener, constrained by both Nazi state and Mormon religious regimes, the closest parallel can be found in Munich's White Rose group. A group of University of Munich students, some of whom were devoutly religious, formed to encourage resistance to Adolf Hitler. They engaged in graffiti campaigns and distributed leaflets. Although siblings Hans and Sophie Scholl produced only six leaflets, in comparison with Hübener's twenty-nine, their printed publications received wider distribution. They mailed them to bartenders and university lecturers. One tract fell into the possession of the Allies, who later dropped millions of copies from aircraft over German cities. When caught, six members of the group, including the Scholl siblings, appeared before the same red-robed jurists of the People's Court in Berlin. Five were guillotined, some within hours of their sentencing. Like Hübener, Sophie Scholl argued defiantly with the judges at her trial.[67]

In comparison to the White Rose group and the July 20, 1944, plot to assassinate Hitler by Claus von Stauffenberg and his associates, Helmuth Hübener's heroism is relatively unknown. Most of this can be attributed to deliberate attempts by individual Mormons and the LDS ecclesiastical leadership to control the focus and intensity of Helmuth's commemorative light. Jakob Schmidt, the building custodian who reported Sophie Scholl to the Gestapo, did not enjoy the protective constituency that shielded Arthur Zander and his fellow émigré Nazis in Utah. Nor were the co-religionists of any other resister group attempting to conduct private diplomacy with a communist state several decades after their defiant bravery.

After the fall of European communism and the passing of many German-American Mormon immigrants, the LDS Church lost its reason to suppress Hübener's memory. But faithful Mormon authors may still consider Arthur Zander and Mormon accommodation of the Nazis to be a sensitive issue. Criticizing church leaders is still considered verboten in the Mormon Culture Region, even those who wore a swastika lapel pin. Like the producers of the documentary and the publishers of the popular biographies, they take comfort in seeking a church official's blessing of their work. That was still happening at the dawn of the twenty-first century, even though the LDS leadership had removed its hand from Helmuth Hübener's commemorative dimmer switch.

The solution may lie in entrusting Hübener's story to non-Mormon authors. As Helmuth's memory becomes secularized, perhaps his heroism can be untangled from the web of religious restrictions that has hindered his recognition during the decades since his martyrdom on Plötzensee Prison's guillotine. Then, Helmuth Hübener, Karl-Heinz Schnibbe, Rudi Wobbe, and even Max Reschke may be free to shine as memory beacons though the murky muck of Mormon accommodation with one of world history's most repulsive regimes.

Conclusion
To Save the Church?

In October 1969, a group of American Latter-day Saint military personnel stationed in Germany convened in Berchtesgaden, a picturesque resort town in the Bavarian Alps that had once been the vacation home of Adolf Hitler. In that Cold War era, the United States military granted time off from work so that troops stationed abroad could attend annual religious retreats staged by the chaplain corps. Prominent denominational leaders were customarily invited. When Mormon servicemen met that year at the General Walker Hotel, an armed forces recreation center in the postwar epoch, they may have been unaware that the chosen venue had its own nefarious past. Formerly *Der Platterhof*, the opulently decorated resort known for its majestic Alpine views had been a favorite meeting place for the governing elites of Hitler's SS and the *Wehrmacht*.

Attendees that day in 1969 came to hear an address by Hugh B. Brown, who for nine years had held the second-ranking position in the Mormon hierarchy, an office known as the First Counselor in the First Presidency. It was not Brown's speech that turned out to be the most impressive. Instead, the recently installed president of the Central German Mission in Dusseldorf, a forty-five-year-old native German who had immigrated to the United States seventeen years before, delivered the most memorable remarks. Speaking in English, Walter H. Kindt began: "As a member of the *Wehrmacht*, I once proudly served my *Führer*. Now, as a member of the church, I proudly serve another *Führer*." According to one army enlisted man in attendance, "There were audible gasps from this audience of American servicemen and their wives." A few Mormons rendered the customary "amen" after Kindt's brief remarks, but others, presumably shocked or offended, said nothing."[1]

Kindt's indelicate introduction may have been nothing more than ill-advised flippancy, or it could have represented an unsuccessful attempt at humor uttered by a recently installed Mormon leader unaccustomed to public speaking in a language that was not his native tongue. Alternatively, it could have constituted another stubborn defense of the Twelfth Article of Faith. To this day, many surviving German Mormons who immigrated to the American Zion after the war steadfastly cling to that justification for their church's accommodating strategy in dealing with the National Socialist government. Likewise, those survivors and many of their apologetic successors stop short of Rudi Wobbe's deeper examination of the Twelfth Article, one he preached from a Mormon pulpit upon his late-life return to the site of the Helmuth Hübener group's heroism in Hamburg. In his 1985 sermon, Wobbe stressed that the Doctrine and Covenants, a book of Mormon scripture, counsels that support of civil government must be tempered by the dictates of conscience.[2]

Kindt, whose words shocked his fellow Mormons in Berchtesgaden, has more recently been depicted in a more delicate way. He appears in the year 2008 work of authors Robert C. Freeman and Jon R. Felt as a seventeen-year-old German soldier struggling to avoid hostilities during the last weeks of the war. That account tells the story of his miraculous, three-hundred-mile hike from his last battlefield at the end of the war to his home in Hamburg. During the trek, he eluded Allied troops who would have captured him, and German soldiers who would have implored him to continue fighting.[3] However humble his circumstances as a young *Wehrmacht* soldier, the middle-aged man who spoke in Berchtesgaden in the midst of the Cold War that day seemed to embrace his role as one of Hitler's stripling warriors.

Kindt is one of many Mormons cast in a new combat role: the battle of memory. In the mid-1970s, when the Helmuth Hübener controversy arose at BYU, competing faithful hands reached for the rheostat of memorialization. Scholars and a playwright wished to ratchet up Helmuth's commemorative light, while German émigrés and church officials wanted to dim the illumination of the lad's memory beacon. The reverberations of that incident have continued to the present date. Faith-promoting publishers have taken a cautious approach toward revealing Hübener's excommunication, to the point that one publishing house omitted its mention entirely in consecutive editions of a Hübener tribute released ten years apart. Another author of faith-promoting works bought the rights to an existing scholarly monograph about Helmuth, presumably to redirect readers toward his own lesser-quality but safer account. When the documentary producers made the extraordinary effort to film on location in Hübener's native Hamburg, they incorporated non-Mormon luminaries such as German novelist Günter Grass and original researcher Ulrich Sander. They nevertheless took pains to prescreen the video for the children of Arthur Zander, who was Hübener's Mormon congregational leader, and for Boyd K. Packer, the senior member of the Quorum of the Twelve Apostles and next in the line of succession as prophet, seer, and revelator.

In the second decade of the twenty-first century, Mormon history in Nazi Germany remains sensitive. While no longer a third-rail issue, discussions are still charged with high-voltage issues that can provoke defensive responses. Believing Mormon authors struggle with how their accounts of Hübener's heroism would reflect on the church. Some remain reluctant to criticize the actions of a priesthood holder like Zander, whose excommunication of the story's protagonist seems not to have been required by the Gestapo. Such sensitivity extends to rank-and-file church members.

At the annual Mormon History Association conference in the summer of 2000 in Aalborg, Denmark, the author of this study presented his preliminary research. The Hübener story appeared unfamiliar to at least half of those who attended a packed conference session. Other historical characters had only recently surfaced, such as the Mormon storm trooper, a "wild" concentration camp commandant, who tortured and murdered Hitler's political opponents. The audience, predominantly LDS by religious affiliation, responded with prideful interest to the story of Hübener's resistance to the Nazis, but with grimaces of discomfort to the details of Erich Krause's torture and murder of prisoners at Berlin's Pape Street prison. At the end of the session, and in informal discussions during the ensuing days of the conference, a consensus seemed to emerge among the attendees: It was unfortunate that Mormons had to collaborate to a measured extent with the Nazis, but such actions were probably necessary "to save the church."

That presumption invites an approach that professional historians tend to eschew: the employment of counterfactual reasoning. If the Mormons had been less accommodating of the Nazis, would the membership have been persecuted and the organization endangered? No one knows for sure, but the available evidence seems to argue against the notion that a lesser degree of accommodation with Hitler's government would have hurt the church. Comparable sized American "new religions" that avoided ingratiating themselves with the Nazis survived the war. They maintain a viable German presence today.

Seventh-day Adventists enjoyed the largest membership among small American sects in in 1933, having thirty thousand adherents among a German population of sixty-five million.[4] Adventists saluted the swastika, served in the German military, and were allowed to continue worshiping, but affiliated soldiers and civil servants lost their Saturday Sabbath exemption from duty. Adventists had fewer influential friends abroad, and they did not pursue an aggressive policy to court favor with the government or party. Although the Nazis temporarily suspended individual congregations' right to worship collectively, all of those revocations were temporary. In 2011, SDA statistics reported a small but viable church in Germany, numbering 35,292 members among a German population of eighty-one million. Several thousand more members live in German-speaking Austria and Switzerland.

Christian Scientists, by contrast, claimed a relatively small number of members in Germany, reported to be only four thousand in 1925.[5] Unlike the Seventh-day Adventists, Christian Scientists were banned from congregational worship in Nazi Germany. They were not resisters, but instead became disfavored because of their American leadership's affiliation with Freemasonry, and conflict with the Nazi doctors' union over their doctrinal refusal to seek medical care. However, individual members who otherwise obeyed the law did not suffer persecution. Christian Science, reported to be a domination that is presently in numerical decline worldwide, still maintains twelve church congregations in eleven German cities.[6]

Surprisingly, the denomination that resisted and consequently suffered intense persecution, the Jehovah's Witnesses, enjoys a substantial membership presence in Germany today. Having lost as many as one-quarter of the sect's twenty thousand German members to death

Conclusion

by execution or concentration camp cruelty, the Witness membership rolls have now rebounded. Jehovah's Witnesses claimed 165,837 German members in 2009.[7] By comparison, the LDS Church, which had no more than fourteen thousand members in Nazi Germany, has 38,739 enrolled members in Germany in 2013.[8] Jehovah's Witnesses, who rebelled against Nazi authority, presently have four times as many German members as do the Mormons—who pursued a different path.

In the decades that follow, Latter-day Saints may eventually conclude that their church was on the wrong side of history in Nazi Germany. Overt efforts to exploit commonalities between Mormonism and Nazism were not needed in order to endure life under the Third Reich. There was no need to ramp up the pace of genealogical research, allow missionaries to train German Olympians, dispatch a mission president's wife to ride with Adolf Hitler and his Nazi women's leader, or employ a bombastic mission president to seek an alliance with the Nazi propaganda ministry. Without these excesses, the Mormons would have probably survived unscathed during the peacetime National Socialist years, 1933–39, as did Catholic and Protestant Germans. When the war came and the American missionaries left, the result would have been the same. German Mormons would have suffered no more or no less than their fellow citizens as a catastrophic consequence of National Socialism.

Instead, the path the Mormons chose left a trail of both paper and memory. Pictures of Hitler-saluting basketball players, a Prophet of God seated before a large swastika, and articles that boast about how Hitler has adopted the practice of Mormon fast Sunday—all of which appeared in the religion section of a church-owned newspaper—will never vanish from the archives and will continue to surface periodically. The consequences of pandering obedience to a godless, tyrannical state have also left a mark on the Mormon psyche that is hard to erase. Helmuth Hübener rebelled as much against the brown and black shirts in his own Hamburg congregation as he did against what Hitler was doing in the Germany outside the walls of his branch's meetinghouse.

Without a dredged-up doctrine that mandated rendering obedience to civil authority, which the Mormons ignored earlier in their German experience, there may have been no need to appoint Arthur Zander to become St. Georg branch president or Alfred C. Rees to become the Berlin mission president. A less enthusiastic advocate of Nazism may have diffused Hübener's rebellion and saved the lad's life. Philemon Kelly's patient approach to solving problems with the government at the lowest possible level would have averted the specter of a pro-Mormon article in the *Völkischer Beobachter*, spiritual radio broadcasts *from* Berlin *to* Utah, and a mission president who said "Heil Hitler" and attended a Nuremberg Nazi Party rally.

In modern times, Helmuth Hübener has become a distraction. His uncharacteristic Mormon resistance to the Nazis acts as a tactical smoke screen that hides the reality of Mormon accommodation in the Third Reich and the collective guilt felt by the postwar German-American LDS community. More than likely, without the enduring defensiveness that German Mormon émigrés felt because of their adherence to the Twelfth Article of Faith, Walter Kindt may have never introduced himself as one who proudly followed the guidance of two *Führers*. Likewise, books and articles that memorialize the struggles of ordinary German soldiers and civilians during the Second World War could be judged on their own merits, rather than prompting suspicion that they serve to divert attention from the less admirable aspects of Mormon history during the Third Reich.

Mormon history in Nazi Germany occurred almost seven decades ago, but battle over how to interpret the memory of those events—or even what to remember and what to forget—continues to this day. It promises to percolate at a low boil, punctuated by occasional eruptions, until the faithful understand the perils involved with conflating God and government. That is a hazard that extends beyond the scope of this narrow historical subject.

Abbreviations

AAU	Amateur Athletic Union
AOC	American Olympic Committee
BBC	British Broadcasting Corporation
BDM	*Bund Deutscher Mädel*
BSA	Boy Scouts of America
BYU	Brigham Young University
BYU Archives	L. Tom Perry Special Collections, Harold B. Lee Library, Brigham Young University, Provo, Utah
Clarkana Papers	Clarkana Papers of Joshua Reuben Clark, Jr., L. Tom Perry Special Collections, Harold B. Lee Library, Brigham Young University, Provo, Utah
Dialogue Journal	*Dialogue: A Journal of Mormon Thought*
FRG	Federal Republic of Germany
GDR	German Democratic Republic
Gestapo	*Geheime Staatspolizei*
HJ	*Hitlerjugend* (Hitler Youth)
IOC	International Olympic Committee
JMH	Journal of Mormon History
KJV	King James Version of the Bible
KPD	German Communist Party
LDS Archives	Archives, Historical Department, The Church of Jesus Christ of Latter-day Saints, Salt Lake City, Utah
LDS Church	The Church of Jesus Christ of Latter-day Saints

Abbreviations

Marriott Archives	Marriott Library Special Collections, University of Utah, Salt Lake City, Utah
MIA	Mutual Improvement Association
NSDAP	National Socialist German Workers Party
NS-*Frauenschaft*	*Nationalsozialistische Frauenschaft* (National Socialist Women's League)
NSV	*Nationalsozialistische Volkswohlfahrt*
PEF	Perpetual Emigration Fund
RLDS	Reorganized Church of Jesus Christ of Latter Day Saints
SA	*Sturmabteilung* (Storm Attachment; "Brownshirts")
S-A MH	Swiss-Austrian Mission Manuscript Histories
SD	*Sicherheitsdienst* (Security Service)
SPD	German Social Democratic Party
SS	*Schutzstaffel*
USOC	United States Olympic Committee
YMMIA	Young Men's Mutual Improvement Association
YWMIA	Young Women's Mutual Improvement Association

Notes

Introduction

1. On November 9, 1938, bands of Nazi thugs set synagogues in Germany and Austria ablaze, destroyed Jewish-owned businesses, and killed at least one hundred Jews and interned thousands of others. Ostensibly motivated spontaneously by the assassination of a German diplomat in Paris by a Jewish youth, the pogrom had actually been planned well in advance by SD chief Reinhard Heydrich, approved by Adolf Hitler, and triggered by Nazi propagandist Joseph Goebbels. Recent scholarship on the origins of *Kristallnacht* includes the release in 1992 of a previously missing section of Goebbels's diary. See Friedländer, *Nazi Germany and the Jews*, 267–80.

2. In this study, the word "Mormon" refers to the Utah-based Church of Jesus Christ of Latter-day Saints, the denomination founded by Joseph Smith, Jr., in western New York in 1830. Except for one brief mention, this study does not examine the Missouri-based Reorganized Church of Jesus Christ of Latter Day Saints, now named the Community of Christ, nor does it discuss various breakaway sects that consider the Book of Mormon to be scripture. The Salt Lake City Mormons numbered approximately fourteen thousand in Germany and more than six hundred thousand worldwide in 1940. Other Mormon sects were much smaller in number.

3. A branch president presides as lay leader of a small Mormon congregation of insufficient numerical strength, or which is not part of the standard ecclesiastical structure, to allow its designation as a ward (parish). Branches in Nazi Germany fell under jurisdiction of a district, whose president, either a German member or American missionary, reported to an American mission president. In areas where church members enjoy significant numerical strength, bishops who govern wards (congregations) report to a stake (diocesan) president.

4. Dixon, "Mormons in the Third Reich," 75.

5. Petty interview, LDS Archives, 27.

6. The term "Mormon Culture Region" emanates from geographer Don Meinig, who in 1965 delimited the area affected by the settlement and subsequent expansive influence of Brigham Young's Mormon pioneers, who migrated to the Great Basin of the intermountain west in 1847. The Mormon Culture Region includes the entirety of Utah and parts of Idaho, Nevada, Arizona, New Mexico, Colorado, and Wyoming. See Meinig, "The Mormon Culture Region," 191–220.

7. King, *Nazi State and New Religions*, 71.
8. Smoot, "Ein Freund von Deutschland."
9. "Europe War Scares Discounted," 8 Sep. 1937.
10. Three authors, all citing official LDS Church membership statistics, have published different membership totals for the Mormon Church's German congregations at the outbreak of the Second World War. In 1970, Gilbert Scharffs listed 13,480 members in Germany in 1940. (See *Mormonism in Germany*, xiv, table 1.) Writing in *Dialogue Journal* in 1972, Joseph Dixon said: "By 1933 there were 14,305 Mormons in Germany, Austria, and Switzerland; by 1939 there were 15,677 in Germany alone." (See "Mormons in the Third Reich," 71.) In 2009, Roger P. Minert, using only the membership statistics of the East and West German missions, listed 13,402 members. (See *In Harm's Way*, 5.) Minert's totals do not include Mormons who lived in the German-speaking Sudetenland of Czechoslovakia, whose country had been absorbed into the Third Reich as the result of the Munich Agreement of September 1938 and Hitler's annexation of the rest of Czechoslovakia in March 1939.
11. Condie, "Let's Follow Dad," 32–37.
12. Scharffs, *Mormonism in Germany*, 116.
13. East German Mission Manuscript History, 21–24 Mar. 1946.
14. The same degree of uncertainty prevails when one assesses the number of casualties inflicted on the German populace. The official German military casualty reporting system broke down late in the war, and for many years historians accepted approximately 3.9 million battlefield deaths, although that excluded battles fought after January 1945. Research conducted at the end of the twentieth century by Rüdiger Overmans estimated that German military losses numbered as high as 5.3 million. See Overmans, *Deutsche militärische Verluste*, 151–204. Similar uncertainty exists regarding civilian casualties. The latest scholarship, conducted by Olaf Groehler, estimated 406,000 civilian casualties from aerial bombardment in Germany and Austria. See *Das Deutsche Reich und der Zweite Weltkrieg*, 9:460.
15. The term "memory beacon" emanates from the writing of military historian Douglas C. Peifer, who specializes in German history on both sides of the Iron Curtain after the Second World War. Unlike Pierra Nora's more commonly used *lieu de mémoire*, a memory beacon can be highlighted but later de-emphasized—or instead totally disregarded—as a society desires to modulate its historical memory. See Peifer, "Formation of Memory Beacons," 1015n10.

Chapter 1

1. Roberts, *A Comprehensive History*, 6:302–17.
2. Smith, *Teachings of the Prophet*, 349.
3. Ostling and Ostling, *Mormon America*, 11.
4. Roberts, *A Comprehensive History*, 6:316; Smith, *Teachings of the Prophet*, 364.
5. *Encyclopedia of Mormonism*, s.v. "Exaltation."
6. Alder, "German-Speaking Immigration to Utah," iii.
7. Holzapfel and Bohn, "Long-Awaited Visit," 5–20.
8. "Official Report of the First Germany, Austria, Holland, Italy, Switzerland, France, Belgium, and Spain Area General Conference," 111.

9. Van Orden, *Building Zion*, 16, 200–201.

10. Brodie, *No Man Knows My History*; Roberts, *Studies of the Book of Mormon*. Brodie argued in 1945, in the first edition of the book that resulted in her excommunication, that Joseph Smith used *View of the Hebrews* as a template for the Book of Mormon. Her view received additional credence with the publication in 1985, by University of Utah researcher Brigham Madsen, of Mormon General Authority B. H. Roberts' early 1920s investigative report that found eighteen distinct points of congruence between the Book of Mormon and *View of the Hebrews*. Roberts was no critic of Mormonism, but instead a staunch defender of his faith. The troubling nature of his findings led him to withhold his early-twentieth-century report from many peers in the Mormon hierarchy.

11. Bushman and Woodworth, *Joseph Smith*, 153.

12. "Church Statistics," Deseret News, *1999–2000 Church Almanac*, 550.

13. *Encyclopedia of Mormonism*, s.v. "Missions of the Twelve to the British Isles."

14. Allen and Leonard, *Story of the Latter-day Saints*, 281.

15. *Encyclopedia of Mormonism*, s.v. "Zion." Mormons refer to Zion as "a group of God's followers or a place where such a group lives." Throughout the nineteenth century, the "gathering to Zion" meant relocation of converts to live with the main body of followers, rather than the establishment of local congregations.

16. *Encyclopedia of Mormonism*, s.v. "Missions." Several of these missions lasted only as long as the terms of service of the establishing missionaries and subsequently closed when those missionaries went home. At the end of 1859, the LDS Church maintained nine permanent missions in the United States and abroad.

17. Scharffs, *Mormonism in Germany*, 1.

18. Ostling and Ostling, *Mormon America*, 92–93, 287.

19. German Mission Manuscript History, Aug. 1852.

20. Scharffs, who spent a career as an instructor and director in the LDS Church's religious education program for high school and college students, is the author of *Truth About the God Makers*, an apologetic rebuttal of evangelical Christian Ed Decker's sensational and factually inaccurate anti-Mormon book and film, *The God Makers*.

21. Scharffs, *Mormonism in Germany*, 2.

22. Allen, *Story of the Latter-day Saints*, 278.

23. Scharffs, *Mormonism in Germany*, 9–11.

24. Ibid., 14.

25. Ibid., 15, 23–24.

26. Anderson, "Mormons and Germany," 10–11.

27. Ibid.

28. Mitchelle, "Mormons in Wilhelmine Germany," 40.

29. Ibid., 104–106, 125.

30. Van Orden, *Building Zion*, 104–106.

31. Ibid., 24.

32. Scharffs, *Mormonism in Germany*, 37–39.

33. Van Orden, *Building Zion*, 104–105.

34. The German-speaking mission headquartered in Switzerland moved to Basel in the late 1870s, a city located on the Swiss side of the border juncture of France, Germany, and Switzerland. Geneva, a French-speaking city, fell under the administration of the Paris mission.

35. Alexander, *Mormonism in Transition*, 213–14.
36. Tobler, "Education, Moral Values," 52.
37. Van Wagoner and Walker, *A Book of Mormons*, 178.
38. Scharffs, *Mormonism in Germany*, 18–19.
39. Ibid., 27.
40. Van Orden, *Building Zion*, 37, 95. Church missionaries in France also published a short-lived French version, *Etoile du Deseret*, in 1851–52.
41. Scharffs, *Mormonism in Germany*, 26–27.
42. Van Wagoner and Walker, *A Book of Mormons*, 180–81.
43. Anderson, "Mormons and Germany," 9n10. Anderson, in his study of Mormons during the Weimar Period, searched extensively for a nineteenth century German statute that expressly outlawed polygamy. He found none. Said Anderson, "Apparently lawmakers saw little need for such laws since regulations regarding moral behavior could generally be cited against the practice."
44. Scharffs, *Mormonism in Germany*, 24–25.
45. Allen, *Story of the Latter-day Saints*, 445.
46. The law prescribed punishment for anyone convicted of polygamy, revoked incorporation of the LDS Church, and limited its real estate holdings to $50,000.
47. Allen and Leonard, *Story of the Latter-day Saints*, 313.
48. Scharffs, *Mormonism in Germany*, 23–24.
49. Ostling and Ostling, *Mormon America*, 70.
50. Scharffs, *Mormonism in Germany*, 24–25.
51. Allen and Leonard, *Story of the Latter-day Saints*, 396–406.
52. *Encyclopedia of Mormonism*, s.v. "Perpetual Emigrating Fund."
53. Scharffs, *Mormonism in Germany*, 37–39.
54. Mitchelle, "Mormons in Wilhelmine Germany," 129.
55. Ibid., 81.
56. Scharffs, *Mormonism in Germany*, 34–36.
57. Ibid., 30.
58. Ibid., 35.
59. Ibid., 41–43.
60. Ibid., 36.
61. Alder, "German-Speaking Immigration," iii.
62. John Taylor, the church president who succeeded Brigham Young and who fought to maintain polygamy as a sacred ordinance while in hiding from federal authorities, had died in 1887.
63. Van Wagoner, *Mormon Polygamy*, 139–43.
64. Alexander, *Mormonism in Transition*, 217.
65. Scharffs, *Mormonism in Germany*, 51, table 3.
66. Ibid., 49.
67. Mitchelle, "Mormons in Wilhelmine Germany," 112–13.
68. Alexander, *Mormonism in Transition*, 227–28.
69. Mitchelle, "Mormons in Wilhelmine Germany," 133.
70. Ibid., 120.
71. Ibid., 134.
72. Utah won statehood in 1896, six years after the LDS Church pledged to bless no more plural marriages, and only after the state's constitutional convention

adopted a plank that specifically barred subsequent polygamous unions. Utah is the only state in the union to outlaw polygamy by constitutional provision; others do so by statute. The Seventeenth Amendment to the United States Constitution, which mandated direct election of senators, did not become effective until 1911. Before then, state legislatures chose United States senators.

73. Quinn, "LDS Church Authority," 9–105.
74. Scharffs, *Mormonism in Germany*, 51.
75. Swiss and German Mission Manuscript History, 4 Apr 1910.
76. Ibid., 27 Aug. 1910.

Chapter 2

1. Rose Valentine Diary in Swiss and German Mission Manuscript History, 25–26 Jul. 1914.
2. Anderson, "Mormons and Germany," 40.
3. Ibid., 40n4.
4. Risenmay Diary, LDS Archives, 2 Aug. 1914.
5. Anderson, "Mormons and Germany," 42–43.
6. Ibid., 44–45.
7. Ibid., 44–45. An exception occurred near in the Prussian town of Tilsit, where the advancing Russian army captured an American missionary named Hunter and his Swiss companion. They remained prisoners for several weeks before being released.
8. *Der Stern*, 15 Oct. 1914.
9. Ibid., 25 Jun. 1915.
10. Swiss and German Mission Manuscript History, 2 Jan. 1916.
11. Ibid., 23 Apr. 1916.
12. Ibid., 31 Dec. 1915.
13. Anderson, "Brothers Across Enemy Lines," 127–28.
14. Ibid., 131.
15. Ibid.
16. *Conference Reports*, 8 Apr. 1917.
17. Swiss and German Mission Manuscript History, 1914–18.
18. Swiss and German Mission Manuscript History, 1 Dec. 1919.
19. Ibid.
20. Swiss and German Mission Manuscript History (year-end report), 1920.
21. Anderson, "Mormons and Germany," 51.
22. Ibid., 83. As Anderson speculates, the pronounced rise in the number of baptisms during the year 1920 may be attributable to Germans joining the church in order to receive relief supplies. The German LDS Church also experienced a similar spike in interest in the immediate post–World War II period, when it became obvious that civilians in the war-torn country were joining the church specifically to take advantage of the extensive relief provided to members. They became known as *Kartoffel Mormonen*.
23. Anderson, "Mormons and Germany," 90.
24. "Der Dank des Kaisers," 1 Feb. 1918.
25. Finck, "Feldpostbrief," 15 Sep. 1917.

26. Mormons are required to be certified as "full tithe payers" as a prerequisite for temple worship, but since there were no LDS temples in Europe until 1955, that restriction did not affect the German members during the First World War. Receipt of the sacrament (Eucharist) is only contingent on a member's faith and good conduct.

27. Hamburg Branch Manuscript History, 1914–18.

28. Heiss interview, LDS Archives, 17–18.

Chapter 3

1. Kolb, *Weimar Republic*, 4.
2. Mitchelle, "Mormons in Wilhelmine Germany," 147.
3. Anderson, "Mormons and Germany," 116.
4. Alexander, *Mormonism in Transition*, 216.
5. Ibid., 215–16.
6. Ibid., 215.
7. Swiss-German Mission Manuscript History, 23 Jan. 1927.
8. Budge, *My Story*, 37
9. German-Austrian Mission Manuscript History, 8 Oct 1930.
10. A relevant parallel occurred with the "Third Convention," a group of rebellious Mexican Mormons who broke from the LDS Church in the 1930s, demanding a mission president of "pure race and blood." The rebels reconciled with the Salt Lake City leadership in the 1940s. See Tullis and Hernandez, "Case of the Third Convention," 1987.
11. Budge, *My Story*, 30.
12. A "stake" is a basic ecclesiastical unit of the LDS Church, approximately equivalent to a Catholic diocese. The word's usage originates from a tent stake used to secure the foundation of the Old Testament Tabernacle. Stakes and their affiliated wards, the equivalent of parishes, exist where the Mormons are numerous enough to support a full-fledged church organization. Stake presidents and ward bishops are lay leaders who devote considerable personal time to ministering to their members. In the foreign mission fields, congregations called branches are grouped into mission districts. (Prior to the 1920s, mission districts were called conferences.) Branch and district presidents may be local members, or they may be missionaries, all of whom report to the mission president, who is the senior ecclesiastical authority. Stakes and wards did not exist in Germany until after the Second World War, when church membership grew sufficiently large enough to free the mission president from the responsibility of overseeing day-to-day religious activities of the local members.
13. German-Austrian Mission Manuscript History, 8 Oct. 1930; Budge, *My Story*, 37.
14. Latter-day Saints embrace the concept of a universal lay male priesthood, customarily bestowed upon spiritually worthy boys at the age of twelve. German Mormons of this epoch generally held priesthood office in the lower of two levels, the Aaronic Priesthood, named for the brother of Moses. Within that level, members held ranks of Deacon, Teacher, or Priest, customarily occupied by adolescent boys in the Mormon Culture Region. The American missionaries, although younger in age, arrived in Germany already ordained to the adult priesthood level,

the Melchizedek—named for an Old Testament priest who appears in Genesis and Psalms, the New Testament book of Hebrews, the Book of Mormon book of Alma, various apocryphal writings, and the Dead Sea Scrolls. Although often much younger than the German congregants, these "Elders" exercised greater authority by virtue of both their priesthood office and their appointed position as ecclesiastical leaders.

15. German-Austrian Mission Manuscript History, 8 Oct 1930; Budge, *My Story*, 38.
16. Budge, *My Story*, 38–39.
17. German-Austrian Mission Manuscript History, 8 Oct. 1930; 19 Jun. 1934.
18. Ibid., 3 Dec. 1926.
19. Van Wagoner, *Mormon Polygamy*, 139–43; Johnson, "Determining and Defining 'Wife,'" 57.
20. German-Austrian Mission Manuscript History, 19 Feb. 1927.
21. "Obituary: Zora LeSieur Galli Newman," 31 Jan. 2003.
22. *Names in Stone Cemetery Maps*, Reed Galli gravesite.
23. Utah Death Certificate, Reed Galli, 17 Aug. 1935.
24. "Trench mouth," *Medline Plus*.
25. "Obituary: Rulon Wieter Jenkins," *Social Security Death Index*, 30 May 1992; and "Obituary: Rulon Wieter Jenkins," *Deseret News*, 30 May 1992.
26. German-Austrian Mission Manuscript History, 19 Feb. 1928; German-Austrian Quarterly Reports, 28 Mar. 1928.
27. German-Austrian Mission Quarterly Reports, 28 Mar. 1928. Present-day responsibility for releasing missionaries from their assignments defers to the young person's hometown stake president, who interviews the returned missionary and issues a certificate of release.
28. German-Austrian Mission Manuscript History, 28 Jan. 1928.
29. Ibid., 19 Feb. 1928.
30. Ibid., 19 Nov. 1930.
31. German-Austrian Mission Manuscript History, 29 Aug. 1928.
32. Ibid., 5 May 1930.
33. Swiss-German Mission Manuscript History, 29 May 1929.
34. German-Austrian Mission Manuscript History, 31 May 1929.
35. Ibid., 17 Sep. 1930.
36. Ibid.
37. Ibid., 4 Apr. 1928
38. Ibid., 19 Dec. 1931
39. German-Austrian Mission Quarterly Reports, 31 Jan. 1932.
40. Scharffs, *Mormonism in Germany*, xiv, table 1.
41. Tilsit is now the city of Sovetsk in the Russian Federation.
42. German-Austrian Mission Manuscript History, 22 Jul. 1926.
43. Swiss-German Mission Manuscript History, 11 Jan. and 9 Sep. 1929.
44. German-Austrian Mission Quarterly Reports, Jun. 1927.
45. German-Austrian Mission Manuscript History, 30 Apr. 1926.
46. German-Austrian Mission Quarterly Reports, Jul. 1927.
47. German-Austrian Mission Manuscript History, 31 Mar. 1926.
48. German-Austrian Mission Quarterly Reports, Sep. 1931.
49. Swiss-German Mission Quarterly Reports, Jul. 1931.

50. Ibid., 31 Oct. 1927.
51. Ibid., 28 Feb. 1932.
52. German-Austrian Mission Quarterly Reports, Jul. 1927.
53. Swiss and German Mission Manuscript History, 30 Jun. 1925.
54. Swiss-German Mission Manuscript History, 3 Dec. 1926.
55. Ibid., 31 Jan. 1929.
56. Ibid., 30 Sep. 1930.
57. Swiss-German Mission Manuscript History, 16 May 1929.
58. Ibid., 27 Mar. 1927.
59. See the New Testament scripture, Matthew 16:4; German-Austrian Mission Quarterly Reports, 27 Apr. 1927.
60. Madison, "RLDS Church in Nazi Germany," 15–30.
61. Swiss-German Mission Manuscript History, 8 Jan. 1931.
62. Ibid., 26 Jul. 1931.
63. Anderson, "Mormons and Germany," 116.
64. Swiss-German Mission Manuscript History, 26 Jun. 1931.
65. Ibid., 20 Dec. 1930.
66. German-Austrian Mission Manuscript History, 29 Sep. 1929.
67. Swiss and German Mission Manuscript History, 12 Jul. and 18 Nov. 1915.
68. German-Austrian Mission Quarterly Reports, 27 Sep. 1927.
69. Ibid., 28 Dec. 1928.
70. Mitchelle, "Mormons in Wilhelmine Germany," 115.
71. The Word of Wisdom is found in Section 98 of the Doctrine and Covenants, one of four books of scripture recognized by the LDS Church.
72. German-Austrian Mission Manuscript History, 17 May 1930.
73. Ibid., 25 Feb. 1932.
74. Mitchelle, "Mormons in Wilhelmine Germany," 116.
75. Various admonitions to live righteously "in the world" while not adopting the hedonistic values "of the world" can be found in the New Testament passages of John 15:19 and 17:14, James 1:27 and 4:4, and 1 John 2:15.
76. Gaeth, "About German Inflation."
77. Ibid.
78. Ibid.
79. German-Austrian Mission Quarterly Reports, 29 Dec. 1929.
80. Swiss-German Mission Manuscript History, 31 Jan. 1931
81. Ibid., 28 Feb. 1931.
82. German-Austrian Mission Manuscript History, 31 Dec. 1931.
83. Swiss-German Mission Manuscript History, Sep. 1932.
84. Ibid., 31 Dec. 1932.
85. Gaeth interview, LDS Archives, 3.
86. Swiss-German Mission Manuscript History, 1 Jul. 1931.
87. Swiss-German Mission Quarterly Reports, May 1932.
88. Wobbe interview by Heiss, LDS Archives, 5–6; Wobbe and Borrowman, *Before the Blood Tribunal*, 2–3.
89. German-Austrian Mission Manuscript History, 31 Jan. 1933.

Chapter 4

1. For a description of the mission headquarters building in Berlin and its environs, see Ollerton, "Visit to the German-Austrian Mission," 21 Oct. 1933.
2. German-Austrian Mission Manuscript History, 7 Sep. 1933.
3. *Encyclopedia of Mormonism*, s.v., "Articles of Faith."
4. Matthew 22:20–22, Mark 12:17, and Luke 20:25 (KJV).
5. Section 134 of the Doctrine and Covenants is the Mormons' equivalent of Romans 13:1–7, a set of statements written by the Apostle Paul to define the relationship between the Christian church and civil government.
6. Scharffs, *Mormonism in Germany*, 85; Budge, *My Story*, 50. Scharffs maintains that Budge "had to appear before the Gestapo," and in 85n17 states that he was "questioned and released." Budge was not taken into custody, nor was he required to appear at the Gestapo office. On the contrary, the records of the German-Austrian mission recount a polite conversation at the mission office. Budge's autobiography also describes a cordial dialogue with the visiting gentleman he called the "Chief of the Secret Service."
7. Today, the German government's Topology of Terror Museum stands at the former No. 8 Prinz-Albrecht-Strasse address. In the Nazi years, the complex of buildings housed an underground Gestapo prison, as well as the desks of Heinrich Himmler, *Reichsführer-SS*, and Reinhard Heydrich, director of the SD, the intelligence branch of the Gestapo and the Nazi Party.
8. For an overview of Nazi natalist attitudes, see Koonz, *Mothers in the Fatherland*, 14, 185–86, 189, 192, 196; and Bock, "Antinatalism, Maternity and Paternity in National Socialist Racism," 121–28.
9. Koonz, *Mothers in the Fatherland*, 149. Regarding Nazi natalism, Koonz said: "Pro-natalist policies in Nazi Germany quickly surpassed similar programs in other nations in terms of funding, the number of people affected, and the policy makers' ingenuity. In underlying goals, too, Nazi planners departed from precedent. Whereas policy makers in the United States and Europe justified their programs in terms of individual happiness and social health, Nazi pamphlets explicitly told Germans, 'Your body does not belong to you but to blood brethren.'"
10. German-Austrian Mission Quarterly Reports, Dec. 1933. The text of Budge's letter posted to Gestapo headquarters, dated 8 Sep. 1933, also appears in Budge's autobiography, *My Story*.
11. *Jehovah's Witnesses, Victims of the Nazi Era*, 6.
12. Budge, *My Story*, 55. In using the term "land church," Budge was referring to the large denominations in Germany, the Catholic and Evangelical (Lutheran) Churches, and his hope that the Nazi government would see the Mormons as their equals.
13. King, *Nazi State and New Religions*, 158.
14. *Jehovah's Witnesses, Victims of the Nazi Era*, 10–14.
15. King, *Nazi State and New Religions*, 160.
16. *Jehovah's Witnesses, Victims of the Nazi Era*, 10–11, 13.
17. Hesse, *Persecution and Resistance of Jehovah's Witnesses*, 10, 145.
18. *Jehovah's Witnesses, Victims of the Nazi Era*, 13.

19. King, *Nazi State and New Religions*, 176.
20. Ibid., 71.
21. King, "Strategies for Survival," 211–34; King, *Nazi State and New Religions*, ix–xv; "Report of the Semiannual General Conference, 1937," 59. Roy Welker, when he returned from his term as a mission president in Berlin (1934–37), reported that the Nazi Government had banned thirty-four small religious denominations. King's research, accomplished decades later, lists forty-two.
22. Swiss-German Mission Manuscript History, May 1934, Oct. 1936; German-Austrian Mission Manuscript History, 30 Apr. 1934; Petty interview, LDS Archives, 26.
23. King, *Nazi State and New Religions*, 40, 97–98.
24. Swiss-German Mission Manuscript History, 31. Dec. 1930. This entry, although obviously referring to the National Socialists, seems to blur the boundary between the Nazis and Alfred Hugenberg's right-wing National German People's Party (DNVP), informally referred to as the "Nationalists," whose paramilitary equivalent to the Nazis' S.A. "storm troopers" was the *Stahlheim* (Steel Helmet) League. The confusion was understandable. The two right-wing parties later forged political cooperation in an alliance called the Harzburg Front, which allowed the Nazis a voting majority in the Reichstag and made Nazism more tolerable to the DNVP's bourgeois right-wing supporters.
25. Swiss-German Mission Quarterly Reports, 1932 (year-end summary).
26. The Nazis fell slightly short of a majority of Reichstag seats in the March 1933 election, but through coalition building with other parties, they managed to achieve a parliamentary voting majority.
27. Swiss-German Mission Manuscript History, March 1933.
28. Ibid., Aug. 1934.
29. German-Austrian Mission Manuscript History, 31 Dec. 1930.
30. Gaeth interview, LDS Archives, 3.
31. Swiss-German Mission Quarterly Reports, Sep. 1934.
32. Ibid., 31 Dec. 1930; German-Austrian Mission Quarterly Reports, Dec. 1930. For example, within the Swiss-German Mission at the end of 1930, the Hamburg District reported 1,094 members and Frankfurt am Main listed 503. In the German-Austrian Mission, Chemnitz enrolled 1,097 while Berlin had 1,082.
33. Swiss-German Mission Manuscript History, Sep. 1932.
34. Kelly to Lyman, in Kelly and Swan, "Philemon Merrill Kelly: A Collection of Memories," LDS Archives, 175.
35. Swiss-German Mission Manuscript History, May 1933.
36. Carter, "Mormons and the Third Reich," 58.
37. "Ein aufklärender Brief," *Der Stern*, 14 Jul. 1933.
38. German-Austrian Mission Manuscript History, 29 Jan. 1934; German-Austrian Mission Quarterly Reports, Jan. 1934.
39. Swiss-German Mission Manuscript History, Jan. 1934.
40. Petty interview, LDS Archives, 26.
41. Swiss-German Mission Manuscript History, Oct. 1936.

Chapter 5

1. Clark, "Mormonism in the New Germany," 9 Dec. 1933; Kirkham, "Record Keeping in Germany," 16 Jul. 1938.
2. Brodie, *No Man Knows My History*, 27.
3. Quinn, *The Mormon Hierarchy: Extensions of Power*, 163. In 1838, Smith declared that those who never heard of Christianity during their lifetime will get a chance to become a Christian in the afterlife: "All those who have not had an opportunity of hearing the Gospel, and being administered to by an inspired man in the flesh, must have it hereafter, before they can finally be judged." On January 19, 1841, Smith declared a revelation from God that authorized posthumous baptisms.
4. Mormons often refer to a verse in the New Testament book of 1 Corinthians (15:29) for biblical justification regarding baptisms for the dead. It says, in the King James Version, "Else what shall they do which are baptized for the dead, if the dead rise not at all? Why are they then baptized for the dead?"
5. *Encyclopedia of Mormonism*, s.vv. "Baptism for the Dead," "Spirit World," "Temples."
6. See Massaquoi, *Destined to Witness*.
7. See *Sinti and Roma: Victims of the Nazi Era*.
8. The Law for the Protection of German Blood and German Honor criminalized marriage or sexual contact between German citizens and Jews, forbade Jews from displaying the national flag, and prohibited Jews from employing female German citizens under the age of forty-five. Ostensibly, the latter "protected" German women of childbearing age from being impregnated by a Jew. The Law for the Protection of Genetic Health of the German People authorized marriage certificates to be issued to couples whom officials certified as being neither biracial nor afflicted with mental deformities or specified physical diseases.
9. A first-degree *Mischling* could be reclassified as a "full Jew" for affiliating with a Jewish synagogue or marrying a Jewish partner. Illegitimately born first-degree *Mischlinge* could also be reclassified as full Jews. The legitimate child of a *Mischling* could be classified as a "full Jew" if his parents married after June 15, 1935. The latter provision discouraged partial Jews from procreating.
10. Fischer, *Nazi Germany*, 386.
11. German-Austrian Mission Manuscript History, 31 Mar. 1926. In the early months of 1926, "Sister Baird of Salt Lake City" traveled throughout Germany, giving instructions with regard to genealogical work.
12. Swiss-German Mission Manuscript History, 8 Jan. 1928. A genealogical "society" was so named because it encouraged its Mormon members to seek participation from nonmembers who did genealogical work as a hobby. Even if nonmembers never joined the LDS Church, the names they researched could be submitted for temple ordinances; thus, their deceased relatives could become Mormons.
13. Ollerton, "Visit to the German-Austrian Mission," 21 Oct. 1933.
14. Swiss-German Mission Manuscript History, Dec. 1933 (year-end report).
15. Clark, "Mormonism in the New Germany," 9 Dec. 1933.
16. Schafft, *From Racism to Genocide*, 43.
17. Swiss-German Mission Manuscript History, Jan. 1934.

18. See Carlson, *The Unfit*.
19. Swiss-German Mission Manuscript History, Jan. 1934.
20. Ibid., Mar. 1934.
21. Ehrenreich, *The Nazi Proof of Genealogy, Race Science, and the Final Solution*, 58.
22. Ibid., 68.
23. West German Mission Manuscript History, 1 Dec. 1945; Scharffs, *Mormonism in Germany*, 88. The speaker is Hamburg District President Otto Berndt, who was interrogated by the Gestapo after the arrest of the Helmuth Hübener group of resisters in 1942.
24. German-Austrian Mission Manuscript History, 30 Sep. 1934; 6 Mar. 1935; 24 Mar. 1935; 12 Jan. 1936; 1 Mar. 1936; 3 May 1936; 23 Jun. 1936.
25. Swiss-German Mission Quarterly Reports, Dec. 1935 (year-end report).
26. German-Austrian Mission Manuscript History, 30 Sep. 1934.
27. Ibid., 6 Sep. 1936.
28. German-Austrian Mission Manuscript History, 15 Oct. 1936.
29. West German Mission Manuscript History, 25 Oct. 1938.
30. Ibid., 26 Jan. 1938.
31. The article included short notes at the end regarding genealogical work done in Tonga and Argentina.
32. Kirkham, "Record Keeping in Germany," 16 Jul. 1938.
33. See Arendt, *Eichmannn in Jerusalem*. Arendt focused on Eichmann as the subject of her book-length condemnation of those who practiced desk genocide, but she referred to all such bureaucratic complicity as the "banality of evil."
34. Scharffs, *Mormonism in Germany*, 84.
35. Bringhurst, *Fawn McKay Brodie: A Biographer's Life*, 75.
36. Brodie to Coolie, Fawn Brodie Papers, Marriott Archives, 16 Nov. 1980. Unfortunately, letters exchanged by Fawn Brodie with members of her immediate family were excluded from the papers she bequeathed to the University of Utah. Correspondence between Brodie and her extended family and intellectual colleagues, in which she expressed skepticism of the Mormons' aims in Germany, survived.
37. Bringhurst, *Fawn McKay Brodie: A Biographer's Life*, 57–64. Fawn's uncle, David O. McKay, who would later become the Mormon prophet, seer, and revelator, went to Chicago in 1936 in a futile effort to dissuade Fawn from marrying outside of her religion. Her father, Thomas E. McKay, wrote to dissuade Fawn from marrying outside of her faith. That letter contained anti-Semitic references. After Fawn published her skeptical biography of Joseph Smith, *No Man Knows My History*, her uncle, David O. McKay, became one of the leading proponents of her 1946 excommunication; that book has never gone out of print. Brodie went on to write critically acclaimed biographies of Thomas Jefferson, Sir Richard Francis Burton, Thaddeus Stevens, and Richard Nixon. Brodie was the first twentieth historian to reintroduce the controversial topic of Jefferson's paternity of Sally Hemings' six children. On the strength of her record as a biographer, Fawn Brodie joined the history faculty at UCLA and eventually achieved the rank of full professor—despite the fact that her highest academic degree was an M.A. in English.
38. Brodie to Brimhall, Brimhall Papers, Marriott Archives, 14 Jun. 1939.

Chapter 6

1. Bennion, "New Ways of Proselyting," 25 Jan. 1936.
2. *Standard Rate & Data Service*, May 1936, 108, 267; *Directory of Newspapers and Periodicals*, 1936, 911. The *Christian Science Monitor* had the highest circulation among daily newspapers that were wholly owned subsidiaries of a religious organization; it had 130,779 paid subscribers in 1936. The *Deseret News*, owned by the LDS Church's Corporation of the President, had 36,735, according to figures published by *Standard Rate and Data Service*. *Directory of Newspapers and Periodicals*, which used different criteria for determining daily circulation data, listed the *Deseret News*'s circulation in 1936 as 36,015.
3. Foster, "Judge May Lose Sports Job," 7 Dec. 1935; Gould, "Olympic Boycott Faction," 9 Dec. 1935.
4. The American Olympic Committee (AOC) was the forerunner to the present-day United States Olympic Committee (USOC). The AAU was the predominant governing body of amateur athletics in the United States in the era before the National Collegiate Athletic Association wielded significant influence.
5. Wenn, "The Commodore Hotel Revisited," 188–201. In those days, the Amateur Athletic Union was the sole authority that certified an athlete's amateur status, and thus eligibility for the Olympic Games. While the AAU had a permanent structure, a new American Olympic Committee formed for every Olympiad. When AOC Chairman Brundage forced Mahoney's resignation as AAU president, Brundage obtained that position, which gave him dictatorial power over which American athletes could compete in the Olympics.
6. Gray and Barney, "Devotion to Whom?" 214–31.
7. Dr. Theodor Lewald, president of the German Olympic Committee in the early 1930s, was one those organizers who put so much effort into the successful German bids for the 1916 and 1936 Olympics. Shortly after Hitler's forced *Gleichschaltung* (coordination) of German sports policies, Lewald was dismissed from his post as head of the Olympic committee. One of his grandmothers was Jewish.
8. Hart-Davis, *Hitler's Games*, 44.
9. Ibid., 45–46.
10. In an effort to mitigate criticism of its exclusion of Jews from the German Olympic team, Reich sports authorities arranged for Helene Mayer, a blue-eyed, blonde-haired daughter of a Christian mother and Jewish father, to compete for Germany on its Olympic fencing team. Like many Jews who were able to flee Nazi Germany, Mayer was living abroad at the time, in Los Angeles, but Mayer agreed to compete for Germany. After she won a silver medal, she mounted the victory stand wearing a swastika and rendered a stiff-arm salute. She later explained that she thought her effort would lead to a greater degree of tolerance for Jews in Germany.
11. Hart-Davis, *Hitler's Games*, 15.
12. Mandell, *The Nazi Olympics*, 58–59; Friedländer, *Nazi Germany and the Jews*, 117.
13. Alexander, *Mormonism in Transition*, 141.
14. German-Austrian Mission Manuscript History, 8 Aug. 1935.
15. German-Austrian Mission Quarterly Reports, Oct. 1935.

16. German-Austrian Mission Manuscript History, 2 Nov. 1935.
17. In later years, the term "display" sports changed to "demonstration" sports.
18. Krueger, "REPLY: 1936 'Nazi' Olympics," 22 Apr. 2000.
19. *Basket-Ball: Die Olympischen Spiele*, 132–33.
20. Merrill, telephone interview with author, 24 Jul. 2001.
21. German-Austrian Mission Manuscript History, 1 Aug. 1936.
22. Scharffs, *Mormonism in Germany*, 86.
23. Organisationskomitee, *The XIth Olympic Games*, 1078–79.
24. Bingham interview, LDS Archives, 3; Friedländer, *Nazi Germany and the Jews*, 117.

Chapter 7

1. Desk Diary, Thomas E. McKay Papers, BYU Archives, 19 Feb.–4 Mar. 1940. McKay, his wife and daughter, and four Mormon missionaries had steamed from Genoa to New York, with intermediate stops in Naples and Gibraltar. Before the war, that trip would have been much shorter. Usually, the SS *Washington* served the Hamburg to New York market.
2. "2 Here to Minimize Blockade Friction," 5 Mar. 1940.
3. *Encyclopedia of Mormonism*, s.v., "Boy Scouting."
4. Blake interview, BYU Archives, 5.
5. The Hitler Youth boys' auxiliaries included the *Deutches Jungvolk* (the German Young Folk) for ages ten through fourteen and the *Hitlerjugend* (the Hitler Youth) for fifteen- to eighteen-year-olds.
6. The Hitler Youth girls' auxiliaries included the *Jungmädelbund* (the League of Young Girls) for ages ten to fourteen and the *Bund deutscher Mädel* (the League of German Girls) for fifteen- to eighteen-year-olds.
7. Beehive groups enrolled Mormon girls ages ten through fourteen. At fifteen, they graduated to the Gleaner Girls.
8. East German Mission Manuscript History, 31 Mar. 1938.
9. Ibid., Oct. 1938.
10. Alexander, *Mormonism in Transition*, 140–41.
11. Ibid., 143.
12. Ibid., 141–42.
13. Rosenthal, *The Character Factory*, 85–86.
14. See Peterson, *The Boy Scouts*.
15. *Encyclopedia of Mormonism*, s.v., "Scouting."
16. Strong, "History of the Young Men's Mutual Improvement Association, 119.
17. Alexander, *Mormonism in Transition*, 143–44.
18. Sullum, *For Your Own Good*, 37.
19. Alexander, *Mormonism in Transition*, 143.
20. *Encyclopedia of Mormonism*, s.v., "Scouting." Within the Aaronic Priesthood, boys are ordained deacons at age twelve and teachers at fourteen. In 1949, Explorer Scouting became the official activities organization for priests, the Aaronic Priesthood ordination bestowed on sixteen-year-old boys.
21. Alexander, *Mormonism in Transition*, 144–45.

22. Walker, *Hitler Youth and Catholic Youth*, 6.
23. Ibid., 8.
24. Peukert, *The Weimar Republic*, 90.
25. Swiss-German Mission Manuscript History, 3 Sep. 1928; German-Austrian Mission Manuscript History, 23 Oct. 1928.
26. Ibid., 6 Nov. 1928; Gaeth interview, LDS Archives. The German-Austrian Mission historical records record the name of the new Scouting organization as the *Deutscher Scoutverbund*. Arthur Gaeth was superintendent of Scouting for the German-Austrian Mission in 1928. He attended the formative meeting and recalls that the Americans agreed to call the new organization the Baden-Powell Council. For registration purposes, the German name prevailed in the official documentation.
27. Carter, "Mormons and the Third Reich," 65.
28. German-Austrian Mission Manuscript History, 3 Dec. 1928; Gaeth interview, LDS Archives. Arthur Gaeth recalled that two small, unaffiliated Scouting councils joined the Mormons in forming the *Deutscher Scoutverbund*.
29. German-Austrian Mission Manuscript History, 3 Dec. 1928.
30. Ibid., 3 Feb 1929; 6 Mar. 1929.
31. German-Austrian Mission Quarterly Reports (year-end report), Dec. 1930; Swiss-German Mission Manuscript History, 16 Aug. 1929; Jul. 1931; 23 Jul. 1932.
32. Gaeth interview, LDS Archives.
33. Swiss-German Mission Manuscript History, 23 Jul. 1932.
34. German-Austrian Mission Manuscript History, 18 Aug. 1929. Kirkham served as president of the Young Men's Mutual Improvement Association.
35. Fischer, *Nazi Germany*, 662; Wistrich, *Who's Who in Nazi Germany*, 222.
36. Stachura, "National Socialist *Machtergreifung*," 255.
37. Walker, *Hitler Youth and Catholic Youth*, 93, 154.
38. Stachura, "National Socialist *Machtergreifung*," 256.
39. Ollerton, "Visit to the German-Austrian Mission," 21 Oct. 1933.
40. Carter, "Mormons and the Third Reich," 67. Carter also said: "Other boys either did not participate or, under pressure, merely went through the motions."
41. Keele and Tobler, "The Führer's New Clothes," 27.
42. Kobs, interview with author, 20 Jul. 2006.
43. Holmes and Keele, *When Truth Was Treason*, 21, 321n30.
44. German-Austrian Mission Quarterly Reports (year-end report), Dec. 1930; Gaeth interview.
45. German-Austrian Mission Manuscript Histories, 30 Apr. 1934.
46. Swiss-German Mission Quarterly Reports, Dec. 1933.
47. German-Austrian Mission Quarterly Reports, 30 Jun. 1934.
48. Rempel, *Hitler's Children*, 266.
49. German-Austrian Mission Quarterly Reports, 30 Jun. 1934.

Chapter 8

1. Dodd and Dodd, *Ambassador Dodd's Diary*, ix, 4, 135–36.
2. King, *Nazi State and New Religions*, 33–34.
3. Ibid., 96.

4. Kershaw, *The Hitler Myth*, 1–10.

5. Taylor, "The Law of the Fast." Joseph Smith established a monthly fast day in order to support church welfare projects in the 1830s. It occurred on a designated Thursday once each month. In the 1890s, because of the experience of English coal miners who would go without pay if they missed work to participate in devotional services held to coincide with the fast day, the LDS Church moved the day and established Fast Sunday.

6. Peukert, *Inside Nazi Germany*, 49, 60, 83. Historian Detlev Peukert said that refusal to prepare the *Eintopf* was one of the few avenues of protest available in Nazi Germany. That protest, however, unfolded within the secrecy of the family home. Few openly refused to contribute if they could afford to do so.

7. Fischer, *Nazi Germany*, 343.

8. Petty interview, LDS Archives, 65; Dixon, "Mormons in the Third Reich," 70; Keele and Tobler, "Führer's New Clothes," 27.

9. Bennett, "All Germany Will Fast," 638–39.

10. Clark, "Mormonism in the New Germany," 9 Dec. 1933.

11. Welker interview, LDS Archives, 58.

12. Pugmire and Babbel, *Roy Anson Welker and Elizabeth Hoge*, 23.

13. *Journal of Discourses*, 12:157–58.

14. Doctrine and Covenants, 89; McCue, "Word of Wisdom," 66–77; Quinn, *The Mormon Hierarchy: Extensions of Power*, 474n18; Arrington, "An Economic Interpretation," 37–49; Alexander, "Principle to Requirement," 47–65; Alexander, *Mormonism in Transition*, 258–71; *Church Handbook of Instructions* 1:192. The Word of Wisdom changed in both its interpretation and obligatory status during the nineteenth century. Originally it prohibited neither beer nor wine, and allowed the use of sacramental wine for several decades after its issuance in 1833. As numerous historians have documented, church members considered it guidance rather than a commandment until the early twentieth century. Leonard J. Arrington provoked a firestorm of controversy when he suggested in a BYU scholarly journal that there were economic implications attendant to the varying degrees of enforcement by church elders. Alarmed university officials suspended the journal *BYU Studies* for a period of time after Arrington's article appeared. Thomas Alexander suggested that the Word of Wisdom became an example of Thomas Kuhn's theory of paradigmatic shifts when Mormons searched for doctrine that would define their church after the demise of polygamy. The LDS Church's *Handbook of Instructions* instructs bishops and stake presidents that the only approved definition of prohibited "hot drinks" is coffee and tea. Many Mormons consider caffeinated sodas to be prohibited in the church's health code.

15. Kershaw, *Hitler Myth*, 3–6, 83–104.

16. Hanfstaengl, *Unheard Witness*, 145; Fischer, *Nazi Germany*, 119.

17. Clark, "Mormonism in the New Germany," 9 Dec. 1933.

18. Carter, "Mormons and the Third Reich," 95.

19. Dixon, "Mormons in the Third Reich," 70.

20. Blake interview, BYU Archives, 5.

21. Bingham interview, LDS Archives, 29.

22. Ibid.

23. Anderson, "Mormons and Germany," 154.
24. King, *Nazi State and the Religions*, 70.
25. Scharffs, *Mormonism in Germany*, 87, 110.
26. Anderson, "Mormons and Germany," 155.
27. Pugmire and Babbel, *Roy Anson Welker and Elizabeth Hoge*, 23–24.
28. Bytwerk, "Party Rally of Honor (1936)."
29. Grunberger, *12-Year Reich*, 280.
30. Pugmire and Babbel, *Roy Anson Welker and Elizabeth Hoge*, 25; Welker, interview, LDS Archives.
31. "Mrs. Daniels" was probably an Anglicized spelling, recorded by a mission office clerk who did not speak German.
32. Pugmire and Babbel, *Roy Anson Welker and Elizabeth Hoge*, 24.
33. German-Austrian Mission Quarterly Reports, Sep. 1936.
34. Pugmire and Babbel, *Roy Anson Welker and Elizabeth Hoge*, 25.
35. During his 1980s-era research on the Helmuth Hübener story, BYU historian Douglas F. Tobler cited information from Roy A. Welker's personal diary, which Tobler read at the archives of the LDS Church's Historian's office in Salt Lake City. Dr. Tobler confirmed the existence of a Welker diary during a phone conversation I had with him on July 17, 2001. The diary contained comments about Elizabeth Welker's interaction with Hitler and Scholtz-Klink. When I tried to access the same diary at the LDS archives, the staff said it could no longer be found, and in fact they could find no record that it had ever been archived there. However, they did produce a volume of Roy Welker's diary that ended on March 22, 1935, and another that began in 1937 after Welker's return to the United States.
36. Welker interview, LDS Archives, 2–3. The surviving documentation of the limousine rides taken by Elizabeth Welker with Hitler and Scholtz-Klink is contained in this oral history interview conducted by Richard L. Jensen, then a member of the LDS Church Historical Department and subsequently a faculty member at BYU, where he served on the staff of the Joseph Fielding Smith Institute for Church History.
37. "Europe War Scares Discounted," 8 Sep. 1937.
38. Friedländer, *Nazi Germany and the Jews*, 162.
39. "Europe War Scares Discounted," 8 Sep. 1937.
40. "Report of the Semiannual General Conference, 1937," 59.
41. "Europe War Scares Discounted," 8 Sep. 1937.
42. Welker, "German Girl of Today," 294–95.

Chapter 9

1. German-Austrian Mission Manuscript History, 3 Apr. 1933; German-Austrian Mission Quarterly Reports, Dec. 1933 (year-end report).
2. Carter, "Mormons in the Third Reich," 73. Steven Carter, using an unpublished paper authored by BYU's Douglas Tobler, cited an undated incident that did not appear in the official records of the two Mormon missions, a reference to a missionary named Reed Bradford whom "Party members . . . nearly beat to death

for refusal to salute the Nazi flag." The citation also does not reveal the location of that attack.

3. Scharffs, *Mormonism in Germany*, 84; Carter, "Mormons in the Third Reich," 73. With regard to the belt-whipping of missionaries Ellsworth and Allen, Scharffs's account differs from the contents of the German-Austrian Mission Manuscript Histories and Quarterly Reports. Scharffs said: "Police refused to do anything about it." The records show that the victims and the assailant appeared before a judge or a magistrate, and that the Mormons declined to press charges.

4. German-Austrian Mission Manuscript History, 31 Mar. 1935.

5. German-Austrian Mission Manuscript History, 2 Apr. 1935; German-Austrian Mission Quarterly Reports, Apr. 1935.

6. Fischer, *Nazi Germany*, 408–409.

7. Blake interview, BYU Archives, 6.

8. Swiss-German Mission Manuscript History, 26 Jun. 1936.

9. Ibid., Jul., Aug., Oct. 1936.

10. "Report of the Semiannual General Conference," 59.

11. Swiss-German Mission Manuscript History, Apr. 1935.

12. Mallmann and Paul, "Omniscient, Omnipotent, Omnipresent?" 176.

13. Johnson, *Nazi Terror*, 48.

14. Swiss-German Mission Manuscript History, Apr. 1935.

15. Bingham interview, LDS Archives, 5.

16. Swiss-German Mission Manuscript History, Feb. 1937.

17. Ibid., Mar. 1937.

18. German-Austrian Mission Manuscript History, 29 Jul. 1937.

19. East German Mission Manuscript History, 1 Jan. 1938; West German Mission Manuscript History, 8 Jan. 1938.

20. Bingham interview, LDS Archives, 8; Swiss-German Mission Manuscript History, Feb. 1936.

21. Bingham interview, LDS Archives, 9.

22. Swiss-German Mission Manuscript History, June 1937.

23. Bingham interview, LDS Archives, 9.

24. Swiss-German Mission Manuscript History, June 1937.

25. Dixon, "Mormons in the Third Reich," 73, 77n13. Dixon's account varies slightly from other sources. Based on an interview he conducted with M. Douglas Wood, the West German Mission President in 1938, a different photographic processor received the second batch of negatives and was the source of denunciation to the Gestapo.

26. Petty interview, LDS Archives, 51.

27. West German Mission Manuscript History, 14 Oct. 1938; Petty interview, LDS Archives, 49.

28. German-Austrian Mission Quarterly Reports, Jan. 1937.

29. German-Austrian Mission Manuscript History, 4 Apr. 1928.

30. *Encyclopedia of Mormonism*, s.v., "Tithing;" Doctrine and Covenants, 119:4.

31. Kelly to Lyman, in Kelly and Swan, "Philemon Merrill Kelly: A Collection of Memories," LDS Archives, 176.

32. Braun, *German Economy in the Twentieth Century*, 84–85.

33. German-Austrian Mission Quarterly Reports, Jan. 1937.

34. East German Mission Manuscript History, 28 Feb. 1938.
35. Blake interview, BYU Archives, 7.
36. Petty interview, LDS Archives, 51–52.
37. Scharffs, *Mormonism in Germany*, 76; "The South American Mission," Feb. 1975; "Council Meeting, Jan. 25, 1940," George Albert Smith Papers. When Mormons began missionary activity in Brazil in 1925, they restricted their efforts to German-speaking inhabitants. In their judgment, this alleviated a concern regarding the inadvertent baptism of Brazilians who had been born as the result of miscegenation between whites and the descendants of black slaves. As late as 1940, minutes of a First Presidency meeting express First Counselor J. Reuben Clark's concern as to "whether or not one drop of negro blood deprives a man of the right to receive the priesthood."
38. *Encyclopedia of Mormonism*, s.v., "Apostasy."
39. Swiss-German Mission Manuscript History, May 1933.
40. Ibid., Jan. 1936.
41. German-Austrian Mission Manuscript History, Sep. 1936.
42. German-Austrian Mission Quarterly Reports, Oct. 1933.
43. Petty interview, LDS Archives, 40.
44. Johnson, *Nazi Terror*, 254.
45. Blake interview, BYU Archives, 6.
46. King, *Nazi State and New Religions*, 44.

Chapter 10

1. "European Mission Presidents Hold Conference," 16 Jul. 1938.
2. Present in Copenhagen were the Mormon mission presidents and "mission matrons" for Great Britain, Denmark, France, Sweden, Norway, Czechoslovakia, the Netherlands, Switzerland-Austria, the two German missions, and their overseer, the European mission president. Leaders of the Palestine-Syrian and South African missions did not attend because of the distance involved.
3. Murdock interview, LDS Archives excerpts, used by permission of Church Historical Department.
4. Ibid.
5. Lindsey interview, LDS Archives, 1; Bingham interview, LDS Archives, 20.
6. Alfred C. Rees, "Im Lande Der Mormonen," 14 Apr. 1939; Ryser interview, LDS Archives, 17; Bingham interview, LDS Archives, 2; Petty interview, LDS Archives, 38; Dixon, "Mormons in the Third Reich," 72.
7. "Germany to Send Broadcast to Utah," 19 Aug. 1939.
8. Rees, "Diary of Ida May Davis Rees," LDS Archives, 1.
9. Ibid., 9–13 Sep. 1937.
10. Bingham interview, LDS Archives, 7.
11. Kelly and Swan, "Philemon Merrill Kelly: A Collection of Memories," LDS Archives, 39–53, 132.
12. Ibid., 132, 135.
13. Ryser interview, LDS Archives, 9.
14. Presiding Bishopric Financial, Statistical, and Historical Reports.

15. Bringhurst, *Fawn McKay Brodie; A Biographer's Life*, 89, 282n72.
16. Petty interview, LDS Archives, 75.
17. Grant married for the first time in 1877 and took two additional wives on successive days in May 1884. By the time Grant became Church President in 1918, only Augusta Winters, his second wife, remained living.
18. Holzapfel and Bohn, "The Long-Awaited Visit," 5.
19. Ibid., 14; Albert E. Blasser, "A Sketch of President Grant's Visit and Its Benefit to the Swiss-German Mission," in Kelly and Swan, "Philemon Merrill Kelly: A Collection of Memories," LDS Archives, 165–67; "President Grant in Frankfurt, Germany," 7 Aug. 1937.
20. Kelly and Swan, "Philemon Merrill Kelly: A Collection of Memories," LDS Archives, 171.
21. Rees, "Diary of Ida May Davis Rees," LDS Archives, 6 Aug. 1937.
22. "Dr. and Mrs. Kelly Transferred to Berlin," 9 Sep. 1937.
23. German-Austrian Mission Manuscript History, 8 Aug. 1937.
24. Petty interview, LDS Archives, 64.
25. Bingham interview, LDS Archives, 2.
26. Lindsey interview, LDS Archives, 2.
27. "A. C. Rees: S. L. Industrial Leader," 23 Jul. 1937.
28. "Editorials: Elder A. C. Rees Honored," 6 Jul. 1937.
29. German-Austrian Mission Manuscript History, 29 Sep. 1937.
30. German-Austrian Mission Manuscript History, 13 Aug. 1937.
31. Swiss-German Mission Manuscript History, Aug. 1937.
32. Rees, "Diary of Ida May Davis Rees," LDS Archives, 7–8, 16–19 Aug. 1937.
33. Ibid., 18 Sep. 1937.
34. Bingham interview, LDS Archives, 17. During the interview, Bingham read from his diary.
35. Swiss-German Mission Manuscript History, Oct. 1937.
36. Lyman to Kelly (second of three letters), in Kelly and Swan, "Philemon Merrill Kelly: A Collection of Memories," LDS Archives, 171–74.
37. Kelly to Lyman, in Kelly and Swan, "Philemon Merrill Kelly: A Collection of Memories," LDS Archives, 175–79.
38. Kelly, Rees, and Thomas E. McKay to Lyman, in Kelly and Swan, "Philemon Merrill Kelly: A Collection of Memories," LDS Archives, 180.
39. Grant and David O. McKay to Kelly, in Kelly and Swan, "Philemon Merrill Kelly: A Collection of Memories," LDS Archives, 198.
40. Kelly to Valdo D. Benson, in Kelly and Swan, "Philemon Merrill Kelly: A Collection of Memories," LDS Archives, 207.
41. West German Mission Manuscript History, 6, 22 Jan. 1938.
42. Ibid., 2 July, 20 Aug. 1938.
43. Swiss Mission Quarterly Reports, 28 Sep. 1939.
44. "Heart Attack," 27 Jul. 1941.
45. "History of the Association." The association Rees founded still exists today; its website logo features a bulldog with protruding lower teeth.
46. "Editorials: Elder A. C. Rees Honored, 6 Jul. 1937; "Heart Attack," 27 Jul. 1941; "Editorials: Alfred Cornelius Rees," 29 Jul. 1941.

47. "Heart Attack," 27 Jul. 1941. In 1947, six years after Rees's death, Congress overrode President Truman's veto of the Taft-Hartley Act, thus fulfilling Rees's dream of outlawing the closed shop labor contract.

48. An apostle is a member of the Quorum of the Twelve. Traditionally, the senior apostle in years of service ascends to the position of prophet, seer, and revelator upon the death of an incumbent church president. When Heber J. Grant invited Clark to become his first counselor in 1934, both men knew Clark would never enjoy the seniority necessary to become the prophet.

49. Quinn, *Elder Statesman*, 82. FDR received 69.3 percent of Utah's vote in the 1936 presidential election.

50. "A. C. Rees: S. L. Industrial Leader," 23 Jun. 1937.

51. Rees, "Diary of Ida May Davis Rees," LDS Archives, 21 Nov. 1937.

52. Ibid., 28 Oct. 1937.

53. Lindsey interview, LDS Archives, 1.

54. Ryser interview, LDS Archives, 18.

55. Rees, "Diary of Ida May Davis Rees," 21 Sep. 1937.

56. Ibid., 27 Oct. 1937.

57. "Alfred Rosenberg," in Wistrich, *Who's Who in Nazi Germany*, 209–12.

58. Rees, "Diary of Ida May Davis Rees," 11 Sep. 1937.

59. Ibid., 28 Sep. 1937.

60. Tansill, *Backdoor to War*, 348.

61. Bingham interview, LDS Archives, 15.

62. Lindsey interview, LDS Archives, 2.

63. "Der Staat im Staate," 22 Nov. 1938.

64. Julius Hermann Moritz Busch wrote *Die Mormonen* upon his return from a trip to the United States in the 1850s. Busch gained notoriety later in life as Otto Von Bismarck's publicist.

65. Lindsey interview, LDS Archives, 2.

66. Ibid.

67. Rees, "Im Lande der Mormonen," 14 Apr. 1939.

68. Lindsey interview, LDS Archives, 2.

69. "Missionary Letter No. 14," 1 Sep. 1938, East German Mission Office Files.

70. "Missionary Letter No. 15, 14 Oct. 1938, East German Mission Office Files.

71. Rees, "Diary of Ida May Davis Rees," 1 May 1939.

72. Quinn, *Elder Statesman*, 287, 538n69.

73. The six-month period of incarceration was probably an exaggeration on Murdock's part. Toronto possibly referred to the arrest of four missionaries for violations of currency exchange regulations, and their confinement in Pankrác Prison in Prague for several months. After returning from Lucerne, Toronto was able to obtain their release by proffering a bribe. Brigham Young University religious history scholar David F. Boone describes their ordeal (see Boone, "Evacuation of the Czechoslovak and German Missions.")

74. Murdock interview, LDS Archives, 114.

75. East German Mission Manuscript History, 18 Dec. 1938.

76. Ibid., 5 Mar. 1939.

77. "Missionary Letter No. 16," 2 Dec. 1938, in East German Mission Office Files.

Chapter 11

1. Fox, *J. Reuben Clark*, 429.
2. Fox, *J. Reuben Clark*, 513–18; Sessions, *Prophesying Upon the Bones*, 46–47. The Monroe Doctrine of 1823 warned European powers against recolonizing or establishing spheres of influence in the Americas. By the time of Theodore Roosevelt's administration at the turn of the twentieth century, Europe no longer threatened the political independence of Latin American republics, but its considerable financial investment in the Americas seemed to invite armed intervention to collect debts. The Roosevelt Corollary asserted the right of the United States to rebuff such European intercession, and went so far as to proclaim the right of preemptory American action in cases of governmental instability in the Americas. When Secretary of State Frank Kellogg concluded negotiations on the Kellogg-Briand Pact in 1929, a treaty that ostensibly outlawed war, Kellogg worried that "Monroe Doctrine cultists" would mount an effort to prevent Senate ratification—similar to the campaign that defeated ratification of the Treaty of Versailles and the League of Nations. Kellogg assigned his undersecretary, J. Reuben Clark, to write a position paper that repudiated the Roosevelt Corollary, claiming that the United States never stated the right to interfere militarily in the internal affairs of sovereign nations.
3. Fox, *J. Reuben* Clark, 196.
4. Quinn, *Elder Statesman*, 427, cover.
5. German-Austrian Mission Manuscript History, 8 Aug. 1937; East German Mission Manuscript History, 24 Jun. 1938.
6. Dodd and Dodd, *Ambassador Dodd's Diary*, 83–84.
7. Sessions, *Prophesying Upon the Bones*, 16.
8. German-Austrian Mission Manuscript History, 6 Oct. 1934; German-Austrian Mission Quarterly Reports, Oct. 1934; Swiss-German Mission Quarterly Reports, Oct. 1934.
9. Grant and David O. McKay to Clark, 23 Mar. 1935, Clarkana Papers, BYU Archives.
10. Grant to Hull, 3 Apr. 1935, Clarkana Papers, BYU Archives.
11. Hull to Grant, 13 Apr. 1935, Clarkana Papers, BYU Archives.
12. Hull to Grant, 21 Jun. 1935, Clarkana Papers, BYU Archives.
13. Wilbur John Clark, Assistant Secretary of State, to J. R. Clark, 15 Apr. 1935, and J. R., Clark to Wilbur Clark, 24 Apr. 1935, Clarkana Papers, BYU Archives.
14. "Memorandum of Conversation of Mr. J. Reuben Clark, Dr. Blessing and Other *Reichsbank* Officials on August 4, 1937," and "Memorandum of Conversation at the Lunch Given to J. Reuben Clark by *Reischsbank* Officials on Thursday, August 5, 1937," Clarkana Papers, BYU Archives.
15. "Conversation at the Lunch," and "Conversation between J. Reuben Clark and Dr. Schacht," Clarkana Papers, BYU Archives.
16. German-Austrian Mission Manuscript History, 8 Aug. 1937.
17. J. Reuben Clark diary, 25 Jun. 1938, Clarkana Papers, BYU Archives.
18. Ibid.; German-Austrian Mission Manuscript History, 24 Jun. 1938.
19. Boone, "Evacuation of Missionaries at the Outbreak of World War II," 65–66.
20. Swiss-Austrian Mission Manuscript History, Sep. 1939.
21. East German Mission Manuscript History, 14 Sep. 1938.

22. Ibid.
23. West German Mission Manuscript History, 14 Sep. 1938.
24. Swiss-Austrian Mission Manuscript History, Sep. 1938.
25. Chamberlain is often misquoted as having said: "Peace *in* our time." Those words, found in the Anglican Book of Common Prayer, were spoken by Prime Minister Benjamin Disraeli when he returned from the Congress of Berlin in 1878.
26. West German Mission Manuscript History, 4 Oct. 1938.
27. East German Mission Manuscript History, 5 Oct. 1938.
28. Lindsey interview, LDS Archives, 14.
29. Petty interview, LDS Archives, 14.
30. Quinn, *Elder Statesman*, 332.
31. King, *Nazi State and the New Religions*, 151–153.
32. J. R Clark diary, 9 Aug. 1937, Clarkana Papers, BYU Archives.
33. Ibid., 6–7 Aug. 1937, 25 Jun. 1938.
34. "An Original 1942 Letter from the Hotel Kaiserhof in Berlin to Reichsleiter Baldur Von Schirach in Wien."
35. "President Grant in Frankfurt Germany," 7 Aug. 1937.
36. "Germany Holds M. I. A. 'Echo of Joy' Festival," 18 Jul. 1936.
37. Bednar, "Hearts of the Children Shall Turn," Oct. 2011.
38. Nelson, "A New Harvest Time," May 1998.
39. Smoot, "Ein Freund von Deutschland," 1 Mar. 1935.
40. Ibid.
41. Ehrenreich, *Nazi Proof of Genealogy*, 58.
42. Swiss-German Mission Quarterly Reports, Mar. 1934.
43. Edna Harker Thomas diary, 20–24 Jul. 1934, Elbert D. Thomas Papers.
44. Ibid., 23, 31 Jul., 5, 30 Aug. 1934.
45. Ibid., 13 Aug. 1934.

Chapter 12

1. W. H. Klopfer, "Childhood in the Big German City," LDS Archives, 1–2; W. H. Klopfer, "Enemy Soldier in the Pulpit," 59–60.
2. W. H. Klopfer, "Childhood in the Big German City," LDS Archives, 1–2; Klopfer, interview with author.
3. W. H. Klopfer, "Childhood in the Big German City," LDS Archives, 1–2.
4. Thomas E. McKay to Barnes, 17 Sep. 1945; Richard Ranglack and Paul Langheinrich to McKay, 5 Jan. 1946; both in Thomas E. McKay Papers, BYU Archives.
5. Erna Klopfer, "Report on the Life of K. Herbert Klopfer," East German Mission Manuscript History. The report is dated December 1957 but is filed in the manuscript histories under the date of 19 Mar. 1945, the date that Klopfer died in a Red Army field hospital.
6. W. H. Klopfer, "Enemy Soldier at the Pulpit," 59–60.
7. East German Mission Manuscript History (year-end report), 31 Dec. 1939.
8. Alfred C. Rees, Missionary Letter No. 11, 15 Aug. 1939, East German Mission Office Files, LDS Archives. Thomas E. McKay, Missionary Letter No. 12, 17 Aug. 1939, East German Mission Office Files.

9. East German Mission Manuscript History (year-end report), 31 Dec. 1939.
10. Boone, "Evacuation of the Czechoslovak and German Missions."
11. Boone, "Evacuation of Missionaries at the Outbreak of World War II," in *Regional Studies in Latter-day Saint Church History*, 65–89. See also Boone, "Worldwide Evacuation of Latter-day Saint Missionaries at the Outbreak of World War II."
12. Montague, *Mine Angels Round About*.
13. Ibid., 23.
14. Ibid., 35–41.
15. Ibid., 60.
16. Ibid., 30, 40, 66.
17. Ibid., 80.
18. Ibid., 52.
19. Ibid., 44.
20. Boone, "Evacuation of the Czechoslovak and German Missions," 148.
21. Kobs, interview with author.
22. This sign appears in Frederick Kempe's book, *Father/Land*. The author observed the sign when Mr. Kobs graciously granted an oral history interview in July 2006.
23. Jared H. B. Kobs, "WW II 1939–1945," 5.
24. In Kempe's book, the author protected the relatives of his murderous distant relative by awarding Erich Krause the pseudonym of Kramer.
25. Kempe, *Father/Land*, 81.
26. Kobs, interview with author, 27 Jul. 2006.
27. Kobs, "WW II 1939–1945," 5.
28. Ibid.
29. Kobs, Letter to author, 15 Aug. 2005.
30. Barth, *Guided and Guarded*, 40; Bickerstaff, "Guarded by Grace," 38–39.
31. Barth, *Guided and Guarded*, 74; Bickerstaff, "Guarded by Grace," 39.
32. Bickerstaff, "Guarded by Grace," 39.
33. Ibid., 22.
34. Freeman and Felt, "German Saints at War," 73.
35. Ibid., 266–68.
36. Corbett, "Disaster Welfare in Germany," LDS Archives, 8.
37. Ibid., 2.
38. Petty interview, LDS Archives, 49.
39. Berndt interview, LDS Archives, 47, 69.
40. Ibid., 84.
41. Beevor, *Berlin*, 410–11.
42. Minert, *In Harm's Way*, 59.
43. East German Mission Manuscript History, 26 Jul.–7 Aug. 1946.
44. Berndt interview, LDS Archives, 50, 70.
45. Corbett, "Disaster Welfare in Germany," LDS Archives, 2–3.
46. W. H. Klopfer, "Childhood in the Big German City," LDS Archives, 4–5; W. H. Klopfer interview.
47. Corbett, "Disaster Welfare in Germany," LDS Archives, 3.
48. Ibid., 7.

49. Reschke, "Would You Forget?" 173. Although the town of Hildesheim was relatively safe during the period in which Horst Reschke lived with his host family, it eventually suffered heavy damage from Allied aerial bombing.

50. The literature on the migration and expulsion of Germans after the Second World War is growing. Two of the most recent scholarly works are Douglas, *Orderly and Humane: The Expulsion of the Germans after the Second World War*, and Merten, *Forgotten Voices: The Expulsion of the Germans from Eastern Europe after World War II*.

51. Schmidt, "An Account of the Mormon Home," LDS Archives, 3; Babbel, *On Wings of Faith*, 41. The literature of the nineteenth-century Mormon handcart migration is extensive. For an overview, see Allen, *Story of the Latter-day Saints*, 292–94, 321; *Encyclopedia of Mormonism*, s.v., "Handcart Companies." For a dissenting historian's view, see Roberts, *Devil's Gate*.

52. Corbett, "Disaster Welfare in Germany," LDS Archives, 15.

53. Marko Schubert to author, 7 May 2007. Entries concerning the Bretschneider property in Wolfsgrün appear in the *Hendelsregister*, the commercial registry of the *Amtsgericht*, the local court, for various dates from 1890 through 1943.

54. Schmidt, "An Account of the Mormon Home," LDS Archives, 4.

55. Lepage, *Hitler Youth, 1922–1945*: 47–49.

56. Kershaw, *Hitler, 1936–45: Nemesis*, 424; Rinderle and Norling, *Nazi Impact on a German Village*, 168.

57. Schmidt, "An Account of the Mormon Home," LDS Archives, 5.

58. Corbett, "Disaster Welfare in Germany," LDS Archives, 14.

59. Carter, "Mormons in the Third Reich, 193.

60. "Homes of Lebensborn," in *Axis History Factbook*. See also Hillel and Henry, *Of Pure Blood*.

61. "The Lebensborn Program," Jewish Virtual Library; "Hitler's Master Race," 26 Apr. 2000.

62. Schmidt, "An Account of the Mormon Home," LDS Archives, 6–8, 10.

63. Ibid., 10–11.

64. Ibid., 18.

65. East German Mission Manuscript History, 24 Mar. 1946.

66. Schmidt, "An Account of the Mormon Home," LDS Archives, 18.

67. Botting, *From the Ruins of the Reich*, 311.

68. Corbett, "Disaster Welfare in Germany," LDS Archives, 9–11.

69. Botting, *From the Ruins of the Reich*, 133.

70. Corbett, "Disaster Welfare in Germany," LDS Archives, 20.

71. Botting, *From the Ruins of the Reich*, 132.

72. Corbett, "Visit of Elder Ezra Taft Benson, 3.

73. Corbett, "Disaster Welfare in Germany," LDS Archives, 13; "Former Missionary Returns," 24 Nov. 1945. Corbett's account identifies Barnes as a major. The *Deseret News* article refers to him as a colonel.

74. Botting, *From the Ruins of the Reich*, 139.

75. "Elder Benson Tells Story," 6 Jul. 1946. See also Dew, *Ezra Taft Benson*.

76. Babbel, *On Wings of Faith*, 35–66; Corbett, "Visit of Elder Ezra Taft Benson," 6–9.

77. East German Mission Manuscript History, 21 Jun.–4 Jul. 1946.

78. Benson, "General Report to the First Presidency," 7 Aug. 1946, in East German Mission Manuscript History, 7 Aug. 1946; "First Church Welfare Supplies," 26 Oct. 1946.

79. Sonne, LDS European Mission President, to the First Presidency, n.d., ca. 1946, included in East German Mission Manuscript History under the date 31 Mar. 1947.

80. East German Mission Manuscript History, 5–23 Oct. 1946; "Elder Benson Reports Second Berlin Shipment," *Deseret News*, 2 Nov. 1946.

81. Holzapfel, "Friends Again: Canadian Grain," 67–70.

82. Mangum and Blumell, *Mormons' War on Poverty*, 152.

83. Ibid.; Ranglack and Langheinrich to Field Marshall Georgy Zhukov, Commander in Chief of the Soviet Occupation Forces in Germany, 9 Aug. 1945, in East German Mission Manuscript History, 9 Aug. 1945.

84. Sokolowski to Ranglack and Langheinrich, East German Mission Manuscript History, 16 Aug. 1945.

85. Ibid., 3.

86. Ranglack and Langheinrich to Zhukov, East German Mission Manuscript History, 9 Aug. 1945.

87. Corbett, "Records from the Ruins," LDS Archives, 5.

88. Ibid., 5–6.

89. Ibid., 11, 13–16; Babbel, *On Wings of Faith*, 57–58.

90. Corbett, "Records from the Ruins," LDS Archives, 13; East German Mission Manuscript History, 9 Aug. 1945.

91. Langheinrich, "Report of Procurement of Church Records," LDS Archives. This report, written by Langheinrich and translated from German, appears in the East German Mission Manuscript History under the date of 16 Aug. 1945. It was undoubtedly written many years later after Langheinrich's immigration to Utah.

92. Wobbe, interview with Heiss, LDS Archives, 79.

93. East German Mission Manuscript History, 16 Feb. 47.

94. Ibid.

95. Ibid., 4 Dec. 1946.

96. Ibid., 26 Feb. 1946.

97. Ibid., 10 Dec. 1946.

98. Ibid., 26 Feb. 1947.

99. Ibid., 7 Apr. 1947.

100. "Walter Krause, Legendary for his Post-War Service," 17 Apr. 2004.

Chapter 13

1. Reschke, *Max*, 61, 75, 81–82; H. Reschke, interview with author, 6 Feb. 2006. Laves-Arzneimittel GmbH, established in 1908 by Wolfgang Laves' father, Dr. Ernst Laves, still flourished in 2014 as a family-owned German pharmaceutical manufacturer.

2. Reschke, *Max*, 79–80; Reschke, interview with author.

3. Reschke, *Max*, 83; Reschke, "There but for the Grace of God," 2; Reschke, interview with author.

4. Reschke, *Max*, 84; H. Reschke, "Scouting in Nazi Germany," 162; Reschke, interview with author.

5. Apparently, the compromise that freed Max Reschke included the stipulation that his son Horst join the Hitler Youth. See Minert, *Under the Gun*, 210, fig. 8.

6. Reschke, *Max*, 83; Reschke, interview with author.

7. Reschke, *Max*, 83.

8. Reschke, "There but for the Grace of God," 2; Reschke, interview with author.

9. Reschke, *Max*, 84; Reschke, interview with author.

10. Reschke, "There but for the Grace of God," 4–6; Reschke, interview with author.

11. Reschke to Schorsch; Reschke, *Max*, 91–92; Reschke, interview with author.

12. Reschke to Blake, 25 Apr. 1982, and Blake to Reschke, 23 May 1982, letters in possession of author; Reschke, "He Understood"; Reschke, *Max*, 84–86; Reschke, interview with author.

13. Reschke, *Max*, 86–88; Reschke, "There but for the Grace of God," 7–8; Reschke, interview with author.

14. Reschke, *Max*, 91; Reschke, interview with author.

15. Reschke, *Max*, 91; Reschke to Ismar Schorsch, 11 Jan. 1993, letter in possession of author.

16. Reschke, *Max*, 91; Reschke, interview with author.

17. See Häsler, *Lifeboat Is Full*.

18. Reschke, *Max*, 91; Reschke, interview with author.

19. *Encyclopedia of Mormonism*, s.v. "Brigham Young University: Jerusalem Center for Near Eastern Studies"; Watzman, "Israeli Cabinet," 33–34.

20. Stone, "Mormon Baptism," 21 Feb. 2012.

21. Tobler, interview with author.

22. Tobler, "Jews, Mormons, and Holocaust," 87.

23. Reschke, "There but for the Grace of God," 2–8; Reschke, interview with author.

24. Quinn, *The Mormon Hierarchy: Extensions of Power*, 826.

25. Mordecai Paldiel, Director, Department of the Righteous, Yad Vashem, to author, 4 Apr. 2000. For statistics on the Righteous, see http://www1.yadvashem.org/yv/en/righteous/statistics.asp.

26. On February 6, 2006, I had the honor of being welcomed into Horst Reschke's home in Riverton, Utah. Mr. Reschke was suffering from an advanced stage of Parkinson's disease and did not feel well enough to submit to a full-fledged oral history interview. However, he kindly confirmed orally all of the important facts about his father that appeared in his book. He also generously provided copies of the other documentation I have cited in this chapter and elsewhere. I asked him, for the second time, if I could assist in nominating his father as a candidate for membership in Righteous Among the Nations. He politely but firmly declined.

27. Reschke, *Max*, 76; Reschke, interview with author.

28. Reschke, *Max*, 76, 77, 99.

29. Ibid., 76, 115.

30. Inge, interview with author, 1. In deference to the courageous woman who shared her story with me, I have elected to redact her surname and hometown from this narrative, and provide her the additional protection of a pseudonym as a given

name. She is the only person afforded such a courtesy. All others are identified by their proper names.

31. Ibid., 4.
32. Jordan, *Structures of Memory*, 159–61; Kempe, *Father/Land*, 262.
33. Kempe, *Father/Land*, 265, 271, 275, 278–79.
34. Ibid., 183, 270.
35. Ibid., 264.
36. East German Mission Manuscript History, 24 Mar. 1946; "East German Mission Head Named," 20 Jul. 1946.
37. Kempe, *Father/Land*, 274, 283.
38. Inge, interview with author, 5–6.
39. Kempe, *Father/Land*, 282.
40. Ibid., 179–80.
41. Inge, interview with author, 6, 10.
42. Inge, interview with author, 9.

Chapter 14

1. "Anschluss & Extermination: The Fate of the Austrian Jews," *Holocaust Education and Archive Research Team*.
2. Ibid.
3. In addition to the LDS First Presidency, Weiss wrote James Rhead, Alfonso G. Pia, and Feramorz Bennion of Salt Lake City; Joseph N. Symons of Hot Lava Springs, Idaho; Roland S. Pond of Fairfield, Idaho; a Brother Woodward of Franklin, Idaho; Andrew L. Larsen of Draper, Utah; and Byron Geslison of Spanish Fork, Utah.
4. Quinn, *The Mormon Hierarchy: Extensions of Power*, 826.
5. Miscellaneous Correspondence of the First Presidency, CR 1/44, Box 111, Folder 6, Headquarters Correspondence, in D. Michael Quinn Papers. First Presidency correspondence files are usually closed to researchers, but Quinn received special dispensation when he wrote the authorized biography of J. Reuben Clark, *The Church Years*, which appeared in 1983.
6. Quinn, *Elder Statesman*, 333, with differences in Quinn, *The Mormon Hierarchy: Extensions of Power*, 827.
7. Miscellaneous Correspondence of the First Presidency, CR 1/44, Box 110, Folder 5, Headquarters Correspondence, in D. Michael Quinn Papers.
8. Quinn, *The Mormon Hierarchy: Extensions of Power*, 827.
9. Clark to Dulles, 11 Apr. 1939, Clarkana Papers, BYU Archives.
10. Quinn, *Elder Statesman*, 319.
11. "The State University," 16 Jun. 1898.
12. Tobler, "Jews, Mormons, and Holocaust," 70; Quinn, *Elder Statesman*, 325.
13. Fox, *J. Reuben Clark*, 415–16.
14. "Ernest Bamberger Chosen," 15 Jul. 1922. Clark actually finished third in the balloting at the 1922 Republican nominating convention, behind Bamberger and another Mormon, William H. Wattis.
15. Ryser interview, LDS Archives, 21.

16. The mission presidents used missionary reports as one source to write the quarterly and year-end reports to Salt Lake City.
17. Petty interview, LDS Archives, 30.
18. "Jews," Office Files, 1939, Clarkana Papers, BYU Archives.
19. "Refugee Ship," 3 Jun. 1939; "Havana Called Waiting Room." 13 May 1941.
20. ""Havana Called Waiting Room," 13 May 1941, and "Suez Must Not be Another Singapore," 28 Feb. 1942; both in "Jews," Office Files, Clarkana Papers, BYU Archives.
21. Quinn, *Elder Statesman*, 331.
22. Clark to Hoover, 14 May 1942, Herbert Hoover Presidential Library.
23. Clark to N. L. Nelson, 24 Jun. 1941, Clarkana Papers, BYU Archives.
24. Quinn, *Elder Statesman*, 326.
25. When I began my research in the LDS Historical Department's archives, I noted that the electronic catalog offered seventeen copies of the *Protocols*. As the story unraveled, I found that J. Reuben Clark had distributed copies liberally to members of the church administration. Presumably, once a recipient retired and donated his office bookshelf material, it enabled the archives to stock many more copies than it would normally have acquired through customary procurement procedures.
26. Clark to Pyramid Book Shop, Houston, 22 Sep. 1958, Clarkana Papers, BYU Archives.
27. Clark to Wilkinson, 5 Feb. 1949, Clarkana Papers, BYU Archives.
28. Clark to Benson, n.d., ca. Dec. 1957, Clarkana Papers, BYU Archives.
29. "Jews," Office Files, Miscellaneous, Clarkana Papers, BYU Archives.
30. Quinn, *Elder Statesman*, 328.
31. Mitsen, "The King-Havenner Bill," 23–32.
32. Mauss, "Mormon Semitism and Anti-Semitism," 11.
33. Mauss, *All Abraham's Children*, 158–161.
34. *Utah History Encyclopedia*, s.v., "The Jewish Community in Utah."
35. "Ernest Bamberger Loses," 8 Nov. 1928.
36. Carter, "Mormons and the Third Reich," 100n110.
37. Kempe, *Father/Land*, 84.
38. Tobler, "Jews, Mormons, and Holocaust," 83.
39. Keele to author, 5 Apr. 2014, copy in my possession.
40. Holmes and Keele, *When Truth Was Treason*, 26.
41. Ibid., 13.
42. Ibid., 14.
43. Ibid., 324n44; Wobbe and Borrowman, *Before the Blood Tribunal*, 27–28.
44. Anna Marie Schwarz, sister of Salomon Schwarz, to Wobbe, 5 Oct. 1987, in Appendix 2, Wobbe interview by Matthew Heiss, LDS Archives, 1988.
45. Ibid. Although Anna Marie Schwarz did not name the person who reported her brother for traveling without his Star of David, all indications point to Arthur Zander. The St. Georg branch president, an enthusiastic Nazi sympathizer, seemed to have maintained a personal vendetta against Salomon Schwarz. Documentation concerning the Helmuth Hübener group, retrieved from the Hamburg Municipal District Archives, the *Stadtteilarchiv*, contains no evidence of any other Mormon who bore a grudge against Schwarz. (Hübener was a member of the same St. Georg branch that Zander led.) Several documents do attest to the enmity that Zander had for Schwarz.

Anna Marie Schwarz's reluctance to name the person who reported her brother to the Gestapo was probably a consideration for the welfare of the large German Mormon postwar expatriate community in Utah. Enthusiastic Nazi sympathizers like Arthur Zander and Nazi opponents like Max Reschke joined hundreds of others in a Mormon diaspora that left Germany for the American Zion after the Second World War. If Zander did not report Salomon Schwarz, it is likely that the person who did so also emigrated after the war. Most émigrés settled in the Salt Lake City metropolitan area, and many lived closer to each other in the United States than they had in Germany.

46. Schwarz to Wobbe, 5 Oct. 1987, LDS Archives.
47. Petty interview, LDS Archives, 36.
48. Dixon, "Mormons in the Third Reich," 75.
49. Keele, "A Latter-day Saint in Hitler's SS," 21–28.
50. *Holocaust Encyclopedia*, s.v. "German Jewish Refugees, 1933–1939."
51. Miscellaneous Correspondence of the First Presidency, CR 1/44, Box 110, Folder 5, Headquarters Correspondence, in D. Michael Quinn Papers.

Chapter 15

1. Holmes and Keele, *When Truth Was Treason*, 241.
2. Mann, *Reminiscences and Reflections*, 292. Initial Hübener scholarship said the executioner wielded an ax. The Third Reich judicial system employed the guillotine, which had been used in Germany since the Napoleonic invasions, for the first few months of 1933 until nativist sensitivities dictated that the "non-German invention" be replaced with an ax or a hangman's rope. After two years, complaints about unskilled ax-wielding executioners and their botched beheadings promoted a return to the guillotine.
3. "Helmuth Hübener Membership Record," LDS Archives.
4. Seisser, "Shedding Light on a Dark Past," Jan. 2009. Sander, the child of a Hamburg wartime resister, made a career of researching the crimes of Nazi Germany committed on the home front. He publicized the transgressions of German military units who carried out atrocities and crusaded to remove the names of known Nazis from streets and public buildings.
5. *Örtlich betäubt* appeared in English in 1970 under the title *Local Anesthetic*. The English translation of *Davor* emerged in 1972, entitled "Max."
6. BYU to Dramatize," 2 Oct. 1976; "BYU Drama: Mormons Caught," 3 Oct. 1976; "Gripping, True Drama," 3 Oct. 1976.
7. Pearson, "Huebener Moving, Powerful New Drama," 8 Oct. 1976; Mary Dickson, "Utah's Huebener," *Salt Lake Tribune*, 17 Oct. 1976.
8. Kunkel interview, LDS Archives, 1.
9. Holmes and Keele, *When Truth Was Treason*, 25. According to Karl Heinz-Schnibbe, "The *Oberbau* was not for those who were on the expensive and elite university track, but were going into some other challenging profession." Hübener desired to attend the university but thought it was out of his reach because of financial limitations. The *Realschule* was a high school of intermediate difficulty between the vocational *Hauptschule* and the college-preparatory *Gymnasium*.
10. Ibid., 178, 276.

11. Keele and Tobler, "The Führer's New Clothes," 21.
12. Holmes and Keele, *When Truth Was Treason*, 29.
13. Ibid., 178; McFarland and Whitaker, *Truth & Conviction*, DVD: 3:59.
14. Sommerfeld interview, LDS Archives, 9.
15. Wobbe and Borrowman, *Before the Blood Tribunal*, 15.
16. Sander, "Helmuth Hübener Gruppe," 326; Holmes and Keele, *When Truth Was Treason*, 277; McFarland and Whitaker, *Truth & Conviction*, DVD: 3:29; Holmes and Keele, *When Truth Was Treason*, Document 27: 193.
17. Holmes and Keele, *When Truth Was Treason*, 29; Wobbe and Borrowman, *Before the Blood Tribunal*, 23.
18. Holmes and Keele, *When Truth Was Treason*, 25.
19. McFarland and Whitaker, *Truth & Conviction*, DVD: 3:12.
20. Wobbe and Borrowman, *Before the Blood Tribunal*, 15.
21. Hugo Hübener held the rank of *Rottenführer*, the SA rank equivalent of a military lance corporal and someone who would be assigned to lead a group of no more than three or four men.
22. Kunkel interview, LDS Archives, 11; Holmes and Keele, *When Truth Was Treason*, 25.
23. Holmes and Keele, *When Truth Was Treason*, 29, 325n58.
24. Wobbe, interview with Heiss, LDS Archives, 6.
25. Sommerfeld interview, LDS Archives, 9.
26. Holmes and Keele, *When Truth Was Treason*, Document 72: 273.
27. Wobbe and Borrowman, *Before the Blood Tribunal*, 21.
28. McFarland and Whitaker, *Truth & Conviction*, DVD: 7:43.
29. Keele to author, 5 Apr. 2014.
30. Holmes and Keele, *When Truth Was Treason*, 26.
31. Berndt interview, LDS Archives, 22, 29. (Read with permission of the Church Archives.)
32. Ibid., 35.
33. Ibid., 31.
34. Wobbe interview with Heiss, LDS Archives, 15.
35. Holmes and Keele, *When Truth Was Treason*, 27.
36. Keele and Tobler, "The Führer's New Clothes," 21; McFarland and Whitaker, *Truth & Conviction*, DVD: 7:43. In McFarland and Whitaker's documentary, the sign on the meeting house door read: "*Juden ist der Zutrittt Verboten!*"
37. Kunkel interview, LDS Archives, 14; Sommerfeld interview, LDS Archives, 7; Wobbe interview with Heiss, LDS Archives, 16. Kunkel said that Otto Berndt consented to baptize Kauffmann. Rudi Wobbe, in his interview with Matthew Heiss, said the baptism was performed by the previous district president, Alwin Brey.
38. Wobbe and Borrowman, *Before the Blood Tribunal*, 31; Wobbe interview with Heiss, LDS Archives, 15. Wobbe declined to name the victim of Zander's temper in his book; however, in his interview with Matthew Heiss of the LDS Church Archives staff, he identified the "elderly sister" as Emma Hasse.
39. Ibid., 19.
40. Ibid., 25–26. In Otto Berndt's interview with Douglas Tobler, Berndt said that Worbs had been confined in Geesthacht concentration camp. This was probably a satellite camp of the main Neuengamme camp near Hamburg.

41. Berndt Interview, LDS Archives, 54.
42. Wobbe interview with Heiss, LDS Archives 22.
43. Wobbe and Borrowman, *Before the Blood Tribunal*, 26; Holmes and Keele, *When Truth Was Treason*, 334n109; Berndt interview, LDS Archives, 54. The official LDS membership records state that Worbs did not die until October 8, 1945, but this is probably a clerical error. Berndt, Wobbe, and Schnibbe—interviewed separately—insist that Worbs died six weeks after his release as a result of maltreatment suffered in the concentration camp.
44. McFarland and Whitaker, *Truth & Conviction*, DVD: 12:39.
45. Holmes and Keele, *When Truth Was Treason*, 29.
46. Wobbe and Borrowman, *Before the Blood Tribunal*, 22.
47. Holmes and Keele, *When Truth Was Treason*, 37.
48. Fischer, *Nazi Germany*, 370.
49. Kunkel interview, LDS Archives, 24.
50. Wobbe and Borrowman, *Before the Blood Tribunal*, 19.
51. Holmes and Keele, *When Truth Was Treason*, 30.
52. Holmes and Keele, *When Truth Was Treason*, Document 28: 194; McFarland and Whitaker, *Truth & Conviction*, DVD: 18:34.
53. McFarland and Whitaker, *Truth & Conviction*, DVD: 11:03.
54. Ibid., 11:31.
55. Ibid., 18:20.
56. Wobbe and Borrowman, *Before the Blood Tribunal*, 36.
57. Ibid.
58. Wobbe interview with Tobler and Keele, 4. LDS Archives.
59. Wobbe and Borrowman, *Before the Blood Tribunal*, 15–16.
60. Wobbe, Interview with Tobler and Keele, 3–4, LDS Archives.
61. McFarland and Whitaker, *Truth & Conviction*, DVD: 18:10, 18:34.
62. Holmes and Keele, *When Truth Was Treason*, Document 10: 156. During Hübener's interrogation by the Gestapo, he stated that he sometimes made up to seven copies at one time. The last edition of a pamphlet, found in the church typewriter when the Gestapo searched his room, consisted of an original and six carbon copies. In Wobbe and Borrwman's *Before the Blood Tribunal*, Rudi claimed Helmuth used the church duplicating machine to reproduce his pamphlets. No other document, including records of Gestapo interrogations or government indictments, verifies this claim.
63. Sander, "Helmuth Hübener Gruppe," 330.
64. Berndt interview, LDS Archives, 36. By this time, Berndt has been promoted to full-fledged district president, in contrast to the "acting" position he filled earlier. Berndt maintained that, contrary to some accounts, Hübener's secretarial position was a district (diocesan) rather than a branch (parish) position. Zander had asked Hübener to write soldiers from the St. Georg branch, and for that purpose the branch president loaned the typewriters to the young man.
65. McFarland and Whitaker, *Truth & Conviction*, DVD: 16:06.
66. The hotel coat closet scene appears in Thomas Rogers' *Huebener* and David Anderson's "Huebener Against the Reich." No historical documentation confirms that particular escapade, although it is possible that Wobbe and Schnibbe recounted that adventure to the playwrights.

67. Ibid., 12:39.
68. Ibid., 22:45.
69. Ibid., 23:09.
70. McFarland and Whitaker, *Truth & Conviction*, DVD: 19:25.
71. Grunberger, *12-Year Reich*, 334.
72. Göring's second wife was German actress Emmy Sonnemann, whom he married in 1935 in a spectacular wedding ceremony during which squadrons of *Luftwaffe* aircraft flew overhead.
73. Holmes and Keele, *When Truth Was Treason*, Document 37: 202.
74. Fisher, *Nazi Germany*, 485–86.
75. Holmes and Keele, *When Truth Was Treason*, 68.
76. "Hitler Appeals for Warm Clothing for Eastern Front," *World War II Today*.
77. Guenther, *Nazi Chic*, 222.
78. Holmes and Keele, *When Truth Was Treason*, Document 42; 206–208. Alan F. Keele translated Hübener's poem from German. I have included only four of the seven stanzas Hübener wrote.
79. Rempel, *Hitler's Children*, 71.
80. Holmes and Keele, *When Truth Was Treason*, Documents 38 and 39; 203–204.
81. Holmes and Keele, *When Truth Was Treason*, Documents 31 and 36; 195, 200–202. A smaller pamphlet, "The Riddle of Hess," is referred to in the attorney general's indictment but does not appear in Holmes and Keele's listing of primary documents.
82. Fisher, *Nazi Germany*, 466–67.
83. "The Fuhrer's Speech," in Holmes and Keele, *When Truth Was Treason*, 212.
84. Holmes and Keele, *When Truth Was Treason*, Document 3; 147.
85. Wobbe and Borrowman, *Before the Blood Tribunal*, 39; Holmes and Keele, *When Truth Was Treason*, Document 27: 188.
86. McFarland and Whitaker, *Truth & Conviction*, DVD: 23:32.
87. Wobbe and Borrowman, *Before the Blood Tribunal*, 39.
88. "Indictment," in Holmes & Keele, *When Truth Was Treason*, Document 27: 189.
89. Wobbe and Borrowman, *Before the Blood Tribunal*, 40.
90. Ibid., 40.
91. Ibid.; McFarland and Whitaker, *Truth & Conviction*, DVD: 26:38. Holmes and Keele, *When Truth Was Treason*, 47, 346n15. In 1950, a German court convicted Heinrich Mohns of "crimes against humanity" for his "denouncement" of Helmuth Hübener. It sentenced Mohns to a term of two years' imprisonment. In a plea reminiscent of the Nuremburg tribunals, Mohns had argued that he was only doing his duty. In 1953 an appeals court overturned the verdict, arguing that Mohns was not guilty as an accessory to Hübener's death, but instead only culpable as an accessory to illegal deprivation of Hübener's freedom. It also ordered the lower court to consider Mohns' conduct in light of emergency laws in effect at the time. In essence, the appeals court agreed that Mohns was doing his duty. Mohns served no time in prison.
92. Wobbe and Borrowman, *Before the Blood Tribunal*, 41.
93. Holmes and Keele, *When Truth Was Treason*, 50.
94. Ibid., 271. Frederich Peters, a member of the St. Georg Branch who was five years older than Helmuth, recalled: "He was the littlest . . . in sports Helmuth was

absolutely nothing . . . we often went to the athletic fields . . . he was never there. He was interested only in intellectual things."

95. Holmes and Keele, *When Truth Was Treason*, Document 6: 148–49.
96. Ibid., Document 72: 273.
97. Ibid., Document 10: 155.
98. McFarland and Whitaker, *Truth & Conviction*, DVD: 28:36.
99. Ibid., 29:26.
100. After Schnibbe's prison term, he was drafted into the army, served on the Eastern front, became a prisoner of the Russians, and did not return to Germany until 1949.
101. McFarland and Whitaker, *Truth & Conviction*, DVD: 36:58.
102. Kola-Fu was an abbreviation for **Ko**zentrations**la**ger **Fu**hlsbüttel. Fuhlsbüttel was a satellite facility of Hamburg's Neuengamme concentration camp.
103. Holmes and Keele, *When Truth Was Treason*, 342n34, 342nn41–45.
104. McFarland and Whitaker, *Truth & Conviction*, DVD: 29:26.
105. Berndt interview, LDS Archives, 41.
106. Wobbe, interview with Tobler and Keele, LDS Archives, 30–31.
107. Wobbe, interview with Heiss, LDS Archives, 22.
108. Wobbe and Borrowman, *Before the Blood Tribunal*, 47.
109. "Statement of Otto Berndt," LDS Archives. Also in Holmes and Keele, *When Truth Was Treason*, Document 65: 257–58.
110. Berndt interview, LDS Archives, 40.
111. For a discussion of the Mormon perspective on excommunication as it applies to one's potential for salvation, see McConkie, *Mormon Doctrine*, 258.
112. District Leader to State Secret Police, in Holmes and Keele, *When Truth Was Treason*, Document 17: 175.
113. Holmes and Keele, *When Truth Was Treason*, Document 27: 189.
114. Ibid., Document 15: 171–73.
115. McFarland and Whitaker, *Truth & Conviction*, DVD: 39:06.
116. Wobbe, *Before the Blood Tribunal*, 69.
117. *Bund Nationalsozialistischer deutscher Juristen.*
118. Wobbe, *Before the Blood Tribunal*, 72.
119. McFarland and Whitaker, *Truth & Conviction*, DVD: 40:27.
120. Wobbe, *Before the Blood Tribunal*, 72.
121. Holmes and Keele, *When Truth Was Treason*, Document 52: 219–20.
122. McFarland and Whitaker, *Truth & Conviction*, DVD: 44:55.
123. Holmes and Keele, *When Truth Was Treason*, Document 6: 239.
124. Ibid., 71.
125. Ibid., Document 62: 241; "Beheadings in the Third Reich," *Axis History Factbook*.
126. Holmes and Keele, *When Truth Was Treason*, Document 59: 238–39.
127. McFarland and Whitaker, *Truth & Conviction*, DVD: 47:57.
128. Berndt interview, LDS Archives, 41.
129. *"Abhören u. Verbreiten ausl. Rundfunksenden."*
130. "Helmuth Hübener Membership Record," LDS Archives.
131. Properly carried out, an excommunication requires that a "church court" be convened and that evidence be heard before a decision is rendered. The accused does

not have to be present, however; *in absentia* excommunications are common. Often, the accused elects not to appear.

132. Kunkel interview, LDS Archives, 21.
133. Holmes and Keele, *When Truth Was Treason*, Document 65: 258. Berndt said: "When I was questioned by the Gestapo, I was told to see that the accused Helmuth [Hübener] was to be cut off by the LDS Church. I flatly refused to do this."
134. Berndt interview, LDS Archives, 30.
135. Dewey, *Hübener vs. Hitler*, 288–92.
136. Klopfer, interview with author.
137. Klopfer, interview with author.
138. Kobs to author, 3 Jul. 2006.
139. Wobbe and Borrowman, *Before the Blood Tribunal*, 147.
140. In postwar West Germany, a citizen who desired privileges such as government housing or a business license needed to be certified to be free of prior connections with the Nazi Party. The old term *Persilschein*, meaning a whitewash, came into popular use when someone with a shady past received a clean political bill of health. The term's root word, *Persil*, is the brand name of a popular laundry detergent in Germany.
141. McFarland and Whitaker, *Truth & Conviction*, DVD: 5:59.
142. Holmes and Keele, *When Truth Was Treason*, 144.
143. Wobbe, *Before the Blood Tribunal*, 143–44, 147–50.
144. *Polk's Salt Lake City Directory*, 1952–1975.
145. Wobbe, *Before the Blood Tribunal*, 152.
146. "Arthur Zander, Obituary," *Deseret News*, 4 Jun. 1989.

Chapter 16

1. Rogers, *Huebener and Other Plays*, v.
2. Ibid.
3. Ibid., 50.
4. Ibid., v.
5. Pearson, "Huebener Moving, Powerful New Drama," 8 Oct. 1976; Dickson, "Utah's Huebener," 17 Oct. 1976.
6. Young, "Doing Huebener," 130.
7. Rogers, interview with author, 23 May 2000.
8. "Huebener's Message Haunts Memories," Nov. 1976.
9. Young, "Doing Huebener," 130.
10. Keele interview with author, 23 May 2000; Keele to author, 19 May 2012.
11. Keele interview with author, 2000; Keele to author, 19 May 2012.
12. Van Orden, *Building Zion*, 201.
13. Rogers interview with author, 2000; Keele interview with author, 2000.
14. Wobbe interview with Heiss, LDS Archives, 69.
15. Wobbe and Borrowman, *Before the Blood Tribunal*, 156.
16. Melich, "New Play," 5 Feb. 1984.
17. Tobler, interview with author, 17 Jul. 2001.
18. Keele to Nelson, 19 May 2012.

19. Rogers interview with author, 2000; Keele interview with author, 2000; Tobler interview with author, 2001.
20. Van Orden, *Building Zion*, 200–201.
21. Tobler, "Before the Wall Fell," 19.
22. In 1985, Benson became president of the LDS Church upon the death of Spencer W. Kimball. Mellowed by age and political reality, his pulpit pronouncements eschewed confrontational politics. Many of the faithful remember his nineteen-year tenure as prophet, seer, and revelator for his repeated pleas to read the Book of Mormon.
23. For an examination of Benson's conflicts with other members of the Mormon hierarchy over the intensity of his anti-communist pronouncements, see Quinn, "Ezra Taft Benson and Mormon Political Conflicts," 1–87.
24. Prince, "The Red Peril, the Candy Maker," 37–94.
25. Tobler, "Before the Wall Fell," 20.
26. "Official Report of the First Germany, Austria, Holland, Italy, Switzerland, France, Belgium, and Spain Area General Conference of the Church of Jesus Christ of Latter-day Saints," 24–26 Aug. 1973, 111.
27. Van Orden, *Building Zion*, 201.
28. Keele interview with author, 2000; Tobler interview with author, 2001.
29. Young, "Doing Huebener," 130.
30. Rogers interview with author, 2000.
31. Keele interview with author, 2000; Tobler interview with author, 2001.
32. Warner, "Helmuth Hübener," 3.
33. Keele interview with author, 2000; Keele to Nelson, 19 May 2012.
34. Keele interview with author, 2000.
35. Keele and Tobler, "The Führer's New Clothes," 20–29.
36. Boone and Cowan, "The Freiberg Germany Temple," 147–67; Kuehne, *LDS Realpolitik*, 89–90; Kuehne, *Mormons As Citizens*, 264.
37. Melich, "New Play," 5 Feb. 1984; Walker, "World Premieres," 5 Feb. 1984.
38. Melich, "Story Worth Telling," 13 Feb. 1984.
39. Warner, "Helmuth Hübener: Antagonist or Protagonist," Mar. 1984.
40. White, "Play About Mormon Youth's War," 15 Feb. 1984; "Huebener Group Lauded in Hamburg," 49.
41. Warner, "Helmuth Hübener: Antagonist or Protagonist," Mar. 1984.
42. Ibid.
43. Anderson, "Huebener Against the Reich," play, 1984.
44. Schnibbe, Keele, and Tobler, *The Price*, 1984.
45. Keele to Nelson, 19 May 2012.
46. Oaks, "Alternate Voices,"
47. "Statement on Symposia," 31 Aug. 1991.
48. Peck, "Origin and Evolution," 13.
49. "Huebener Group Lauded," 48–49; Hale, "Prisoners of Conscience," 52–61.
50. "German Democratic Republic," 74–75.
51. Wobbe interview with Heiss, LDS Archives, 69. Wobbe made these comments about Zander in August 1988, ten months before Zander's death.
52. Chandler, "Appeal to a Lower Court," 27–50.
53. Melich, "BYU's Huebener Plays it Safe," 8 Apr. 1992.

54. Swenson, "Utah Under Cover," 25 Oct. 1992.
55. Wobbe and Borrowman, *Three Against Hitler*.
56. Keele to Nelson, 19 May 2012.
57. Keele to Nelson, 19 May 2012.
58. Apparently, Dewey runs his publishing house from a facility in Provo that sells computer parts. When one searches directories or online databases, the Academic Research Foundation of Provo, Utah, appears among listings for "computer motherboards, computer power supplies, removable media devices, external drives, peripherals, optical drives, keyboards, and computer mice."
59. Dewey, *Hübener vs. Hitler*, 352.
60. Keele to Nelson, 19 May 2012.
61. Tunnell, *Brothers in Valor* (Kindle edition), chap. 1.
62. Berson, *Young Heroes in World History*.
63. Bartoletti, *The Boy Who Dared*.
64. M. Heiss, "Online Review: The Boy Who Dared," *Amazon Prime*, 24 Oct. 2011.
65. Peukert, *Inside Nazi Germany*, 118–19.
66. Ibid., 154–55, 166–67.
67. The literature on the White Rose group is extensive. The first English-language news appeared relatively early, in a March 29, 1943, article in the *New York Times*, entitled "Nazis Execute 3 Munich Students For Writing Anti-Hitler Pamphlets." In 1952, one of the surviving White Rose conspirators, Inge Scholl, wrote *Students Against Tyranny*. Wesleyan University Press published her book in English in 1970. Since then, a number of books, movies, and dramatic presentations have commemorated the group's sacrifice. One of the more recent is Frank McDonough's *Sophie Scholl: The Real Story of the Woman Who Defied Hitler*.

Conclusion

1. Quinn, Personal Journal, October 1969, excerpt included in email to author, 24 Oct. 2012.
2. Doctrine and Covenants, 134:2–5.
3. Freeman and Felt, *Saints at War*, 126–28.
4. King, *The Nazi State and the New Religions*, 224.
5. Ibid., 226.
6. "The Christian Science Journal Directory."
7. "Statistics: 2009 Report of Jehovah's Witnesses Worldwide."
8. "Facts and Statistics, Germany," Mormon Newsroom.

Bibliography

Archives and Manuscript Collections

BYU Archives are located in Provo, Utah.
LDS Archives are located in Salt Lake City.
Marriott Archives are located in Salt Lake City.

Bartsch, Hans-Jurgen Ingo. Interview by Matthew K. Heiss, Berlin, 8 Oct. 1991. LDS Archives.
Berndt, Dieter Hermann Erich. Interview by Matthew K. Heiss, Berlin, 7 Oct. 1991. LDS Archives.
Berndt, Otto Herman Willy. "Autobiography," n.d. LDS Archives.
Berndt, Otto, and Frieda M. Berndt. Interview by Douglas F. Tobler, Salt Lake City, 1–15 Oct. 1974. LDS Archives.
Blake, George R. "Autobiography," 1996. LDS Archives.
Blake, George R. Interview by Michael Van Wagenen, Provo, 8 Jan. 1992. BYU Archives.
Bleyl, Lorenzo Antinius. "A Legacy to Our Posterity," n.d. LDS Archives.
Bingham, Stanford M. Interview by Douglas F. Tobler and Alan F. Keele, Provo, Utah, 1974. LDS Archives.
Brimhall, Dean R., Papers. Marriott Archives.
Brodie, Fawn McKay, Papers. Marriott Archives.
Clarkana Papers of J. Reuben Clark, L. Tom Perry Special Collections, Harold B. Lee Library, Brigham Young University.
Clayson, Eli. Interview by Douglas F. Tobler, Provo, Utah, 9 Dec. 1985. LDS Archives.
Corbett, Donald Cecil. "Disaster Welfare in Germany," n.d., c.a. 1966. LDS Archives.
———. "Records from the Ruins," n.d., c.a. 1996. LDS Archives.
———. "Visit of Elder Ezra Taft Benson to Berlin, Germany, 1946," n.d., c.a. 1966. LDS Archives.
"Council Meeting, Jan. 25, 1940." George Albert Smith Papers, Marriott Archives.
East German Mission Manuscript History and Quarterly Reports (1938–57). LDS Archives.
East German Mission Office Files (1938–57). LDS Archives.
Gaeth, Arthur. Interview by Douglas F. Tobler, Denver, 19 Apr. 1980. LDS Archives.

Bibliography

German Mission Manuscript History (1852–55). LDS Archives.
German-Austrian Mission Manuscript History and Quarterly Reports (1925–38). LDS Archives.
Gillispie, J. Robert. Interview by Douglas F. Tobler, Provo, Utah, 9 Dec. 1985. LDS Archives.
Hamburg Branch Manuscript History (1918–19, 1961–). LDS Archives.
Heiss, Frank. Interview by Matthew K. Heiss, 9 Apr. 1987. LDS Archives.
Heller, Johannes Manfred. Interview by Matthew K. Heiss, Dresden, 13 Oct. 1991. LDS Archives.
"Helmuth Hübener Membership Record with Excommunication Notation." Hamburg District Record of Members. LDS Archives.
Henkel, Karl Friedrich. Interview by Matthew K. Heiss, Freiberg, 15 Oct. 1991. LDS Archives.
Herold, Johannes Emil. Interview by Matthew K. Heiss, Freiberg, 15 Oct. 1991. LDS Archives.
Kelling, Hans-Wilhelm Ludvig. Interview by Douglas F. Tobler, Salt Lake City, 1974. LDS Archives.
Kelly, Ralph S., and Connie Kelly Swan. "Philemon Merrill Kelly: A Collection of Memories," n.d. LDS Archives.
Kindt, Gabriele B. "Statistical Study: Emigration of German Members of the Church of Jesus Christ of Latter-Day Saints, 1945–62." Undergraduate paper, BYU, 1977. LDS Archives.
Klopfer, W. Herbert. "Childhood in the Big German City of Berlin: The Ravages of World War II. My Father's Life and Church Leadership," n.d., ca. 1980. LDS Archives.
———. "Escape to Freedom," n.d. LDS Archives.
———. "Fellowship With the Saints Through the Tune of a Hymn," n.d. LDS Archives.
———. "Reminiscenses," n.d. LDS Archives.
———. "Supplement to My Father's Experiencces in Esbjerg, Denmark," n.d. LDS Archives.
Kunkel, Gerhardt. Interview by Douglas F. Tobler and Alan F. Keele, Salt Lake City, 1974. LDS Archives.
Langheinrich, Paul. "Report of Procurement of Church Records, Films, and Photocopies," n.d., ca. 1960. LDS Archives.
Lehmann, Rudi Paul Willi. Interview by Matthew K. Heiss, Freiberg, 15 Oct. 1991. LDS Archives.
Lindsey, Ralph Mark. Interview by Matthew K. Heiss, Oakmont, Calif., 1991. LDS Archives.
Loeffler, Kurt Peter Max. Interview by Matthew K. Heiss, Berlin, 8 Oct. 1991. LDS Archives.
Loscher, John Peter. "Autobiography." Salt Lake City, 1976. LDS Archives.
Loscher, Johann Peter. Interview by Douglas F. Tobler, Provo, Utah, 22 Jan. 1975 (excerpts, 21–25). LDS Archives.
McKay, Thomas E. Papers, BYU Archives.
Meyer, Joachim. Interview by Matthew K. Heiss, Salt Lake City, 27 Feb. 1989. LDS Archives.

Bibliography

Morgan, Dale L. Papers. Marriott Archives.
Muller, Gerhard Rudolf Ernst. Interview by Matthew K. Heiss, Halle, Germany, 16 Jun. 1993. LDS Archives.
Murdock, Franklin J. Interview by Richard L. Jensen, Salt Lake City, 21–27 Mar. 1973. LDS Archives.
Panitsch, Michael and Mary. Interview by Douglas F. Tobler, Munich, 30 Mar. 1974. LSD Archives.
Petty, Donald M. Interview by Douglas F. Tobler, 6 Aug. 1985. LDS Archives.
Presiding Bishopric Financial, Statistical, and Historical Reports of Wards, Stakes, and Missions, 1884–1955. Provided by LDS Archives staff.
Quinn, D. Michael, Papers. Beinecke Rare Book & Manuscript Library, Yale University, New Haven, Conn.
Rees, Ida May Davis. "Diary of Ida May Davis Rees, 1937–39." LDS Archives.
Risenmay, George H., Diary. LDS Archives.
Ryser, Sterling. Interview by Douglas F. Tobler, 1975. LDS Archives.
Schiele, Walter Gerd. Interview by Matthew K. Heiss, Leipzig, 11 Oct. 1991. LDS Archives.
Schmidt, Arnold. "An Account of the Mormon Home in Wolfsgruen, 1945–47." LDS Archives.
Schult, Hans Gunter Erich. Interview by Matthew K. Heiss, Berlin, 7 Oct. 1991. LDS Archives.
Schult, Johannes Erich Michael. Interview by Matthew K. Heiss, Berlin, 12 Jun. 1993. LDS Archives.
Schwarz, Anna Marie to Rudi Wobbe, 5 Oct. 1987, in Appx. 2, Rudolf Gustav Wobbe oral history, interviewed by Matthew K. Heiss, Aug. 1988, LDS Archives.
Seeber, Helga. "Werden und Werken der Mormonen in Munchen." Undergraduate paper, Ludwig-Maximillian University, Feb. 1977. LDS Archives.
Sommerfeld, Marie. Interview by Douglas F. Tobler. Salt Lake City, 1974. LDS Archives.
Speidel, Walter A. Interview by Douglas F. Tobler, 1975. LDS Archives.
Speidel, Walter Hans. Interview with Jeff Anderson, Provo, Utah, Oct. 1985. LDS Archives.
Swiss and German Mission Manuscript History (1868–1898, 1904–25). LDS Archives.
Swiss Mission Manuscript History and Quarterly Reports (1939). LDS Archives.
Swiss-Austrian Mission Manuscript History and Quarterly Reports (1938–39). LDS Archives.
Swiss-German Mission Manuscript History and Quarterly Reports (1925–38). LDS Archives.
Thomas, Elbert D., Papers. Utah State Historical Society. Salt Lake City.
Warnke, Klaus Jurgen. Interview by Matthew K. Heiss, Frankfurt, 8 Sep. 1991. LDS Archives.
Welker, Roy Ansen. Interview by Richard L. Jensen, Star, Idaho, 2–3 Feb 1993. LDS Archives.
Welker, Roy Anson, Papers. LDS Archives.
Wenzel, Maja Busche. "How Was the Mormon Church in Germany Affected by Hitler's Rule?" Undergraduate paper, Brigham Young University, Nov. 18, 1982. LDS Archives.

Bibliography

West German Mission Manuscript History and Quarterly Reports (1938–1959). LDS Archives.
Winkler, Sigurd Kark Max. Interview by Matthew K. Heiss, Berlin, 13 Jun. 1993. LDS Archives.
Wunderlich, Jean. Interview by James B. Allen, Oram, Utah, 1972. LDS Archives.
Wobbe, Rudolph Gustav. Interview by Douglas F. Tobler and Alan F. Keele (1st interview), Salt Lake City, 1974. LDS Archives.
Wobbe, Rudolph Gustav. Interview by Matthew K. Heiss (2nd interview), Salt Lake City, 1988. LDS Archives.

Interviews with Author and Notes to Author

Babbel, Rhoda, daughter of Roy and Elizabeth Welker. Telephone interview with author, 25 May 2000.
"Inge." Interview with author, Salt Lake City, 1 Feb. 2006.
Keele, Alan F. Telephone interview with author, 23 May 2000.
Keele, Alan F., to author, 19 May 2012; 5 Apr. 2014.
Klopfer, W. Herbert. Interview with author, Salt Lake City, 19 Sep. 2006.
Kobs, Jared H. B. Interview with author, Sandy, Utah, 20 Jul. 2006.
Merrill, Vinton M. Telephone interview with author, 24 Jul. 2001.
Paldiel, Mordecai, Director, Department of the Righteous, Yad Vashem, to author, 4 Apr. 2000.
Quinn, D. Michael. Personal Journal. Excerpt emailed to author (unpublished).
Reschke, Horst. Interview with author, Riverton, Utah, 2 Feb. 2006.
Rogers, Thomas F. Telephone interviews with author, 23 May 2000 and 19 May 2012.
Schubert, Marko, to author, 7 May 2007, letter in my possession.
Tobler, Douglas F. Telephone inteview with author, 17 Jul. 2001.

All Other Sources

"A. C. Rees: S. L. Industrial Leader To Preside Over New German Division." *Deseret News*, 23 Jul. 1937.
Alder, Douglas D. "The German-Speaking Immigration to Utah 1850–1950." Master's thesis, University of Utah, 1959.
Alexander, Thomas G. *Mormonism in Transition: A History of the Latter-day Saints, 1890–1930*. Urbana: University of Illinois, 1996.
———. "The Word of Wisdom: From Principle to Requirement." *Dialogue Journal* 14-3 (Autumn 1981): 80–90.
Anderson, David A. "Huebener Against the Reich." Unpublished stage play, 1984.
Allen, James B., and Glen M. Leonard. *The Story of the Latter-day Saints*. Salt Lake City: Deseret, 1976.
Anderson, Jeffery L. "Brothers Across Enemy Lines: A Mission President and a German Soldier Correspond During World War I." *BYU Studies* 41-1 (2002): 127–39.

Bibliography

Anderson, Jeffery L. "Mormons and Germany, 1914–1933: A History of the Church of Jesus Christ of Latter-Day Saints and its Relationship with the German Governments from World War I to the Rise of Hitler." Master's thesis, Brigham Young University, 1991.

"An Original 1942 Letter from the Hotel Kaiserhof in Berlin to Reichsleiter Baldur Von Schirach in Wien." Kaisserhof Hotel Berlin Letter. USM Books. http://usmbooks.com/kaiserhof_schirach.html

Arendt, Hannah. *Eichmann in Jerusalem: A Report on the Banality of Evil*. New York: Viking, 1963.

"Arthur Zander, Obituary." *Deseret News*, 4 Jun. 1989.

Arrington, Leonard J. *Adventures of a Church Historian*. Urbana: University of Illinois, 1998.

———. "An Economic Interpretation of the Word of Wisdom." *BYU Studies* 1 (1959): 37–49.

———. *Great Basin Kingdom: An Economic History of the Latter-day Saints, 1830–1900*. 2nd ed. Lincoln: University of Nebraska, 1968.

Axis History Factbook. http://www.axishistory.com/.

Babbel, Frederick W. *On Wings of Faith: My Daily Walk with a Prophet*. Salt Lake City: Bookcraft, 1972.

Bacque, James. *Crimes and Mercies: The Fate of German Civilians under Allied Occupation, 1944–1950*. Toronto: Little, Brown and Co., 1997.

Barth, Fredrick H. *Guided and Guarded: German War-Corporal Turns to Mormonism*. Salt Lake City: Self-published, 1981.

Bartoletti, Susan Campbell. *The Boy Who Dared: A Novel Based on the True Story of a Hitler Youth*. New York: Scholastic, 2008.

Basket-Ball: Die Olympischen Spiele in Berlin und Garmish-Partenkirchen 1936. Hamburg, 1936.

Baugh, Alexander L. "A Call to Arms: The 1838 Mormon Defense of Northern Missouri." Ph.D. dissertation, Brigham Young University, 1996.

Baugh, Alexander L. "Joseph Young's Affidavit of the Massacre at Haun's Mill." *BYU Studies* 38–1 (1999): 188–202.

Beard, Mary R. *Women as a Force in History: A Study in Traditions and Realities*. New York: Collier, 1971.

Bednar, David A. "The Hearts of the Children Shall Turn." *Ensign* (Oct. 2011).

Beevor, Anthony. *Berlin: The Downfall, 1945*. London: Viking, 2002.

Bell, William S. "Miracle on the Vistula: The Founding of the Church of Jesus Christ of Latter-Day Saints in Poland." Student Religious Studies Symposium, Brigham Young University, Provo, 2001.

Bennett, Richard S. "All Germany Will Fast." *Millennial Star* 95 (28 Sep. 1933): 638–39.

Bennion, Glenn. "New Ways of Proselyting and the Reason Therefor." *Deseret News*, 25 Jan. 1936.

Benson, Lee, and Doug Robinson. *Trials and Triumphs: Mormons in the Olympic Games*. Salt Lake City: Deseret, 1992.

Benson, Ezra T. "Letter from Elder Ezra Taft Benson." *Improvement Era* (May 1946): 287.

———. "Special Mission to Europe." *Relief Society Magazine* (May 1947): 293–94.
———. "Be True to the Faith." *Improvement Era* (Dec. 1955): 949–50.
Berson, Robin Kadison. *Young Heroes in World History*. Westport, Conn.: Greenwood, 1999.
Bickerstaff, George. "Guarded by Grace." *This People* (Apr. 1992): 38–39.
Bitton, Davis. "Ten Years in Camelot: A Personal Memoir." *Dialogue Journal* 16–3 (Autumn 1983): 9–19.
Blake, Stanley, to Horst Reschke, 23 May 1982. Letter in author's possession.
Bock, Gisela. "Antinatalism, Maternity and Paternity in National Socialist Racism." In *Nazism and German Society*, edited by David F. Crews, 121–28. London: Routledge, 1994.
Boone, David F. "The Evacuation of Missionaries at the Outbreak of World War II." In *Regional Studies in Latter-day Saint History*. Mormon History Association, 35th Annual Meeting, Aalborg, Denmark, Jun. 2000.
———. "The Evacuation of the Czechoslovak and German Missions at the Outbreak of World War II." *BYU Studies* 40–3 (2001): 122–54.
———. "The Worldwide Evacuation of Latter-day Saint Missionaries at the Outbreak of World War II." Master's thesis, Brigham Young University, 1981.
Boone, David F., and Richard O. Cowan. "The Freiberg Germany Temple: A Latter-day Miracle." In *Regional Studies in Latter-day Saint Church History: Europe*, edited by Donald Q. Cannon and Brent L. Top. Provo, Utah: Brigham Young University, 2003.
Botting, Douglas. *From the Ruins of the Reich: Germany, 1945–1949*. New York: New American, 1986.
Braun, Hans-Joachim. *The German Economy in the Twentieth Century*. London: Routledge, 1990.
Bringhurst, Newell G. *Fawn McKay Brodie: A Biographer's Life*. Norman: University of Oklahoma Press, 1999.
———. "Fawn Brodie and Her Quest for Independence." *Dialogue Journal* 22–2 (Summer 1989): 79–95.
———, ed. *Reconsidering No Man Knows My History: Fawn M. Brodie and Joseph Smith in Retrospect*. Logan, Utah: Utah State, 1996.
Broadbent, Thomas L. "The Salt Lake Beobachter; Mirror of an Immigration." *Utah Historical Quarterly* 26 (Oct. 1958): 329–52.
Brodie, Fawn McKay. *No Man Knows My History: The Life of Joseph Smith*. New York: Knopf, 1945.
Brokaw, Tom. *The Greatest Generation*. New York: Random House, 1998.
Brooks, Juanita. *History of the Jews in Utah and Idaho*. Salt Lake City: Western Epics, 1973.
Budge, Oliver. *My Story*. Privately published, n.d., ca. 1950. Copy in LDS Archives.
Bullock, Alan. *Hitler, A Study in Tyranny*. New York: Bantam, 1958.
Bushman, Richard L. "The Crisis in Europe and Hugh B. Brown's First Mission Presidency." *Dialogue Journal* 21–2 (Summer 1988): 51–60.
Bushman, Richard L., and Jed Woodworth. *Joseph Smith: Rough Stone Rolling*. New York: Knopf, 2005.
Bytwerk, Randall. "The Party Rally of Honor (1936)." *German Propaganda Archive: Calvin College*. http://www.calvin.edu/academic/cas/gpa/pt36.htm.

Bibliography

"BYU Drama: Mormons Caught in Nazi Toils." *Salt Lake Tribune*, 3 Oct. 1976.

"BYU to Dramatize Mormon vs. Nazis." *Deseret News*, 2 Oct. 1976.

Cannon, Donald Q. "The King Follett Discourse: Joseph Smith's Greatest Sermon in Historical Perspective." *BYU Studies* 18–2 (1978): 179–92.

Carlson, Elof A. *The Unfit: the History of a Bad Idea*. Cold Spring Harbor, N.Y.: Lab Press, 2001.

Carter, Steven E. "The Mormons in the Third Reich, 1933–1946." Ph.D. dissertation, University of Arkansas, 2003.

Chandler, Neal. "Appeal to a Lower Court." *Sunstone* 14–6 (Dec. 1992): 27–50.

Chatecism of the Catholic Church. United States Conference of Catholic Bishops.

"The Christian Science Journal Directory: Churches and Societies." http://goo.gl/B5RUdG.

Church Handbook of Instructions: Book 1, Stake Presidencies and Bishoprics. Salt Lake City: The Church of Jesus Christ of Latter-day Saints, 1989.

Clark, Dale. "Mormonism in the New Germany." *Deseret News*, 9 Dec. 1933.

Clark, J. Reuben, to Herbert Hoover. Herbert Hoover Presidential Library, West Branch, Iowa.

Condie, Dorothea Spech. "Let's Follow Dad—He Holds the Priesthood." In *Behind the Iron Curtain: Recollections of Latter-day Saints in East Germany, 1945–1989*, edited by Gordon N. Davis and Norma S. Davis. Provo, Utah: Brigham Young University, 2000.

Conference Reports. Salt Lake City: LDS Church, 1917, 8 Apr. 1917.

Crew, David F. *Nazism and German Society, 1933–1945, Rewriting Histories*. London: Routledge, 1994.

Das Deutsche Reich und der Zweite Weltkrieg. 16 vols. Stuttgart: Deutsche Verlags-Anstalt, 2008.

"Der Dank des Kaisers." *Der Stern*, 1 Feb. 1918.

"Der Staat im Staate." *Völkischer Beobachter*, 22 Nov. 1938.

Deseret News. *1999–2000 Church Almanac*. Salt Lake City: Deseret, 1999.

Dew, Sheri L. *Ezra Taft Benson: A Biography*. Salt Lake City: Deseret, 1989.

Dewey, Richard Lloyd. *Hübener vs. Hitler: A Biography of Helmuth Hübener, Mormon Teenage Resistance Leader*. Provo, Utah: Academic Research Foundation, 2003.

Dickson, Mary. "Utah's Huebener: A Brilliant, Powerful Work." *Salt Lake Tribune*, 17 Oct. 1976

Directory of Newspapers and Periodicals. Philadelphia: W. Ayer & Son, Inc., 1936.

Dixon, Joseph M. "Mormons in the Third Reich 1933–45." *Dialogue Journal* 7–1 (1972): 70–78.

Dodd, William Edward, and Martha Dodd, eds. *Ambassador Dodd's Diary, 1933–1938*. New York: Harcourt Brace, 1941.

Douglas, R. M. *Orderly and Humane. The Expulsion of the Germans after the Second World War*. New Haven: Yale, 2012.

"Dr. and Mrs. Kelly Are Transferred to Berlin." *St. Anthony News*, 9 Sep. 1937.

"East German Mission Head Named." *Deseret News*, 20 Jul. 1946.

"Editorials: Alfred Cornelius Rees." *Deseret News*, 29 Jul. 1941.

"Editorials: Elder A. C. Rees Honored." *Deseret News*, 6 Jul. 1937.

Ehrenreich, Eric. *The Nazi Proof of Genealogy, Race Science, and the Final Solution*. Bloomington: University of Indiana, 2007.

Bibliography

"Ein aufklärender Brief." *Der Stern*, 14 Jul. 1933.
"Elder A. C. Rees Honored." *Deseret News*, 6 Jul. 1937.
"Elder Benson Reports Second Berlin Shipment." *Deseret News*, 2 Nov. 1946.
"Elder Benson Tells Story of Church Welfare in Germany." *Deseret News*, 6 Jul. 1946.
"Emigration." *Der Stern* 84 (1958): 343–46.
Encyclopedia of Mormonism: The History, Scripture, Doctrine, and Procedure of the Church of Jesus Christ of Latter-day Saints, edited by Daniel H. Ludlow. 4 vols. New York: Macmillan, 1992.
"Ernest Bamberger Chosen Republican Senatorial Nominee." *Deseret News*, 15 Jul. 1922.
"Ernest Bamberger Loses in Utah Senate Race." *Jewish Telegraph Agency: Jewish News Archive*, 8 Nov. 1928.
"European Mission Presidents Hold Conference." *Deseret News*, 16 Jul. 1938.
"Europe War Scares Discounted; L.D.S. Officers tell of Nazi Desire to Prevent Strife." *Salt Lake Tribune*, 8 Sep. 1937.
"Facts and Statistics, Germany." Mormon Newsroom. http://www.mormonnewsroom.org/facts-and-statistics/country/germany.
Finck. "Feldpostbrief." *Der Stern*, 15 Sep. 1917.
"First Church Welfare Supplies Reach Members in Berlin Area." *Deseret News*, 26 Oct. 1946.
Fischer, Klaus P. *Nazi Germany: A New History*. New York: Continuum, 1995.
Flake, Kathleen. *The Politics of American Religious Identity: The Seating of Senator Reed Smoot, Mormon Apostle*. Chapel Hill: University of North Carolina, 2004.
"Former Missionary Returns to Mission as Army Officer." *Deseret News*, 24 Nov. 1945.
Foster, Michael J. "Judge May Lose Sports Job; Boycott Forces to Carry On—Fund Block Hinted." *Deseret News*, 7 Dec. 1935.
Fox, Frank W. *J. Reuben Clark: The Public Years*. Provo, Utah: Brigham Young University, 1980.
Freeman, Robert C., and Dennis A. Wright. *Saints at War: Experiences of Latter-day Saints in World War II*. American Fork, Utah: Covenant, 2001.
Freeman, Robert C., and Jon R. Felt. *German Saints at War*. Springville, Utah: Cedar Fort, 2008.
Friedländer, Saul. *Nazi Germany and the Jews: The Years of Persecution, 1933–39*. New York: HarperCollins, 1997.
Gaeth, Arthur. "About German Inflation." *Deseret News*, 2 Nov. 1935.
"German Democratic Republic to Welcome Missionary Work." *Ensign* (Jan. 1989): 74–75.
"Germany Holds M. I. A. 'Echo of Joy' Festival." *Deseret News*, 18 Jul. 1936.
"Germany to Send Broadcast to Utah: Church Leaders to Speak." *Deseret News*, 19 Aug. 1939.
Gould, Alan. "Olympic Boycott Faction Will Continue to Fight Against U.S. Participation." *Deseret News*, 9 Dec. 1935.
Grunberger, Richard. *The 12-Year Reich: A Social History of Nazi Germany, 1933–1945*. New York: Ballantine, 1971.
Gray, Wendy, and Robert Knight Barney. "Devotion to Whom?: German-American Loyalty on the Issue of Participation in the 1936 Olympic Games." *Journal of Sports History* 17-2 (Summer 1990): 214–31.

Bibliography

"Gripping, True Drama Relates Terror of Nazi Tyrrany in Original BYU Play." *Provo Herald*, 3 Oct. 1976.
Guenther, Irene. *Nazi Chic: Fashioning Women in Nazi Germany*. New York: Berg, 2004.
Hanfstaengl, Ernst. *Unheard Witness*. Philadelphia: Lippincott, 1957.
Hale, Steve. "Prisoners of Conscience." *Utah Holiday* (May 1985): 52.
Hall, Bruce W. "And the Last Shall Be First: The LDS Church in the German Democratic Republic." Mormon History Association, 35th Annual Meeting, Aalborg, Denmark, Jun. 2000.
———. "Gemeindegeschichte Als Vergleichende Geschichte: The Church of Jesus Christ of Latter-Day Saints in East Germany 1945–1989." Master's thesis, Brigham Young University, 1998.
———. "Render until Caesar: State, Identity and Minority Churches in the German Democratic Republic, 1945–1989." Ph.D. dissertation, State University of New York–Buffalo, 2003.
Hansen, Klaus J. "Growing up in Hitler's Germany." *Queen's Quarterly* 103–1 (1996): 73–85.
———. "Under Kaiser and Führer: The Story of a Mormon Family." *The Third Eye: The Canadian Journal of Mormon Studies* 1–1 (1996): 14–30.
Hart-Davis, Duff. *Hitler's Games*. New York: Harper & Row, 1986.
Häsler, Alfred A. *The Lifeboat Is Full: Switzerland and the Refugees, 1933–1945*. New York: Funk & Wagnalls, 1969.
"Havana Called Waiting Room for Refugees." *New York Herald Tribune*, 13 May 1941.
"Heart Attack Causes Death of A. C. Rees: Became Known as LDS and Business Leader." *Salt Lake Tribune*, 27 Jul. 1941.
Heiss, M. "Online Review: The Boy Who Dared." *Amazon Prime*, 24 Oct. 2011.
Helmreich, Ernst Christian. *The German Churches Under Hitler: Background, Struggle, and Epilogue*. Detroit: Wayne State, 1979.
Hesse, Hans. "Foreword." In *Persecution and Resistance of Jehovah's Witnesses During the Nazi Regime, 1933–1945*, edited by Hans Hesse. Chicago: Courier, 2001.
Heston, Leonard L., Renate Heston, and Albert Speer. *The Medical Casebook of Adolf Hitler: His Illnesses, Doctors, and Drugs*. New York: Cooper Square, 2000.
Hillel, Marc, and Clarissa Henry. *Of Pure Blood*. New York: Pocket Books, 1978.
"History of the Association." *Utah Taxpayers Association: Your Tax Watchdog*. www.utahtaxpayers.org.
"Hitler Appeals for Warm Clothing for Eastern Front." *World War II Today*. http://ww2today.com/20th-december-1941-hitler-appeals-for-warm-clothing-for-eastern-front-troops
"Hitler's Master Race." ABC News documentary, televised 26 Apr. 2000.
Hollister, Ovando James. *Life of Schuyler Colfax*. New York: Funk & Wagnalls, 1886.
Holmes, Blair R., and Alan F. Keele. *When Truth Was Treason: German Youth against Hitler*. Urbana: University of Illinois, 1995.
Holmes, Judith. *Olympiad 1936: Blaze of Glory for Hitler's Reich*. New York: Ballantine, 1971.
Holocaust Education and Archive Research Team. www.holocaustresearchproject.org.
Holocaust Encyclopedia. United States Holocaut Memorial Museum. www.ushmm.org.

Holzapfel, Richard Neitzel. "Friends Again: Canadian Grain and the German Saints." *JMH* 23–2 (Fall 1997): 46–76.
Holzapfel, Richard Neitzel, and Marc Alain Bohn. "A Long-Awaited Visit: President Heber J. Grant in Switzerland and Germany, 1937." *BYU Studies* 42, 3–4 (2003): 4–20.
"Huebener Group Lauded in Hamburg." *Sunstone* 10–2 (March 1985): 48–49.
"Huebener's Message Haunts Memories in Remarkable Drama." *BYU Today* (Nov. 1976).
Hutchison, E. P. *Immigrants and Their Children: A Volume in the Census Monograph Series.* New York: John Wiley & Sons, 1956.
Jehovah's Witnesses, Victims of the Nazi Era. Washington, D.C.: U.S. Holocaust Memorial Museum, 1995.
Jewish News Archive. Jewish Telegraph Agency. http://archive.jta.org.
Jewish Virtual Library. http://www.jewishvirtuallibrary.org.
Johnson, Jeffery Ogden. "Determining and Defining 'Wife': The Brigham Young Households." *Dialogue Journal* 20–3 (Fall 1987): 57–72.
Johnson, Eric A. *Nazi Terror: The Gestapo, Jews, and Ordinary Germans.* New York: Basic Books, 1999.
Jordan, Jennifer A. *Structures of Memory: Understanding Urban Change in Berlin and Beyond.* Palo Alto: Stanford University Press, 2006.
Journal of Discourses. 26 vols. London: LDS Book Depot, 1854–86.
Keele, Alan F. "A Latter-day Saint in Hitler's SS: The True Story of a Mormon Youth Who Joined and Defected from the Infamous *Schutzstaffel.*" *BYU Studies* 42, 3–4 (2003): 21–18.
Keele, Alan F., and Douglas F. Tobler. "The Führer's New Clothes: Helmuth Hübener and the Mormons in the Third Reich." *Sunstone* 25 (Nov.–Dec. 1980): 20–29.
Kempe, Frederick. *Father/Land: A Personal Search for the New Germany.* New York: G.P. Putnam's Sons, 1999.
Kershaw, Ian. *Hitler, 1936–45: Nemesis:* New York: Norton, 2000.
———. *The Hitler Myth: Image and Reality in the Third Reich.* Oxford: Oxford University Press, 1987.
King, Christine Elizabeth. *The Nazi State and the New Religions: Five Case Studies in Non-Conformity.* New York: Mellen, 1982.
———. "New Religious Movements: A Perspective for Understanding Society." In *Studies in Religion and Society*, vol. 3, edited by Eileen Barker. New York: Mellen Press, 1982.
———. "Some Lesser-Known Victims of Totalitarian Persecution." *Patterns of Prejudice* 16–2 (1982): 15–26.
———. "Strategies for Survival: Sectarian Experience in the Third Reich." In *Of Gods and Men: New Religious Movements in the West. Proceedings of the 1981 Conference of the British Sociological Association Sociology of Religion Study Group.* Macon, Ga.: Mercer University Press, 1981.
———. "Strategies for Survival: An Examination of the History of Five Christian Sects in Germany 1933–45." *Journal of Contemporary History* 14–2 (1979): 211–34.
Kirkham, James M. "Record Keeping in Germany." *Deseret News,* 16 Jul. 1938.
Klopfer, W. Herbert. "Enemy Soldier in the Pulpit." *Ensign* (Jun. 1990): 59–60.

Bibliography

Kobs, Jared H. B. "WW II 1939–1945—Unforgettable Days at 'The Gates of Hell.'" Unpublished memoir, n.d., ca. 2000.

Krueger, Arnd. akrueger@gwdg.de, "REPLY: 1936 'Nazi' Olympics." In H-ARETE, 22 Apr. 2000. https://www.h-net.org/~arete/

Kuehne, Raymond M. "The Frieberg Temple—an Unexpected Legacy of a Communist State and a Faithful People." *Dialogue Journal* 37-2 (Summer 2004): 95–131.

———. *Henry Burkhardt and LDS Realpolitik in Communist East Germany*. Salt Lake City: University of Utah Press, 2011.

———. *Mormons As Citizens of a Communist State: A Documentary History of the Church of Jesus Christ of Latter-day Saints in East Germany, 1945–1990*. Salt Lake City: University of Utah Press, 2010.

Kolb, Eberhart. *The Weimar Republic*. Translated by P. S. Falla. London: Unwin Hyman, 1988.

Koonz, Claudia. *Mothers in the Fatherland: Women, the Family, and Nazi Politics*. New York: St. Martin's Press, 1987.

Larson, Gustive O. "The Story of the Perpetual Emigration Fund." *The Mississippi Valley Historical Review* 18-2 (Sep. 1931): 184–94.

Lepage, Jean-Denis *Hitler Youth, 1922–1945: An Illustrated History*. Jefferson, N.C.: McFarland, 2009.

Madison, R. Ben. "National Socialist and Social Idealists: The RLDS Church in Nazi Germany, 1933–1945." *John Whitmer Historical Association Journal* 16 (1996): 16–30.

Mallmann, Klaus-Michael, and Gerhard Paul. "Omniscient, Omnipotent, Omnipresent? Gestapo, Society, and Resistance." In *Nazism and German Society*, edited by David F. Crews. London: Routledge, 1994.

Mandell, Richard D. *The Nazi Olympics*. New York: McMillian, 1971.

Mangum, Garth, and Bruce Blumell. *The Mormons' War on Poverty: A History of LDS Welfare, 1830–1990*. Salt Lake City: University of Utah, 1993.

Mann, Galo. *Reminiscences and Reflections: A Youth in Germany*. New York: Norton, 1990.

Massaquoi, Hans J. *Destined to Witness: Growing Up Black in Nazi Germany*. New York: Morrow, 1999.

Matheson, Peter. *The Third Reich and the Christian Churches*. Grand Rapids: W. B. Eerdmans, 1981.

Mauss, Armand L. *All Abraham's Children: Changing Mormon Conceptions of Race and Lineage*. Urbana: University of Illinois, 2003.

———. "Mormon Semitism and Anti-Semitism." *Sociological Analysis* 29-1 (Spring 1968): 11–27.

McConkie, Bruce R. *Mormon Doctrine*. 2nd ed. Salt Lake City: Bookcraft, 1966.

McCue, Robert J. "Did the Word of Wisdom Become a Commandment in 1851?" *Dialogue Journal* 14 (Autumn 1981): 66–77.

McDonough, Frank. *Sophie Scholl: The Real Story of the Woman Who Defied Hitler*. Charleston, S.C.: History, 2009.

McFarland, Rick, and Matt Whitaker. *Truth & Conviction: The Helmuth Hübener Story*. DVD. Salt Lake City: Covenant, 2002.

McLaws, Monte B. "The Attempted Assassination of Missouri's Ex-Governor, Lilburn W. Boggs." *Missouri Historical Review* 60-1 (Oct. 1965): 50–62.

Meinig, D. W. "The Mormon Culture Region: Strategies and Patterns in the Geography of the American West, 1847–1964." *Annals of the Association of American Geographers* 55-2 (June 1965): 191–220.

Melich, Nancy. "A Story Worth Telling and a Satisfying Play." *Salt Lake Tribune*, 13 Feb. 1984.

———. "BYU's Huebener Plays it Safe with Tough Play." *Salt Lake Tribune*, 8 Apr. 1992.

———. "New Play Treats Life of Helmuth Huebener, a German Youth Who Gave His Life for the Truth." *Salt Lake Tribune*, 5 Feb. 1984.

Merrill, Milton R. *Reed Smoot: Apostle in Politics, Western Experience*. Logan: Utah State, 1990.

Merten, Ulrich. *Forgotten Voices: The Expulsion of the Germans from Eastern Europe after World War II*. New Brunswick, N.J.: Transaction, 2012.

Milton, Sybil. "Jehovah's Witnesses as Forgotten Victims." In *Persecution and Resistance of Jehovah's Witnesses During the Nazi Regime, 1933–1945*, edited by Hans Hesse. Chicago: Courier, 2001.

Minert, Roger P. *"In Harm's Way: East German Latter-day Saints in World War II*. Provo, Utah: Brigham Young University, 2009.

———. *Under the Gun: West German and Austrian Latter-day Saints in World War II*. Provo, Utah: Brigham Young University, 2011.

Mitchelle, Michael. "The Mormons in Wilhelmine Germany, 1870–1914. Making a Place for an Unwanted American Religion in a Changing German Society." Master's thesis, Brigham Young University, 1974.

Mitsen, Hannah L. "The King-Havenner Bill of 1940: Dashed Hopes for a Jewish Immigration Haven in Alaska." *Alaska History* 14 (Spring–Fall 1999): 23–32.

Monson, Thomas S. *Faith Rewarded: A Personal Account of Prophetic Promises to the East German Saints*. Salt Lake City: Deseret, 1996.

Montague, Terry Bohle. *Mine Angels Round About: Mormon Missionary Evacuation from Western Germany, 1939*. 2nd ed. Orem, Utah: Granite, 2000.

Mulder, William. *Homeward to Zion: The Mormon Migration from Scandinavia*. Minneapolis: University of Minnesota, 2000.

Names in Stone Cemetery Maps. Orem, Utah: Gateway Mapping Company. http://www.namesinstone.com.

Nelson, David C. "The Hübener Syndrome: How Mormons Remember Church History in Nazi Germany." Mormon History Association, 35th Annual Meeting, Aalborg, Denmark, Jun. 2000.

Nelson, Russell M. "A New Harvest Time." *Ensign* (May 1998).

Nibley, Preston R. "The East German Mission." *Relief Society Magazine* (Aug. 1956): 512–13.

Norling, Bernard. *The Nazi Impact on a German Village*. Lexington: University Press of Kentucky, 1993.

Oaks, Dallin. "Alternate Voices." *Ensign* (May 1989).

"Obituary: Rulon Wieter Jenkins." *Deseret News*, 30 May 1992.

"Obituary: Rulon Wieter Jenkins." *Social Security Death Index*, 30 May 1992. http://search.ancestry.com/search/db.aspx?dbid=3693.

"Obituary: Zora LeSieur Galli Newman." *Deseret News*, 31 Jan. 2003.

Bibliography

"Official Report of the First Germany, Austria, Holland, Italy, Switzerland, France, Belgium, and Spain Area General Conference of the LDS Church." 24–26 Aug. 1973: III (primary source).

Oleschinski, Brigitt. *Plötzensee Memorial Center*. Berlin: German Resistance Memorial Center, 1996.

Ollerton, Fay. "A Visit to the German-Austrian Mission." *Deseret News*, 21 Oct. 1933.

Organisationskomitee für die XI. Olympiade Berlin 1936 E.V. *The XIth Olympic Games, Berlin, 1936: Official Report*. Vol. II. Berlin: Limpert, 1936.

Ostling, Richard N., and Joan K. Ostling. *Mormon America: The Power and the Promise*. San Francisco: Harper, 1999.

Overmans, Rüdiger. *Deutsche militärische Verluste im Zweiten Weltkrieg*. Munich: Oldenberg, 2000

Pearson, Howard. "Huebener Moving, Powerful New Drama." *Deseret News*, 8 Oct. 1976.

Peck, Elbert Eugene. "The Origin and Evolution of the Sunstone Species." *Sunstone* 115 (Dec. 1999): 13.

Peifer, Douglas C. "Commoration of Mutiny, Rebellion, and Resistance in Postwar Germany: Public Memory, History, and the Formation of 'Memory Beacons.'" *The Journal of Military History* 65–4 (Oct. 2001): 1015n10.

Peterson, Robert, *The Boy Scouts: An American Adventure*. New York: American Heritage, 1984.

Penton, M. James. *Jehovah's Witnesses and the Third Reich: Sectarian Politics under Persecution*. Toronto: University of Toronto Press, 2004.

Peukert, Detlev. *Inside Nazi Germany: Conformity, Opposition, and Racism in Everyday Life*. New Haven: Yale, 1987.

———. *The Weimar Republic: The Crisis of Classical Modernity*. Translated by Richard Daveson. New York: Hill and Wang, 1989.

Polk's Salt Lake City Directory. Southfield, Mich.: R. L. Polk & Company, 1952–1975 editions.

Porter, Marlow Rich. *Impressions of the German Mission 55 Years Ago: From the Journal of M. Rich Porter, Former President of Swiss-German Mission*. Salt Lake City: Privately published, 1960.

Powell, Allan Kent. "The Jewish Community in Utah." In *Utah History Encyclopedia*. http://www.uen.org/utah_history_encyclopedia/

"President Grant in Frankfurt Germany." *Deseret News*, 7 Aug. 1937.

Prince, Gregory A. "The Red Peril, the Candy Maker, and the Apostle: David O. McKay's Confrontation with Communism." *Dialogue Journal* 37-2 (Summer 1994): 37–94.

Pugmire, Ruth Welker, and Rhoda Babbel. *Roy Anson Welker and Elizabeth Hoge: Their History*. Logan, Utah: Privately published, LDS Archives, 1987.

Purple Triangles. VHS Tape. Brooklyn, N.Y.: Watchtower Bible and Tract Society, 1991.

Quinn, D. Michael. *Elder Statesman: A Biography of J. Reuben Clark*. Salt Lake City: Signature, 2002.

———. "Ezra Taft Benson and Mormon Political Conflicts." *Dialogue Journal* 26-2 (1992): 1–87.

———. *J. Reuben Clark: The Church Years*. Provo, Utah: Brigham Young University, 1983.

———. "A Marketplace of Ideas, A House of Faith, and a Prison of Conformity." *Sunstone* 64 (March 1988): 6–7.

———. *The Mormon Hierarchy: Extensions of Power*. Salt Lake City: Signature, 1997.

———. *The Mormon Hierarchy: Origins of Power*. Salt Lake City: Signature, 1994.

———. "LDS Church Authority and New Plural Marriages, 1890–1904." *Dialogue Journal* 18–1 (Spring 1985): 9–105.

Rauschning, Hermann. *Gespräch Mit Hitler*. New York: Europa, 1940.

Rees, Alfred C. "Im Lande Der Mormonen." *Völkischer Boebachter*, 14 Apr. 1939.

"Refugee Ship Sails from Cuba, then Anchors; May Go Back: Americans Reported Intervening to Let Jews In." *New York Herald Tribune*, 3 Jun. 1939.

"Religious Movements in the West." In *Proceedings of the 1981 Conference of the British Sociological Association, Sociology of Religion Study Group*. Macon, Ga.: Mercer University Press, 1981.

Rempel, Gerhard. *Hitler's Children: The Hitler Youth and the SS*. Chapel Hill: University of North Carolina Press, 1989.

"Report of the Semiannual General Conference of the LDS Church, October, 1937." Salt Lake City, Utah.

Reschke, Horst. "Scouting in Nazi Germany: A Mormon Family's Experience." *Der Blumenbaum: Sacramento German Genealogy Society* 21–4 (Apr.–Jun. 2004): 162

———. "He Understoood." Unpublished memoir, n.d.

———. *Max: A West Prussian Odyssey*. Salt Lake City: Privately published, 1998.

———. "There but for the Grace of God." Lecture, University of Utah, n.d., ca. 1998.

——— to Ismar Schorsch, 11 Jan. 1993. Letter in author's possession.

——— to Stanley Blake, 25 Apr. 1982. Letter in author's possession.

———. "Would You Forget? An Explanation on Horst Reschke's Comments Above." *Der Blumenbaum: The Sacramento German Genealogical Society Journal* 20–4 (Apr.–Jun. 2003): 173.

Rinderle, Walter, and Bernard Norling. *The Nazi Impact on a German Village*. Lexington: University Press of Kentucky, 1993.

Roberts, B. H. *A Comprehensive History of the Church of Jesus Christ of Latter-Day Saints, Century I*. Salt Lake City: Deseret, 1930.

———. *Studies of the Book of Mormon*, edited by Brigham D. Madsen. Urbana: University of Illinois Press, 1985.

Roberts, David. *Devil's Gate: Brigham Young and the Mormon Handcart Tragedy*. New York: Simon & Schuster, 2008.

Rogers, Thomas F. *Huebener and Other Plays*. Salt Lake City: Poor Robert's, 1992.

Rosenthal, Michael. *The Character Factory: Baden Powell and the Origins of the Boy Scout Movement*. London: Collins, 1986.

Sander, Ulrich. "Helmuth Hübener Gruppe." In *Streiflichter aus dem Hamburger Widerstand 1933–1945*, edited by Ursel Horchmuth and Gerhard Meyer. Frankfurt: Roderberg Verlag, 1969.

———. *Jugend Widerstand im Krieg: Die Helmuth-Hübener-Gruppe, 1941–1942*. Bonn: Paul-Krgenste in Verlag Nach Folger GmbH, 2002.

Bibliography

Schafft, Gretchen E. *From Racism to Genocide: Anthropology in the Third Reich.* Urbana: University of Illinois, 2004.

Scharffs, Gilbert W. "The Branch That Wouldn't Die." *Ensign* (Apr. 1971): 30–33.

———. *Mormonism in Germany; A History of the Church of Jesus Christ of Latter-Day Saints in Germany between 1840 and 1970.* Salt Lake City: Deseret, 1970.

Schnibbe, Karl-Heinz, Alan F. Keele, and Douglas F. Tobler. *The Price: The True Story of a Mormon Who Defied Hitler.* Salt Lake City: Bookcraft, 1984.

Scholtz-Klink, Gertrud. *Die Frau im Dritten Reich.* Tübingen: Grabert, 1978.

Seisser, Hanjo. "Shedding Light on a Dark Past: German Nazi Hunter Ulrich Sander has Never Let Go." *Atlantic Times,* Jan. 2009. http://www.atlantic-times.com/archive_detail.php?recordID=1619.

Sessions, Gene Allred. *Prophesying Upon the Bones: J. Reuben Clark and the Foreign Debt Crisis, 1933–39.* Urbana: University of Illinois, 1992.

Shirer, William L. *The Rise and Fall of the Third Reich.* New York: Simon & Schuster, 1960.

Sinti and Roma: Victims of the Nazi Era. Washington, D.C.: United States Holocaust Memorial Museum.

Smith, D. Brent. "LDS Pioneers in Post–World War II Germany, Both East and West." Mormon History Association, 31st Annual Meeting, Snowbird, Utah, Jun. 1996.

Smith, Joseph Fielding, ed. *Teachings of the Prophet Joseph Smith.* Salt Lake City: Deseret, 1938.

Smoot, Reed. "Ein Freund von Deutschland." *Der Stern,* 1 Mar. 1935.

"The South American Mission." *Ensign,* Feb. 1975. https://www.lds.org/ensign/1975/02/the-south-american-mission?lang=eng

Speer, Albert. *Inside the Third Reich.* New York: Simon & Schuster, 1970.

Stachura, P. D. "The National Socialist *Machtergreifung* and the German Youth Movement: Co-ordination and Reorganization, 1933–34." *Journal of European Studies* 5 (1975): 255–72.

Standard Rate & Data Service, Newspaper Section 18–5. Chicago: B & B Service Corp., 1936.

"The State University: The Twenty-ninth Annual Commencement Exercises; J. Reuben Clark's Masterly Effort." *Salt Lake Herald,* 16 Jun. 1898.

"Statement on Symposia." *Deseret News,* 31 Aug. 1991.

Stark, Rodney, and Reid Larkin Neilson. *The Rise of Mormonism.* New York: Columbia University Press, 2005.

"Statistics: 2009 Report of Jehovah's Witnesses Worldwide." http://www.watchtower.org/statistics/worldwide_report.htm.

Stern, Norton B. "The Founding of the Jewish Community in Utah." *Western States Jewish Historical Quarterly* 8–1 (Oct. 1975): 65–69.

Stone, Andrea. "Mormon Baptism Targets Anne Frank—Again." *Huffington Post,* 21 Feb. 2012.

Strong, Leon M. "A History of the Young Men's Mutual Improvement Association: 1875–1938." Master's thesis, Brigham Young University, 1939.

"Suez Must Not be Another Singapore: What Reason Can There be NOW for the British Government Not to Create a Jewish Army in the Middle East?" *New York Herald Tribune,* 28 Feb. 1942.

Sullum, Jacob. *For Your Own Good: The Anti-Smoking Crusade and the Tyranny of the Public Sector*. New York: Simon & Schuster, 1999.

Swenson, Paul. "Utah Under Cover: Area Books and Authors." *Salt Lake Tribune*, 25 Oct. 1992.

Tansill, Charles Callan. *Backdoor to War: The Roosevelt Foreign Policy, 1933–41*. Chicago: Regnery, 1952.

Taylor, Henry D. "The Law of the Fast." *Ensign* (Nov. 1974).

Tobler, Douglas F. "Before the Wall Fell: Mormons in the German Democratic Republic, 1945–89." *JMH* 25–4 (Winter 1992): 11–30.

———. "Education, Moral Values, and Democracy: Lessons from the German Experience." *BYU Studies* 28–3 (1988): 47–63.

———. "The Jews, the Mormons, and the Holocaust." *JMH* 18–1 (Spring 1992): 59–92.

"Trench Mouth." *Medline Plus*. U.S. National Library of Medicine, National Institutes of Health. http://www.nlm.nih.gov/medlineplus/ency/article/001044.htm.

Tullis, F. Lamond, and Elizabeth Hernandez. "Mormons in Mexico: Leadership, Nationalism, and the Case of the Third Convention." 1987. http://www.orsonpratt brown.com/MexicanMission/third-convention.html.

Tunnell, Michael O. *Brothers in Valor: A Story of Resistance*. New York: Holiday, 2001.

"2 Here to Minimize Blockade Friction." *New York Times*, 5 Mar. 1940.

United States Bureau of the Census. Decennial censuses of the United States. Washington, D.C.: U.S. Government Printing Office.

Utah Death Certificate, Reed Galli, Division of Vital Records and Statistics, Utah Departent of Health, Salt Lake City, 17 Aug. 1935.

Utah History Encyclopedia. Salt Lake City: University of Utah. http://www.uen.org/utah_history_encyclopedia/.

Van Orden, Bruce A. *Building Zion: The Latter-day Saints in Europe*. Salt Lake City: Deseret, 1996.

Van der Vat, Dan. *The Good Nazi: The Life and Lies of Albert Speer*. New York: Houghton-Mifflin, 1997.

Van Wagoner, Richard S. *Mormon Polygamy: A History*. 2nd ed. Salt Lake City: Signature, 1989.

Van Wagoner, Richard S., and Steven C. Walker. *A Book of Mormons*. Salt Lake City: Signature, 1982.

Walker, Joseph. "World Premieres: Two Salt Lake Theaters Debut Plays by Utah Playwrights." *Deseret News*, 5 Feb. 1984.

Walker, Lawrence D. *Hitler Youth and Catholic Youth 1933–1936*. Washington, D.C.: Catholic University of America Press, 1970.

"Walter Krause, Legendary for his Post-War Service, Dies." *Deseret News*, 17 Apr. 2004.

Warner, Cecelia. "Helmuth Hubener: Antagonist or Protagonist?" *Sunstone Review* 3–5 (Mar. 1984): 3–4.

Warnke, Jürgen. "The Legal History of the Church of Jesus Christ of Latter-Day Saints in Germany." Mormon History Association, 35th Annual Meeting, Aalborg, Denmark, June 2000.

Watters, Leon L. *The Pioneer Jews of Utah*. New York: American Jewish Historical Society, 1952.

Bibliography

Watzman, Haim. "Israeli Cabinet agrees to investigate Brigham Young's Jerusalem Center." *Chronicle of Higher Education* 31 (1986): 33–34.

Welker, Elizabeth H. "The German Girl of Today." *Improvement Era* (May 1937): 294–95.

Wenn, S. "The Commodore Hotel Revisited: An Analysis of the 1935 AAU Convention." *Proceedings—Sixth Canadian Symposium on the History of Sport and Physical Education*. London, Ontario: University of Western Ontario, 1988.

White, David. "Play About Mormon Youth's War on Hitler Stirs Conflict in the Church." *New York Times*, 15 Feb. 1984.

Widmer, Kurt. *Unter Zions Panier: Mormonism and Its Interaction with Germany and Its People*. Stuttgart: Franz Steiner Verlag, 2013.

Widtsoe, John H., ed. *Discourses of Brigham Young*. Salt Lake City: Deseret, 1954.

Wistrich, Robert S. *Who's Who in Nazi Germany*. London: Routledge, 1995.

Wobbe, Rudolf Gustav, and Jerry Borrowman. *Before the Blood Tribunal*. American Fork, Utah: Covenant, 1992.

———. *Three Against Hitler: A Compelling Story of Three LDS Teens' Fight for Freedom* American Fork, Utah: Covenant, 2002.

Wright, Clyde J., ed. *Protocols of the Learned Elders of Zion*. Houston: Pyramid, Feb. 1934.

Young, Margaret Blair. "Doing Huebener." *Dialogue Journal* 2–4 (1988): 127–32.

Index

Page numbers in *italics* indicate illustrations.

Aaronic Priesthood, 123–24, 126, 283, 360n20
Academic Research Foundation, 334, 383n58
Adams, Ray H., 76
Adorf, Germany, 37
Ahnenpass, 110–11
alcohol, 5, 34, 138–39
Alexander, Thomas G., 43, 125
Allen, James B., 36
Allen, Preston C., 167, 364n3
Allende, Salvador, 324
All Quiet on the Western Front (Remarque), 85
Amateur Athletic Union (AAU), 116, 359nn4–5
American Indians, 23–24, 281
American Olympic Committee (AOC), 359n4
Anderson, David, 238, 327, 378n66
Anderson, Jeffery L., 56, 140, 350n43
Anschluss, 176, 197, 215
anti-Semitism: of Clark, 6–7, 154, 275–76, 277–80, 375n25; Ida Rees and, 202; *Kristallnacht* pogrom, 3, 115, 259–61, 347n1; LDS Church and, 6, 114–15, 280–81, 287; of McKay, 358n37; Nuremberg Race Laws and, 107, 142–43, 219, 357nn8–9; Olympic Games of 1936 and, 117, 118, 120–21; of Schirach, 130; signs barring Jews, *157,* 284, 293–94, 375n45; of Smoot, 12, 218–19. *See also* Jews
apostles, defined, 367n48
Appeal to a Lower Court (Chandler), 331
Arendt, Hannah, 113, 358n33
Argentina, 324
Arrington, Leonard J., 362n14
Ashton, Marvin A., 71–72
Augsburg, Germany, 80, 81
Augustine, St., 230
Austria: Jews in, 272–73; Nazi occupation of, 176, 197, 215
Ausweisung der Mormonen, 45

Baden-Powell, Robert, 126
Ballif, Serge, 56
Bamberger, Ernest, 275–76, 281
"banality of evil," 113, 358n33
baptism, posthumous: of Jews, 249–50, 261; Mormon doctrine of, 105, 106, 247, 357nn3–4
Barmbek Branch, 284
Barnes, John R., 245
Bartels, Adolf, 130
Barth, Frederick H., 232–33
Bartoletti, Susan Campbell, 335–36
Basel, Switzerland, 31, 349n34
basketball: German national team photo, *146;* Mormon tradition in, 118–19; Mormon training of German team, 117, 119–21

403

Index

Bavaria, 34, 37
Beck, John, 28
Beer Hall Putsch, 139, 201
Beevor, Anthony, 237
Bennett, John, 27
Benson, Ezra Taft, 323, 382n22; anti-communism of, 323–24; and genealogical records, 249; and post-war relief effort, 7, 245, 313
Berlin: Allied bombing of, 223, 236, 239, 301; in Imperial Germany, 39, 42, 45; mission office in, 32, 71, 93, 103, 135, 179; Mormon meetings in 1930s, 207, 213, 217; Nazi prisons in, 231, 267, 312, 341; Olympic Games in, 118, 121–22; post-war relief efforts in, 244–45, 246; power struggle over mission presidency in, 187–88, 190–97; Red Army in, 237, 244; refugees in, 238–39, 241; during Weimar Republic, 71, 85, 140
Berlin Wall, 224, 331
Berndt, Otto, *162*, 237, 238, 358n23; Gestapo interrogation of, 309–10, 381n133; and Hübener, 300, 308–309, 312, 313, 378n64; immigration to U.S. of, 313–14; and Worbs, 294–95, 377n40; on Zander, 292–93
Berson, Robin K., 335
Biehl, Frederick L., 215
Bielefeld, Germany, 81
Bingham, Stanford H., 177, 192, 195, 202–203
blacks, 106; proscription of ordination of, 182, 365n37
Blaine, James G., 43
Blake, George R., *153*, 172, 180–81, 184
Blessing, Karl, 213
Blum, Leon, 278
Böhm, Bruno, 69
Book of Mormon, 24, 281, 349n10; and Hitler Myth, 140, 328; sales of, 24, 81; Smith and, 20
Boone, David F., 227
Borkhardt, Johannes, 55
Borrowman, Jerry, 332
Boyce, William, 126

Boy Scouting, 123–34; Hitler Youth absorption of Mormons, 12–13, 98, 123, 124, 132–34; LDS Boy Scouts, 128–29; Mormonism and, 123–24, 125–26; in pre-Nazi Germany, 127–30
Boy Scouts of America (BSA), 126
The Boy Who Dared (Bartoletti), 335–36
Bradford, Reed, 363–65n2
Brandenburg, Germany, 80, 120, 180, 236
Braunschweig, Germany, 80
Bremen, Germany, 42, 57
Breslau, Germany, 52, 80, 111; rebellion in Central Branch of, 61, 62–64, 101
Bretschneider, C. G., 241
Brey, Alwin, 175, 293
Brigham Young University (BYU), 32, 317, 362n14; and *Huebener* play, 161, 289–90, 318–20, 321, 327, 332
Brimhall, Dean, 114
Bringhurst, Newell, 114, 191
Brinkmann, Rudolf, 213
Brodie, Bernard, 114, 358n37
Brodie, Fawn McKay, 114, 358n36; career of, 358n37; on genealogical research, 114–15; on Smith and Mormon beliefs, 23, 106, 349n10
Bromberg, Samuel, 28
Brothers in Valor (Tunnell), 335
Brown, Hugh B., 339
Brundage, Avery, 117, 359n4
Buchanan, James, 36
Buchenwald, 96
Budge, Oliver H., 61–64, 71, 101, 144, 188, 219; dealings with Third Reich, 64, 93–95, 355n6, 355n12; enforcement of discipline by, 69–70, 102
Budge, William, 33
Bund deutscher Mädel (BDM), 141–42
Burkardt, Paul Max, 207
Busch, Julius Hermann Moritz, 203, 367n64
Bushman, Richard L., 24
BYU Studies, 326

Index

Calder, Edwin H., 77
Canada, 24, 246
Cannon, Angus J., 54–55, 82
Cannon, Hugh J., 38, 44, 45
Cannon, Joseph J., 196
Carn, Daniel, 28, 38
Carter, Steven E., 129, 131, 140, 167, 281, 363–64n2
Chai Ling, 335
Chamberlain, Houston Stewart, 130
Chamberlain, Neville, 214, 215, 369n25
Chandler, Neal, 331
Chemnitz, Germany, 76, 77, 179, 215, 356n32
Chile, 324
Christensen, Jerome J., 121
Christian Science Monitor, 359n2
Christian Scientists, 12, 98, 136, 184, 342
Clark, J. Reuben, *154,* 209–16, 365n37; anti-Semitism of, 6–7, 154, 275–76, 277–80, 375n25; biographical background, 210; and evacuation of missionaries, 214, 225, 229–30; German financial officials' negotiations with, 12, 154, 205, 209, 210–13; and German Mormons, 212, 213, 215–16; "Memorandum on the Monroe Doctrine," 210–11, 368n2; Nazis' respect for, 216; opposition to Jewish immigration, 273–75; and Rees, 192, 199; "Right to Protect Citizens in Foreign Countries by Landing Forces," 211
Clay, Lucius D., 248
Cologne, Germany, 52, 61
Common Sense, 279
Communist Party (KPD), 88, 99, 291–92
concentration camps, 5, 14–15, 265–67, 286
conversions and baptisms, 21, 24–25, 34, 39, 44, 56
Corbett, Donald C., 62–63, 242, 244, 245, 248–49
Covenant Communications, 332, 333–34
Covey, Theron, 77

Crosland, Ivan, 320, 321–22, 332
Cuba, 277
Cullom-Struble Bill, 43
Cumming, Alfred, 36
Czechoslovakia, 176, 207, 214, 367n73

Dahl, Friedrich, 52
Damke, Emilie, 35
Dautel, Eugene, 234
demonic possession, 77
Deseret News, 11, 105, 115, 131, 199, 224–25; circulation of, 359n2; on genealogical work in Germany, 109, 112–13; and Hitler Myth, 137–38, 139–40; on Olympic Games of 1936, 116–17; on persecution of Jews, 276–77; on plays about Hübener, 320, 327; on Rees, 193, 199, 206; swastikas and Nazi salute depicted in, 117, *146,* 217
"desk genocide," 113
Deutscher Scoutverbund, 129, 361n26
Deutsches Jungvolk, 132
Dewey, Richard Lloyd, 334, 383n58
Dittmer, August A., 173
Dixon, Joseph, 285–86, 348n10, 364n25
Doctrine and Covenants: Section 89 of, 138; Section 93 of, 159; Section 134 of, 4, 93, 232, 330, 355n5
Dodd, William E., 135–36, 211–12, 213, 219
Doyle, Arthur Conan, 36
Dresden, Germany, 65, 70, 83; International Hygiene Exposition in, 83–84, 219–20; mission headquarters in, 71, 82; U.S. consulate in, 83–84
Dulles, Allen, 274–75
Düwer, Gerhard, 305, 306, 310–11, 333

East Germany (German Democratic Republic), 22, 246; and Mormon genealogical research, 247–48, 249; Mormon negotiations and relations with, 22, *166,* 251–52, 321, 323, 324, 326–27, 330; unification with West, 233, 331; and Wolfsgrün facility, 242–44

Index

Ebert, Friedrich, 59
Edelweiss Pirates, 36
Edmunds Act (1882), 37
Edmunds-Tucker Act (1887), 38
Edwards, Jonathan, 23
Ehrenreich, Eric, 110, 219
Eichmann, Adolf, 273, 358n33
Einbeck, Germany, 80
Einsatzgruppen, 15
Einstein, Albert, 85
Eintopfsonntag, 137, 362n6
Elder's Reference, 61
Elgren, Ossman, 77
Ellsworth, P. Blair, 167, 364n3
Elmshorn, Germany, 80
emigration: after World War II, 246, 314–17; of German Jews, 273–74, 277, 286, 287; Nazi laws on, 224, 314; in nineteenth century, 8, 30–31, 43; statistics on, 246, 315; during Weimar Republic, 72
Ensign, 330
Evangelical Church, 30
exaltation, 21
excommunication, 65–66, 72, 207; of Hübener, 15, 288, 309, 312–13, 332, 334, 340–41, 343; procedure in, 70, 380n131; reasons for, 70, 312; of Reschke, 253, 264

fasting, 137, 362n5
Father/Land (Kempe), 231
Federal Republic of Germany. *See* West Germany
Felt, Jon R., 231, 340
Fischer, Klaus P., 107, 137
Flögel, Bertha, 304–305, 306
Fluckiger, Norville, 172, 173
Ford, Henry, 130
Forsberg, Norman W., 77
Forst, Germany, 81, 182–83
Fox, Frank, 275–76
Frankfurt, Germany, 11, 52, *158*, 181, 217, 326–27; West German mission office in, 176, 190, 191–92, 195, 197, 198, 203, 206, 215, 226, 237, 250
Freeman, Robert C., 231, 233–34, 340

Freiberg, Germany, 22, 52; Mormon temple in, 326, 327
Friedländer, Saul, 142–43
Friedrich Wilhelm IV, 29–30

Gaeth, Arthur, 83, 88, 101, 132, 361n26
Galli, Reed, 65–66, 67
Geh Voran, 175
genealogical societies, 108, 357n12
Genealogical Society of Utah, 112
genealogy, 105–15; Mormon-Nazi collaboration around, 4, 105–106, 107–10, 111–12, 113–14, 218, 219, 357nn11–12; Mormon research after World War II, 247–50; Nazi use of, 106–107, 110–11
General Walker Hotel, 339
Geneva, Switzerland, 31, 349n34
German-American Bund, *156*
German-Austrian Mission Association, 103
German Saints at War, 234
German Society for Racial Hygiene, 109
Germany. *See* East Germany; Imperial Germany; Third Reich; Weimar Republic; West Germany
girls' organizations, Mormon, 124, 360n7
Gitlow, Benjamin, 278
Gleiwitz, Germany, 111
Goebbels, Joseph, 137, 299, 347n1; *Deseret News* admiration of, 139; Radio Measures decree of, 296; Rees and, 186, 204, 208
Goldman, Emma, 278
Göring, Hermann, 301, 379n72
Gorschig, G., 132–33
Graff, Mark B., 214
Grant, Heber J., 126, 189, 197, 274, 287; and Clark, 211, 212; polygamy practiced by, 191, 366n17; speech before swastika banner, 11, 217; visit to Nazi Germany by, 22, *152*, 191, 193, 196
Grass, Günter, 289, 333, 341
Great Britain, 25, 126

Index

Great Depression, 86–87, 101
Green, William, 117
Groß Wartenberg, Germany, 80
Großräschen, 80
Guided and Guarded (Barth), 232
Gypsies, 106, 182

Haas, Otto, 200
Haeberle, Arminius T., 82, 83–84
Hamburg, Germany, 42, 52, 57, *164*, 189–90; Allied bombing of, 238; mission headquarters in, 44, 176; political climate in, 291–92. *See also* Hübener, Helmuth; St. Georg Branch
Hanover, Germany, 80, 110, 254, 257, 258, 259; American consul in, 45, 79; *Kristallnacht* in, 3, 260–61
Hasse, Emma, 335, 377n38
Hawkes, Heber, 119
Hegewald, Clemens, *147*
"Heil Hitler" salutation, 133, 319; Mormon use of, 134, 144, 186, 288, 344. *See also* Nazi salute
Heismann, Erich, 171
Helmuth Hübener-Haus, *164*, 329–30
Helmuth-Hübener-Weg, *165*
Hess, Rudolf, 303, 379n81
Heydrich, Reinhard, 94, 284, 347n1, 355n7
Hildesheim, Germany, 240, 371n49
Hilgenfeldt, Erich, 241–42
Hill, David Jayne, 47
Himmler, Heinrich, 94, 97, 242, 355n7
Hindenburg, Germany, 79, 111, 167
Hindenburg, Paul von, 100
Hitler, Adolf, 88, 118, 171, 214, 293, 312, 347n1; and alcohol, 138–39; assumption of power by, 64, 100; *Deseret News* on, 112; Hübener on, 301–302, 304; Mormon leaders in presence of, 141, 142, 216, 220, 255, 363nn35–36; public image of, 137, 139
Hitler Myth, 136–37; *Deseret News* on, 137–38, 139–40; Hitler as secret Mormon, 13, 140, 328; and Hitler's non-drinking and non-smoking image, 5, 138–40; and Nazi welfare scheme, 137–38; Welker version of, 5, 138, 140, 143
Hitler Youth, *147*, 255; auxiliary organizations of, 360nn5–6; girls camp of, 142; Hübener and, 290–91, 292, 303; membership of, 134; Mormon Boy Scouts absorbed by, 12–13, 98, 123, 124, 132–34; Mormon youth active in, 131–32; rise of, 130
Hoehle, Robert, 132–33
Hoffmann, Edward, 51
Holland, Philip, 82
Holmes, Blair, 332–33, 334
homosexuals, 140
Honecker, Erich, *166*, 325, 330
Hoover, Herbert, 211
Horne, Joseph S., 31
Horsley, Burt, 229
Horst Wessel Song, 6, 292
Houtz, Jacob, 29–30
Howard, James, 25, 26
Howe, Eber D., 24
Hübener, Helmuth, 288–317; anti-Nazi viewpoint adopted by, 292, 295; arrest of, 306–307; brochures and handbills by, 297, 298–304, 305, 378n62; cockiness of, 300; continuing Mormon discomfort over, 341; controversy over legacy of, 318–38; denunciation of, 304–306; dimmer switch applied to memory of, 15–16, 288–89, 324, 328; excommunication of, 15, 288, 309, 312–13, 332, 334, 340–41, 343; excommunication reversal, 313; execution of, 15, 288, 312, 376n2; and foreign radio broadcasts, 296–98, 299, 303; Gestapo interrogation of, 307–308, 320; and Hitler Youth, 290–91, 292; on invasion of Soviet Union, 295, 302; job of, 299, 305–306; LDS Church eventual embracing of, 253, 332–35; other resisters compared to, 336–37; and persecution of Jews, 304; photos, *161*, *163*; recent books on, 332–36;

407

Index

Hübener, Helmuth (*continued*)
revolutionary objectives of, 295, 299;
in school, 290, 376n9; step father of,
291, 377n21; Tobler-Keeler article in
Sunstone on, 325–26; trial of, 310–12;
and Worbs imprisonment, 294, 295
Hübener, Hugo, 291, 309
Hübener vs. Hitler (Dewey), 334
Hübner, Karl, 63
Huebener (Rogers), 378n66;
fictionalization of events in, 318–20;
Mormon hierarchy suppression
of, 161, 289–90, 321–22, 327;
performances of, 289, 318, 320, 332
"Huebener Against the Reich"
(Anderson), 327, 328, 378n66
Hugenberg, Alfred, 356n24
Hull, Cordell, 212
Hull, Thomas, 125–26
Hunter, Howard W., 232
Hyde, Orson, 25–27
hyperinflation, 85–86

immigration. *See* emigration
Imperial Germany, 9; church-state
relations under, 78–79; harassment
of Mormon missionaries in, 21–22,
36–38, 42; map of, *40–41*; Mormon
missionary work in, 43–45
Improvement Era, 143–44
International Hygiene Exposition,
83–84, 219–20
The International Jew (Ford), 130
International Olympic Committee
(IOC), 117–18
International Red Cross, 246

Jacobi, Franz, 282, 293, 309, 313;
depiction in plays, 318, 328
Japan, 60
Jay, John, 44
Jehovah's Witnesses: Nazi persecution
of, 12, 96–97, 136, 216, 342–43;
Statement of Principles by, 95–96
Jenkins, Rulon W., 66–68
Jensen, Dilworth, 114
Jensen, Richard L., 142

Jews, *157*, 272–87; American Indians
and, 23–24; in Austria, 272–73;
Clark's view of, 6–7, 154, 275–76,
277–80, 375n25; *Deseret News* on
persecution of, 276–77; emigration
attempts by, 229, 273–74, 277,
286–87; exclusion from German
sports, 118, 121, 359n10; genealogical
research on, 106–107, 110–11,
247–50; German LDS churches'
barring of, 282, 284, 293–94,
375n45; German Mormons' stance
toward, 182, 285; Ida Rees on,
194, 202; *Kristallnacht* pogrom of,
3, 115, 259–61, 347n1; *Mischling*,
107, 283, 284, 357n9; Mormons'
posthumous baptizing of, 249–50,
261; Nuremberg Race Laws on, 107,
142–43, 219, 357nn8–9; relationship
toward in Utah, 281; Welker on, 13,
142, 143. *See also* anti-Semitism
Johnson, Albert Sidney, 36
Johnson, Eric A., 174, 183–84
Judd, Edward G., 121
Jünger, Ernst, 85

Karlsruhe, Germany, 29, 31, 37
Kaufmann, Rudolph, 294
Keele, Alan F.: on Hübener, 289, 297,
299, 325–26, 332–33, 334–35; and
Hübener story, 318, 322–23, 325,
328–29, 333; on Mormons and Nazis,
131, 281, 286; and Zander, 320–21
Kellogg-Briand Pact, 210, 368n2
Kelly, Philemon M., 102, 179, 188, 254,
344; biographical background, 187,
189; and mission presidency power
struggle, 190–97; and Schoenhals,
177, 189
Kempe, Frederick, 231, 265, 266, 268,
269
Kennedy, John F., 211
Kererbeck, Helmuth Friedrich Michael
Walter, 52
Kershaw, Ian, 136–37, 139
Kessler, Wilhelm, 52–54
Kest, John Robert, 227

Index

Kiefer, Johann, 178
Kiel, Germany, 37, 39, 172, 173
Kimball, Heber C., 25
Kindt, Walter H., 339–40, 343
King, Christine Elizabeth, 96, 97, 136, 184; on Nazi-Mormon common worldview, 11, 99
King, William H., 84, 280, 281
Kirkham, James M., 112–13
Kirkham, Oscar A., 130
Kleinert, Erich, 132
Klopfer, Karl Herbert, *159*, 215, 235, 239; as memory beacon, 223–25
Klopfer, W. Herbert, 314
Knox, Philander, 45
Knutti, Frank, 228–29
Kobs, Jared H. B., 132, 282; as memory beacon, 230–32
Köhler, Paul, 63
Königsberg, Germany, 52, 80, 238
Kranz, Werner, 305–306
Krause, Erich, 231, 265–71, 341; daughter of, 266–67, 270–71; Mormon leadership defense of, 269–70; as Nazi torturer and murderer, 14–15, 265, 267; trial of, 268–69; uncovering past of, 265–66
Krause, Walter, 251–52, 324
Krisch, Wilhelm, 234–35
Kristallnacht, 3, 115, 259–61, 347n1
Krueger, Arnd, 120
Kunkel, Gerhard, 291, 296, 313

labor unions, 198–99, 255, 367n47
LaGuardia, Fiorello, 117
Lambert, Paul H., 206
Landon, Alf, 199
Langheinrich, Paul, 235–36, 239–40, 242; and genealogical research, 247, 248–49
Laves, Wolfgang, 254
Lazarus, Kurt and Kaete, 256–58, 264
LDS Boy Scouts, 128–29
LDS Church discipline: Galli case, 65–66; Jenkins case, 66–68; of proselytizing elders, 69–70; Rees enforcement of, 207; Richter case, 71–72; Schwab case, 68–69. *See also* excommunication
LDS Church doctrine and practices: on American Indians, 23–24, 281; basketball as proselytizing tool, 118–19; and Boy Scouting, 123–24, 125–26; fast days and offerings, 137, 362n5; on genealogical research, 106, 218; on Jews' return to Holy Land, 25; "King Follett Discourse" outlining of, 19–20; liturgy, 6, 57, 73, 76, 237, 250, 352n26; on living in and of the world, 84–85, 354n75; on miracles, 26, 73, 76–78; on obedience to civil authority, 4, 9, 38, 93, 94–95, 97–98, 122, 173, 225, 232, 312, 330, 340, 343, 344, 355n5; overseas missions, 25, 349n16; plural marriage, 27, 30, 35–36, 59–60, 65, 191, 350n62, 350–51n72, 366n17; on posthumous baptisms, 105, 106, 247, 357nn3–4; priesthood concept of, 62, 63, 352–53n14; pro-natalism of, 94, 205, 355n9; tithing system, 57, 64, 175, 179, 205, 237, 352n26; Word of Wisdom dietary and health code, 34, 60, 83, 85, 138, 219–20, 354n71, 362n14
LDS Church founding, 24
LDS Church governance: authoritarian style of, 22, 59, 62, 97, 252; changes in Nazi Germany to, 100–102; intolerance of criticism, 337; local structure of, 347n3, 352n12; rebellions against, 61–63, 352n10; role of mission presidents, 61–65, 187–88, 190–97; Salt Lake City as base of, 176, 250–52, 347n2
LDS Church membership: in 1830s, 24; in Germany, 34, 42, 47, 72, 107, 343, 348n10, 356n32
Lebensborn program, 242
Lee, Harold B., 22, 324
Lehmann, Daniel H., 170–71
Leignitz, Germany, 111
Lenin, Vladimir, 278
Lewald, Theodor, 359n7

Index

Liebknecht, Karl, 278
Liebknecht, Wilhelm, 278
Lincoln, Abraham, 36
Lindsey, Ralph Mark, 192, 199–200, 203, 204, 205, 215
Lion, Alexander, 127
Los Angeles Times, 202, 327
Ludwig, Willie, *147*
Ludwigsburg, Germany, 81
Ludwigshafen Tageblatt, 39
Lute, Allen, 177–78
Luxemburg, Rosa, 278
Lyman, Francis D., 38
Lyman, Francis M., 61
Lyman, Richard R., 181, 193, 195–96

Madsen, Brigham, 349n10
Maeser, Karl, 32–35, 205
Mahoney, Jeremiah T., 117
Mann, Heinrich, 295
Mann, Henry, 213
Marx, Karl, 278
Mather, Cotton, 23
Mauss, Armand, 280–81
Max: A West Prussian Odyssey (Reschke), 262
Mayer, Helene, 359n10
McFarland, Rick, 333
McKay, David O., 22, 191, 280, 358n57; anti-communist pronouncements by, 323–24; and Rees, 192–93, 197
McKay, Thomas, Jr., 114
McKay, Thomas E., 32, 47–48, 188, 226; and daughter Fawn, 114, 358n37; as head of Swiss-Austrian Mission, 151, 198, 215; and mission presidency power struggle, 191–97; photo, *151*; on relations with Third Reich, 123
Meinig, Don, 347n6
Melchizedek Priesthood, 124, 313, 353n14
Melich, Nancy, 332
memory beacons, defined, 348n15
Merrill, Joseph F., 11, 217
Merrill, Vinton M., 120–21
Mexican Revolution, 211
The Millennial Star, 34, 137, 193

Millerites, 23
Mine Angels Round About (Montague), 227–28
Minert, Roger P., 237, 348n10
miracles, 26, 73, 76–78
missionaries: code of conduct for, 85; divided views on Nazi Germany among, 5–6; European-wide conference of (1902), 44; German authorities' early clashes with, 9, 21–22, 26, 27, 28, 29, 30–31, 36–38, 42, 45; and German language and culture, 9, 61; in Imperial Germany, 21–22, 36–38, 42, 43–45; initial overseas efforts, 24–25, 26–27; Maeser and, 32–35; Nazi regime confrontations with, 167, 170–72, 176–80, 182–83, 363–64nn2–3; in pre-Imperial Germany, 25–31, 39; prewar evacuation of American, 7, 214, 225–30; releasing from assignment of, 69, 353n27; relief work by, 54–56, 351n22; screening of, 60–61; self-reliance of, 94; and swastika, *153*, 177–78; toleration of prejudices by, 281–82; training programs for, 10, 61; under Weimar Republic, 54–56, 79, 351n22; during World War I, 50–51, 351n7
Mitchell, Michael, 30
mob violence, 37, 42
Mohns, Heinrich, 305–306, 379n91
Molotov-Ribbentrop pact, 225
Monroe Doctrine, 210–11, 368n2
Monson, Thomas S.: and East Germany relations, 22, *166*, 321, 323, 330; and *Huebener* play, 320, 322, 327
Montague, Terry, 227–28
Mormon Church. *See* LDS Church
Mormon Culture Region, defined, 347n6
Die Mormonen (Busch), 203, 367n64
The Mormon Hierarchy (Quinn), 262
Mormon History Association, 341
Mormonism in Germany (Scharffs), 121
Mormon-Nazi accommodation and collaboration, 4–8, 10–13; around

Index

genealogical research, 4, 105–106, 107–10, 111–12, 113–14, 218, 219, 357nn11–12; attempts to suppress discussion of, 161, 289–90, 321–22, 327, 341–42; in basketball, 117, 119–21; common worldview seen, 11, 97, 98, 99, 105–106; justifications for, 4, 94–95, 98, 122, 173, 225, 232, 312, 340, 341–42, 344; merger of Boy Scouts into Hitler Youth, 12–13, 98, 123, 124, 132–34; ongoing consequences of, 343–44; search for commonalities, 5, 137–40, 144, 205, 343; skill navigating Nazi bureaucracy, 172–74, 180–81; withdrawal of material offensive to Nazis, 6, 98, 103–104, 114, 182, 184

Mormons, German: as concentration camp mechanics, 5, 286; confrontations with Third Reich by, 170–72, 176–80, 182–83; congregational leadership positions taken by, 10, 100–102, *148*; conversions and baptisms by, 34, 39, 44, 56; ecclesiastical control over, 176, 250–52, 347n2; genealogical work by, 107–108, 247–50, 357nn11–12; hooligan attacks on, 37, 42, 79–80; and LDS-RLDS conflict, 80–81; membership figures of, 31, 34, 42, 47, 72, 89, 107, 343, 347n3, 348n10, 356n32; myth of Nazi persecution of, 167–84; as Nazis, 265–71, 281, 282–83, 284, 292–93; patriotism of, 57–58, 97–98, 109, 215; social activities by, *149*; St. Georg Branch of, *162*, 282–83, 284, 292–94, 308–309, 312, 375n45; tracting by, 173–74; weddings by, *160*; youth activities of, 124–25. *See also* missionaries; Mormon-Nazi accommodation and collaboration

Moroni, 20

Morrell, David M., 119

Morrill Anti-Bigamy Act, 36, 37, 350n46

Morris, Charles, 44

Morrow, Dwight, 210

Mueller, Ernst F., 28, 37

Müller, Ludwig, 131

Munich, Germany, 52, 88, *165*, 336–37; Beer Hall Putsch in, 139, 201

Munich Conference (1938), 214, 348n10

Murdock, Franklin J., 185, 207, 215, 227

Mussolini, Benito, 186, 202–203, 303

Mutual Improvement Association (MIA), 125–26

Naismith, James, 118

Napoleon Bonaparte, 295

National German People's Party (DNVP), 356n24

National Socialists. *See* Nazi Party

Nationalsozialistich Volkswohlfahrt (NSV), 241–42

Nazi Germany. *See* Third Reich

Nazi Labor Front, 3, 5, 96, 107, 220, 255

Nazi Party: assumption of power by, 64, 100; auxiliary organizations of, 241–42; election results of, 88, 99, 100, 356n26; growth of, 131; Mormon membership in, 281; and National German People's Party, 356n24; Nuremberg rallies of, 141, 186, 201–202, 256; street violence organized by, 88–89, 99, 291–92

Nazi salute, 5, 12, 116, 117, *146*, 185–86. *See also* "Heil Hitler" salutation

Neibaur, Alexander, 20–21

Netherlands, 226–27, 229, 230

Neumünster, Germany, 172–73

New York Times, 327

Nichols, Paul, *153*

Niebuhr, Hermann, 120

Nixon, Richard, 324

Noack, Hermann, 175

Notes for Missionaries (Lyman), 61

Nuremberg branch, 42

Nuremberg Nazi rallies, 141, 186, 201–202, 256

Nuremberg Race Laws, 107, 142–43, 219, 357nn8–9

Oaks, Dallin, 320, 322–23, 325–26, 329

Oberbau, 290, 376n9

411

Offenbach, Germany, 80
Ollerton, Fay, 108, 131
Olympic Games of 1936, *146*; anti-Semitic signs removed during, 120–21; awarded to Germany, 118; boycott movement, 117, 146; Mormon training of German basketball team, 117, 119–21; U.S. participation in, 117
Overmans, Rüdiger, 348n14
Owen, William, 44

Packer, Boyd K., 334, 341
Paldiel, Mordecai, 263
Paulus, Friedrich von, 231
Peifer, Douglas C., 348n15
Penn, William, 23
Perón, Isabel, 324
Perschon, Charles A., 121
Persilschein, 314, 381n140
Peters, Frederick, 379–80n94
Petty, Donald M., 178, 191, 192, 237, 277, 285; experience with Nazi authorities, 181–82, 183
Peukert, Detlev, 128, 336, 362n6
Pfadfinder movement, 127–28, *129*; Hitler Youth absorption of, 131, 132
Pinochet, Augusto, 324
Plath, Helmuth, 133, 134
Plauen, Germany, 80, 235
Pohlsander, Walter, 109
Poland Act, 37
Poll, Richard, 229
polygamy, 35–42; German civil authorities and, 8, 30, 37–38, 42, 350n43; as Mormon practice, 27, 30, 35–36, 65, 191, 350n62, 366n17; Mormon prohibition of, 43, 46, 59–60; sensationalist stories about, 8, 36, 43, 45, 46; U.S. laws against, 36, 37, 38, 350n46, 350–51n72
Popel, H., 77
Porter, William, 73
The Practical Guide for Genealogical and Temple Work, 110
Pratt, Orson, 27, 30
Preuss, Hugo, 60
priesthood, 62, 63, 352–53n14

Prohibition, 126
prostitutes, 60, 140
The Protocols of the Learned Elders of Zion, 201, 279, 375n25
Prussia, 29–31

Quinn, D. Michael, 199, 262, 323; on Clark, 211, 273–74
Quorum of the Twelve, 12, 25, 27, 39, 43, 45, 320, 322, 323, 324, 329, 334, 341, 367n48

Ranglack, Richard, 235–36
rape, 237–38
Rathke, Walter, 77
Rattei, Marie Elizabeth, 70
Rees, Alfred C., 152, 180, 188, 343; biographical background, 198; church discipline enforced by, 207; collaboration with Nazis by, 5, 150, 185–87, 200–203, 208; conservative political advocacy by, 198–99; and mission presidency power struggle, 190–97; personal qualities of, 200; photo, *150*; *Völkischer Beobachter* article by, 5, 150, 186, 203–206, 344
Rees, Ida, 192–93, 194, 200, 206; on Nuremberg rally, 201–202
refugees: ethnic German, 240–41; Wolfsgrün home for, 241–44; during World War II, 238–39
Reichstag fire, 100
Reiser, George, 28
relief efforts: after World War I, 54–56, 351n22; after World War II, 7–8, 244–46, 313–14; during World War II, 236–37
Remarque, Erich, 85
Reorganized Church of Jesus Christ of Latter Day Saints (RLDS), 80–81
Reschke, Horst, 256, 260, 262, 271; father's special recognition not sought by, 14, 263, 373n26; *Max: A West Prussian Odyssey*, 262
Reschke, Lilly, 258, 263, 264
Reschke, Max, 253–65; character traits of, 259; excommunication of, 253, 264; final years of, 271; hatred

for Nazis, 254–56; and historical remembrance, 3–4, 14, 253, 261–62; and *Kristallnacht,* 3, 259–61; Lazarus couple protected by, 256–58, 264; as pharmaceutical firm manager, 240, 254, 255; as philanderer, 14, 263–65; photo, *145*; Polish slave laborer saved by, 258; religious life of, 254; and "Righteous Among the Nations" list, 3, 262–63; Russian POW saved by, 258–59, 264; in World War I, 254
Reschke, Wilma, 260, 263
Revelation, Book of, 25
Ribbentrop, Joachim von, 171
Richards, LeGrand, 50
Richter, Bruno Ernst, 71–72
Riley, James H., Jr., 171
Roberts, B. H., 349n10
Roderick, John, 77
Rogers, Thomas, 289, 318, 322, 325, 327, 332
Roosevelt, Franklin D., 135, 199, 211, 219, 278, 280
Roosevelt, Theodore, 44, 55
Roosevelt Corollary, 210–11, 368n2
Rosenberg, Alfred, 201
Rosenhan, Emma, 228
Röttger, Wilhelm, 312
Ruf, Erwin, 175
Ein Ruf aus der Wüste, 26
Runderlass decree, 30, 39, 45
Rutherford, Joseph Franklin, 216
Ryser, Sterling, 276–77

sacrament (Eucharist), 57, 237, 250, 352n26
Saints at War (Freeman and Felt), 231
Saints at War Project, 233–34
Salt Lake Tribune, 142, 143, 322, 332
Salzner, Francis, 101–102, 144, 188; on genealogical research, 110, 113–14, 219
Sander, Ulrich, 289, 333, 376n4
Schacht, Hjalmar, 12, 154, 209, 210, 211, 212, 213
Scharffs, Gilbert, 14, 26, 113, 121, 348n10, 355n6; on belt-whipping incident, 167, 364n3; career of, 349n20

Schirach, Baldur von, 130–31, 134
Schmidt, Alfred, 284, 285
Schmidt, Arnold, 242, 243
Schmidt, Jakob, 337
Schmidt, Walter, 285
Schmuhl, Albert, 79
Schnibbe, Karl-Heinz, 291, 292, 304, 333; anti-Nazi conspiratorial work by, 298–99, 300, 305; arrest and interrogation of, 307–308, 320; emigration to U.S. by, 316; expulsion from Hitler Youth, 132; honoring of, 320, 329–30; and Hübener, 290, 291, 295, 296–97, 306–307; photos, *161, 162*; published account by, 328, 333; trial of, 310–11; on Zander, 282, 283, 293
Schoenhals, Alvin J., 6, 176–77, 189
Scholl, Hans and Sophie, 337
Scholtz-Klink, Gertrude, 5, 141–42, 143, 363nn35–36
Schultz, Hans W., 170–71
Schutzstaffel (SS), 5, 94, 286, 355n6
Schwab, Edgar C., 68–69
Schwarz, Anna Marie, 284, 285, 375n45
Schwarz, Salomon, 283–85, 286, 375n45; denied entry to church, 157, 284, 293–94; deportation and death of, 284
Schwermer, Helga Abel and Horst, *160*
Seamons, Myron, *153*
Second Great Awakening, 23
Seibold, Norman George, 226, 227
Seifart, Otto, 79
Seifert, Paul, 70
Sessions, Lawrence A., 171
Seventh-day Adventists, 23; Nazi persecution of, 12, 98, 136, 342
Shakers, 23
Sicherheitsdienst (SD), 94
Siebenschein, Richard, 274, 286, 287
Skidmore, William, 119
Smelser, Ronald, 262
Smith, Emma, 138
Smith, Ethan, 23–24, 349n10
Smith, George Albert, 313
Smith, Hyrum J., 282
Smith, Hyrum Mack, 49–50

Index

Smith, Jessie Ella Evans, *150*
Smith, John Henry, 44
Smith, Joseph: on American Indians, 23–24; on baptism and salvation, 105; and Book of Mormon, 20, 349n10; founding of Mormon Church by, 24; on genealogical research, 218, 219; on German language and Germans, 8, 20, 21, 22–23; "King Follett Discourse" of, 19–20, 21; monthly fast day established by, 137, 362n5; and Mormons' Word of Wisdom, 138; overseas missionaries dispatched by, 25, 26–27; and polygamy, 27, 65
Smith, Joseph F., 21, 39, 46
Smith, Joseph Fielding, *150*, 225–26
smoking and tobacco, 68, 72, 126, 139, 142; Word of Wisdom prohibition of, 60, 83, 138
Smoot, Reed, 44, 45–46, 55, 135; "A Friend of Germany" article by, 217–18; anti-Semitism of, 12, 218–19
Social Democratic Party (SPD), 88, 291, 292
Sokolowski, Wasili, 247–48
Sommerfeld, Marie, 290, 292, 312, 316
Soviet Union, 295, 297, 302
Spandau, Germany, 52
Spencer, Orson, 29–30
Stachura, P. D., 131
stake, defined, 362n12
St. Anthony News, 192
Starke, Oskar, 235
Stauffenberg, Claus von, 337
Der Stern, 53, 56–57, 95, 103, 175, 218; on Boy Scouting movement, 129; founding of, 34; genealogy articles in, 111–12
St. Georg Branch, *162*, 282–83; conflict around Schwarz in, 283–84; and Hübener case, 308–309, 312; Nazism of, 292–93, 309; sign barring Jews in, 284, 293–94, 375n45
Stollbert, Otto, 128, 129
The Storm of Steel (Jünger), 85
Stover, Walter, 250, 251, 268–69
Stucki, Vergil, 172, 173

A Study in Scarlet (Doyle), 36
Sturmabteilung (SA), 5, 131, 283
Stuttgart, Germany, 28, 52, 175
Sudentanland, 176, 207, 214, 215
Suhrke, Ludwig, 39
Sunstone magazine, 329, 331
The Sunstone Review, 325
Sunstone Symposium, 329
swastika, 12, *158*; American missionaries and, *153*, 177–78; as Mormon adornment, 205–206, 292; Mormons speaking from podiums draped with, 11, 191, 217
Swenson, Paul, 332
Switzerland, 31–32, 349n34

Tadje, Frederick, 76, 128
Taft, William Howard, 211
taxes, 179–80
Taylor, John, 37–38, 350n62
Taylor, John H., 126
theft and embezzlement, 71
Third Convention, 352n10
Third Reich: banning of small religious denominations by, 97, 356n21; bureaucracy of, 172, 180, 208; exclusion of Jews from sports, 118, 121, 359n10; financial negotiations under, 12, 154, 205, 209, 210–13; genealogical interests of, 106–107, 110–11; Law Against Malicious Attacks on the State and the Party for Protection of the Party Uniform, 177; map of in 1939, *168–69*; militarization program of, 171–72, 213; Mormon battle plan in, 93–104; myth of Mormon persecution under, 167–84; pro-natalist policies of, 94, 355n9; public works projects under, 180; Race Laws under, 107, 110, 142–43, 219, 357nn8–9; relief programs under, 137, 302–303; resistance to Nazis under, 288–317; taxation in, 179–80; unintentional violations as inevitable feature of, 174–75. *See also* Mormon-Nazi accommodation and collaboration
Thomas, Edna Harker, 219, 220

Index

Thomas, Elbert D., 12, *155*, 218, 280; tour of Germany by, 135, 136, 155, 219–20
Three Against Hitler, 332
Tilsit, Germany, 73, 80, 351n7, 353n41
Times of London, 328
tithing, 57, 64, 175, 179, 205, 237, 352n26
tobacco. *See* smoking and tobacco
Tobler, Douglas F., 87, 282, 324, 363n35; on Hübener, 289, 292, 297, 304, 325–26; and Hübener story, 318, 322–23, 325, 328, 329, 333; on Mormons and Nazis, 132, 281; on Reschke, 261–62; and Zander, 320–21
Toronto, Wallace F., 207, 367n73
totalitarianism, 97
Totenkopfverbände (Death's Head SS brigade), 5, 283
Tower, Charlemagne, Jr., 44
Tracks of the Jew Throughout the Ages (Rosenberg), 201
tracting, 173–74
Transcontinental Railroad, 36
Trotsky, Leon, 278
Truth & Conviction (McFarland and Whitaker), 304
Tunnell, Michael O., 335
Twelfth Article of Faith, 9, 38; about, 93; as justification for Nazi collaboration, 4, 94–95, 98, 122, 173, 225, 232, 312, 340, 344; Wobbe lesson on, 330, 340
Tyler, John, 33

Uchtdorf, Dieter F., 22, 166
Uder, Karoline, 78
United States embassy and consulates, 10, 44–45, 82–84
Ursenbach, Octave, 33–34
Utah: 1857–59 war in, 27, 36; and polygamy, 350–51n72

Valentine, Hyrum, 82, 128, 214, 224; and disciplinary tribunal, 65, 68–69; and World War I, 49, 50, 51, 52, 53–54

Valentine, Rose Ellen, 49, 51
Van Orden, Bruce A., 31
Versailles Treaty, 171, 278
View of the Hebrews (Smith), 23–24, 349n10
Völkischer Beobachter, 5, 150, 186, 203–206, 344

Waldenburg, Germany, 111
Walker, Lawrence D., 127
Wandervogel movement, 127–28, 131
Weber, Max, 85
weddings, *160*
Wehnes, Friedrich, 52
Wehrmacht: invasions by, 216, 229, 295, 297, 302; Mormons serving in, 5, 14, 224–25, 230–35, 339–40
Weimar Constitution, 59, 60, 100
Weimar Republic, 9–10, 59–89; church-state relations during, 78–81; emigration of Mormons during, 72; genealogical societies under, 108, 357n12; Great Depression impact on, 86–87; hyperinflation during, 85–86; map of, *74–75*; missionaries' relief work in, 54–56, 351n22; Mormon membership during, 72; as "republic without republicans," 59; street violence in, 88–89, 99, 291–92; U.S. consulate during, 82–84
Weiss, Egon Engelbert, 272, 273, 286
Weißenfels, Germany, 83
Welker, Elizabeth Hoge: on German racial superiority, 143–44; and Nazi leadership, 5, 141–42, 143, 363nn35–36
Welker, Roy A., 142, 173, 356n21; German-Austrian mission presidency of, 188, 190, 196; Hitler Myth held by, 5, 138, 140, 143; on Nazis and Jews, 13, 142, 143
Wesche, John, *153*
West Germany (Federal Republic): Economic Miracle in, 289; honoring of Hübener by, 329–30; *Persilschein* in, 314, 381n140; unification with East, 233, 331

When Truth Was Treason (Keele and Holmes), 332–33, 334–35
Whitaker, Matt, 333
White, David, 327
White, Walter, 117
White Rose, 337, 383n67
Whitmer, Peter, 20, 24
Whitney, Newel K., 138
Williams, Roger, 23
Wilson, Woodrow, 211
Wirthlin, Joseph, 324
Wobbe, Rudi, 132, 304, 309, 322, 332; anti-Nazi conspiratorial work by, 298–99, 300, 305; arrest of, 308; emigration to U.S. by, 316; honoring of, 320, 329–30; and Hübener, 290, 291, 295, 296, 297–98, 306–307; photos, *161, 162*; trial of, 310–11; on Twelfth Article of Faith, 330, 340; witnessing of street violence by, 88–89, 291; on Worbs incident, 294, 295; on Zander, 293, 321, 330
Wolfsgrün refugee home, 241–44
Wolters, Royal V., 177–78
women, 7, 237–38
Wood, Evelyn, 206–207
Wood, M. Douglas, 188, 197, 364n25; disagreement with Rees on Nazis, 206, 207; and evacuation of missionaries, 226, 227–28
Woodruff, Wilford, 43
Worbs, Heinrich, 294–95, 377n40, 378n43
Word of Wisdom, 60, 83, 85, 219–20, 354n71; changes in interpretation and status of, 362n14; and Hitler Myth, 138
World War I, 8; American Mormon missionaries during, 50–51, 351n7; German patriotic fervor during, 56–57; Mormons in German army during, 52–54, 97; onset of, 49–50; postwar relief efforts, 54–56

World War II, 7, 13, 229, 233; Allied bombing during, 236, 238, 239–40, 301; German casualties during, 14, 348n14; German home front during, 235–40; invasion of Poland, 216, 229; invasion of Soviet Union, 295, 297, 302; refugees during, 238–39; Soviet army rapes during, 237–38
Wright, Dennis, 233–34
Wunderlich, Gene, 250–51
Württemberg, Germany, 34

Yad Vashem: Righteous Among the Nations list, 3–4, 262–63
Young, Brigham, 8, 36, 125, 230; emissaries to Prussian monarchy sent by, 29–30, 45; polygamy by, 65; sending of overseas missionaries by, 25
Young, Margaret Blair, 320
Young Heroes of World History (Berson), 335

Zacheile, Willie, 67
Zander, Arthur, *162*; appointment as branch president, 293, 343; depiction of in plays and media, 318, 328, 331, 332, 333, 335; excommunication of Hübener by, 309, 312–13, 332; and Hitler portrait, 6, 293; and Hübener case, 306, 308–309, 312; immigration to U.S. by, 314, 316; life in Utah of, 313, 317, 320–21, 326, 330; as Nazi enthusiast, 282–83, 284, 292–93; as POW, 313; sign barring Jews posted by, *157*, 284, 293–94, 375n45
Zenger, Albert, 69
Zhukov, Georgy, 247
Ziburski, Käthe Elsa Antonie, 268
Zion, defined, 349n15
Zwickau, Germany, 52, 125, 238

www.ingramcontent.com/pod-product-compliance
Ingram Content Group UK Ltd.
Pitfield, Milton Keynes, MK11 3LW, UK
UKHW041438190426
11946UKWH00030B/141/J